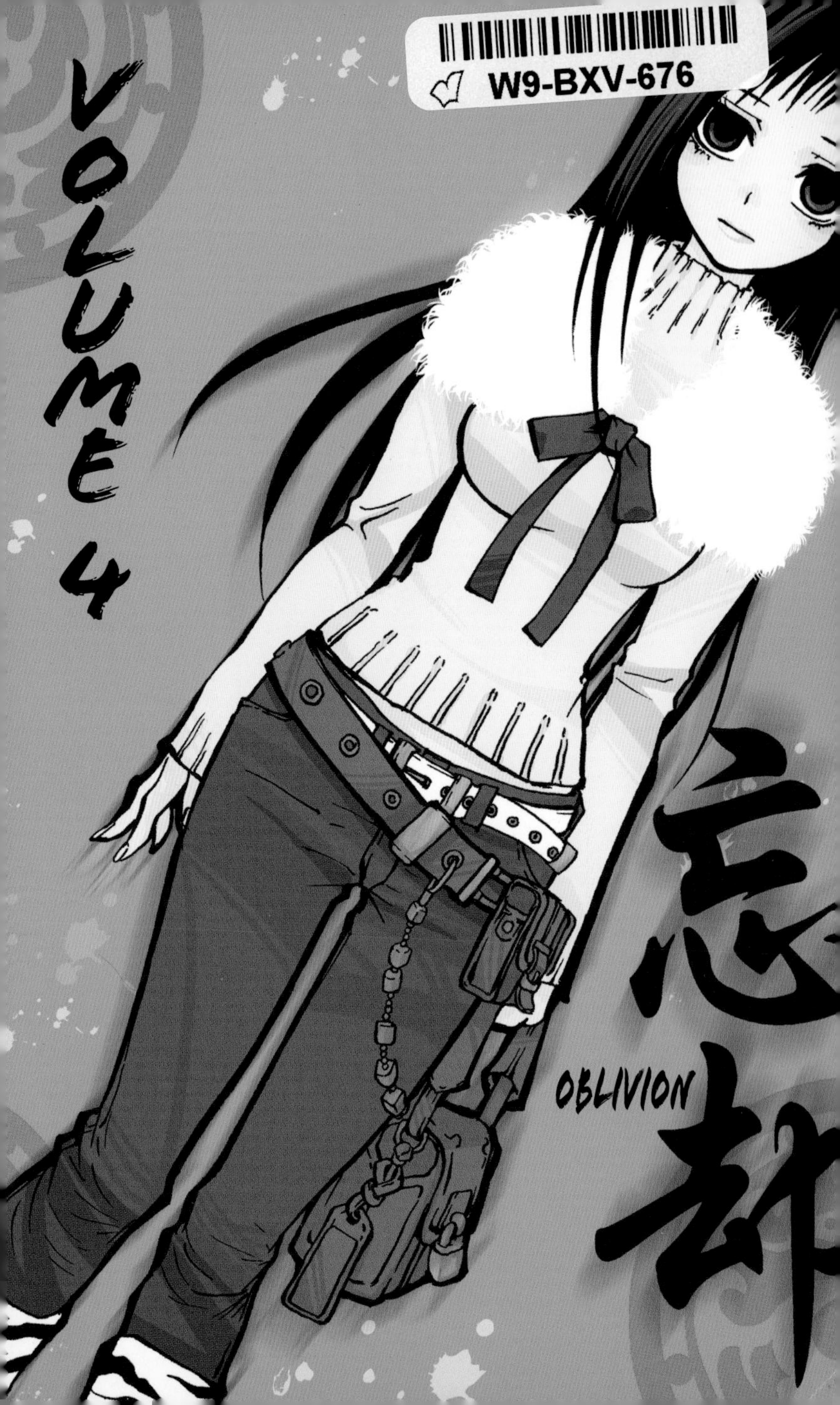
VOLUME 4
忘却
OBLIVION

SUMMARY

Laon is a fox with nine tails, each one taking one hundred years to collect. With one more tail, she would've been able to become a maegu, a deity with her own planet. But when she angered Queen Mago, Laon was expelled to Earth without her tails or ears.
This episode is about Laon finding her second tail. In the middle of idol singer Eunbi's song, Laon hears the voice of her "Singing Tail." Laon runs into the broadcasting studio in search of the source of the voice.

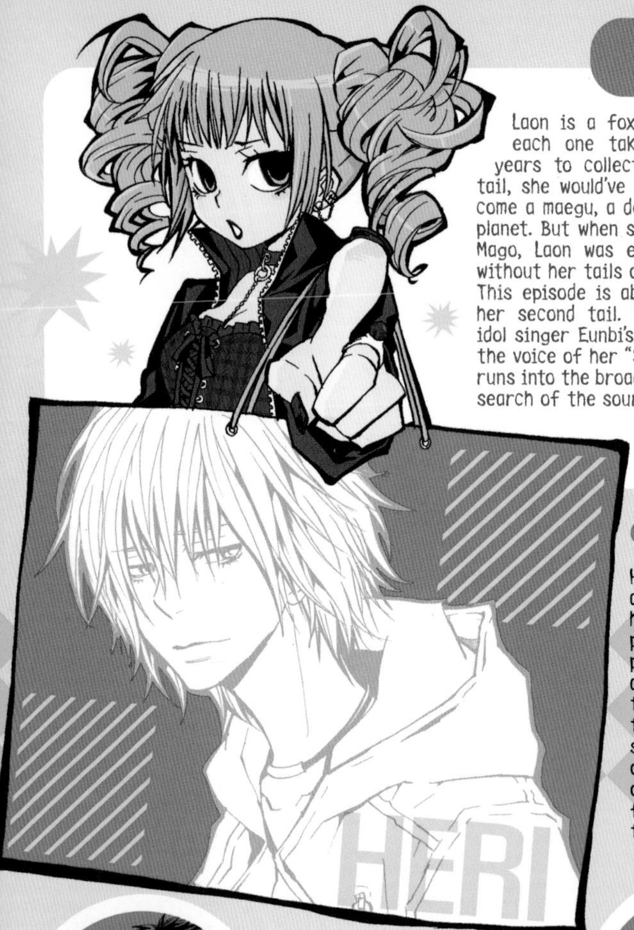
HERI

SECOND TAIL?

Heri is a singer at the height of his fame. With a perfect sense of pitch, he has the ability to stir the emotions of those who hear his songs. But do the occasional flashes of sadness on his face indicate a tragic past?

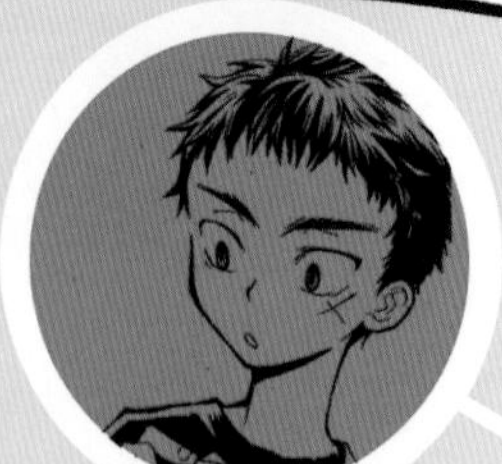

NAMELESS BOY

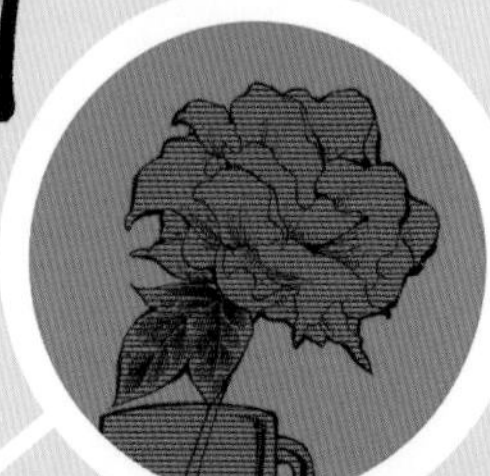

GHOST FLOWER

And what's the mystery behind the flower left by the boy who wanted to protect his sister even after his own death?

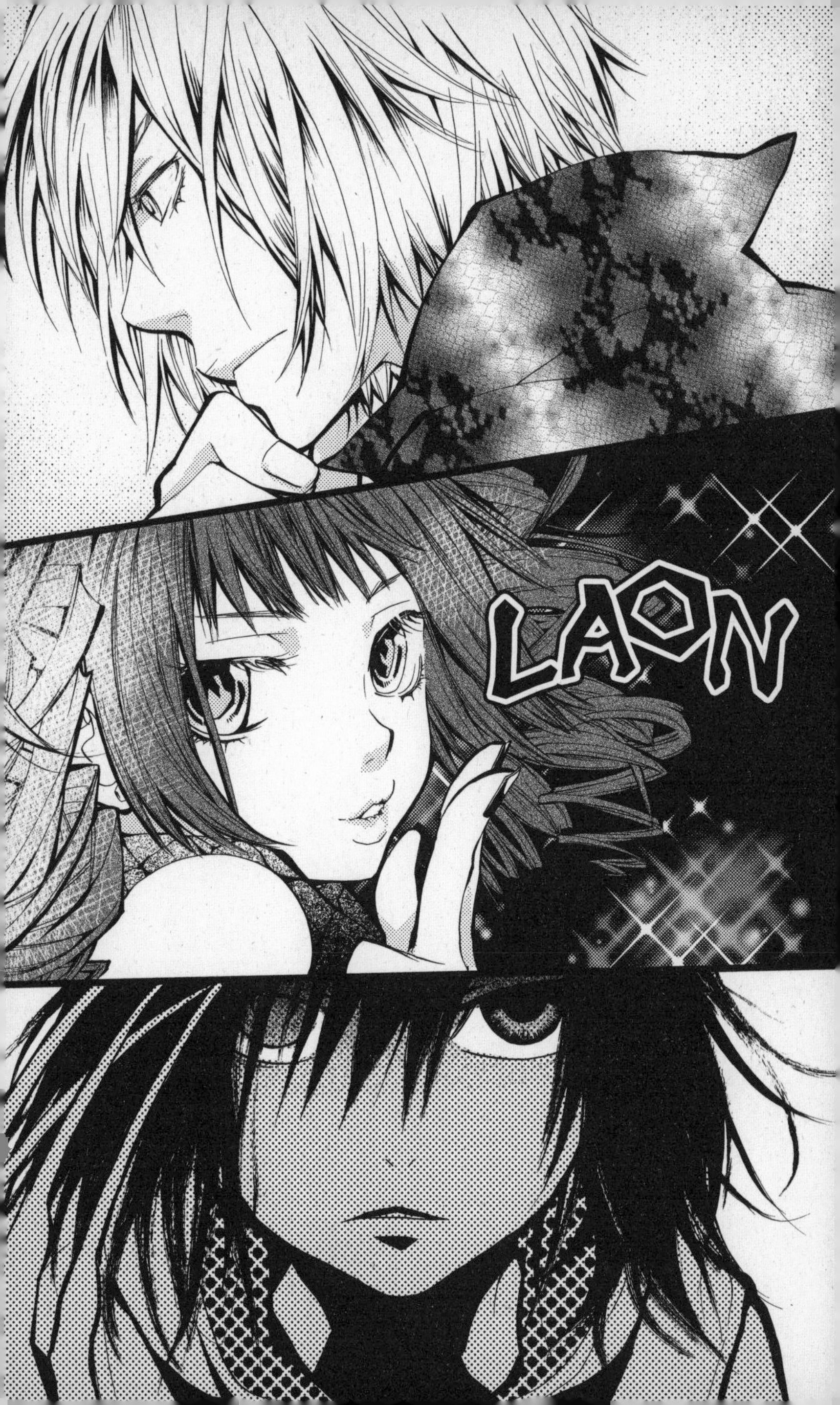
LAON

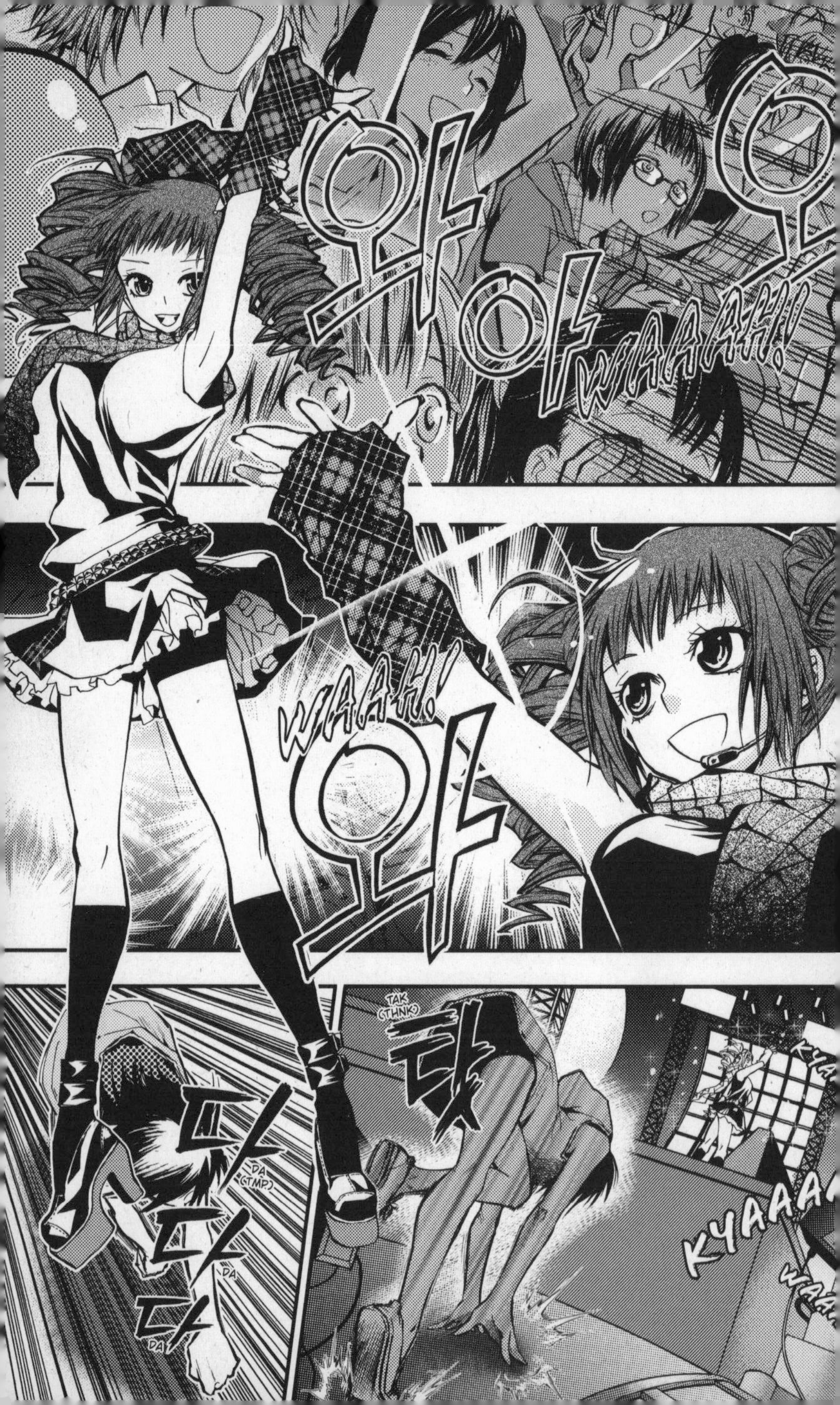
와아
WAAAAH!
WAAH!
와
다
DA
(TMP.)
다
DA
다
DA
TAK
(THNK)
탁
KYAAA
KYAAAA
WAAA

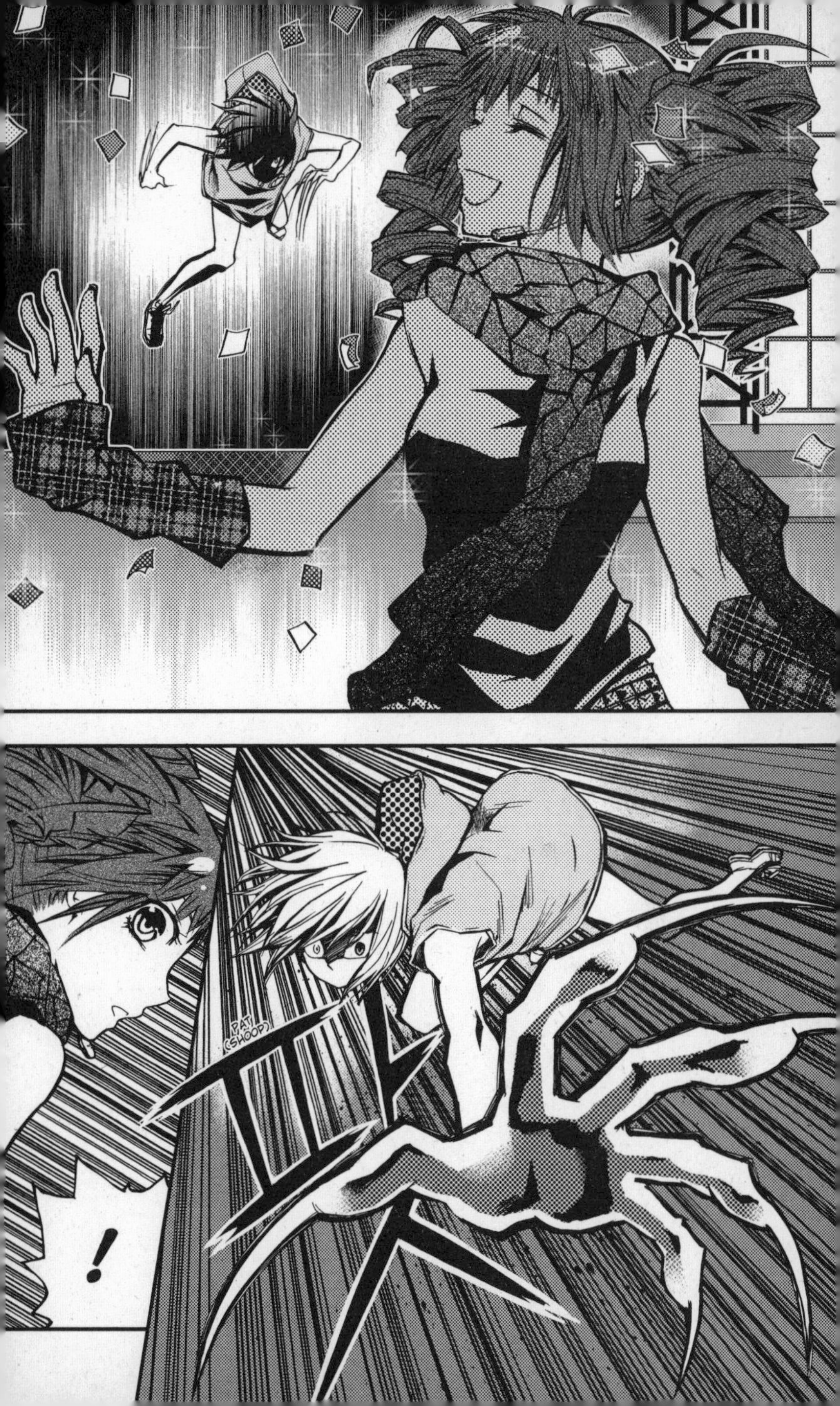
PAT
(SHOOP)
!

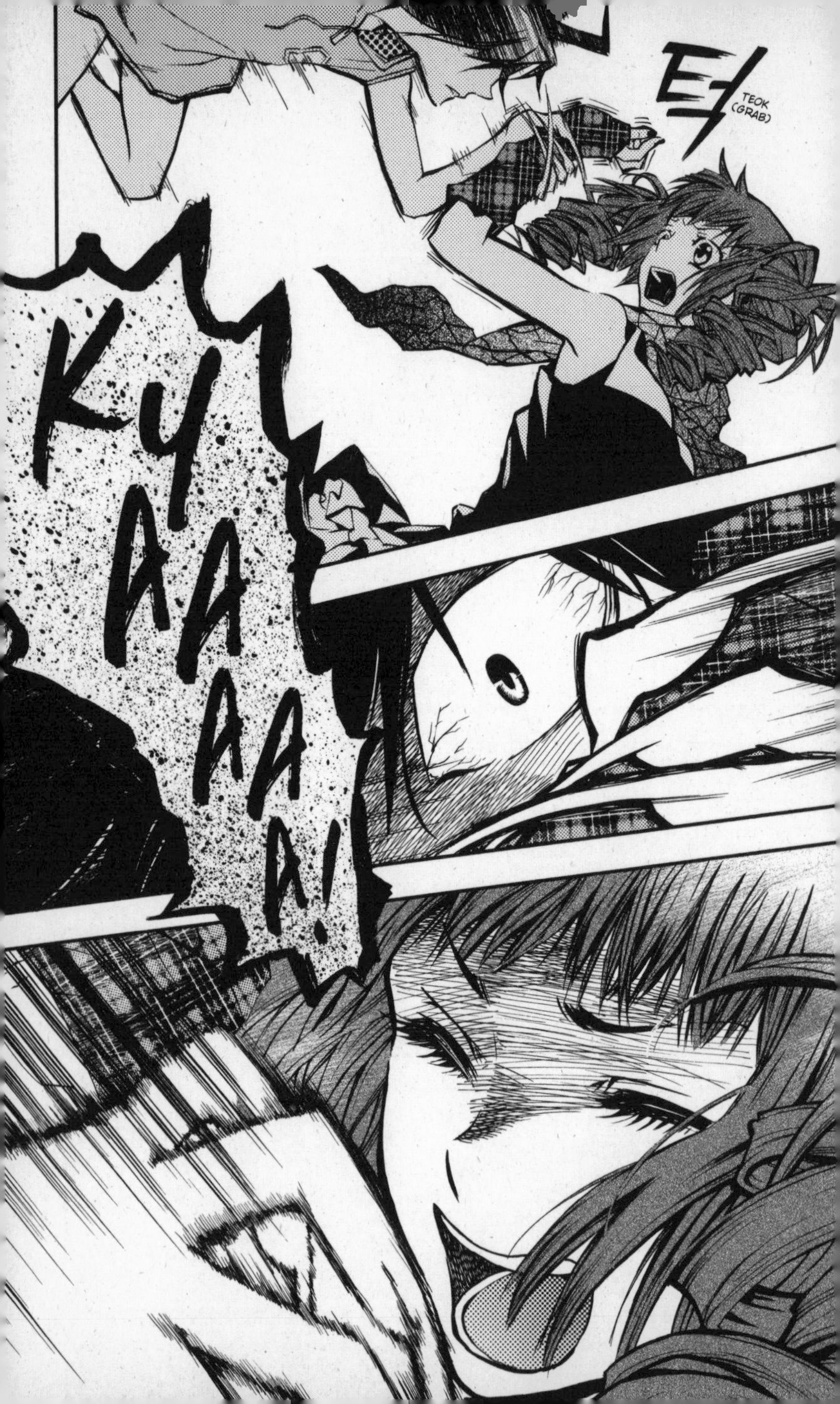

터
TEOK (GRAB)
KYAAAAAA!

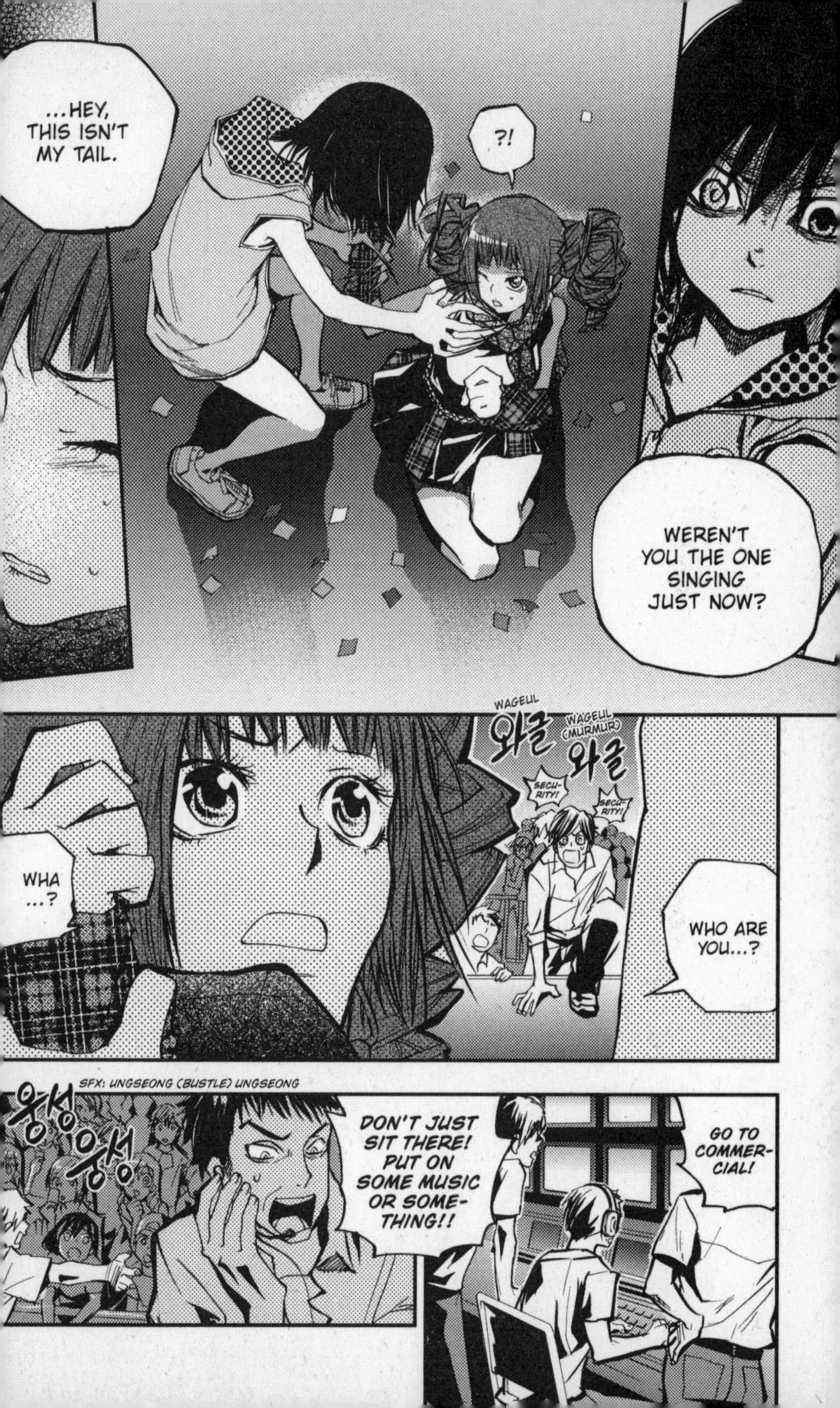
...HEY, THIS ISN'T MY TAIL.
?!
WEREN'T YOU THE ONE SINGING JUST NOW?
WHA ...?
WAGEUL
와글
WAGEUL (MURMUR)
와글
SECU-RITY!
SECU-RITY!
WHO ARE YOU...?
SFX: UNGSEONG (BUSTLE) UNGSEONG
웅성웅성
DON'T JUST SIT THERE! PUT ON SOME MUSIC OR SOME-THING!!
GO TO COMMER-CIAL!

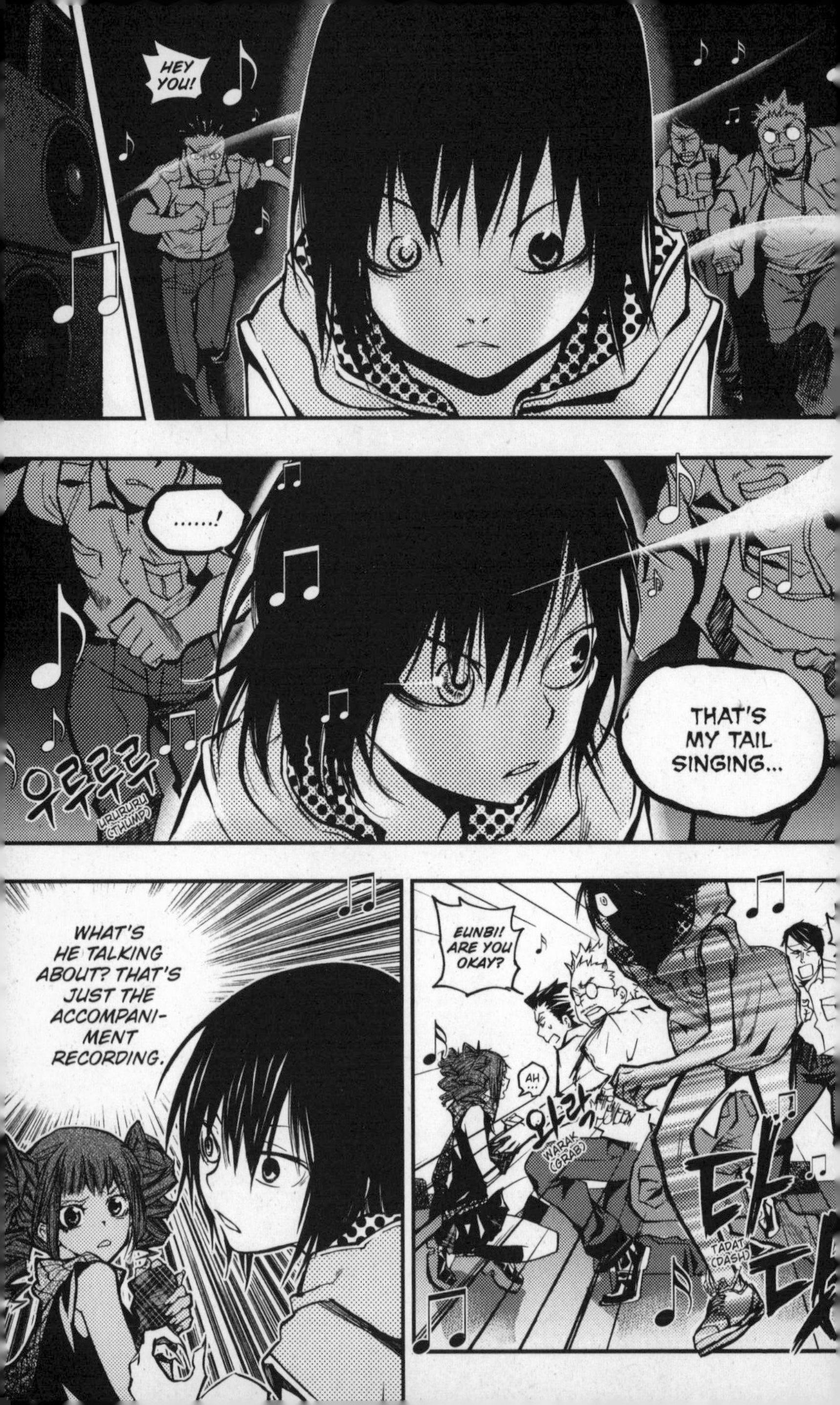
HEY YOU!
.......!
우루루루
URURURU (THUMP)
THAT'S MY TAIL SINGING...
WHAT'S HE TALKING ABOUT? THAT'S JUST THE ACCOMPANI-MENT RECORDING.
EUNBI! ARE YOU OKAY?
AH ...
와락
WARAK (GRAB)
타닥
TADAT (DASH)

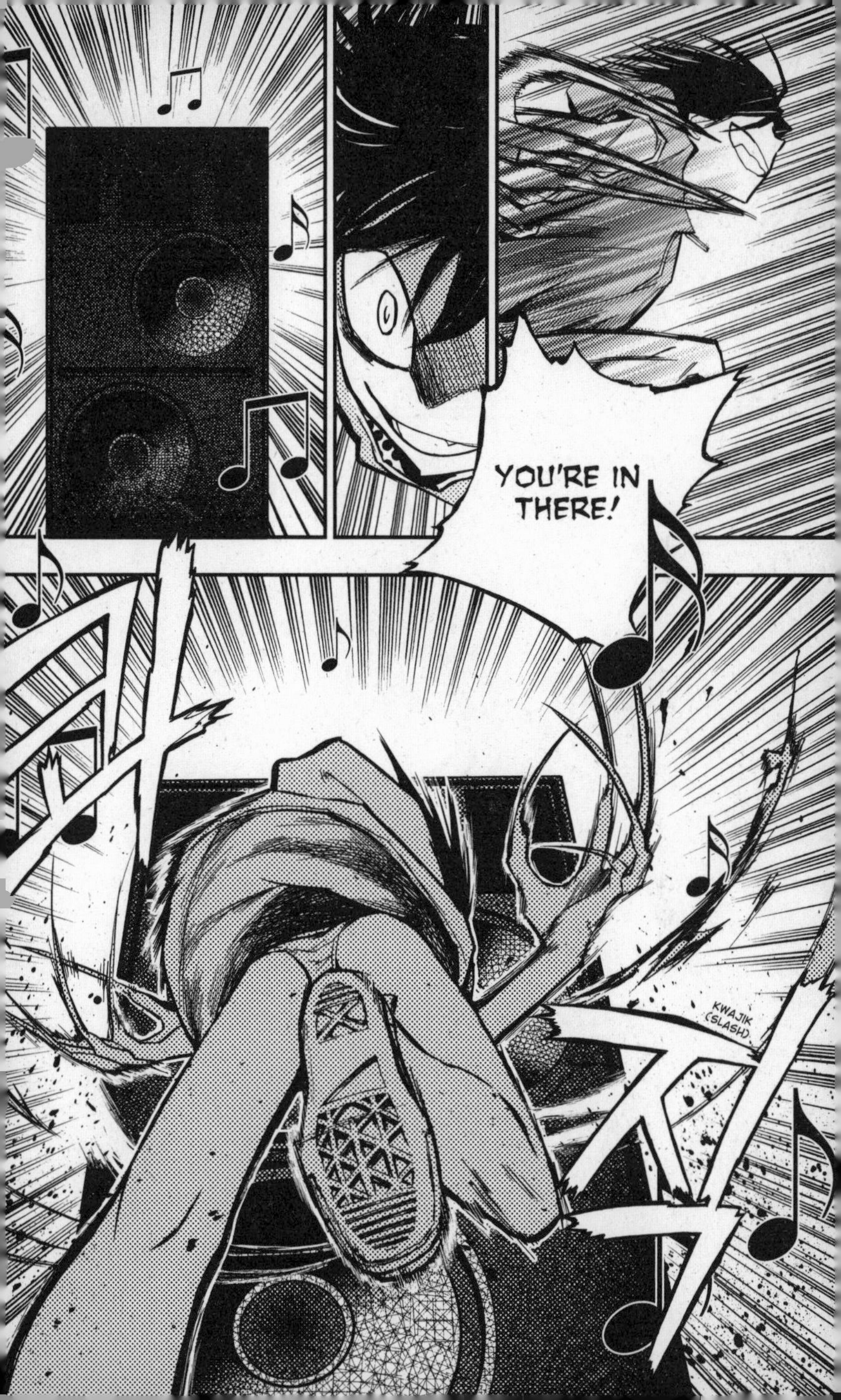
YOU'RE IN THERE!
KWAJIK (SLASH)

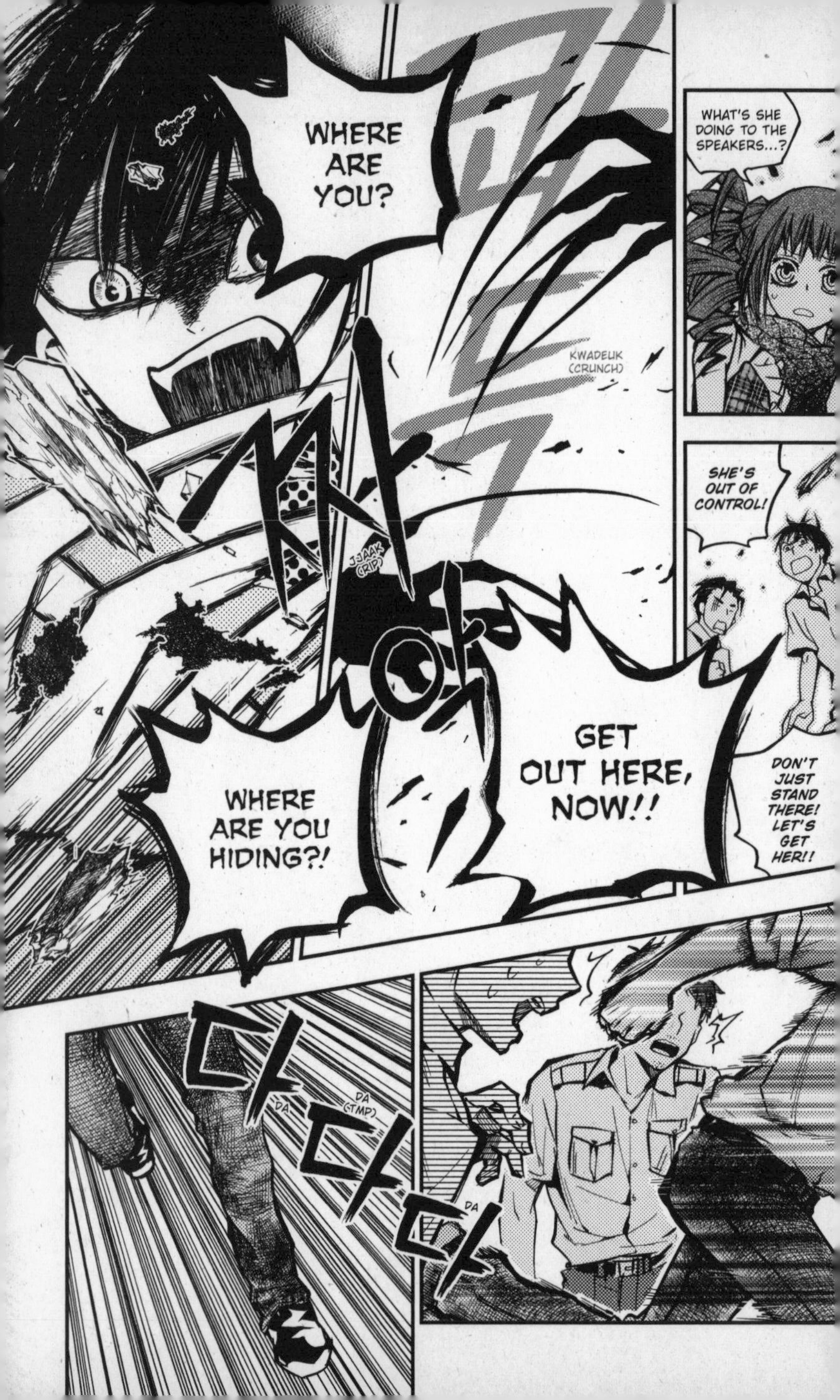
WHERE ARE YOU?
KWADEUK (CRUNCH)
JJAAK (RIP)
WHERE ARE YOU HIDING?!
GET OUT HERE, NOW!!
WHAT'S SHE DOING TO THE SPEAKERS...?
SHE'S OUT OF CONTROL!
DON'T JUST STAND THERE! LET'S GET HER!!
DA
DA (TMP)
DA

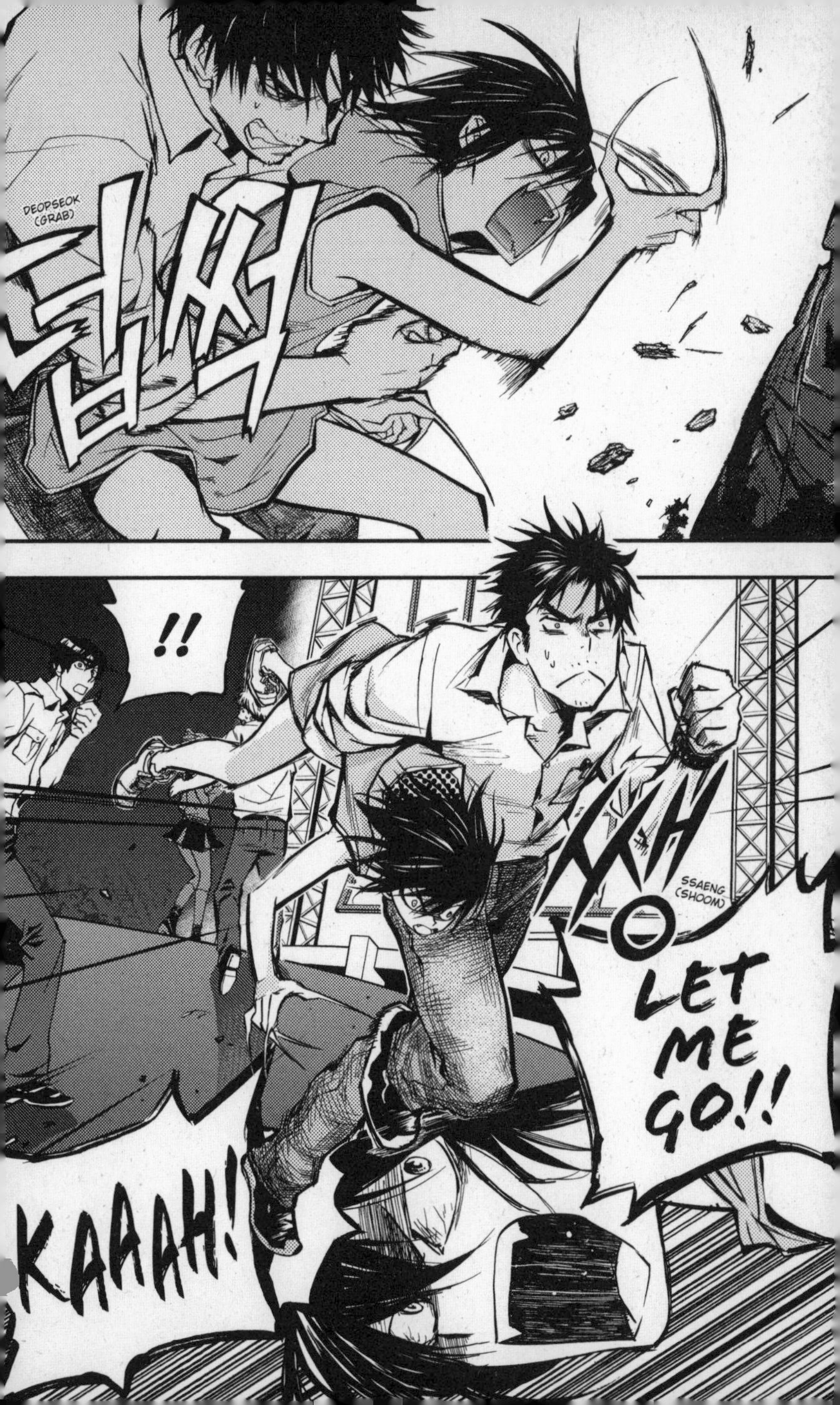
DEOPSEOK (GRAB)
!!
SSAENG (SHOOM)
LET ME GO!!
KAAAH!

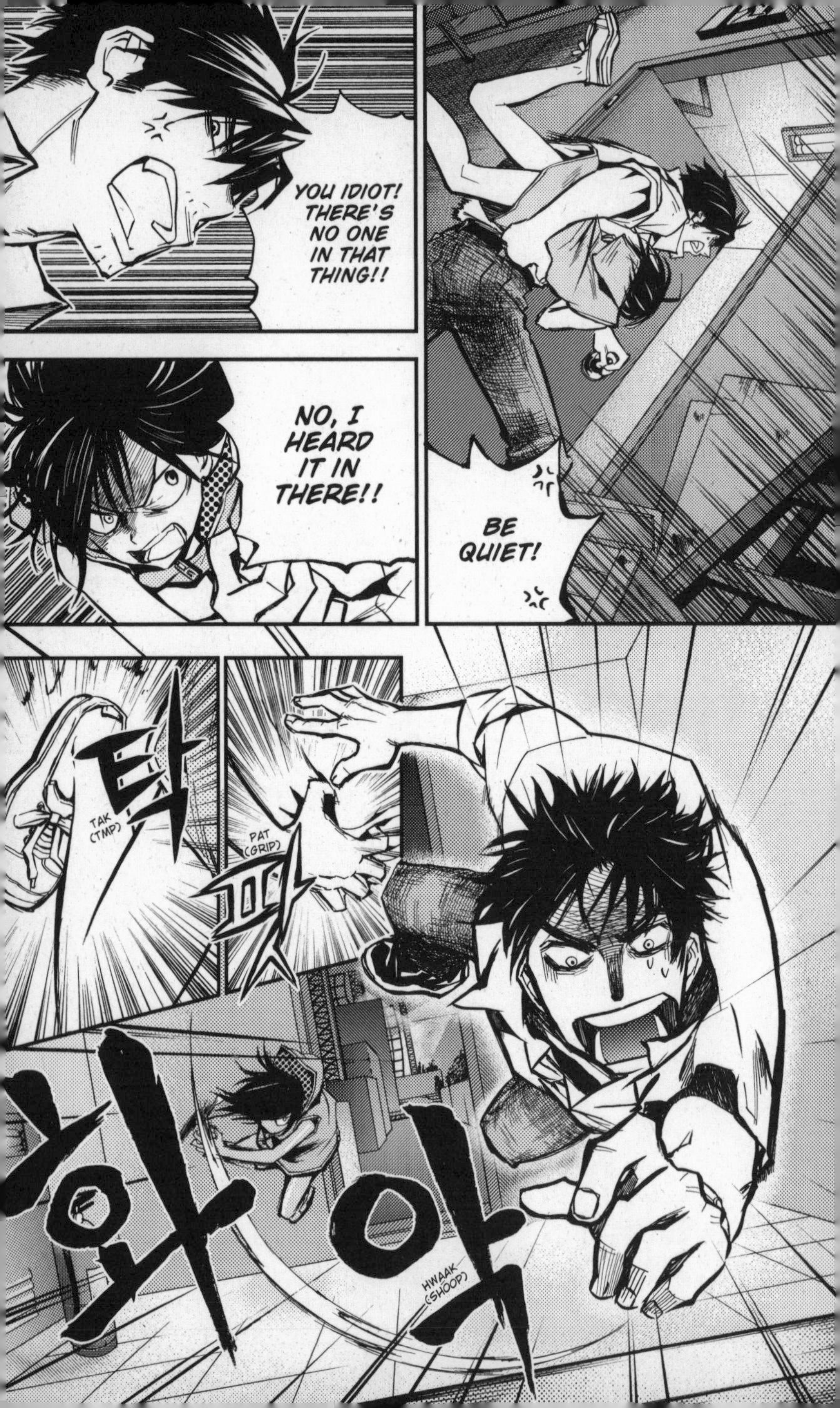
YOU IDIOT! THERE'S NO ONE IN THAT THING!!
NO, I HEARD IT IN THERE!!
BE QUIET!
탁
TAK (TMP)
파
PAT (GRIP)
화아
HWAAK (SHOOP)

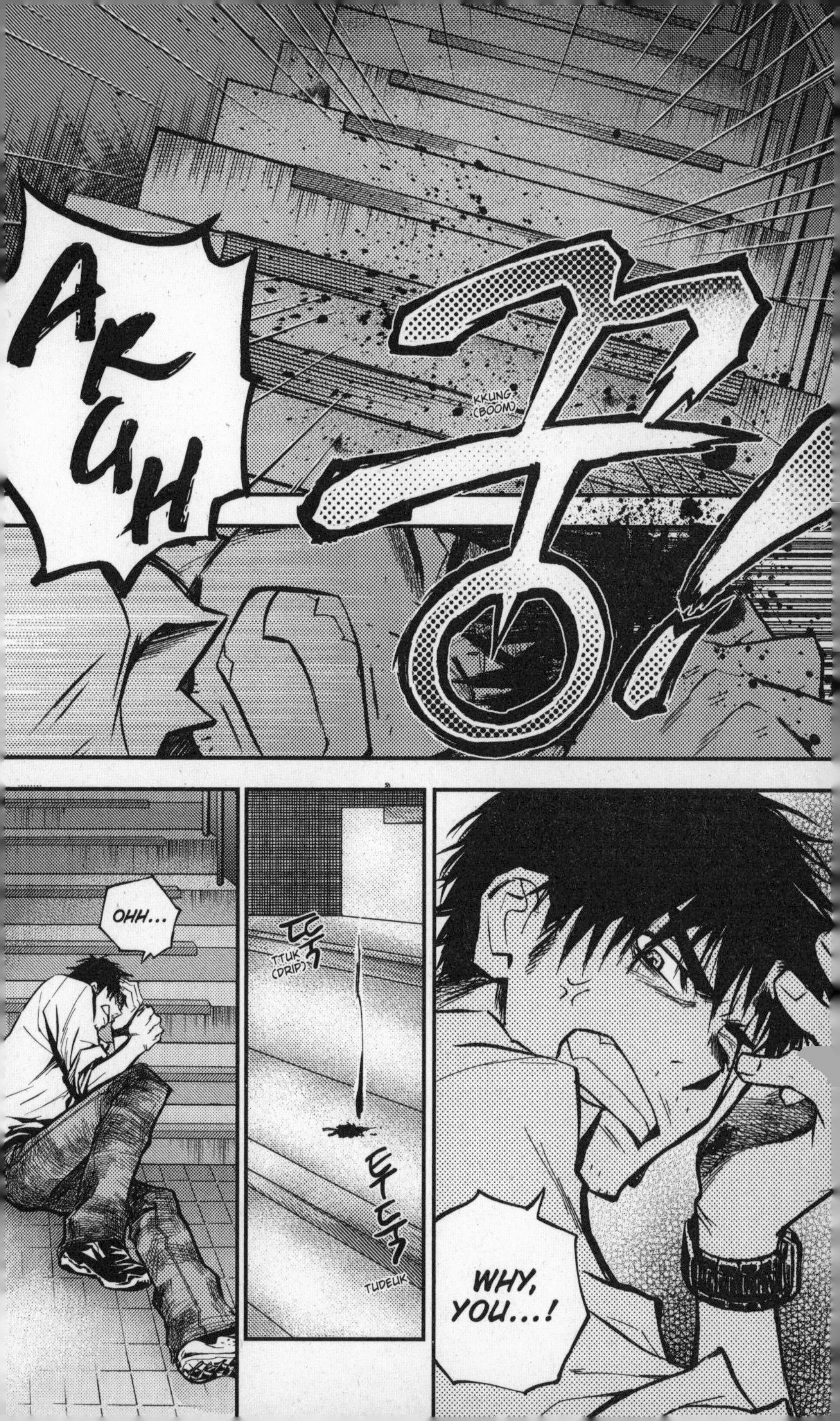
AKUH
KKUNG (BOOM)
OHH...
TTUK (DRIP)
TUDEUK
WHY, YOU...!

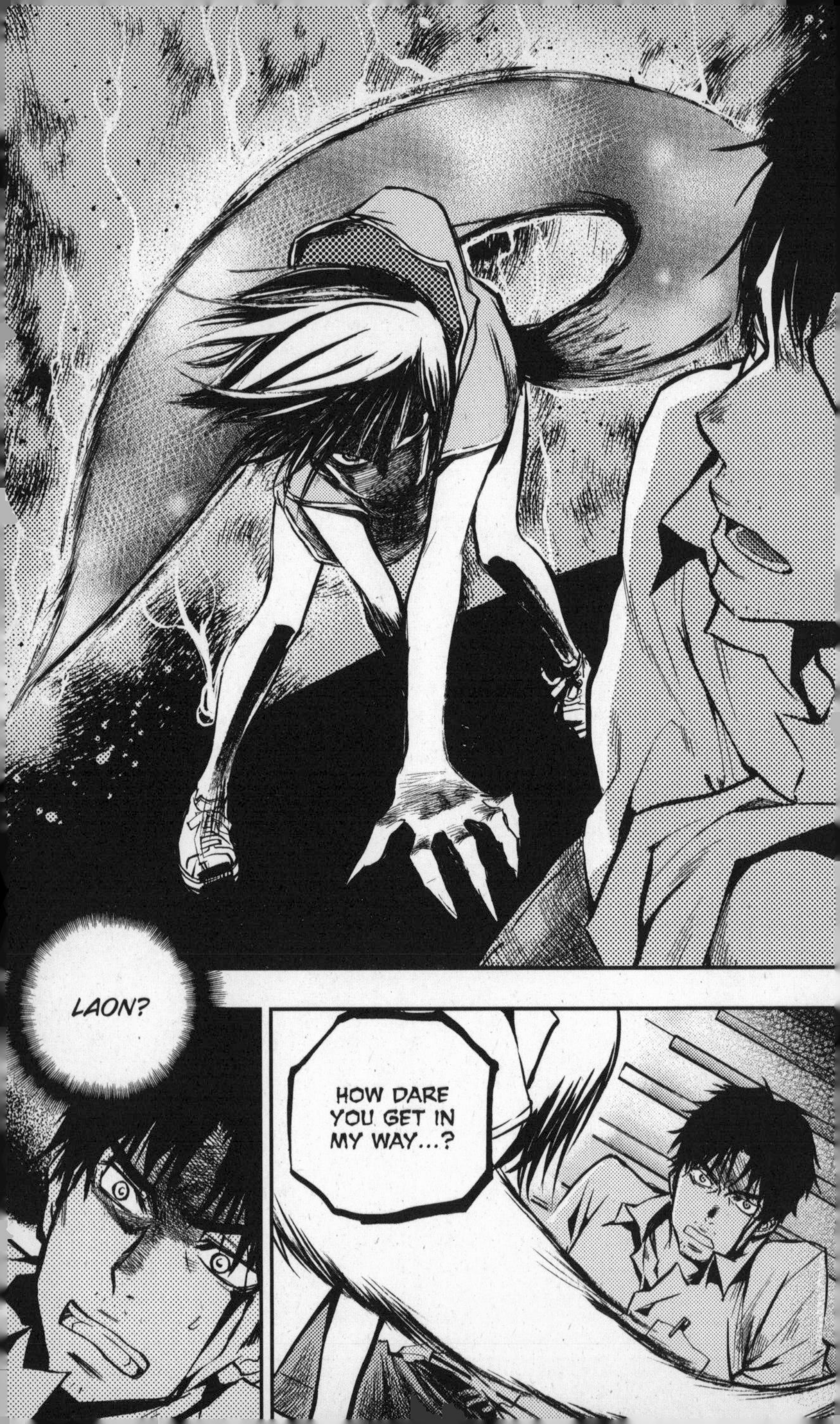
LAON?
HOW DARE YOU GET IN MY WAY...?

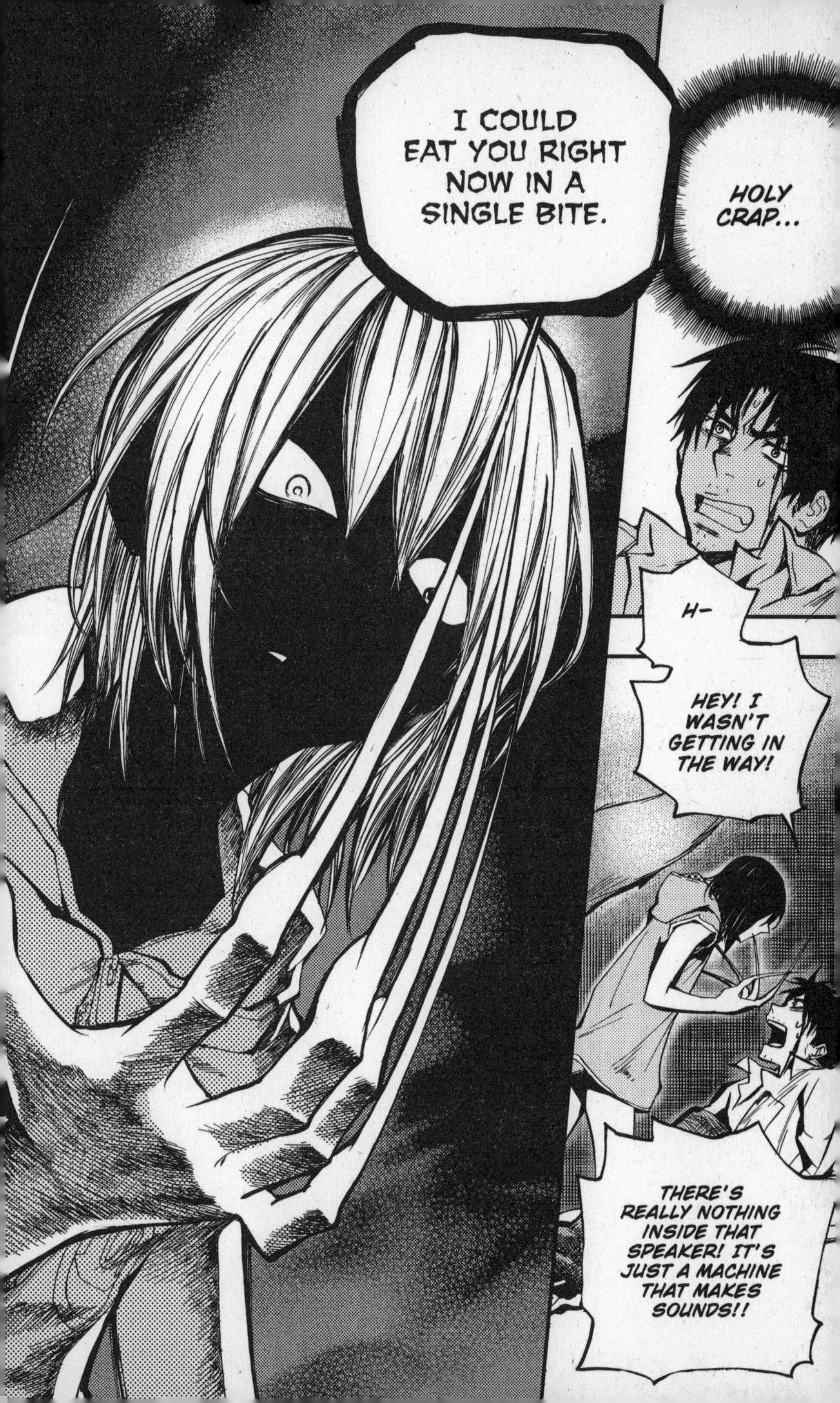
I COULD EAT YOU RIGHT NOW IN A SINGLE BITE.
HOLY CRAP...
H-
HEY! I WASN'T GETTING IN THE WAY!
THERE'S REALLY NOTHING INSIDE THAT SPEAKER! IT'S JUST A MACHINE THAT MAKES SOUNDS!!

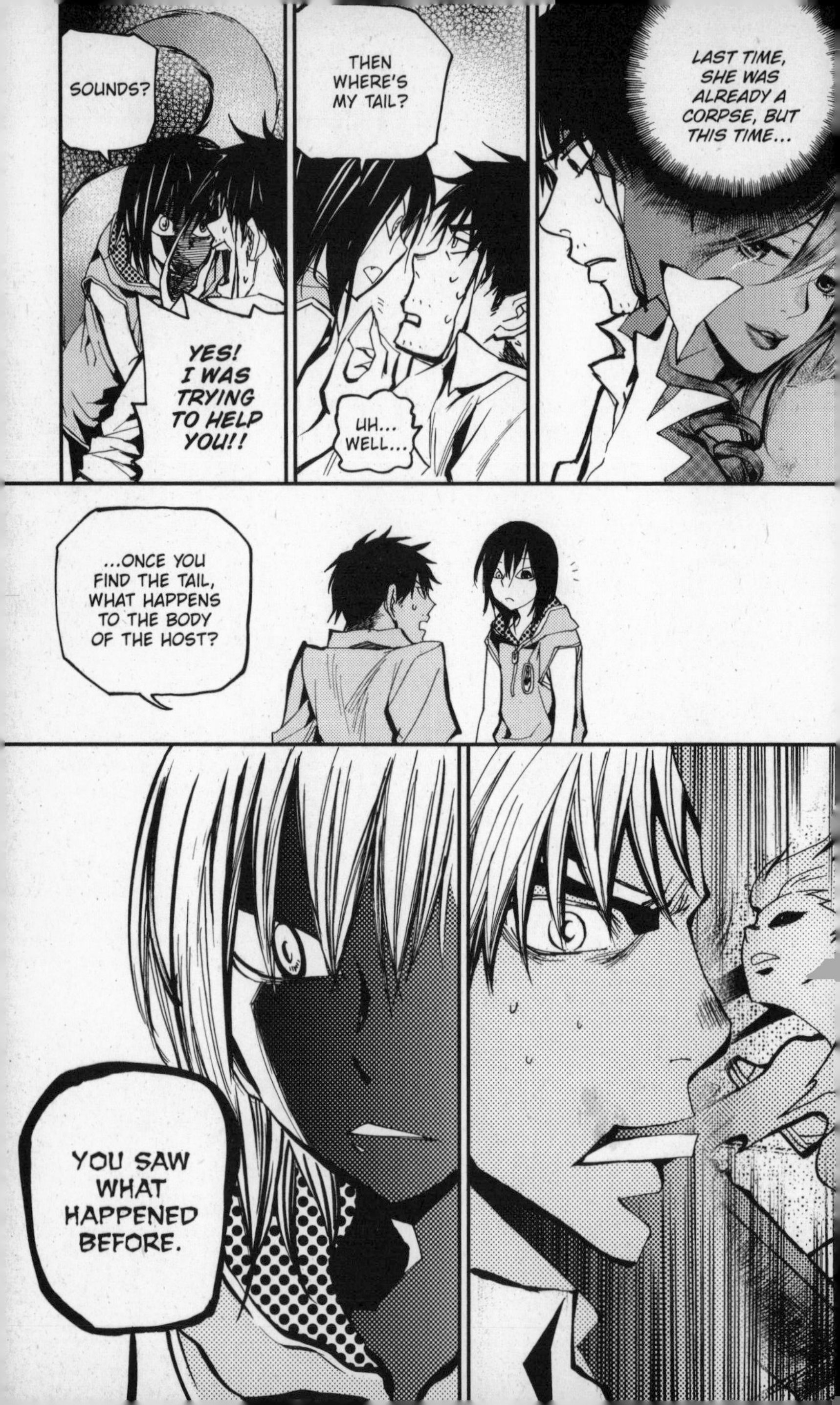
SOUNDS?
YES! I WAS TRYING TO HELP YOU!!
THEN WHERE'S MY TAIL?
UH... WELL...
LAST TIME, SHE WAS ALREADY A CORPSE, BUT THIS TIME...
...ONCE YOU FIND THE TAIL, WHAT HAPPENS TO THE BODY OF THE HOST?
YOU SAW WHAT HAPPENED BEFORE.

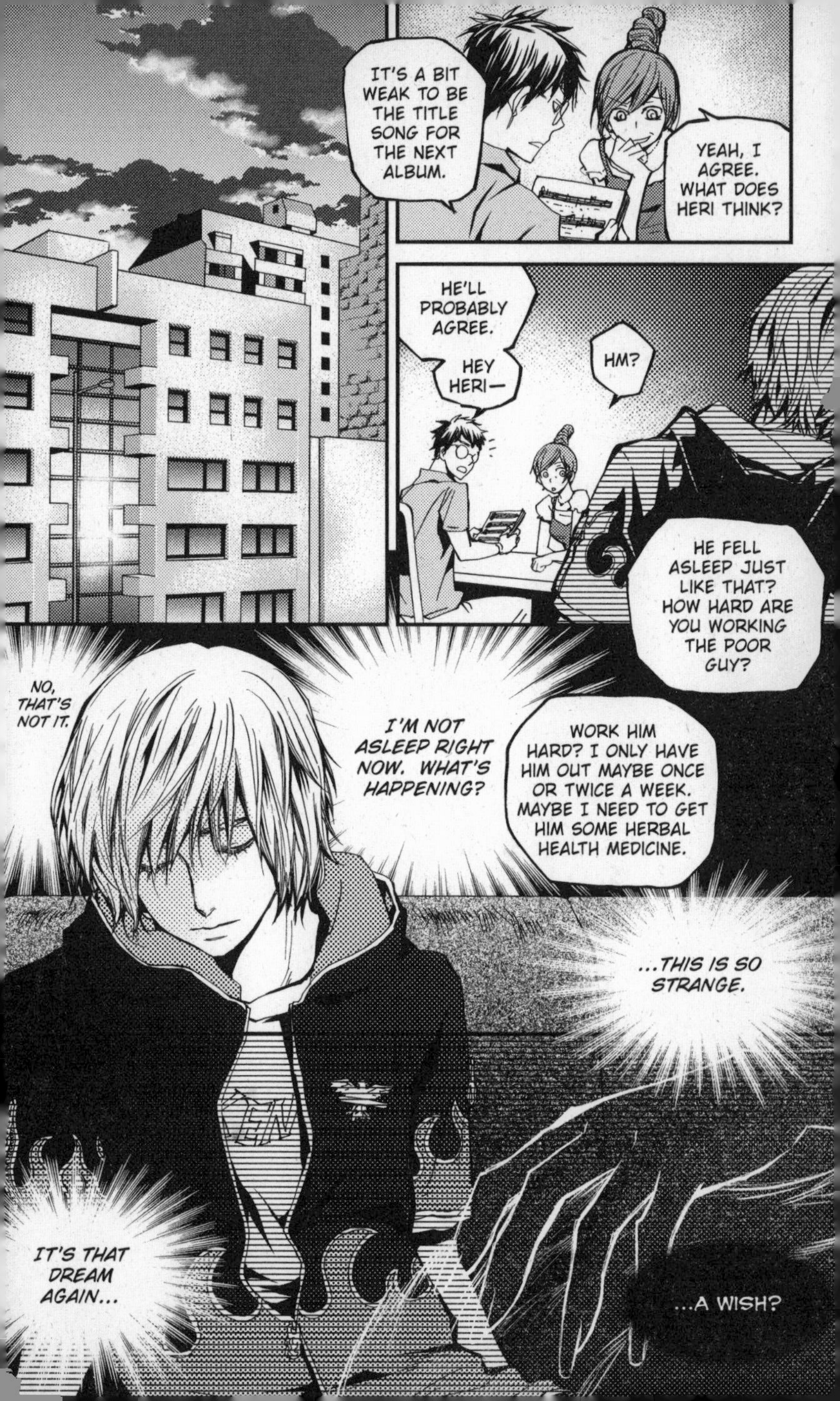

IT'S A BIT WEAK TO BE THE TITLE SONG FOR THE NEXT ALBUM.
YEAH, I AGREE. WHAT DOES HERI THINK?
HE'LL PROBABLY AGREE.
HEY HERI—
HM?
HE FELL ASLEEP JUST LIKE THAT? HOW HARD ARE YOU WORKING THE POOR GUY?
NO, THAT'S NOT IT.
I'M NOT ASLEEP RIGHT NOW. WHAT'S HAPPENING?
WORK HIM HARD? I ONLY HAVE HIM OUT MAYBE ONCE OR TWICE A WEEK. MAYBE I NEED TO GET HIM SOME HERBAL HEALTH MEDICINE.
...THIS IS SO STRANGE.
IT'S THAT DREAM AGAIN...
...A WISH?

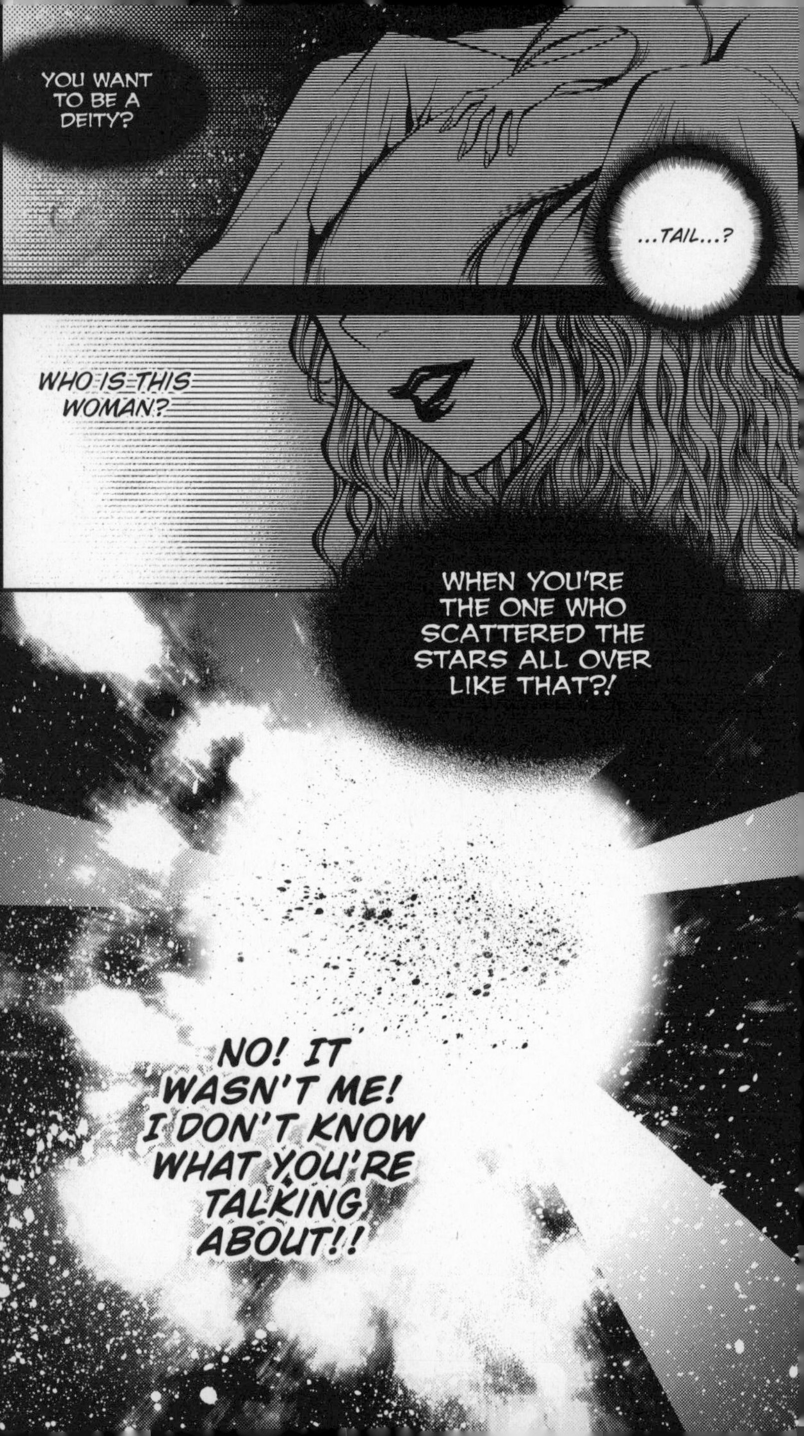
YOU WANT TO BE A DEITY?
...TAIL...?
WHO IS THIS WOMAN?
WHEN YOU'RE THE ONE WHO SCATTERED THE STARS ALL OVER LIKE THAT?!
NO! IT WASN'T ME! I DON'T KNOW WHAT YOU'RE TALKING ABOUT!!

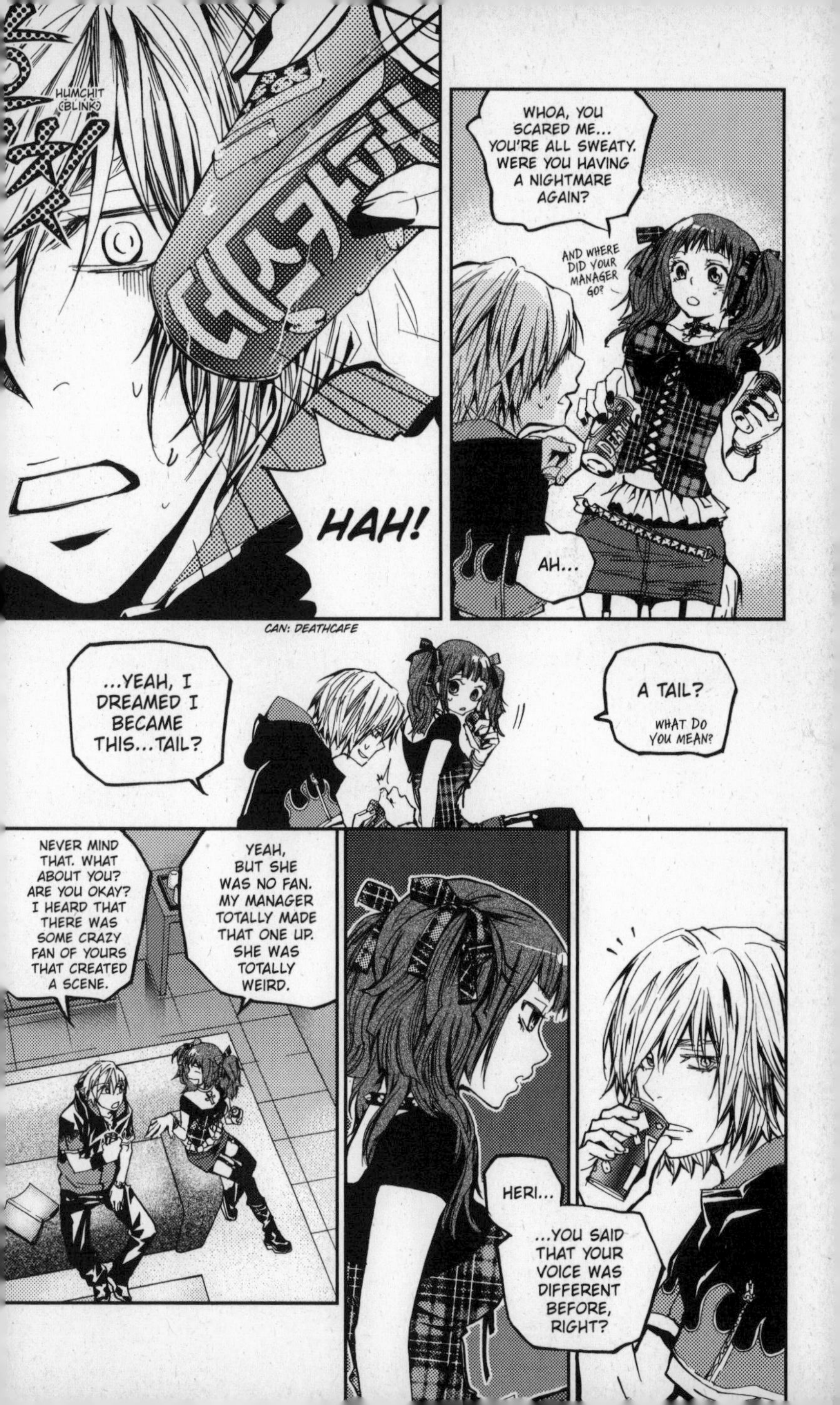
HUMCHIT (BLINK)
HAH!
WHOA, YOU SCARED ME... YOU'RE ALL SWEATY. WERE YOU HAVING A NIGHTMARE AGAIN?
AND WHERE DID YOUR MANAGER GO?
AH...
CAN: DEATHCAFE
...YEAH, I DREAMED I BECAME THIS...TAIL?
A TAIL?
WHAT DO YOU MEAN?
NEVER MIND THAT. WHAT ABOUT YOU? ARE YOU OKAY? I HEARD THAT THERE WAS SOME CRAZY FAN OF YOURS THAT CREATED A SCENE.
YEAH, BUT SHE WAS NO FAN. MY MANAGER TOTALLY MADE THAT ONE UP. SHE WAS TOTALLY WEIRD.
HERI...
...YOU SAID THAT YOUR VOICE WAS DIFFERENT BEFORE, RIGHT?

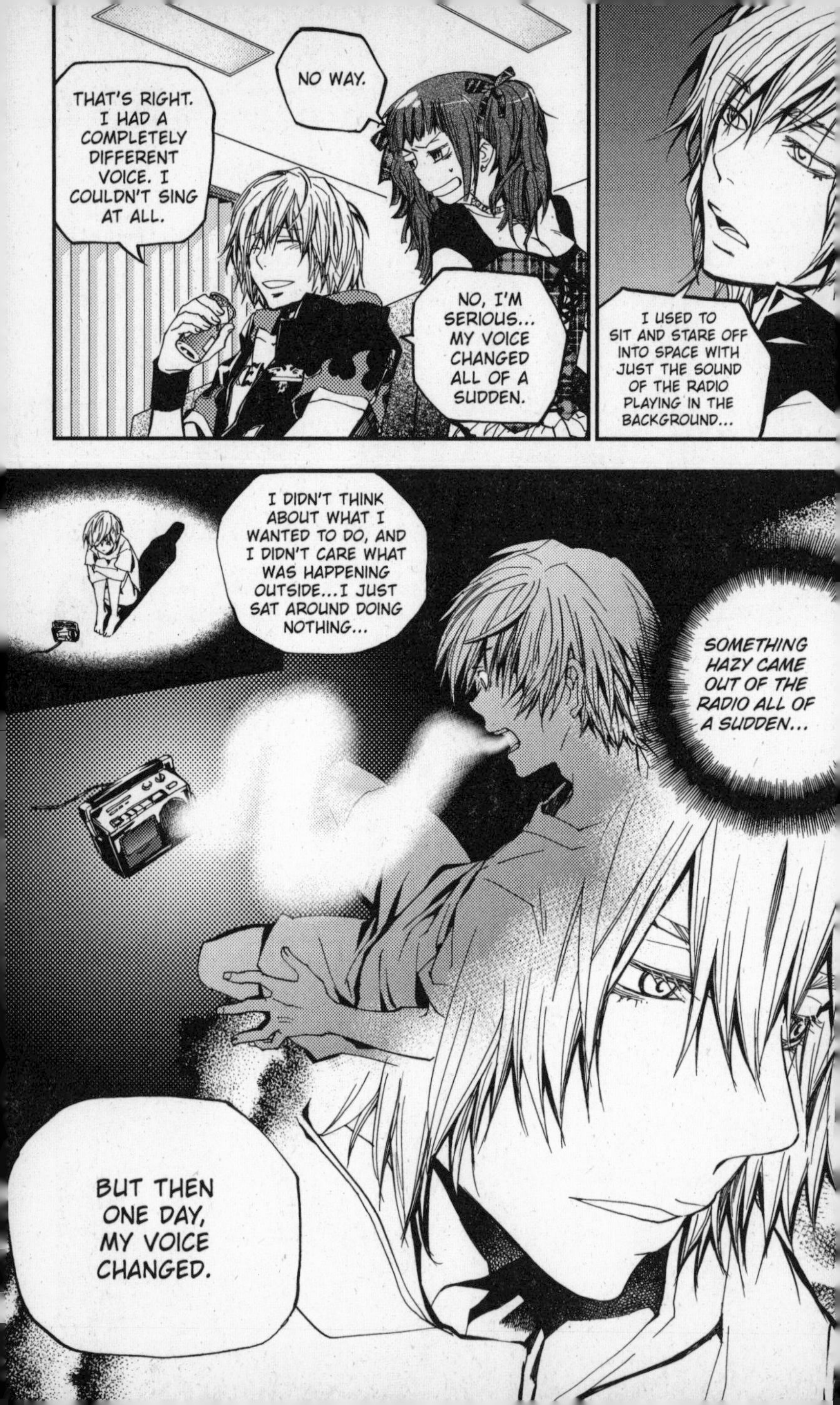
THAT'S RIGHT. I HAD A COMPLETELY DIFFERENT VOICE. I COULDN'T SING AT ALL.
NO WAY.
NO, I'M SERIOUS... MY VOICE CHANGED ALL OF A SUDDEN.
I USED TO SIT AND STARE OFF INTO SPACE WITH JUST THE SOUND OF THE RADIO PLAYING IN THE BACKGROUND...
I DIDN'T THINK ABOUT WHAT I WANTED TO DO, AND I DIDN'T CARE WHAT WAS HAPPENING OUTSIDE...I JUST SAT AROUND DOING NOTHING...
SOMETHING HAZY CAME OUT OF THE RADIO ALL OF A SUDDEN...
BUT THEN ONE DAY, MY VOICE CHANGED.

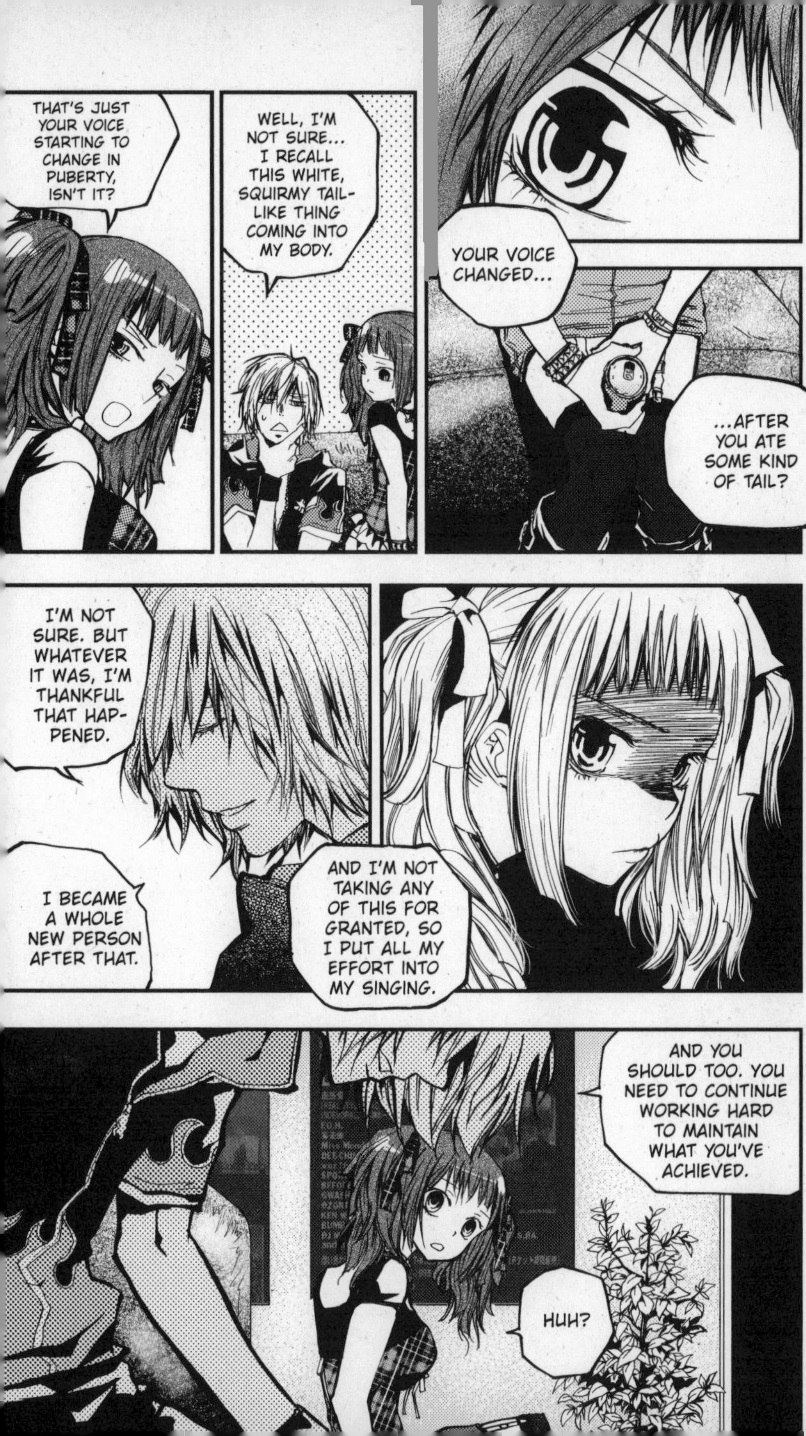
THAT'S JUST YOUR VOICE STARTING TO CHANGE IN PUBERTY, ISN'T IT?
WELL, I'M NOT SURE... I RECALL THIS WHITE, SQUIRMY TAIL-LIKE THING COMING INTO MY BODY.
YOUR VOICE CHANGED...
...AFTER YOU ATE SOME KIND OF TAIL?
I'M NOT SURE. BUT WHATEVER IT WAS, I'M THANKFUL THAT HAPPENED.
I BECAME A WHOLE NEW PERSON AFTER THAT.
AND I'M NOT TAKING ANY OF THIS FOR GRANTED, SO I PUT ALL MY EFFORT INTO MY SINGING.
AND YOU SHOULD TOO. YOU NEED TO CONTINUE WORKING HARD TO MAINTAIN WHAT YOU'VE ACHIEVED.
HUH?

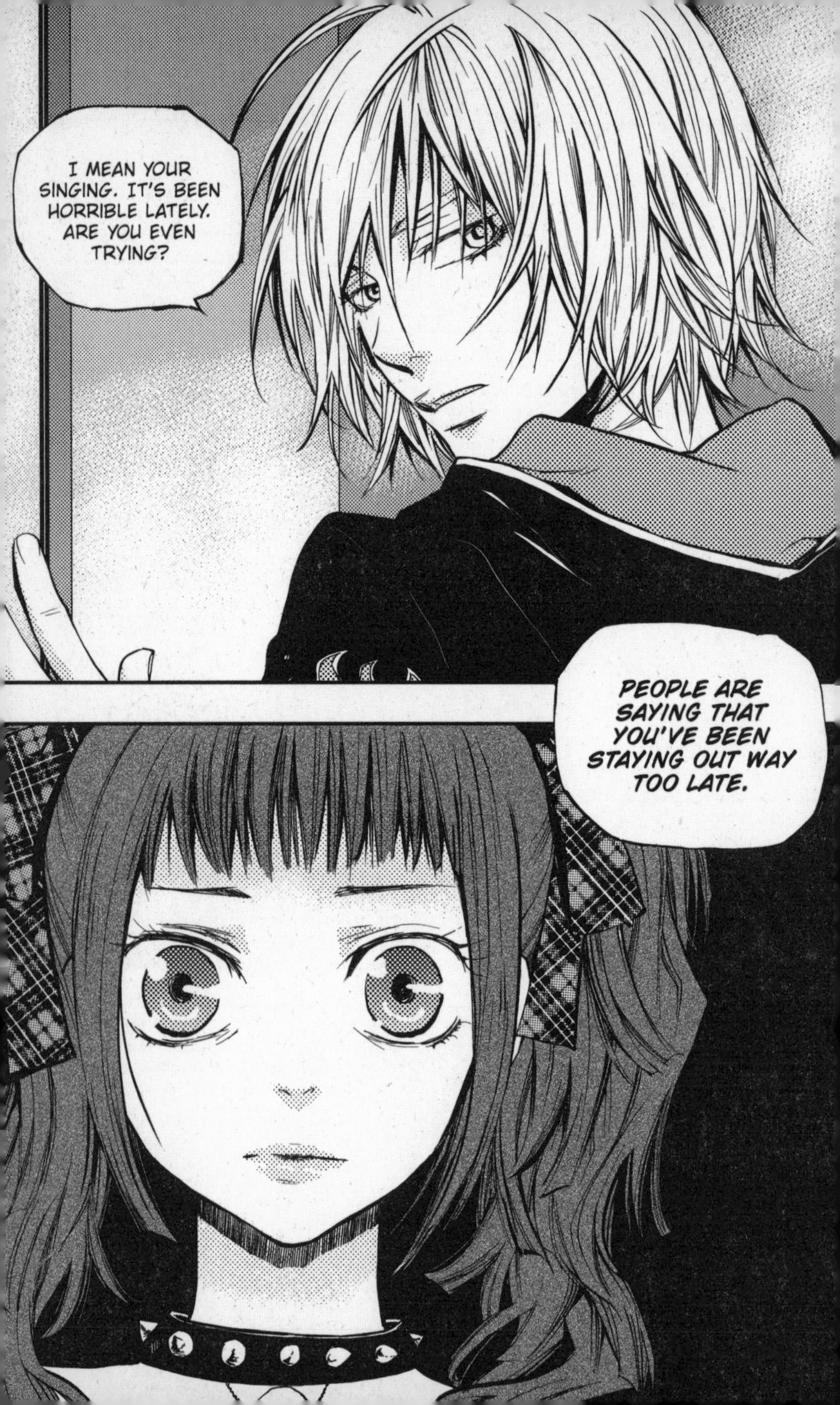

I MEAN YOUR SINGING. IT'S BEEN HORRIBLE LATELY. ARE YOU EVEN TRYING?
PEOPLE ARE SAYING THAT YOU'VE BEEN STAYING OUT WAY TOO LATE.

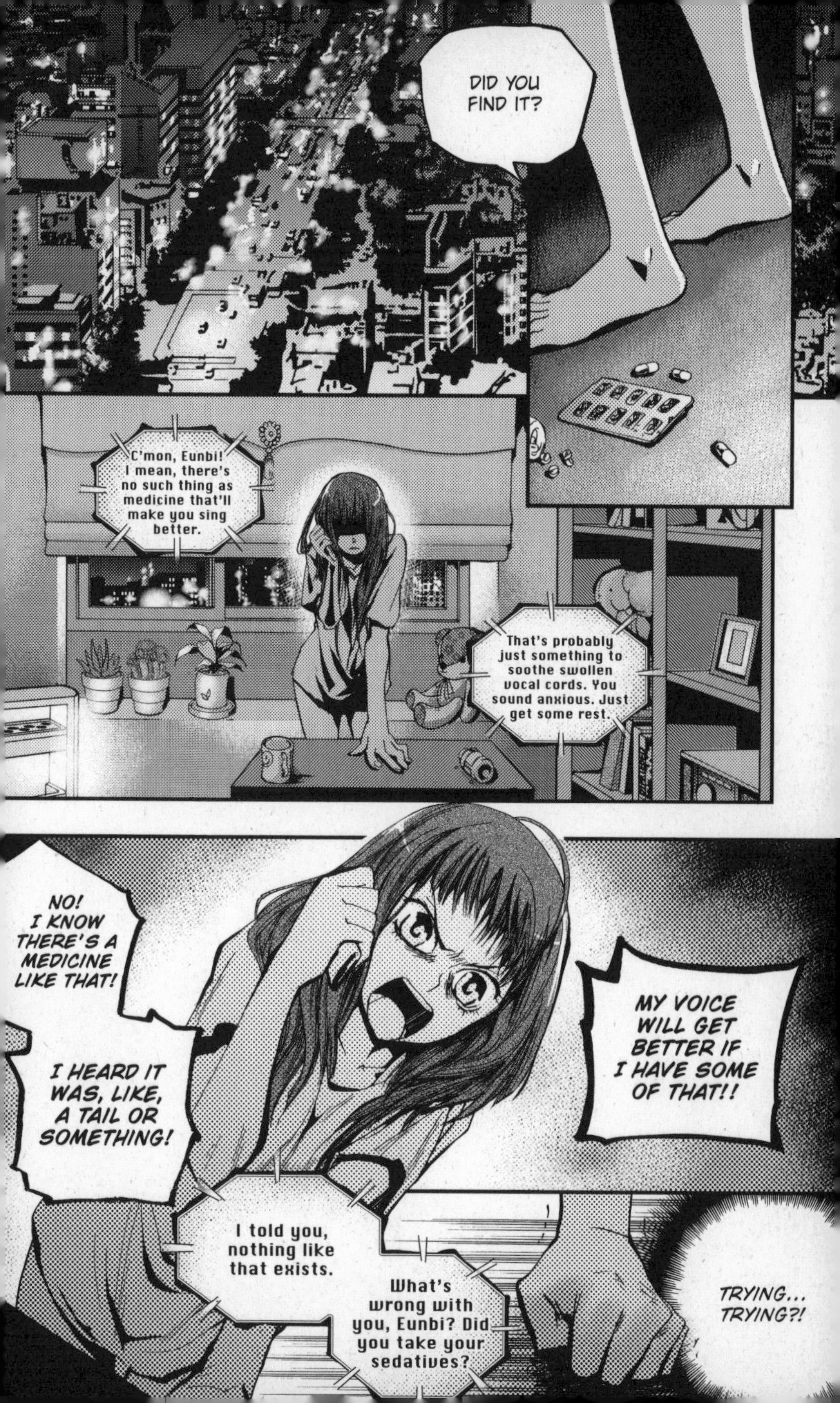
DID YOU FIND IT?
C'mon, Eunbi! I mean, there's no such thing as medicine that'll make you sing better.
That's probably just something to soothe swollen vocal cords. You sound anxious. Just get some rest.
NO! I KNOW THERE'S A MEDICINE LIKE THAT!
I HEARD IT WAS, LIKE, A TAIL OR SOMETHING!
MY VOICE WILL GET BETTER IF I HAVE SOME OF THAT!!
I told you, nothing like that exists.
What's wrong with you, Eunbi? Did you take your sedatives?
TRYING... TRYING?!

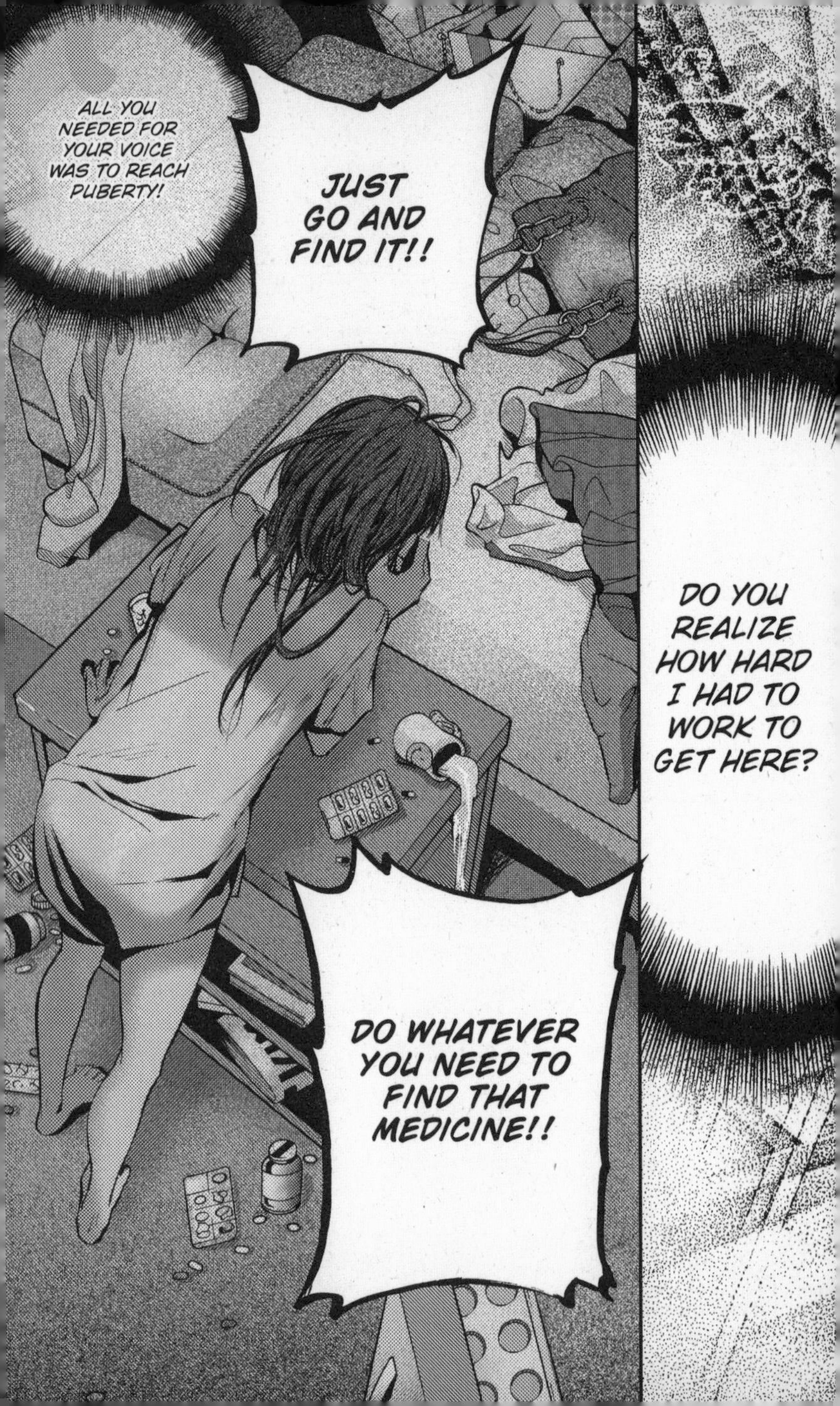
ALL YOU NEEDED FOR YOUR VOICE WAS TO REACH PUBERTY!
JUST GO AND FIND IT!!
DO WHATEVER YOU NEED TO FIND THAT MEDICINE!!
DO YOU REALIZE HOW HARD I HAD TO WORK TO GET HERE?

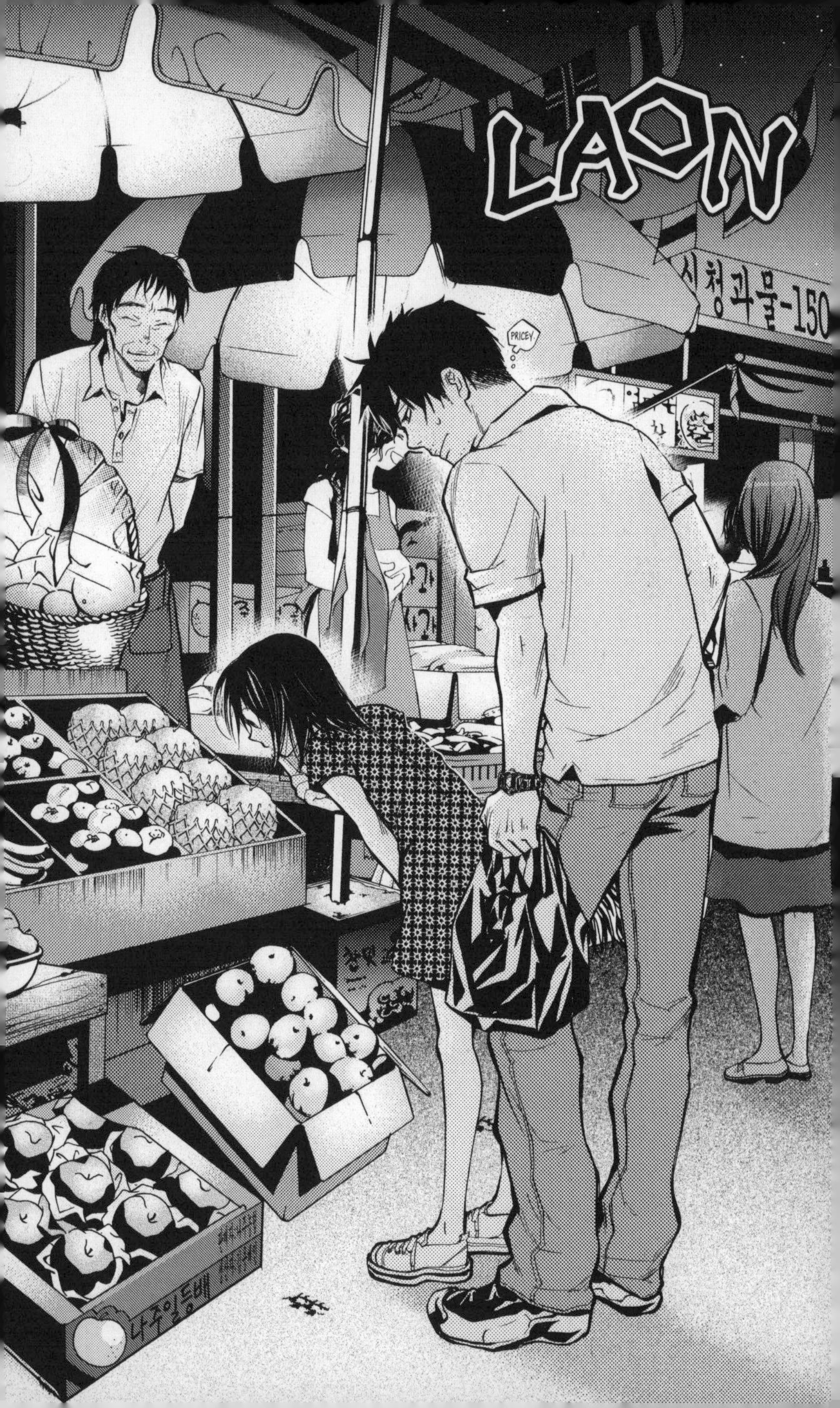
LAON
PRICEY.
시청과물-150
나주일등배

MAGAZINE: EUNBI, A WORLD COVERED IN SILVER

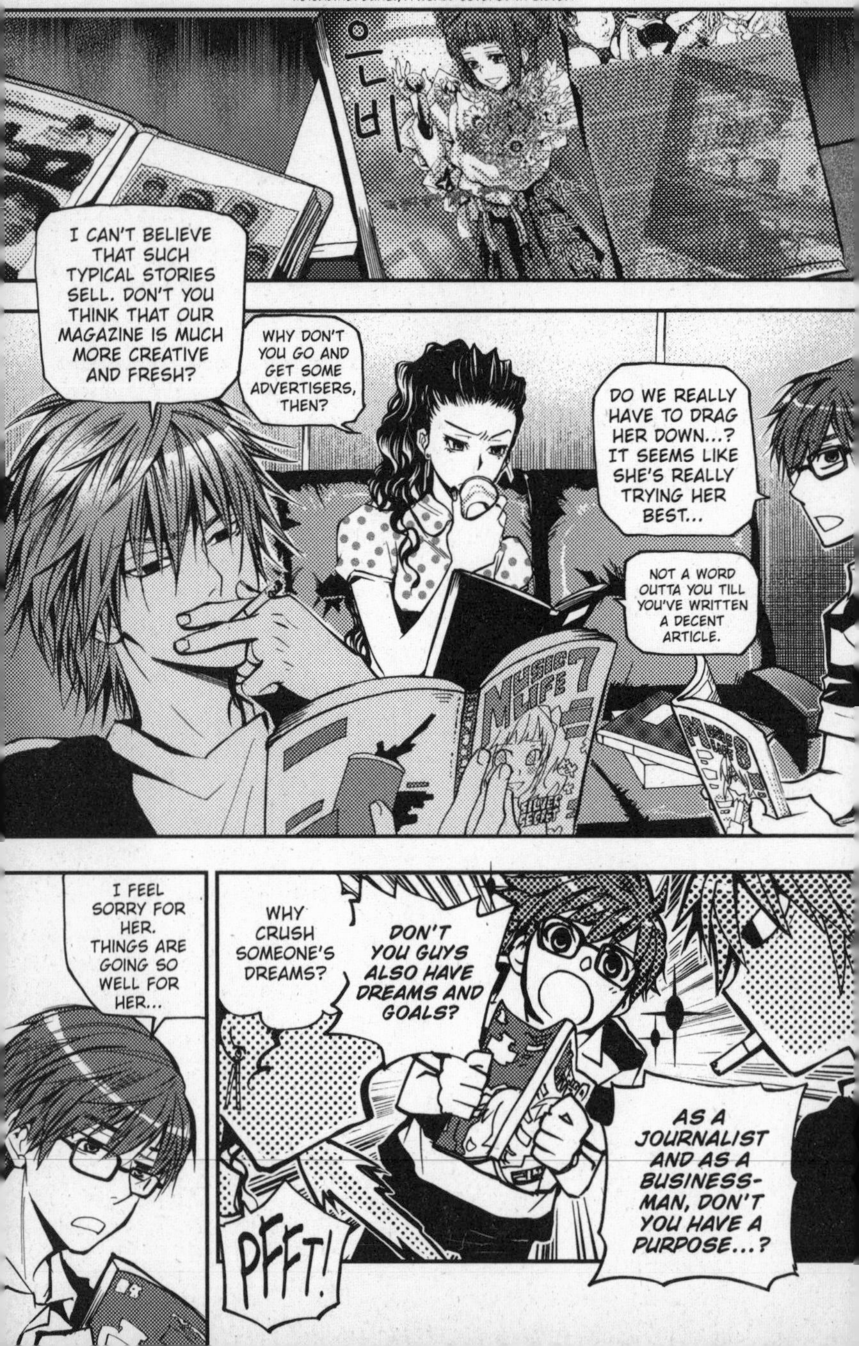
I CAN'T BELIEVE THAT SUCH TYPICAL STORIES SELL. DON'T YOU THINK THAT OUR MAGAZINE IS MUCH MORE CREATIVE AND FRESH?
WHY DON'T YOU GO AND GET SOME ADVERTISERS, THEN?
DO WE REALLY HAVE TO DRAG HER DOWN...? IT SEEMS LIKE SHE'S REALLY TRYING HER BEST...
NOT A WORD OUTTA YOU TILL YOU'VE WRITTEN A DECENT ARTICLE.
MUSIC LIFE 7
SILVER SECRET
I FEEL SORRY FOR HER. THINGS ARE GOING SO WELL FOR HER...
WHY CRUSH SOMEONE'S DREAMS?
DON'T YOU GUYS ALSO HAVE DREAMS AND GOALS?
AS A JOURNALIST AND AS A BUSINESS-MAN, DON'T YOU HAVE A PURPOSE...?
PFFT!

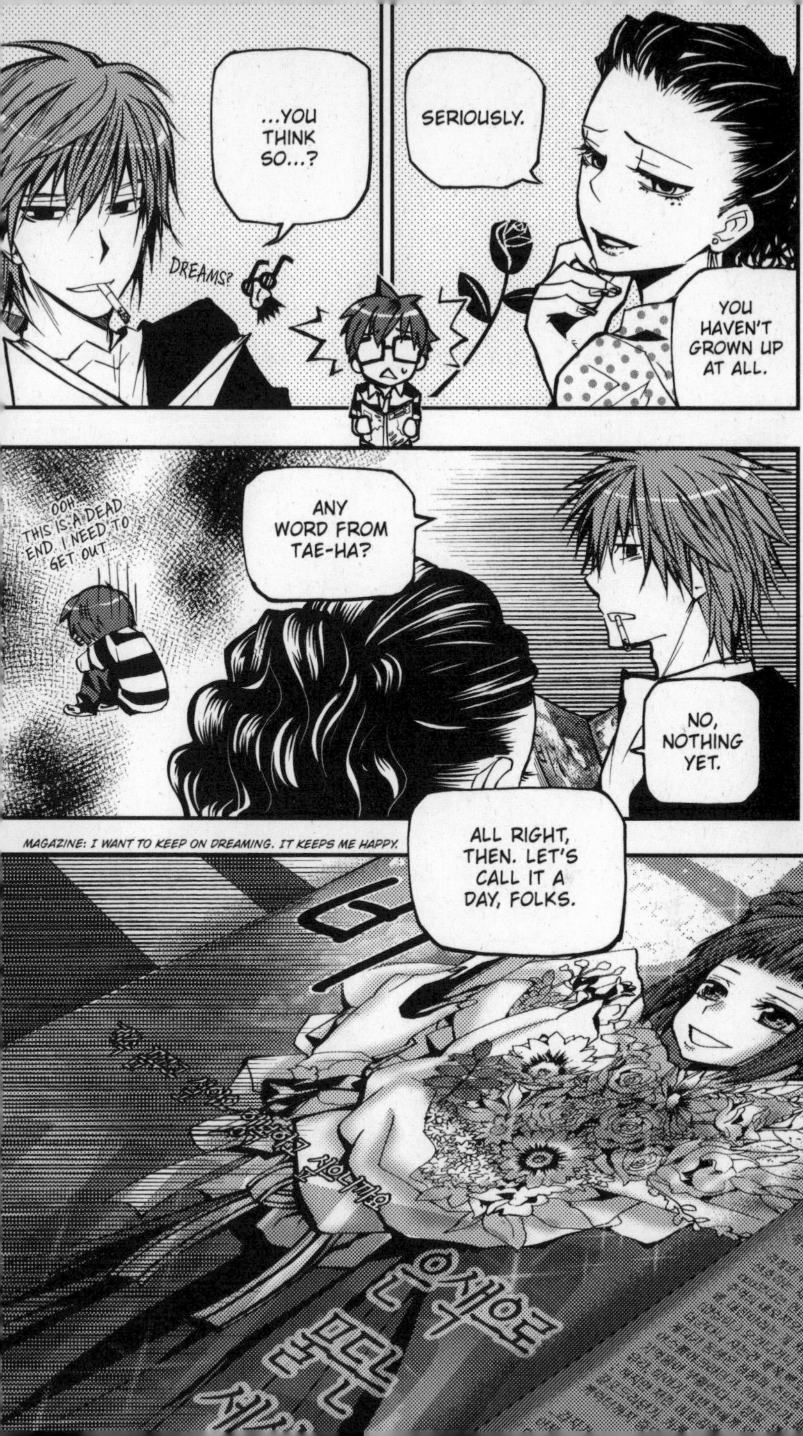
...YOU THINK SO...?
DREAMS?
SERIOUSLY.
YOU HAVEN'T GROWN UP AT ALL.
OOH... THIS IS A DEAD END. I NEED TO GET OUT...
ANY WORD FROM TAE-HA?
NO, NOTHING YET.
MAGAZINE: I WANT TO KEEP ON DREAMING. IT KEEPS ME HAPPY.
ALL RIGHT, THEN. LET'S CALL IT A DAY, FOLKS.

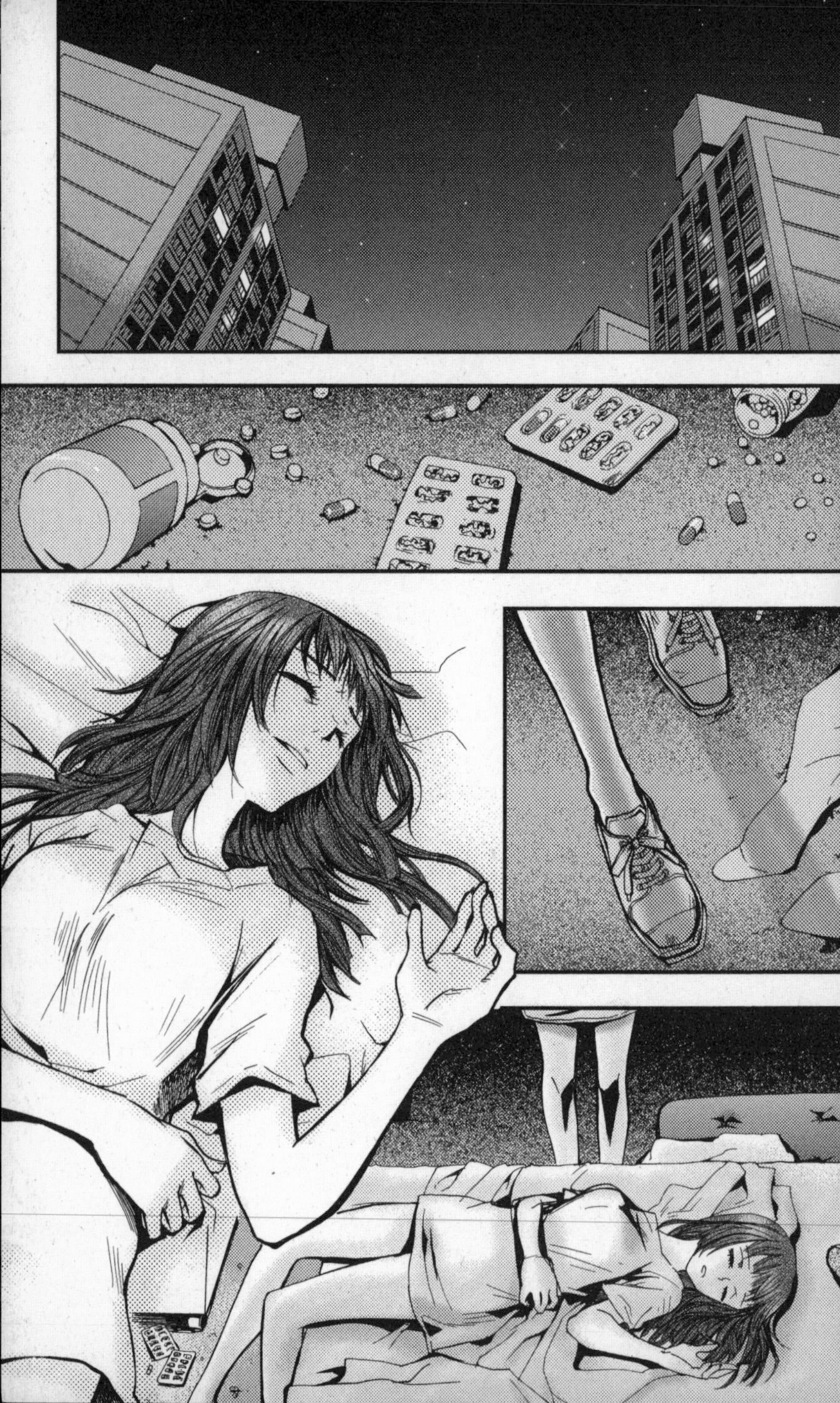

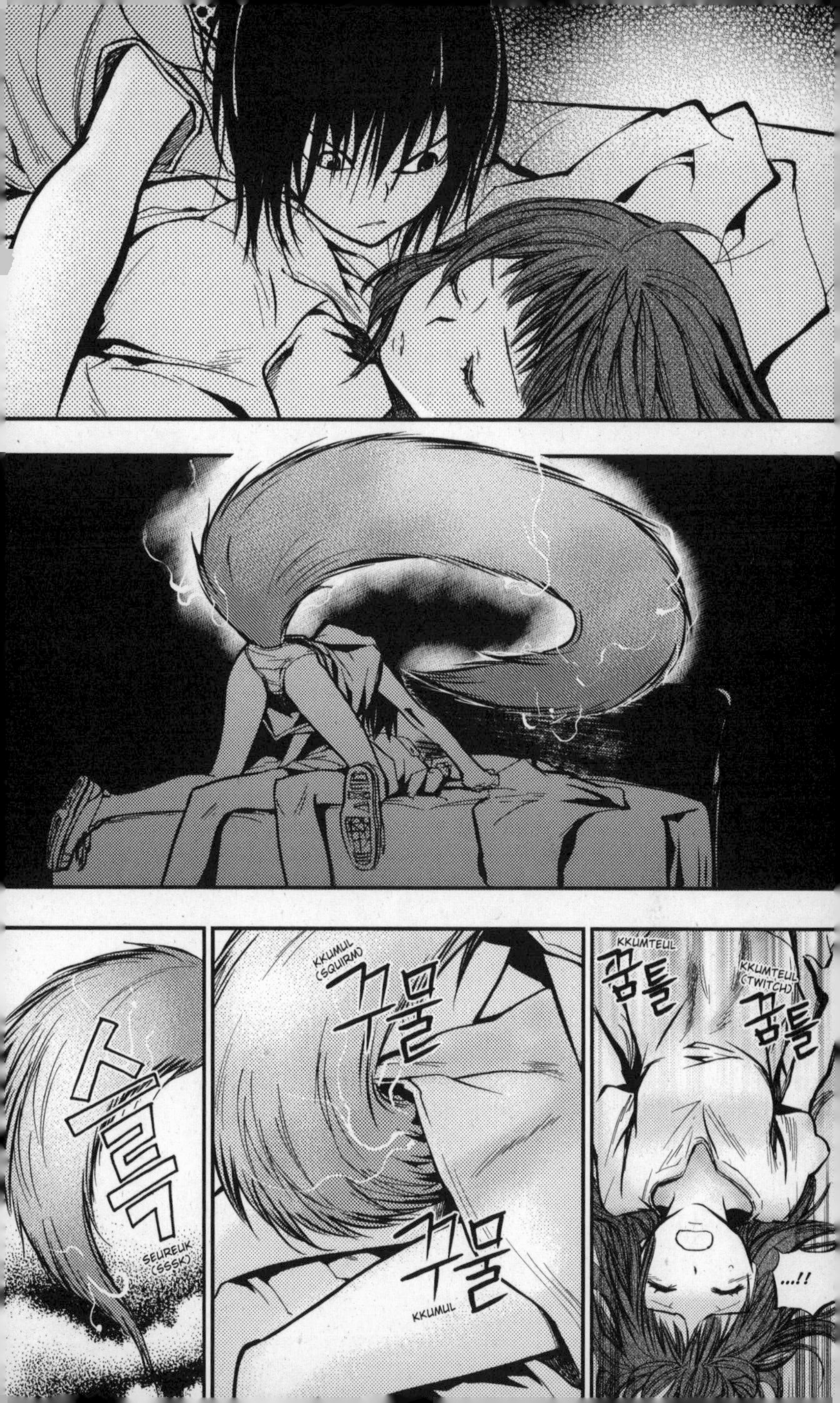
스르륵
SEURELIK (SSSK)
KKUMUL (SQUIRM)
꾸물
꾸물
KKUMUL
KKUMTEUL
꿈틀
KKUMTEUL (TWITCH)
꿈틀
...!!

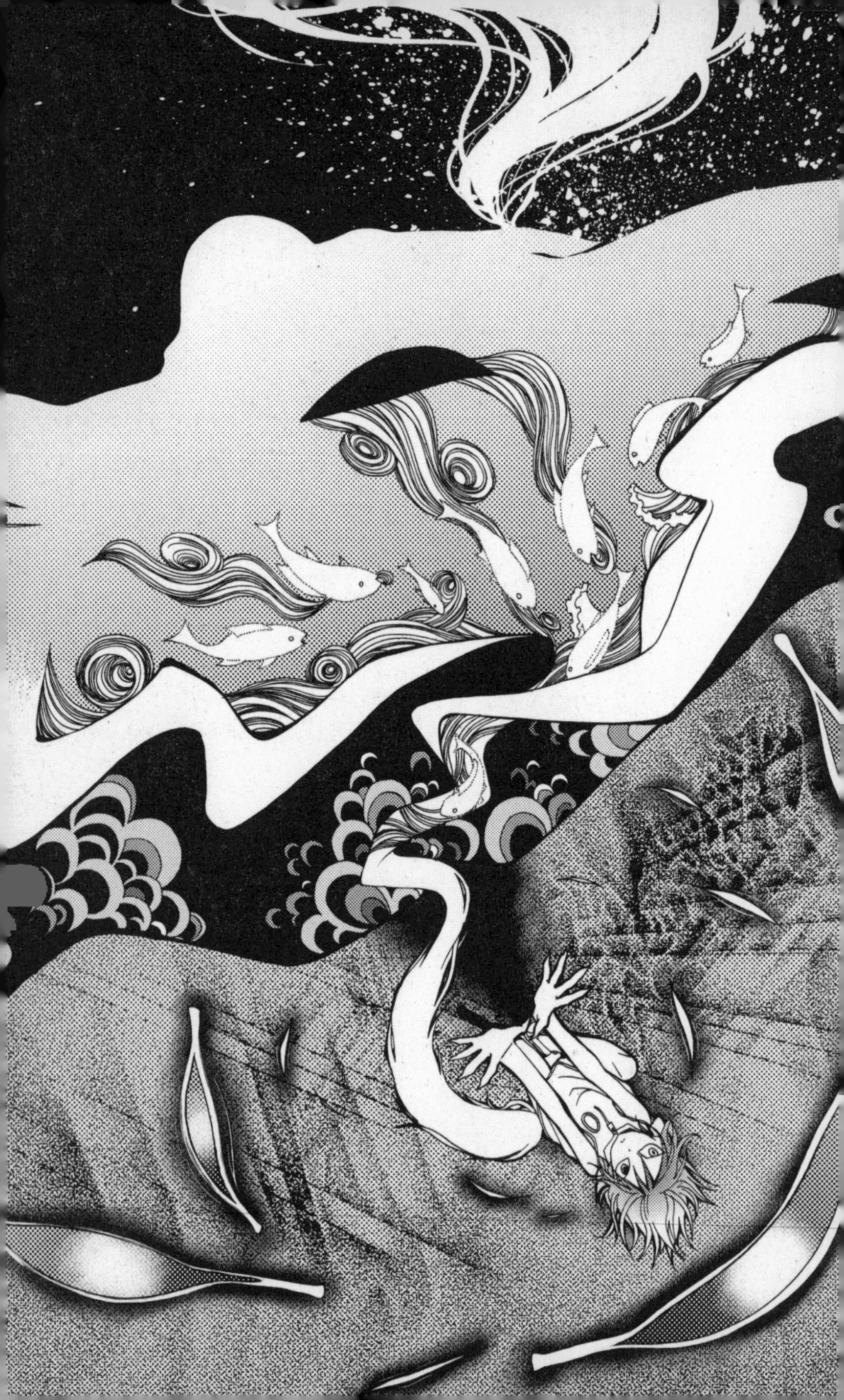

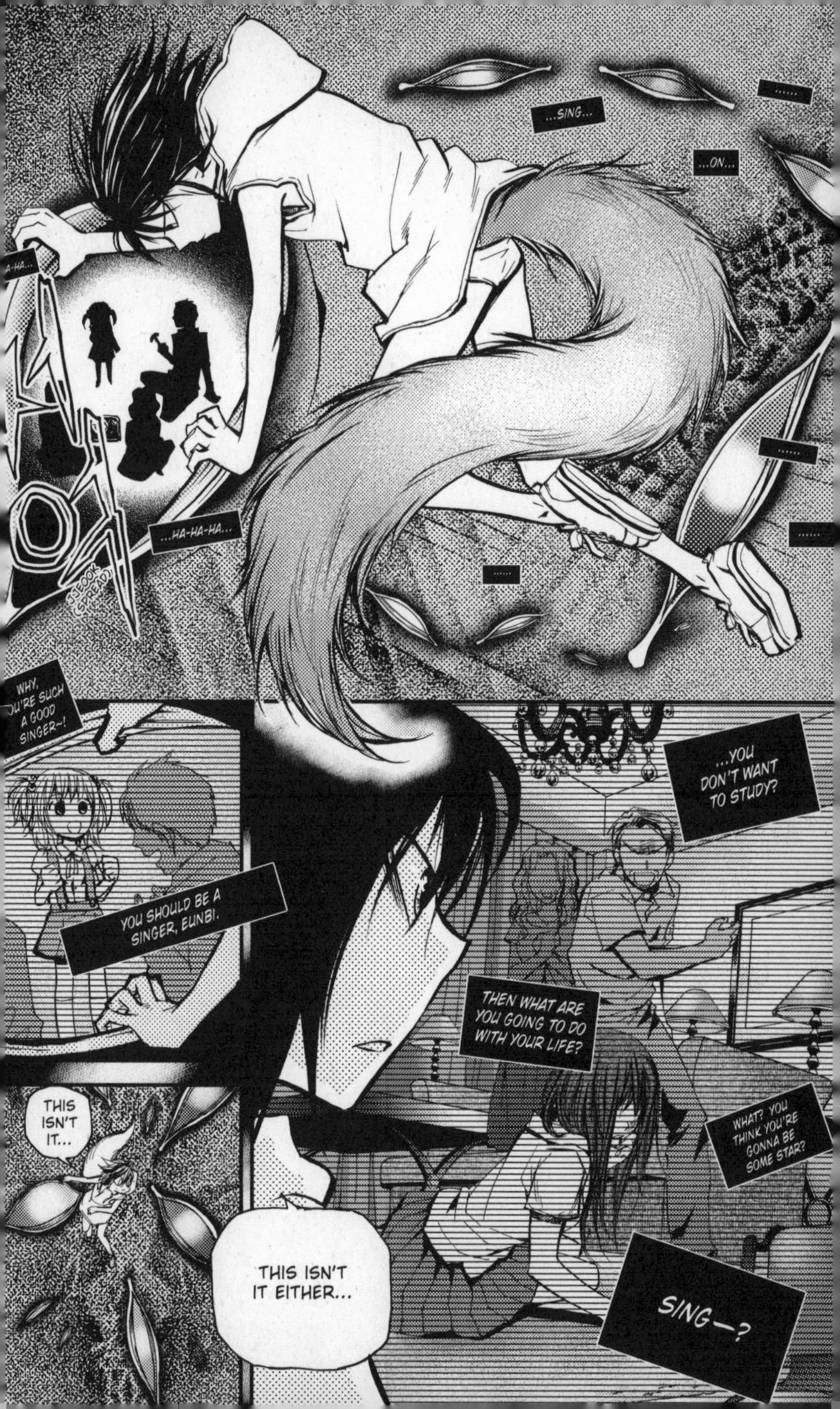
A-HA...
JJEOOK (SPREAD)
...HA-HA-HA...
...SING...
......
...ON...
......
......
......
WHY, OU'RE SUCH A GOOD SINGER~!
YOU SHOULD BE A SINGER, EUNBI.
...YOU DON'T WANT TO STUDY?
THEN WHAT ARE YOU GOING TO DO WITH YOUR LIFE?
WHAT? YOU THINK YOU'RE GONNA BE SOME STAR?
SING—?
THIS ISN'T IT...
THIS ISN'T IT EITHER...

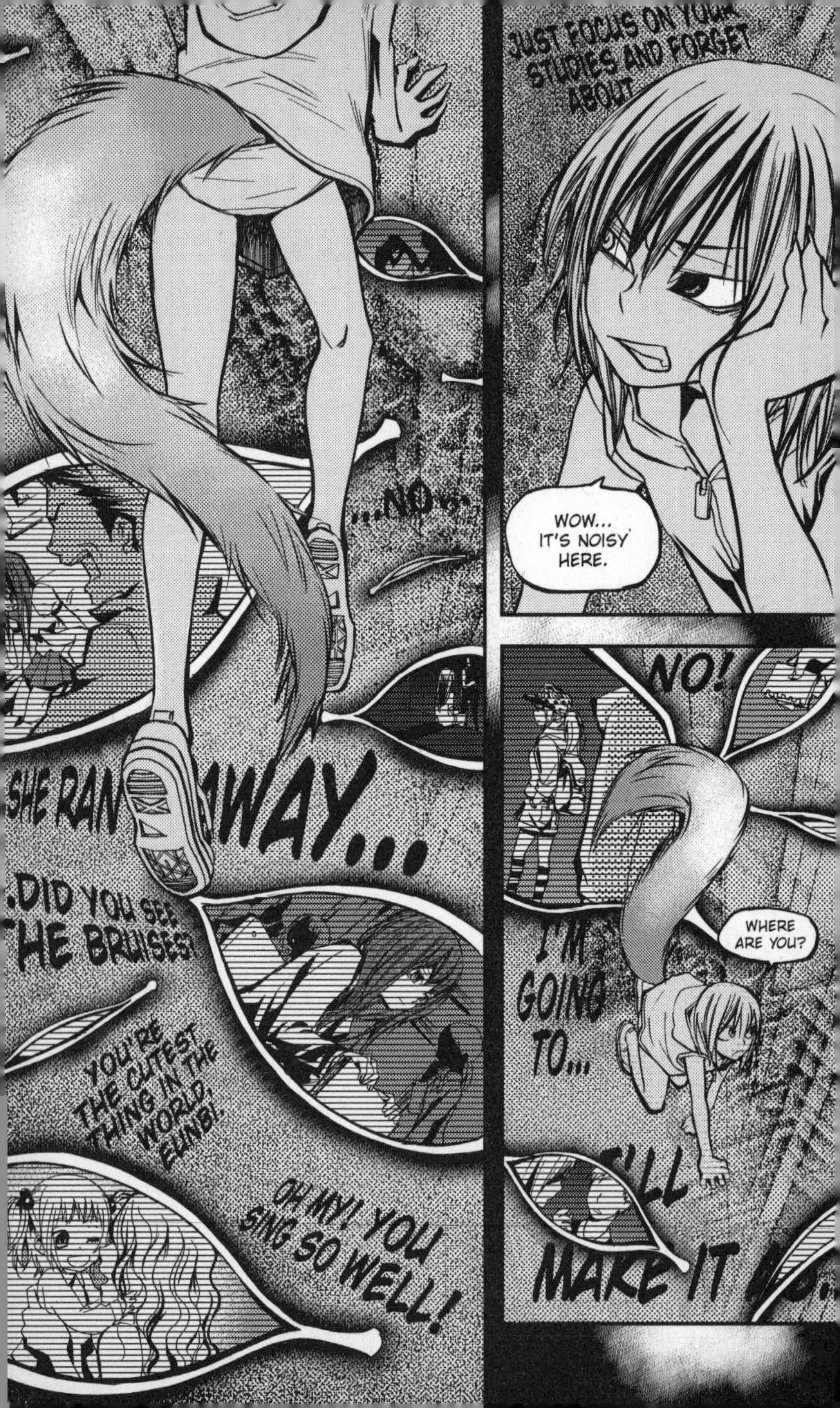

...NO...
SHE RAN AWAY...
.DID YOU SEE THE BRUISES?
YOU'RE THE CUTEST THING IN THE WORLD, EUNBI.
OH MY! YOU SING SO WELL!
JUST FOCUS ON YOUR STUDIES AND FORGET ABOUT
WOW... IT'S NOISY HERE.
NO!
WHERE ARE YOU?
I'M GOING TO...
MAKE IT

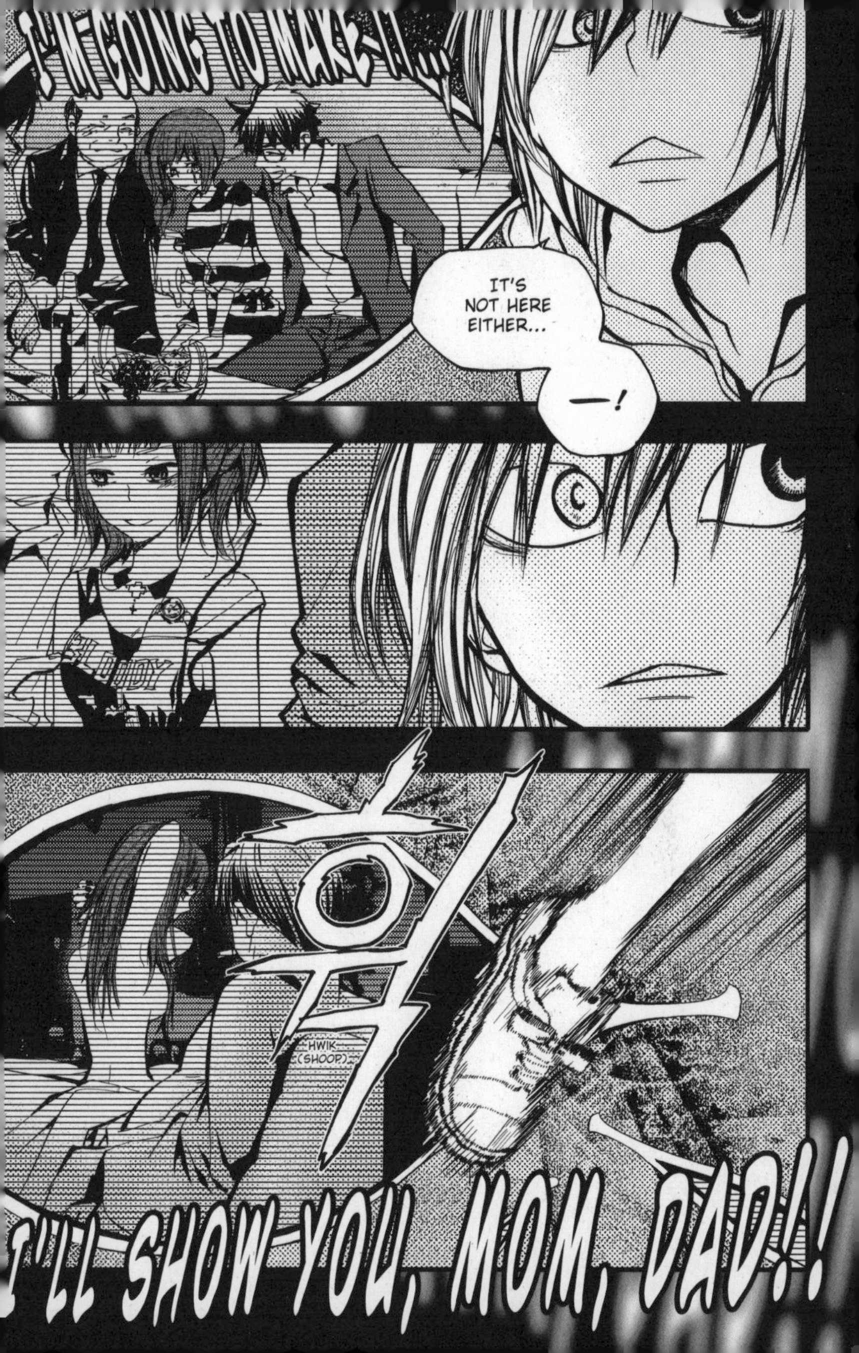
I'M GOING TO MAKE IT...
IT'S NOT HERE EITHER...
—!
HWIK (SHOOP)
I'LL SHOW YOU, MOM, DAD!!

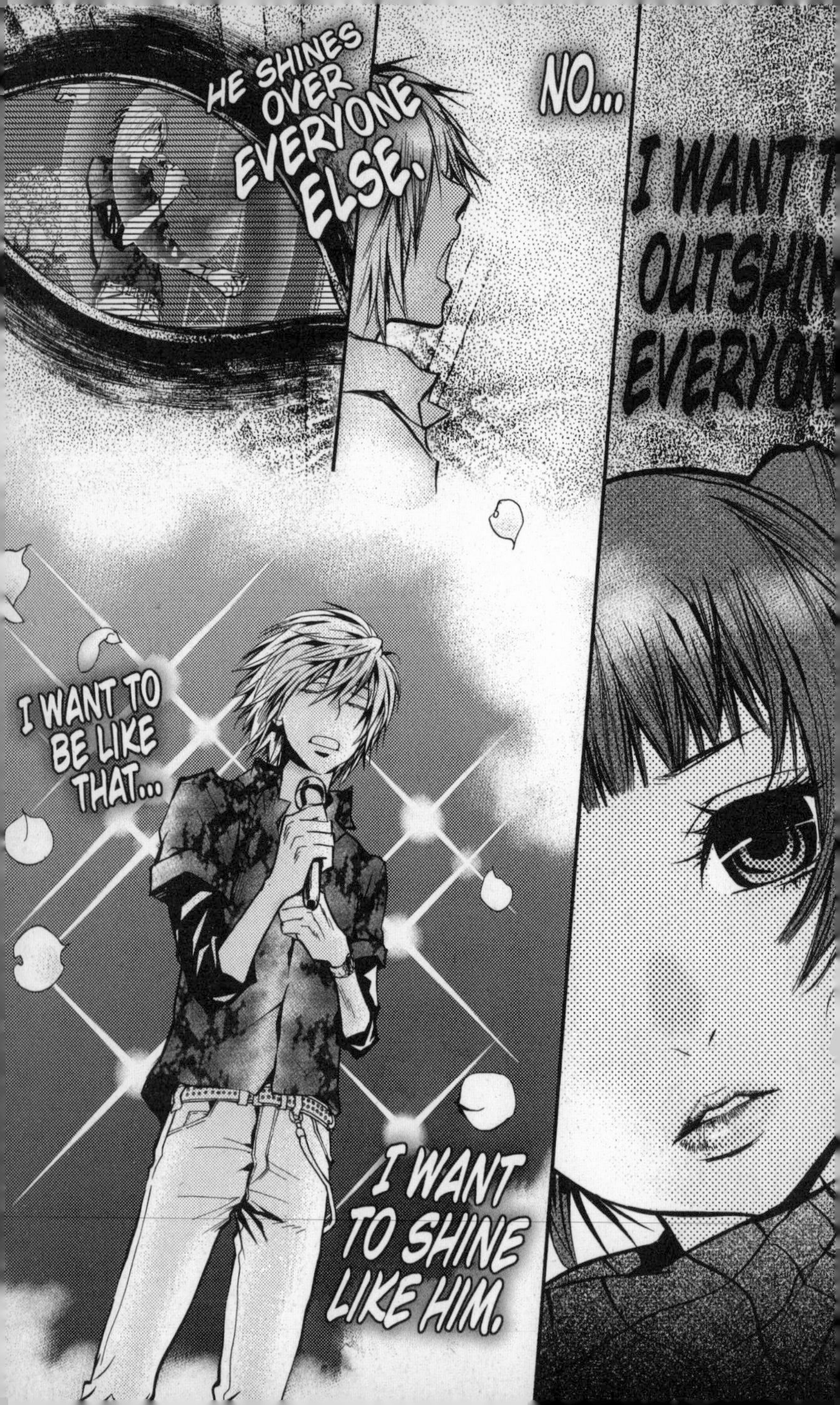
HE SHINES OVER EVERYONE ELSE.
I WANT TO BE LIKE THAT...
I WANT TO SHINE LIKE HIM.
NO...
I WANT T
OUTSHIN
EVERYON

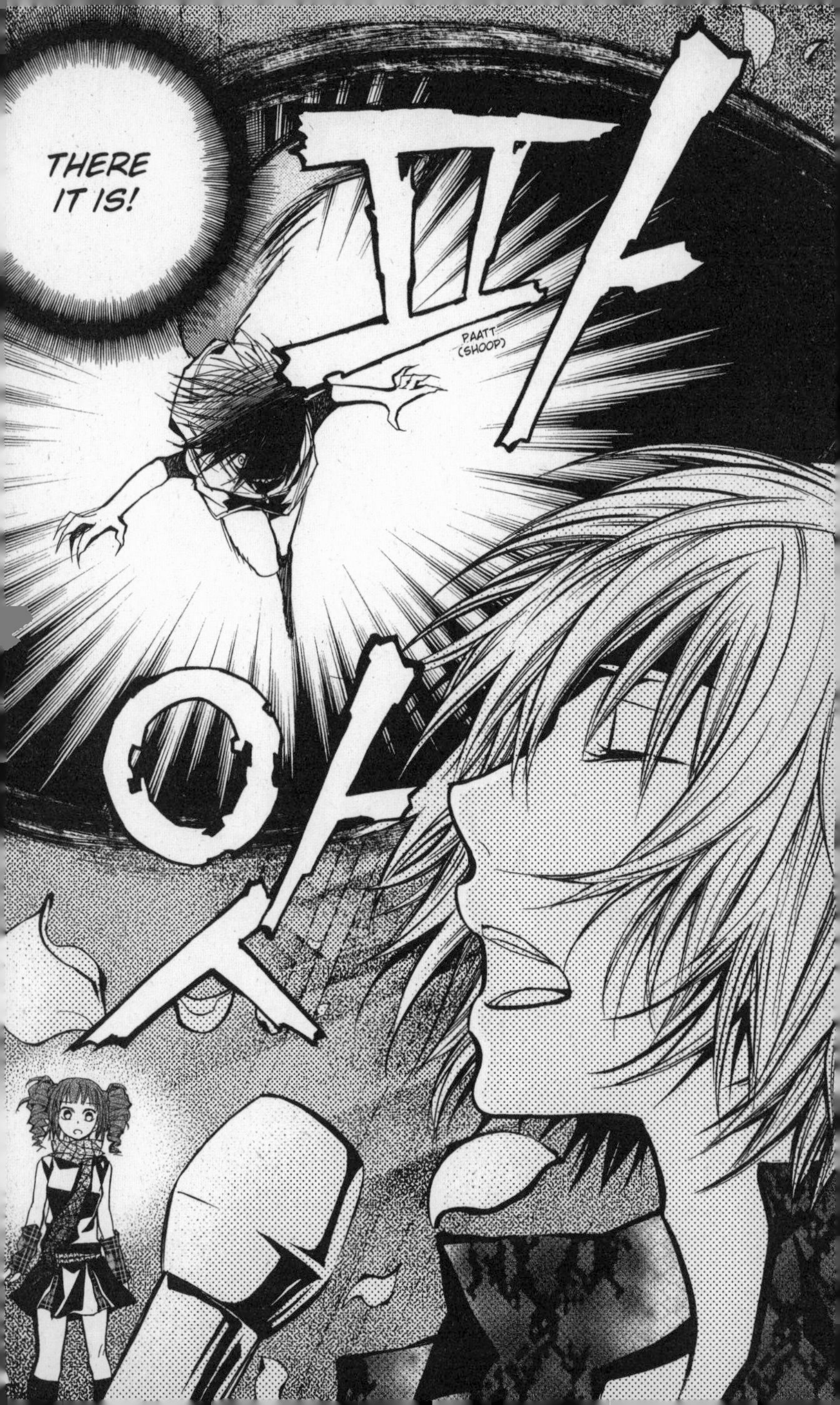
THERE IT IS!
PAATT (SHOOP)

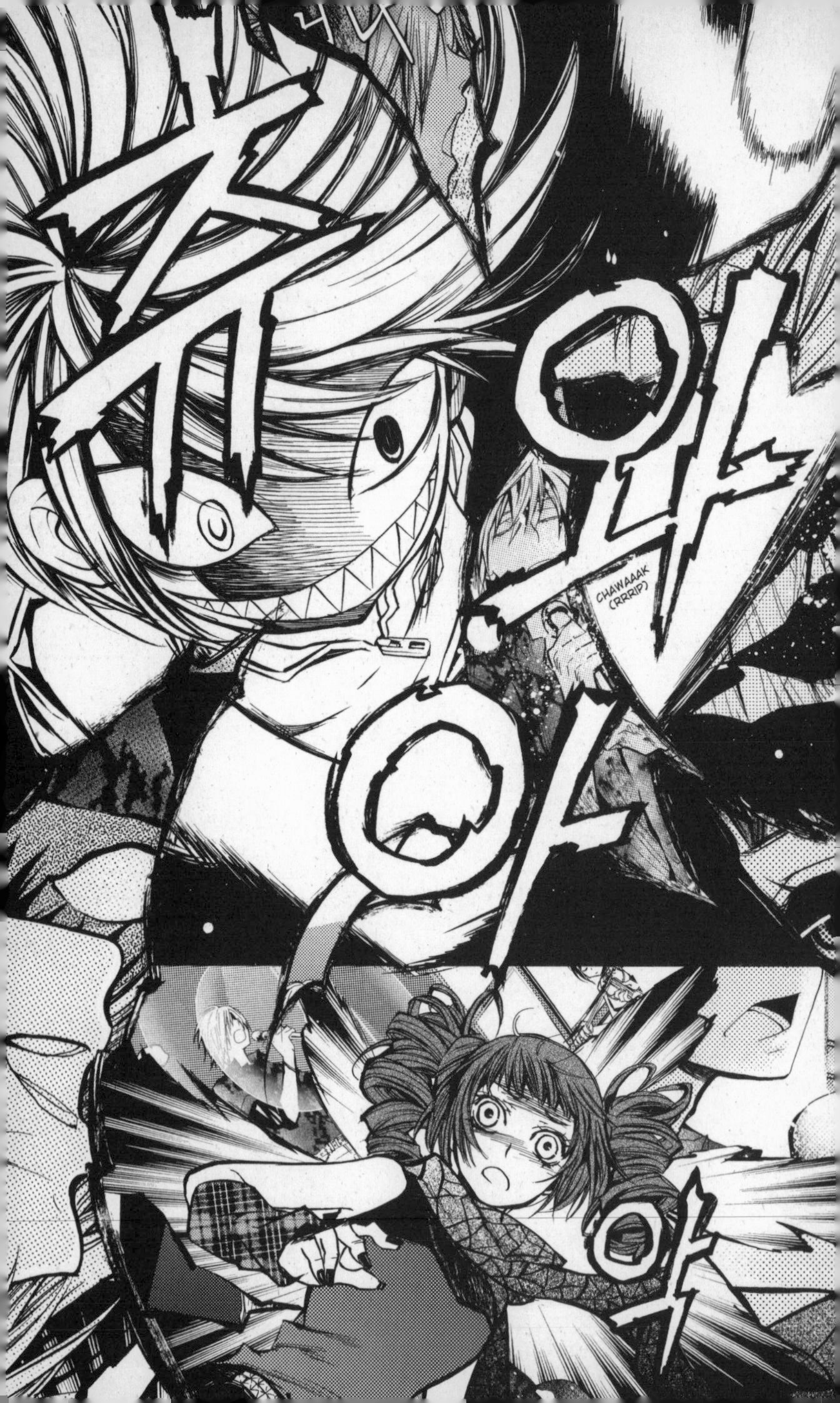
CHAWAAAK
(RRRIP)

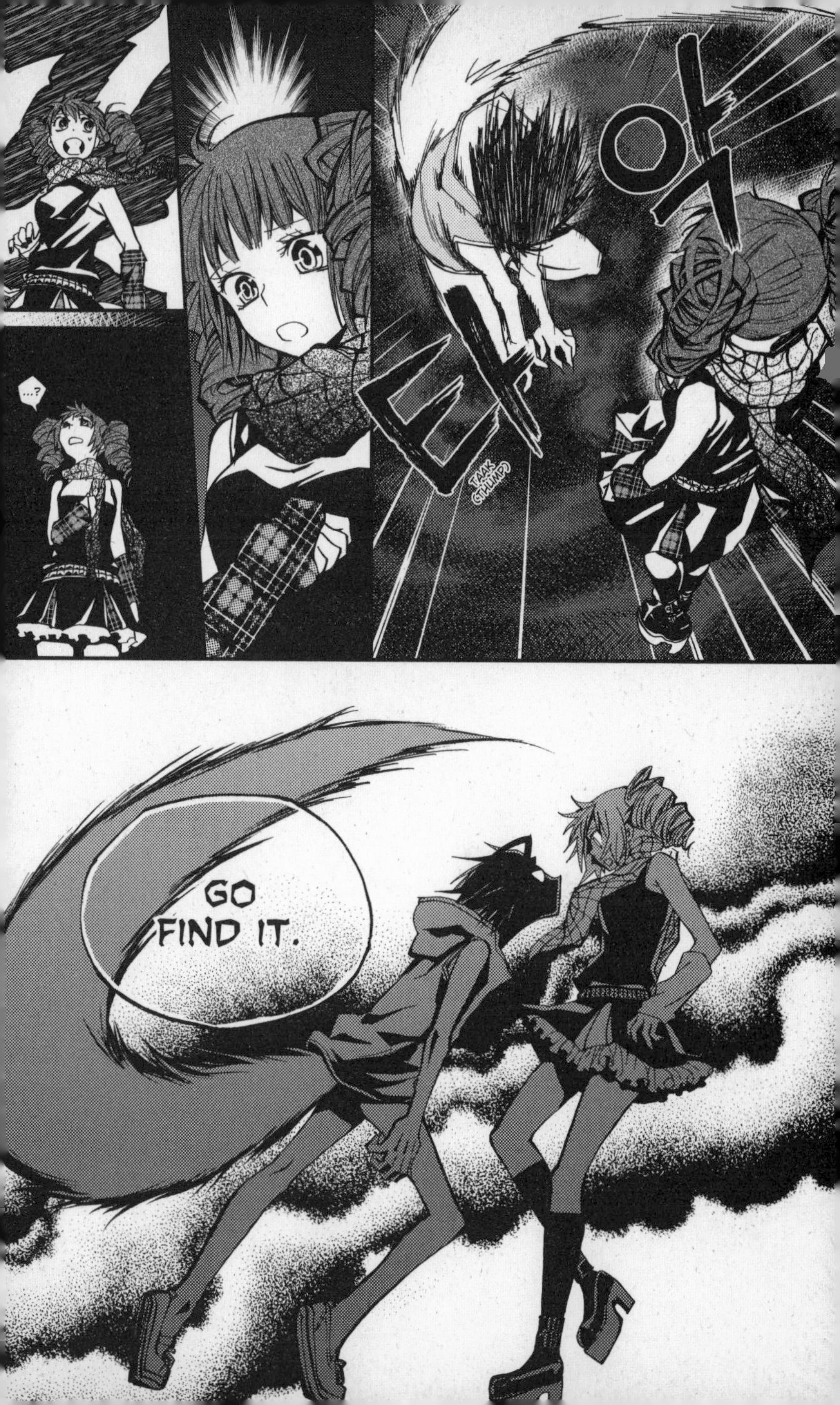
...?
TAAK (THUMP)
GO FIND IT.

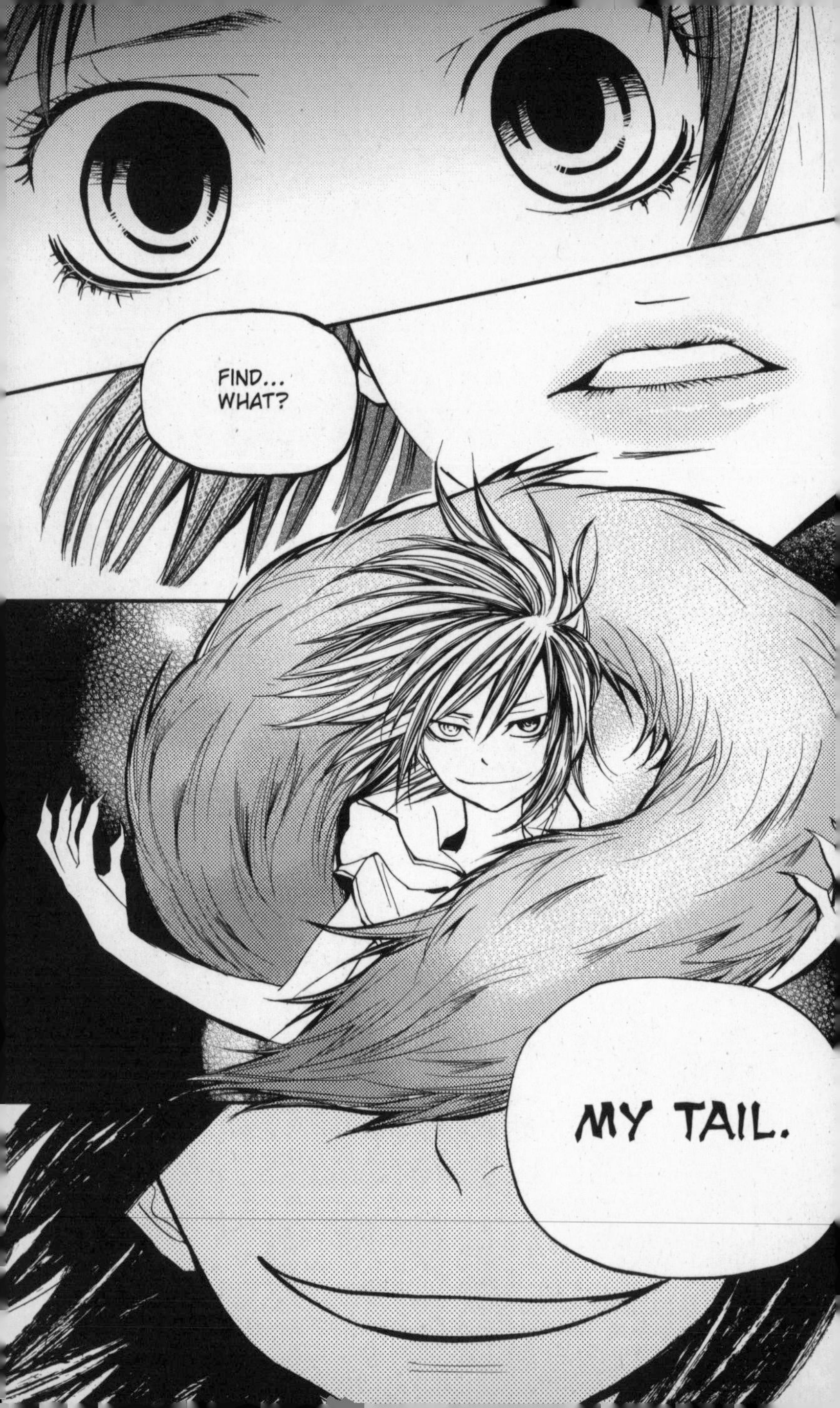
FIND... WHAT?
MY TAIL.

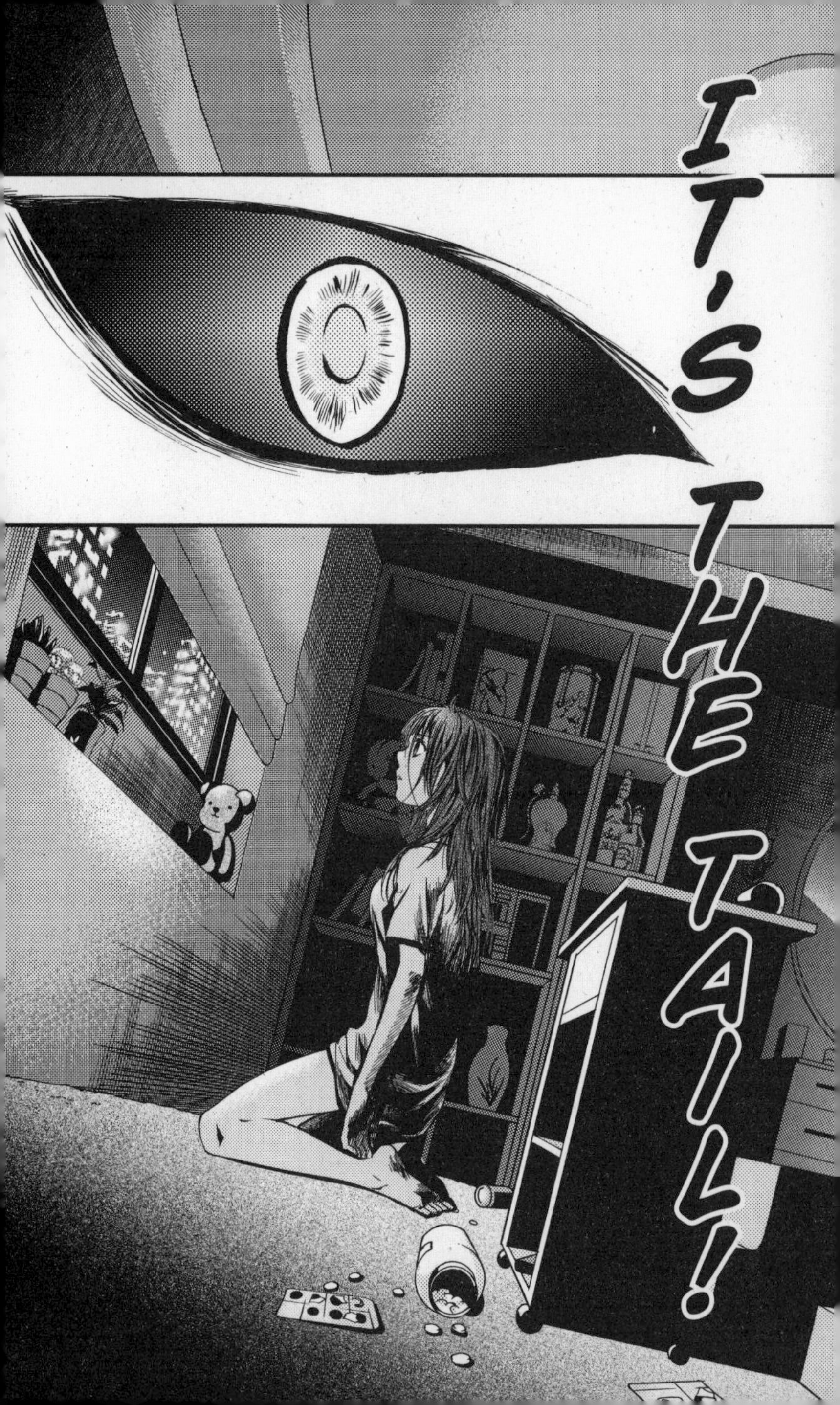
IT'S THE TAIL!

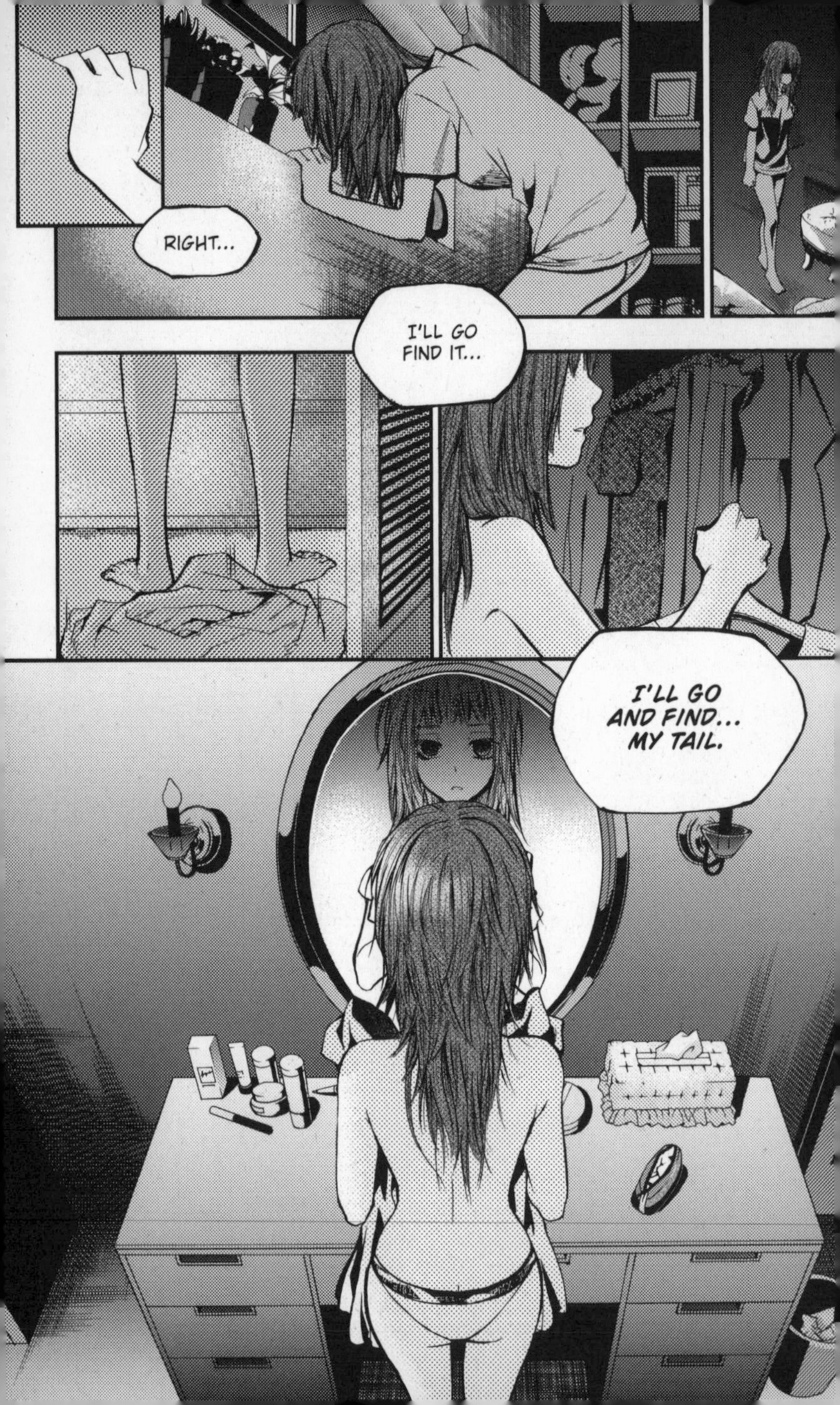
RIGHT...
I'LL GO FIND IT...
I'LL GO AND FIND... MY TAIL.

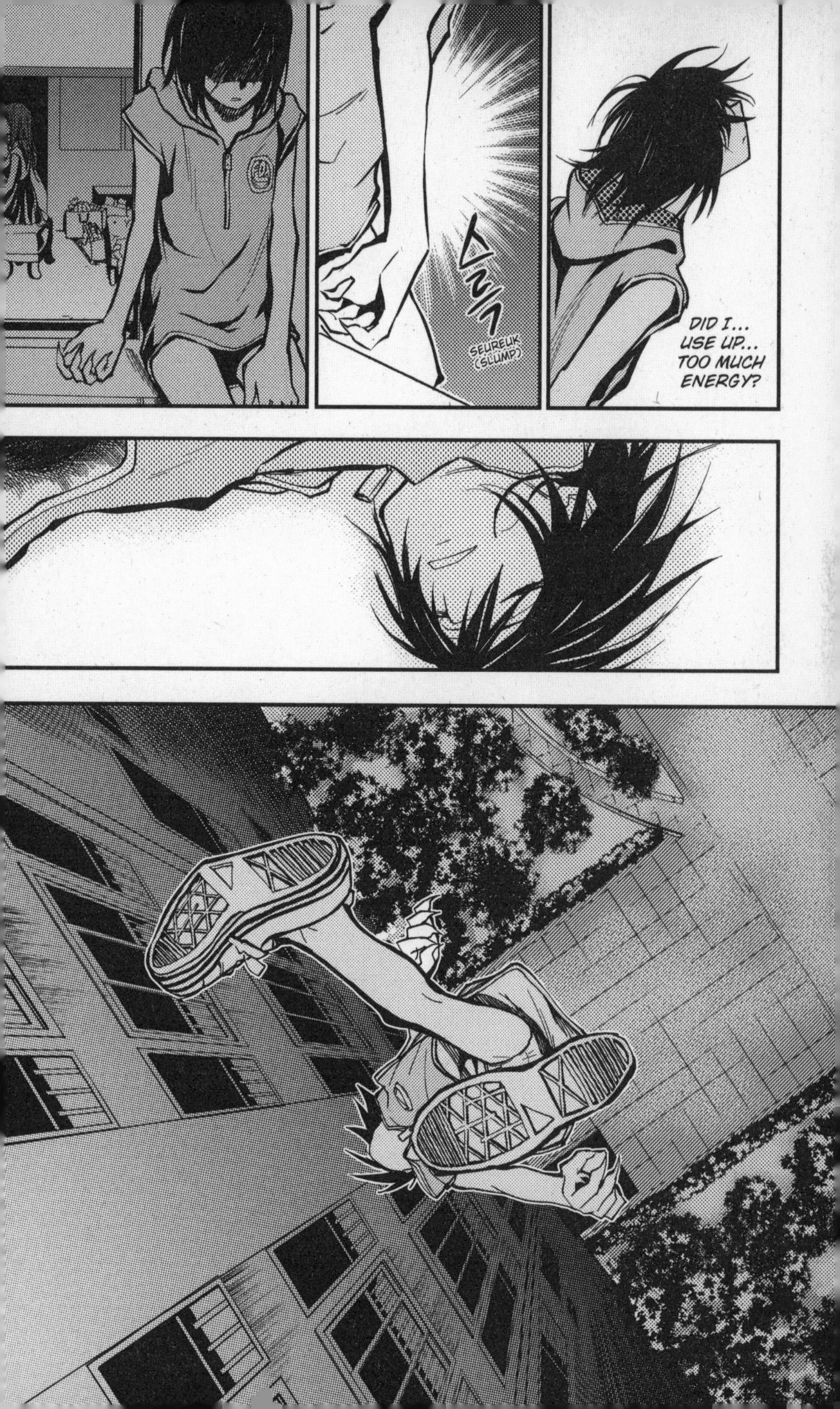
SEUREUK (SLUMP)
DID I... USE UP... TOO MUCH ENERGY?

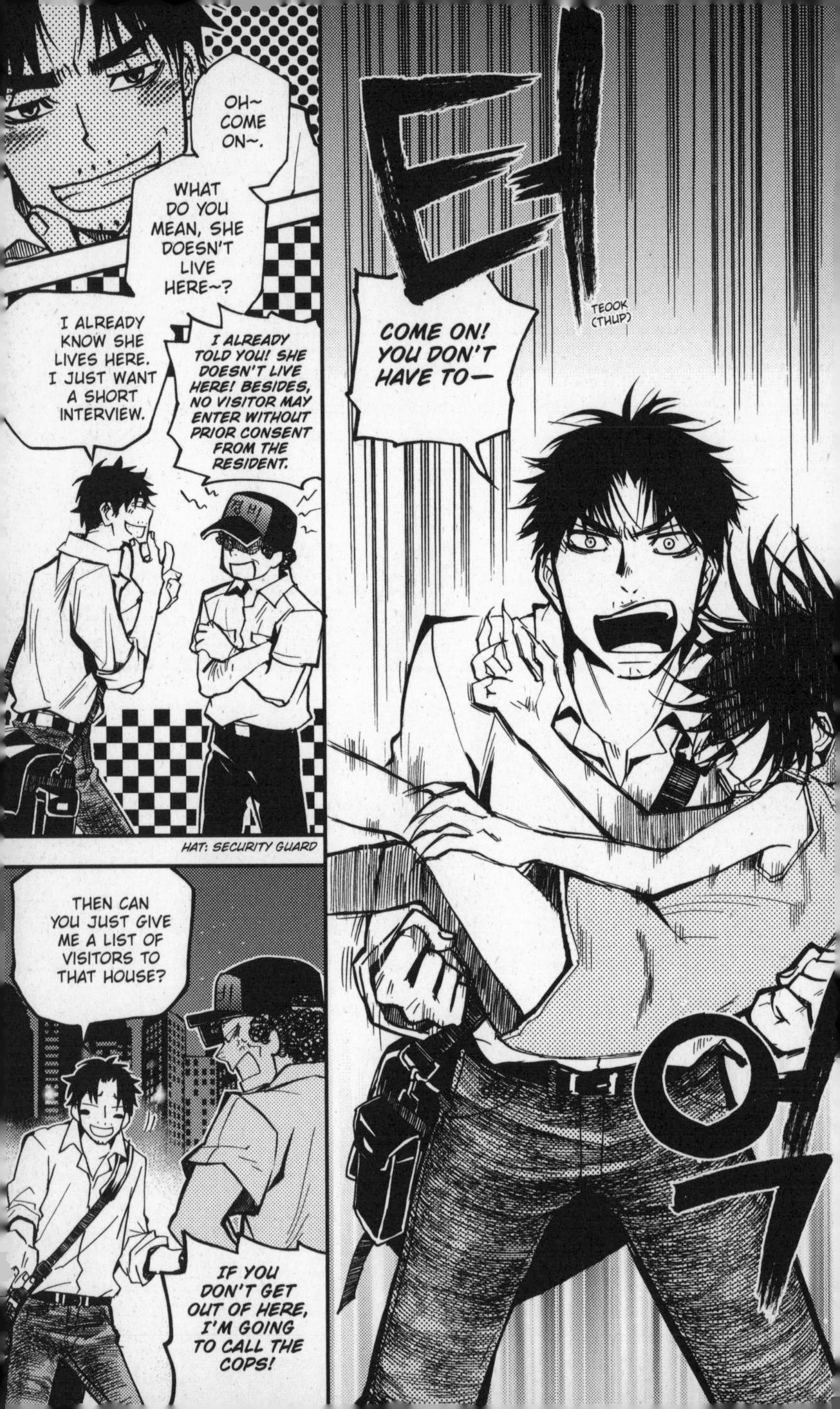
OH~ COME ON~.
WHAT DO YOU MEAN, SHE DOESN'T LIVE HERE~?
I ALREADY KNOW SHE LIVES HERE. I JUST WANT A SHORT INTERVIEW.
I ALREADY TOLD YOU! SHE DOESN'T LIVE HERE! BESIDES, NO VISITOR MAY ENTER WITHOUT PRIOR CONSENT FROM THE RESIDENT.
HAT: SECURITY GUARD
THEN CAN YOU JUST GIVE ME A LIST OF VISITORS TO THAT HOUSE?
IF YOU DON'T GET OUT OF HERE, I'M GOING TO CALL THE COPS!
TEOOK (THUP)
COME ON! YOU DON'T HAVE TO—

LA...LAON?!

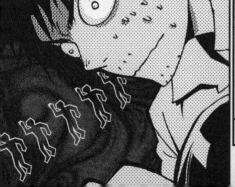

AH...

MM...

UHH...

WHAT'S GOING ON HERE?

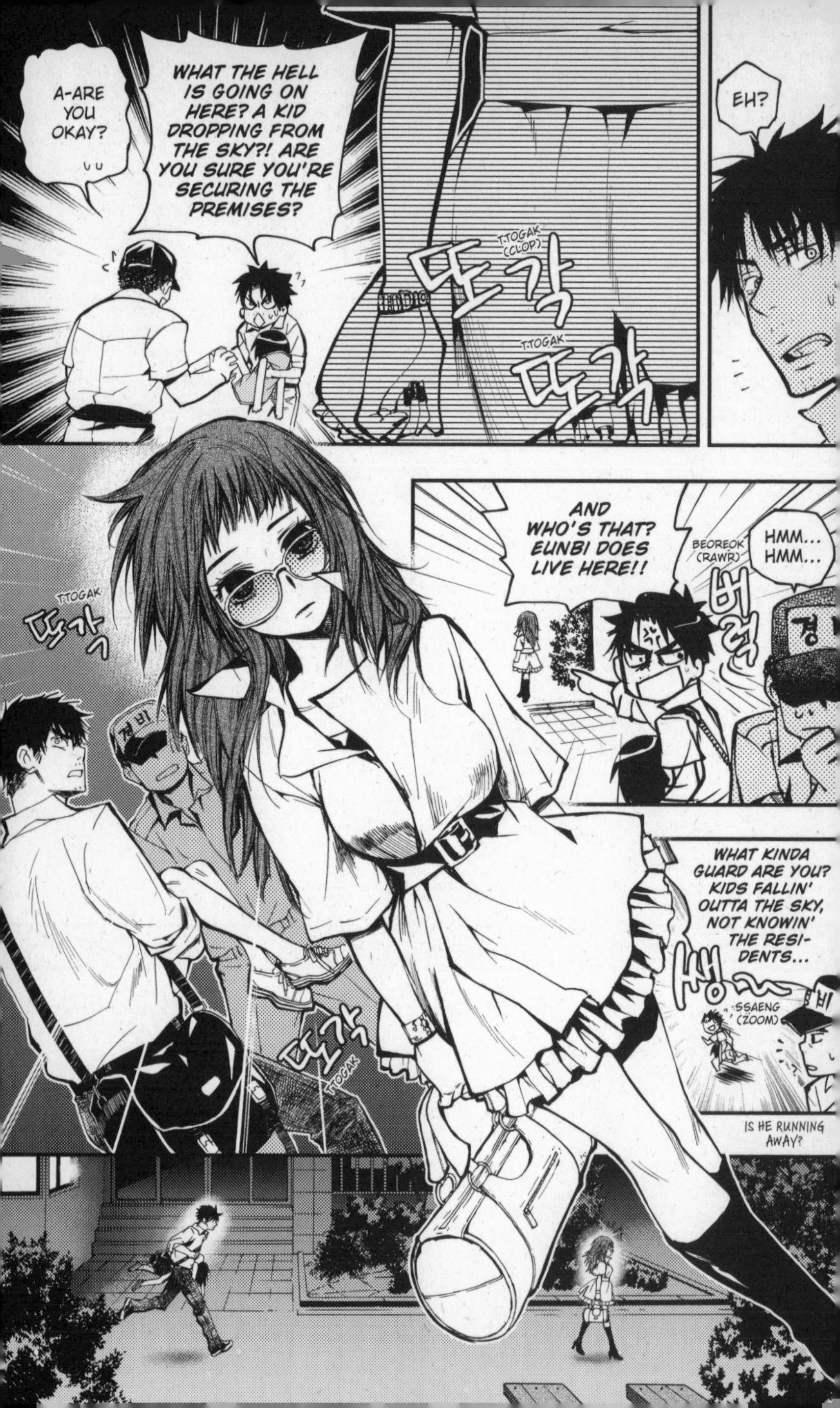
A-ARE YOU OKAY?
WHAT THE HELL IS GOING ON HERE? A KID DROPPING FROM THE SKY?! ARE YOU SURE YOU'RE SECURING THE PREMISES?
T.TOGAK (CLOP)
또각
T.TOGAK
또각
EH?
T.TOGAK
또각
또각
T.TOGAK
AND WHO'S THAT? EUNBI DOES LIVE HERE!!
BEOREOK (RAWR)
버럭
HMM... HMM...
WHAT KINDA GUARD ARE YOU? KIDS FALLIN' OUTTA THE SKY, NOT KNOWIN' THE RESI-DENTS...
쌩~~
SSAENG (ZOOM)
IS HE RUNNING AWAY?

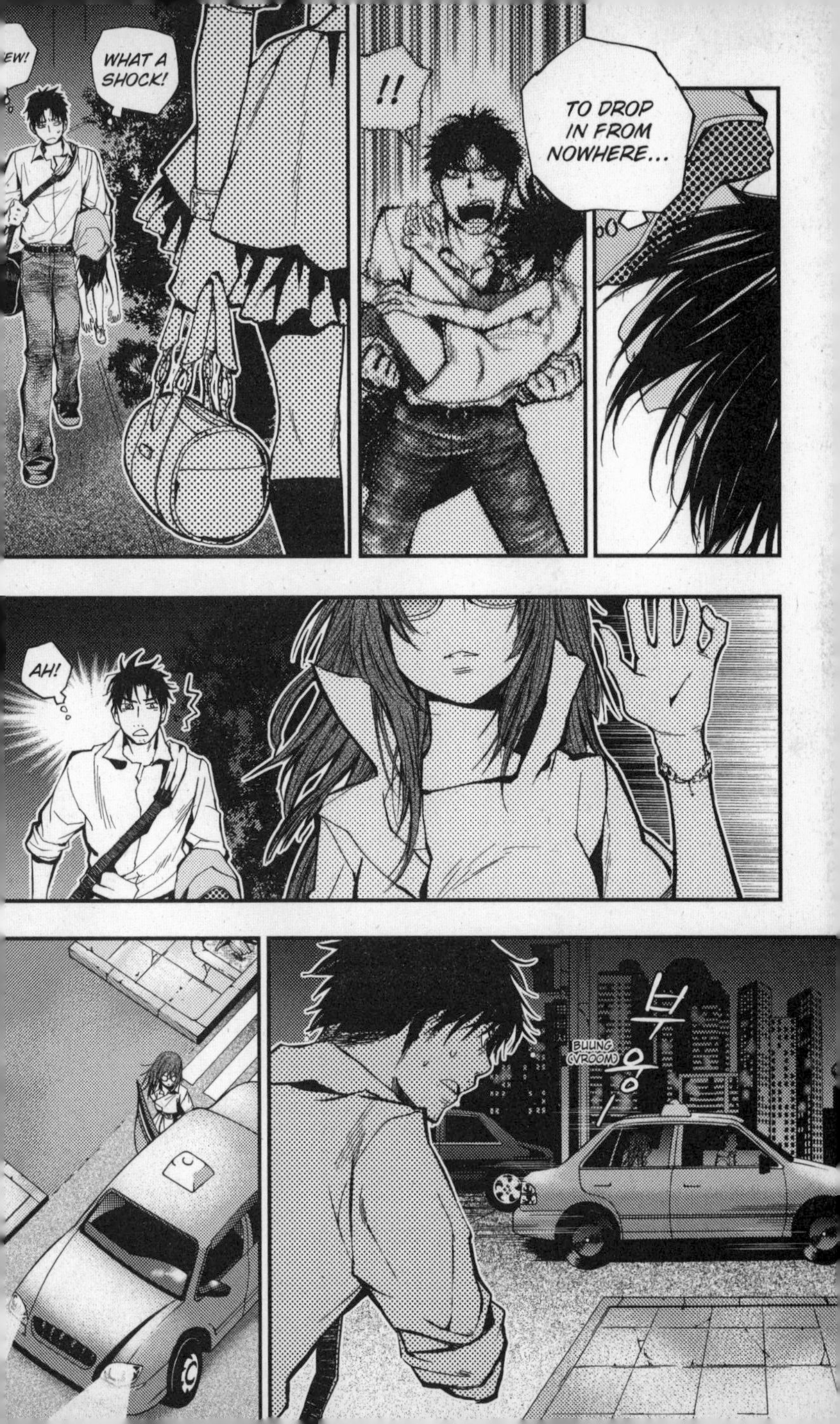
EW!
WHAT A SHOCK!
!!
TO DROP IN FROM NOWHERE...
AH!
부웅-
BUUNG (VROOM)

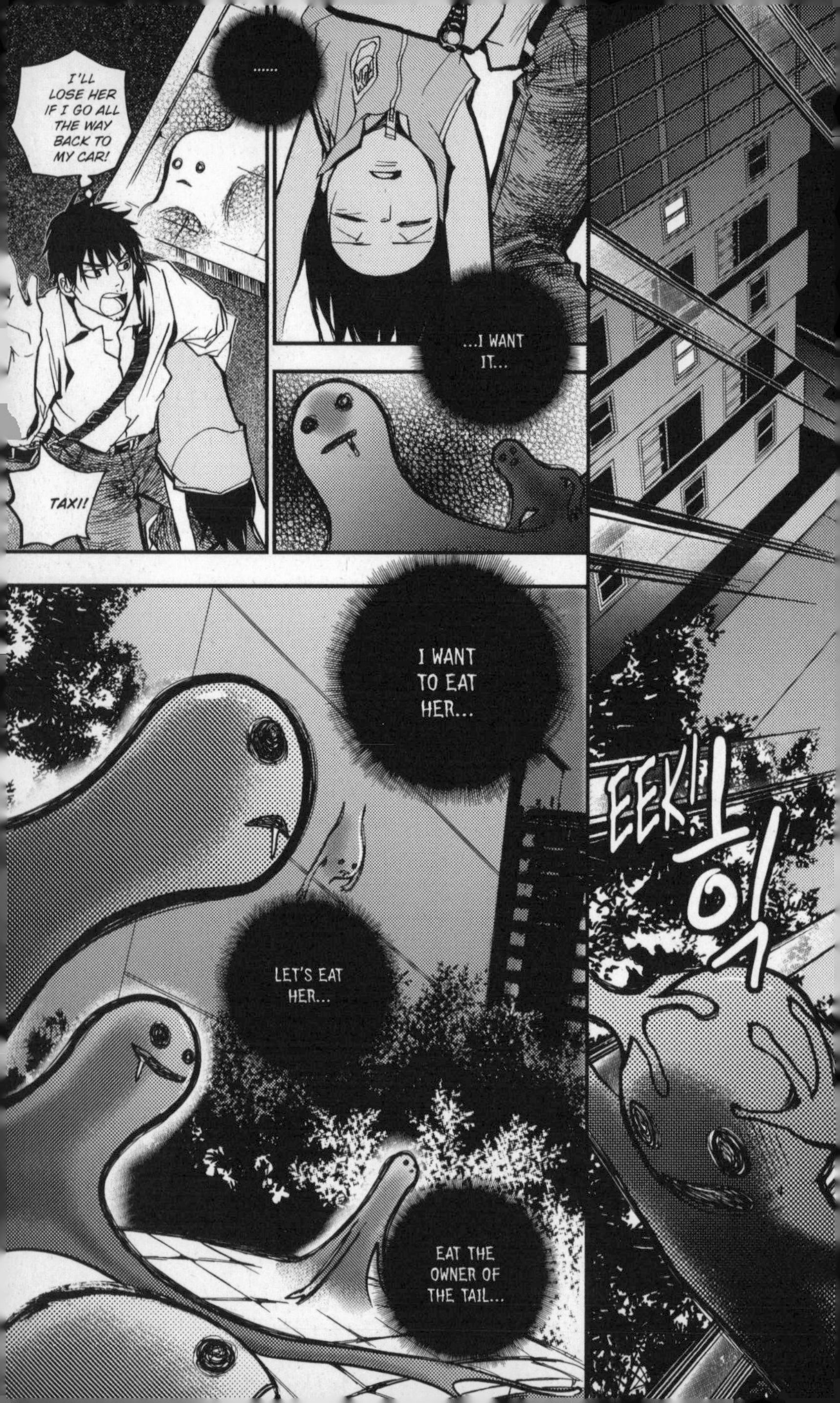
I'LL LOSE HER IF I GO ALL THE WAY BACK TO MY CAR!
TAXI!!
......
...I WANT IT...
I WANT TO EAT HER...
LET'S EAT HER...
EAT THE OWNER OF THE TAIL...
EEK!!

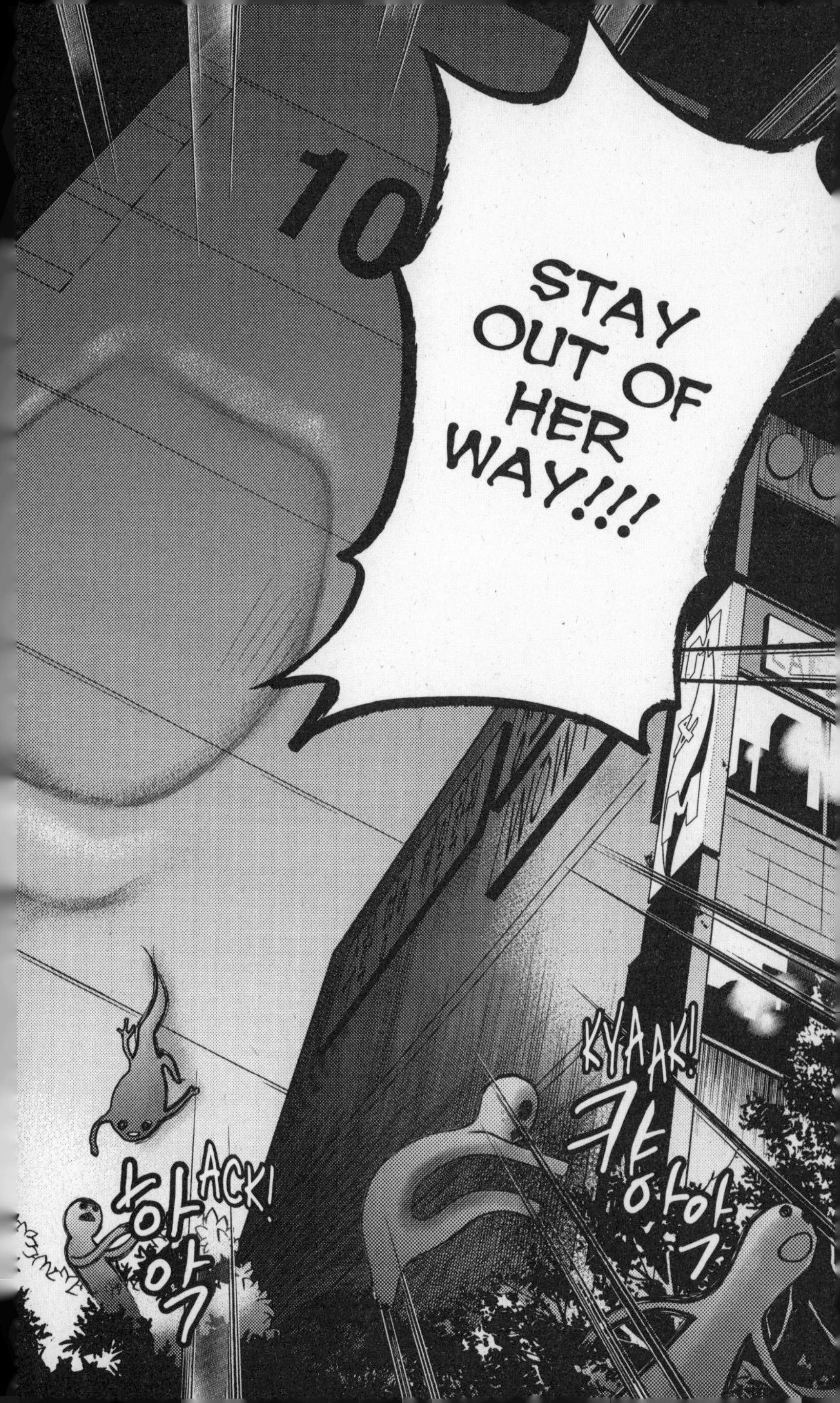
STAY OUT OF HER WAY!!!
ACK!
KYAAK!
캬아악

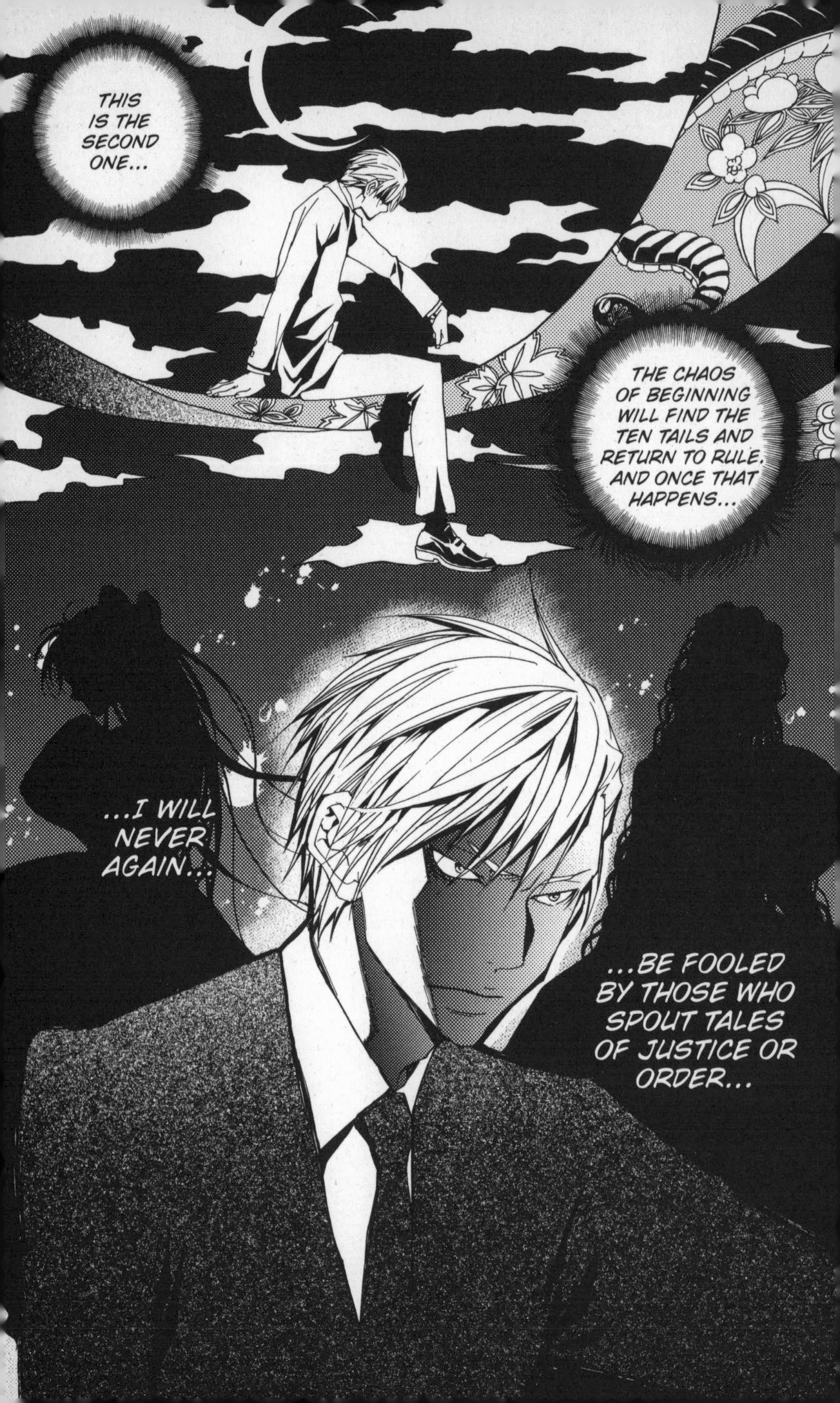
THIS IS THE SECOND ONE...
THE CHAOS OF BEGINNING WILL FIND THE TEN TAILS AND RETURN TO RULE. AND ONCE THAT HAPPENS...
...I WILL NEVER AGAIN...
...BE FOOLED BY THOSE WHO SPOUT TALES OF JUSTICE OR ORDER...

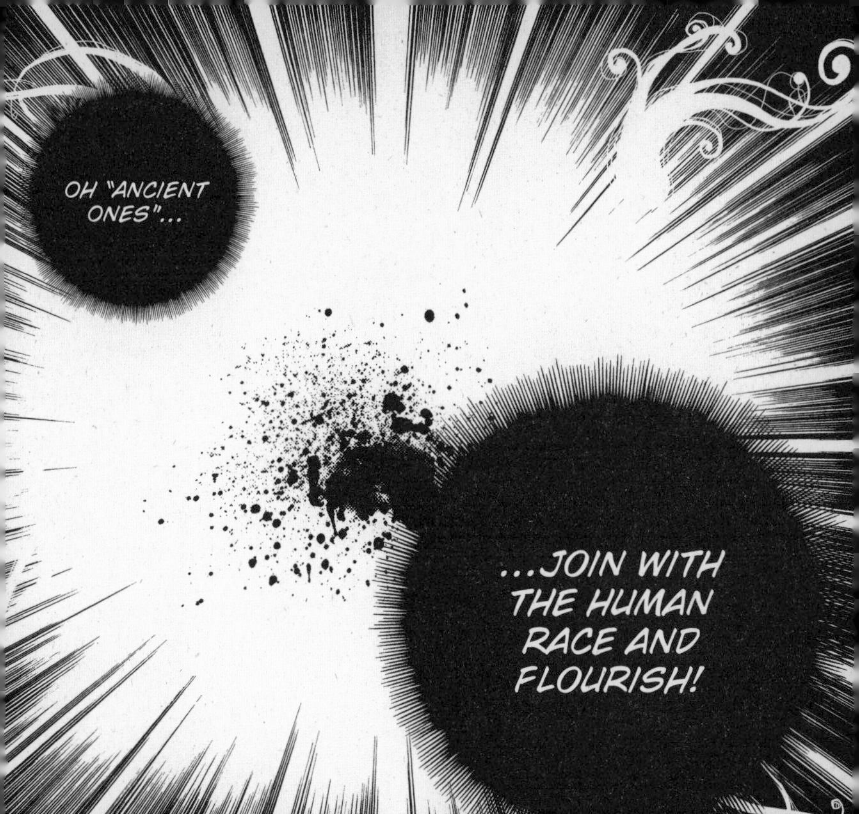
OH "ANCIENT ONES"...
...JOIN WITH THE HUMAN RACE AND FLOURISH!

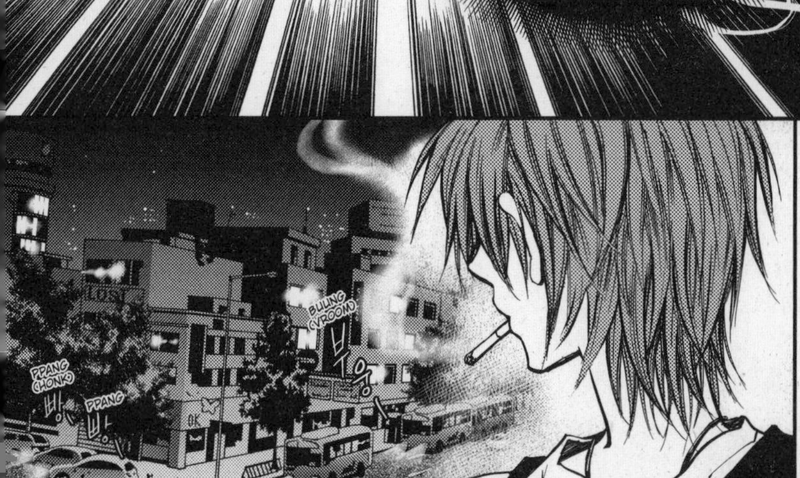
PPANG (HONK)
PPANG
BULING (VROOM)

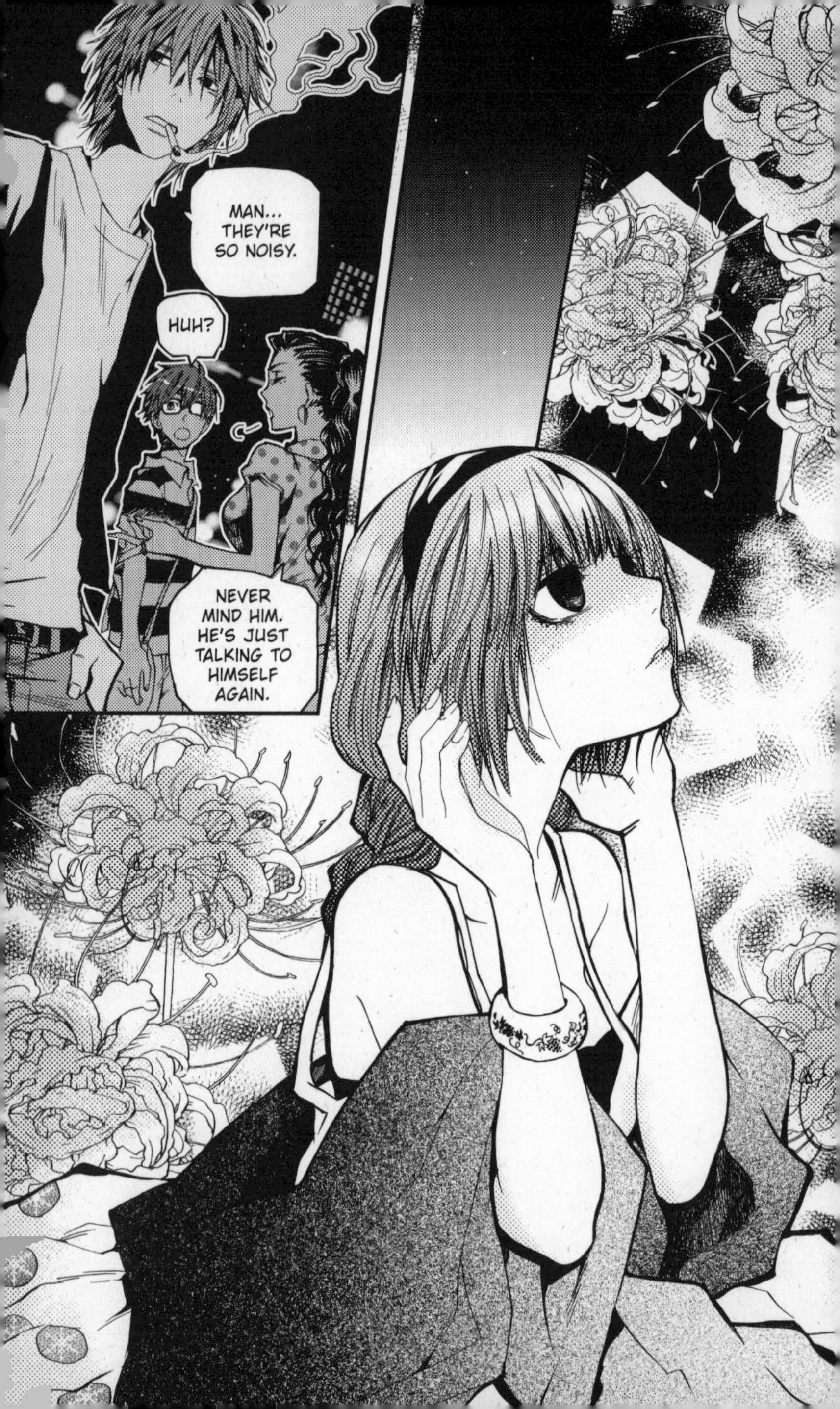
MAN... THEY'RE SO NOISY.
HUH?
NEVER MIND HIM. HE'S JUST TALKING TO HIMSELF AGAIN.

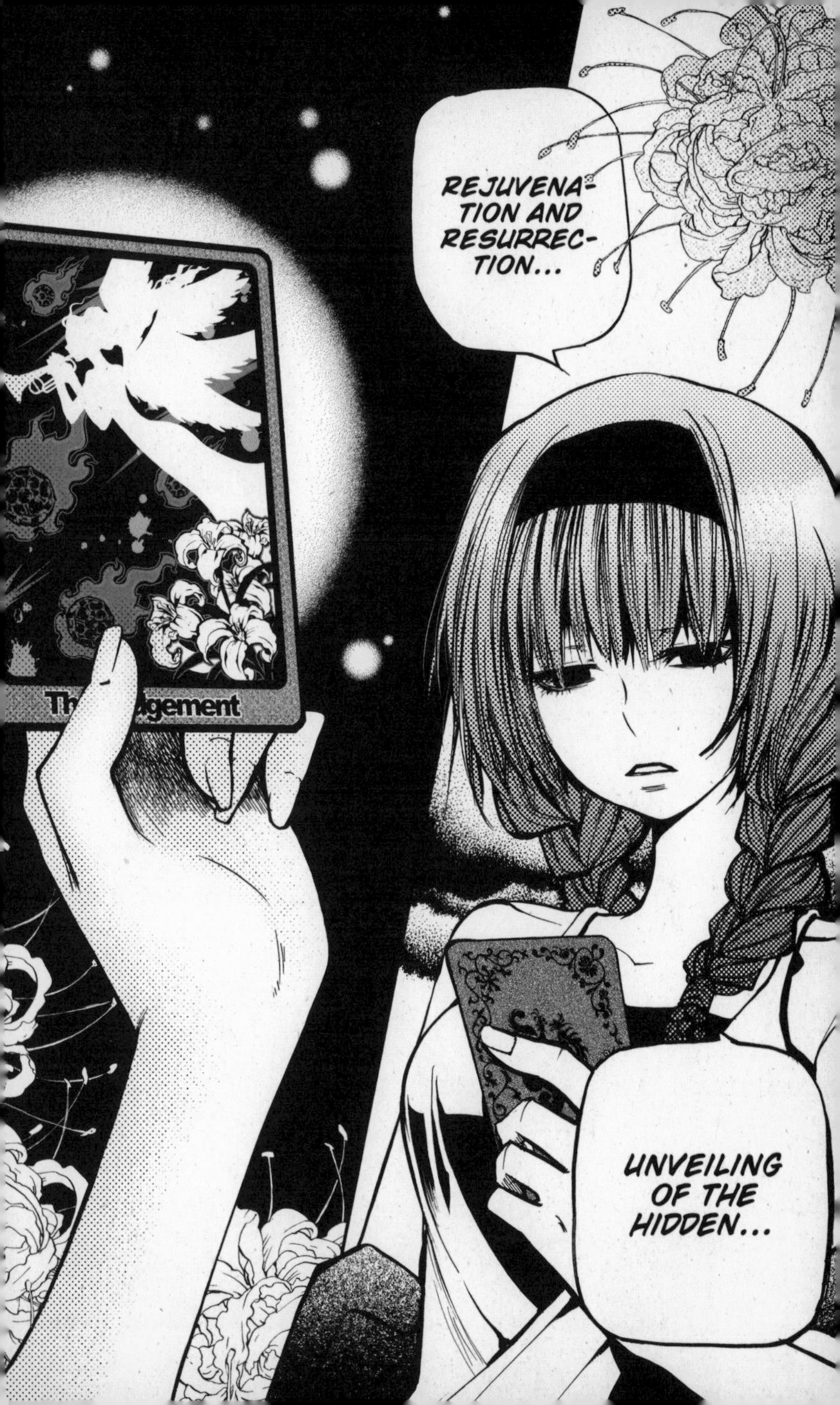
REJUVENATION AND RESURRECTION...
UNVEILING OF THE HIDDEN...

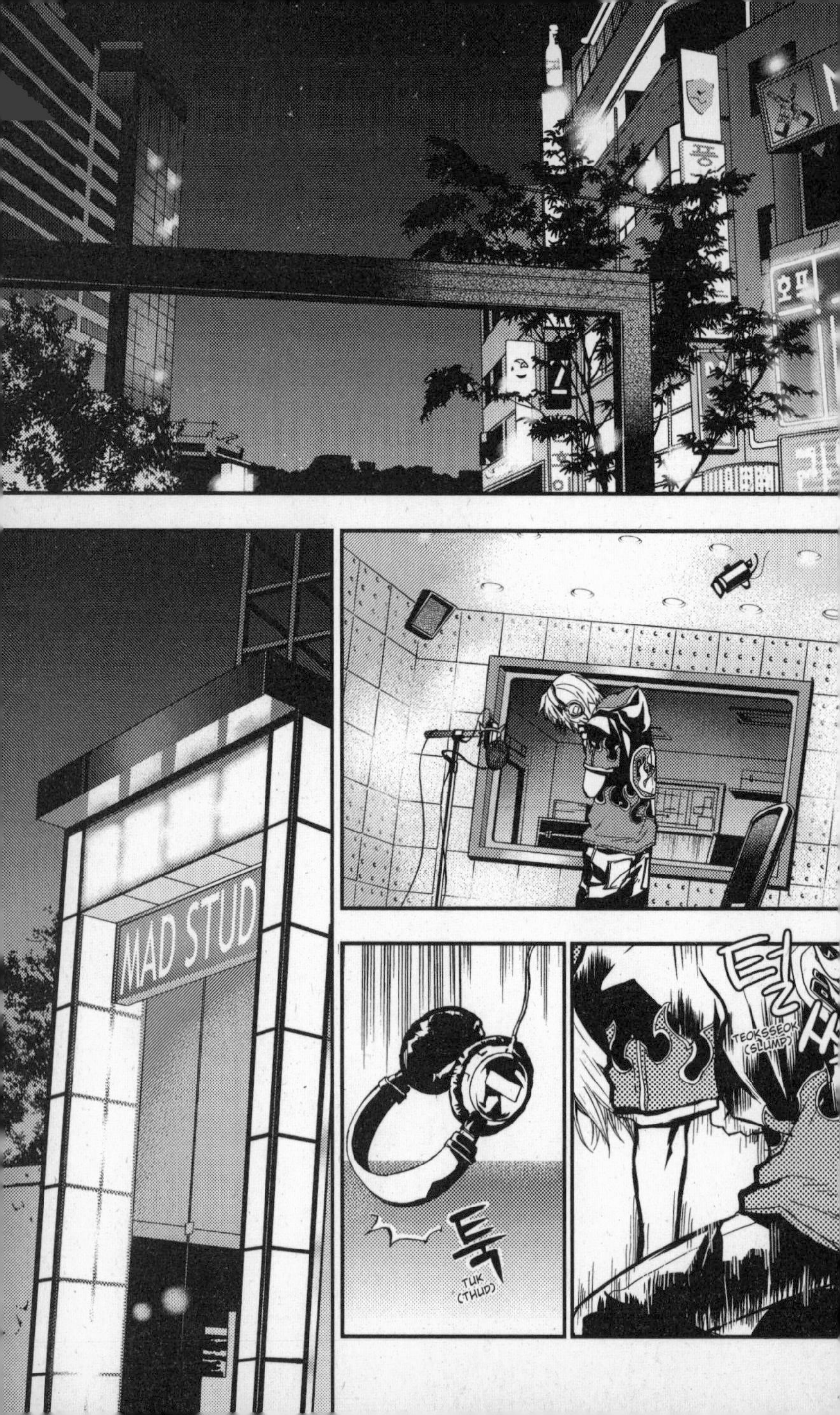
MAD STUD
TUK (THUD)
TEOKSSEOK (SLUMP)

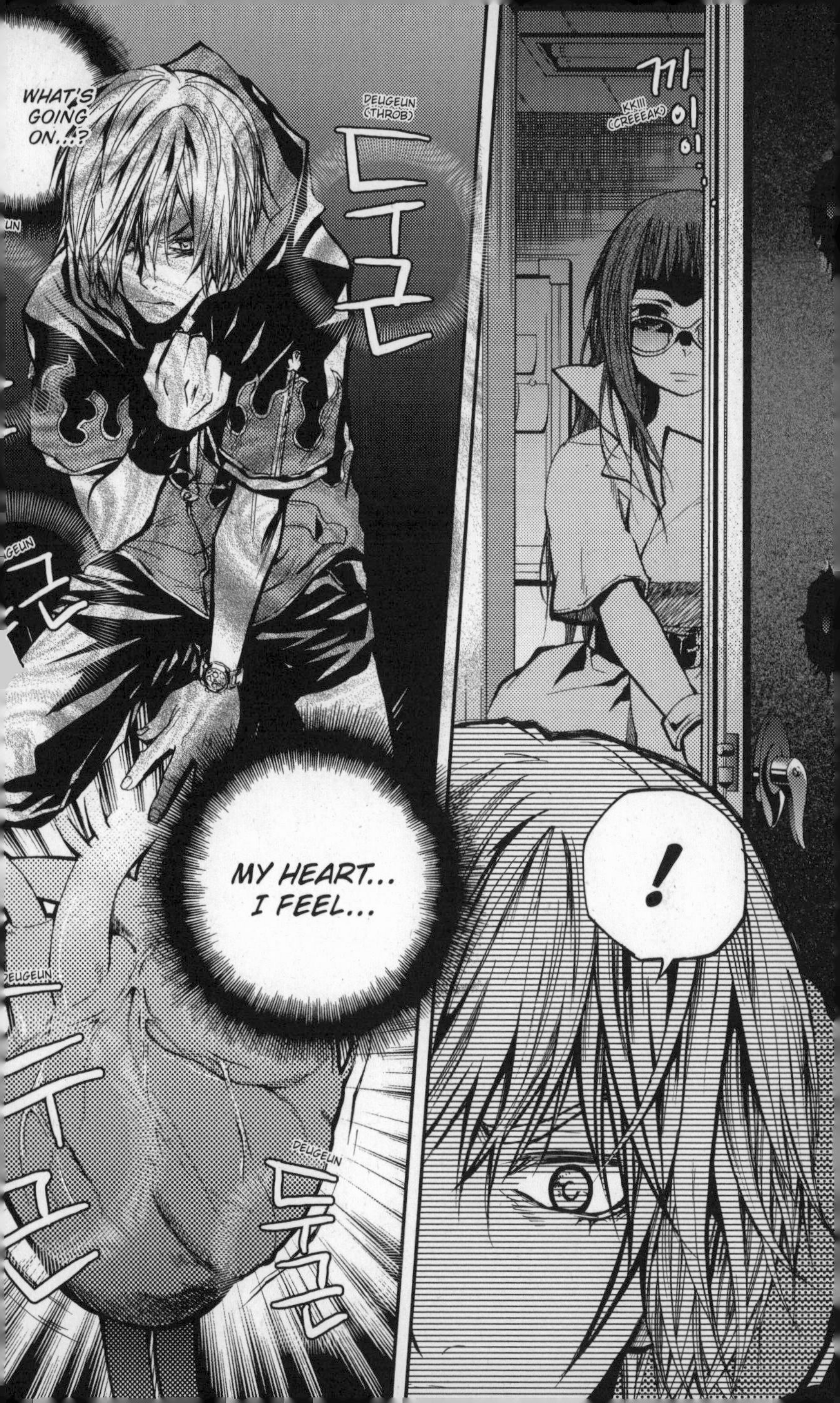
WHAT'S GOING ON...?
DEUGEUN (THROB)
DEUGEUN
MY HEART... I FEEL...
DEUGEUN
KKIII (CREEEAK)
!

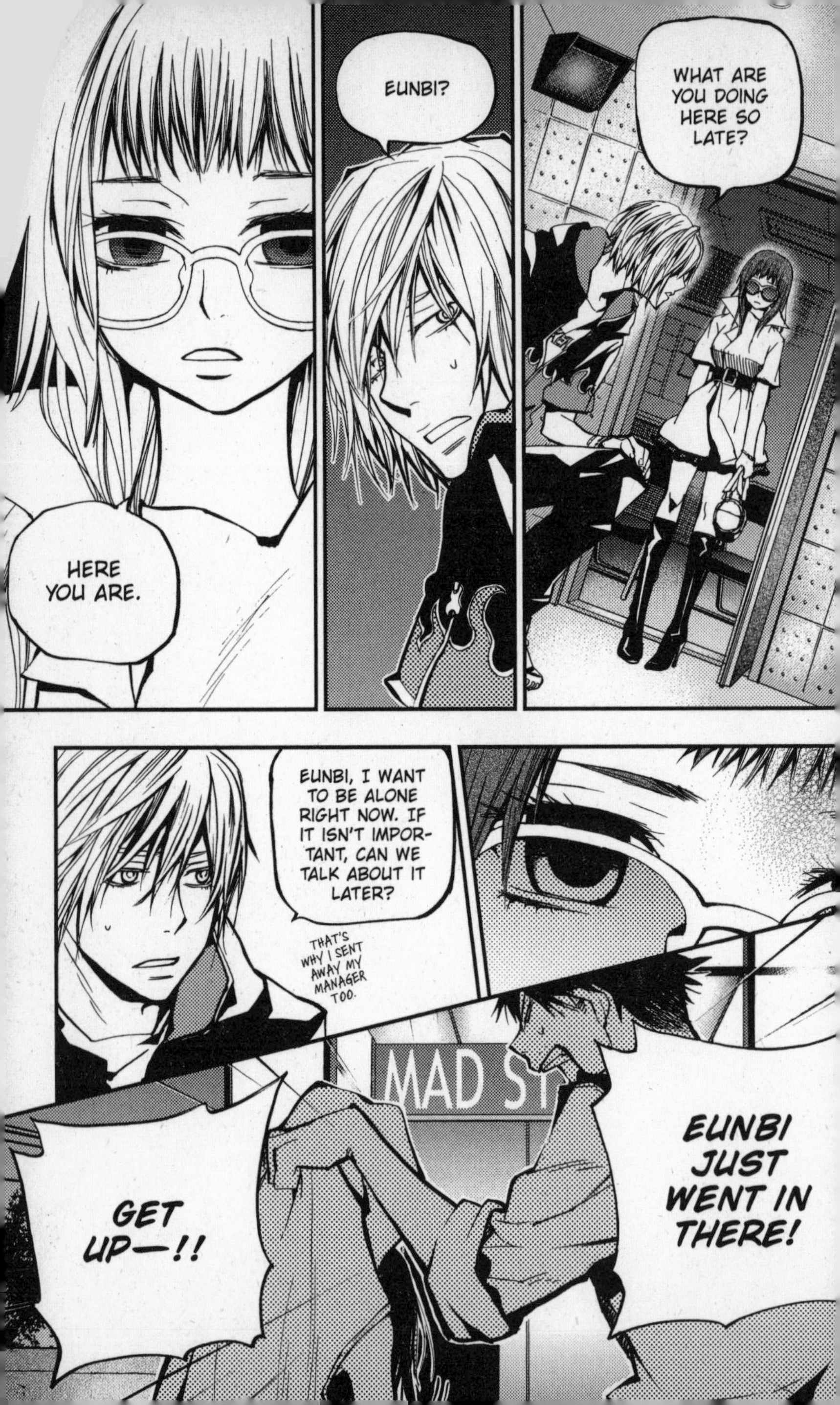
HERE YOU ARE.
EUNBI?
WHAT ARE YOU DOING HERE SO LATE?
EUNBI, I WANT TO BE ALONE RIGHT NOW. IF IT ISN'T IMPORTANT, CAN WE TALK ABOUT IT LATER?
THAT'S WHY I SENT AWAY MY MANAGER TOO.
MAD ST
GET UP—!!
EUNBI JUST WENT IN THERE!

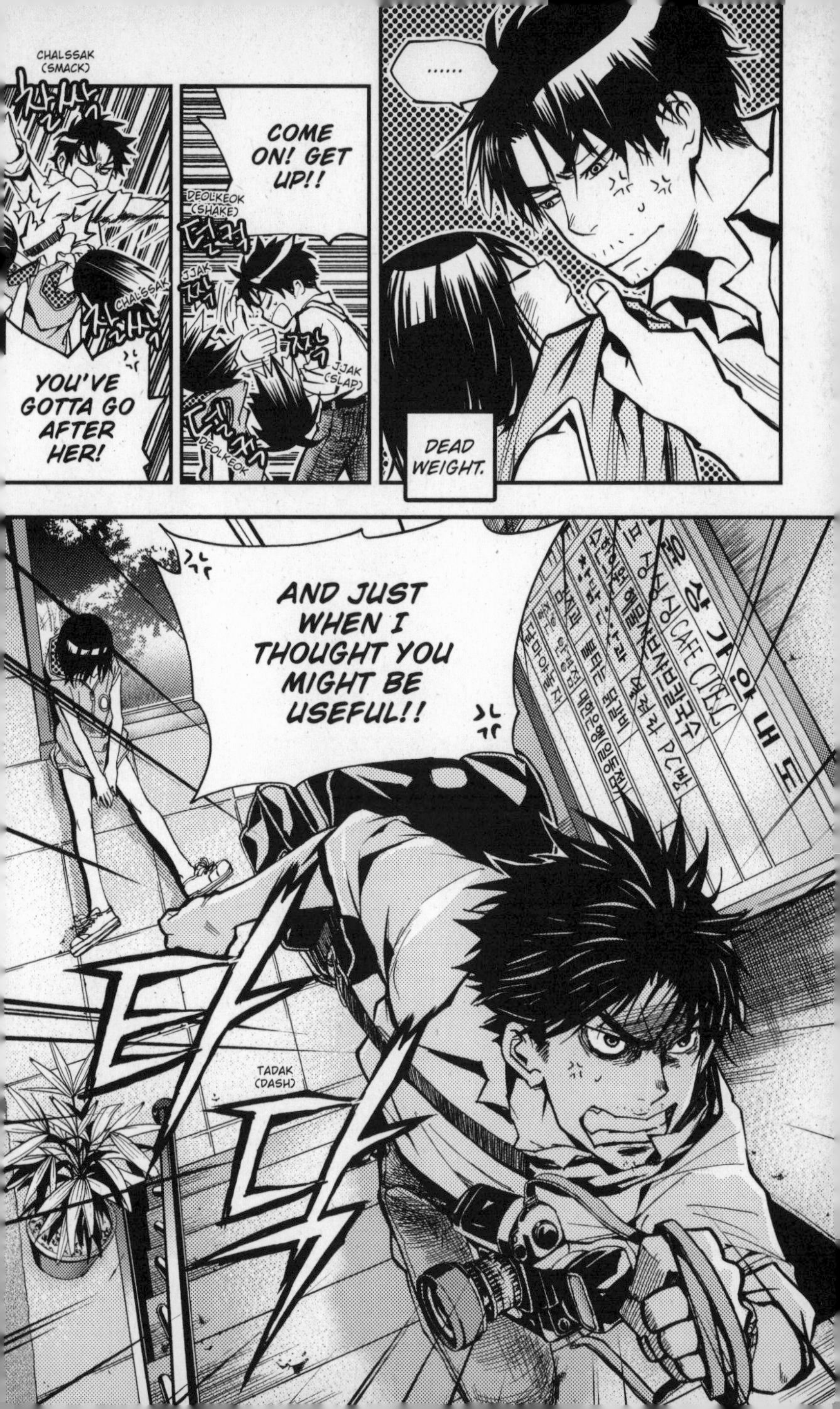
CHALSSAK (SMACK)
CHALSSAK
YOU'VE GOTTA GO AFTER HER!
COME ON! GET UP!!
DEOLKEOK (SHAKE)
JJAK
JJAK (SLAP)
DEOLKEOK
......
DEAD WEIGHT.
AND JUST WHEN I THOUGHT YOU MIGHT BE USEFUL!!
TADAK (DASH)

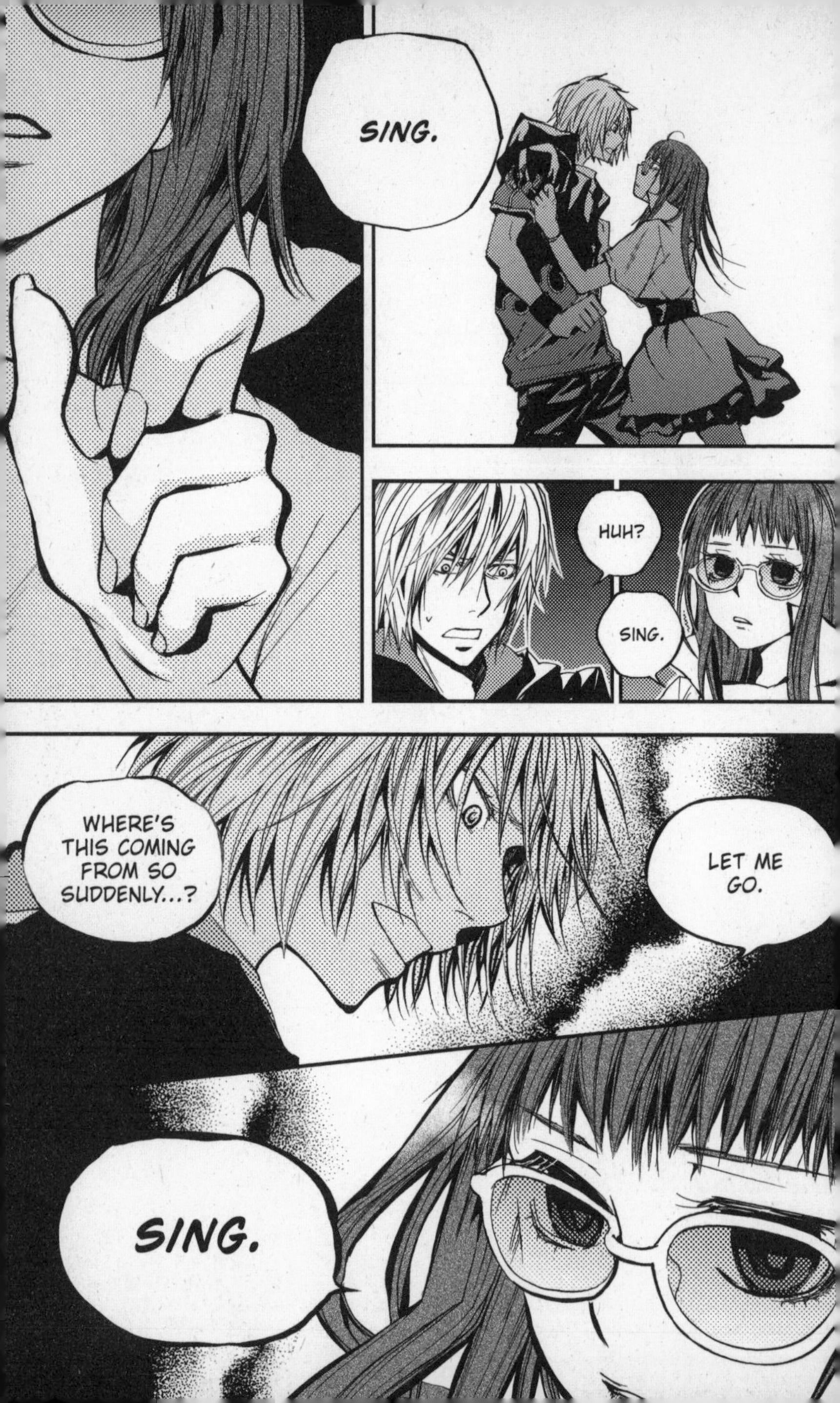
SING.
HUH?
SING.
WHERE'S THIS COMING FROM SO SUDDENLY...?
LET ME GO.
SING.

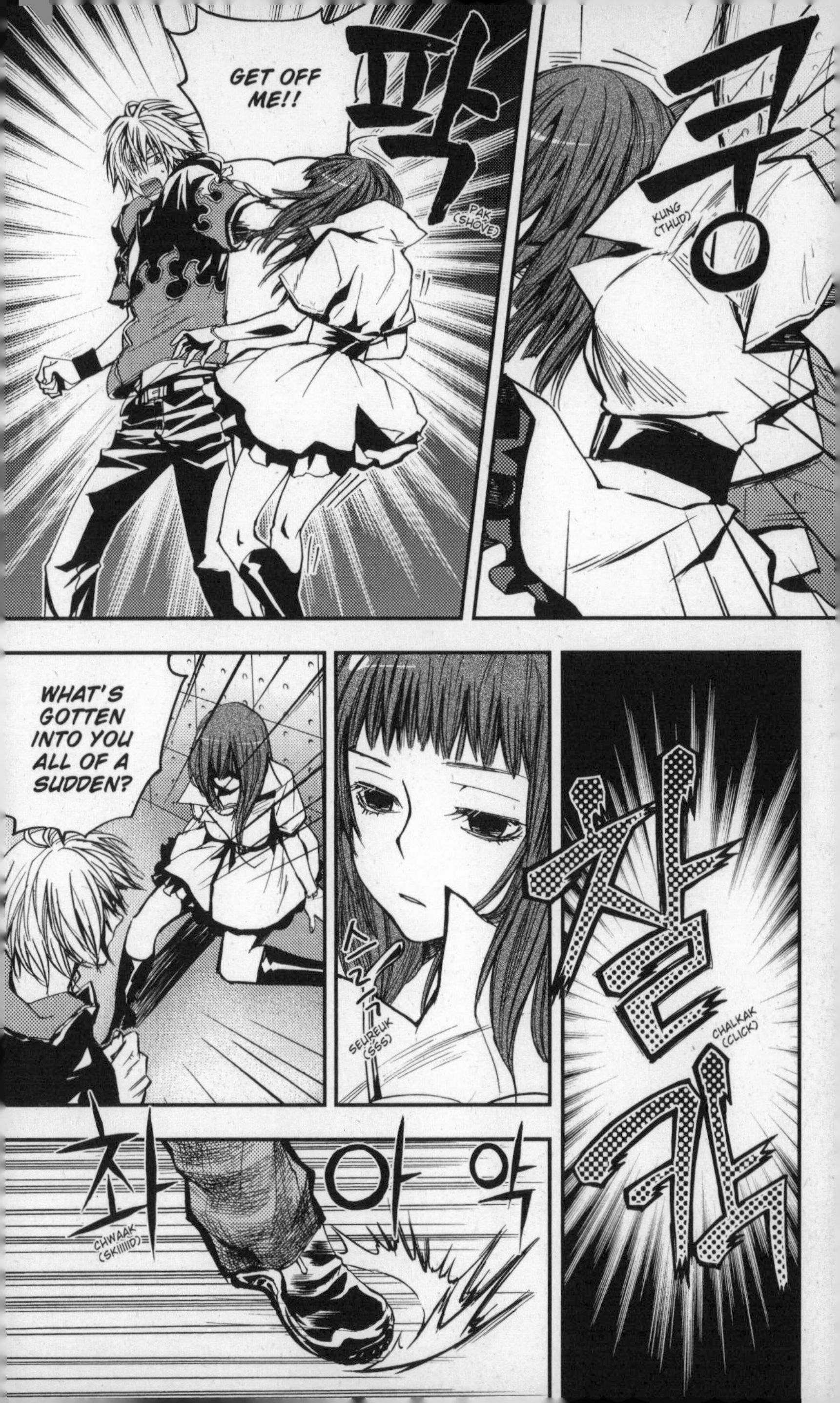
GET OFF ME!!
PAK (SHOVE)
KUNG (THUD)
WHAT'S GOTTEN INTO YOU ALL OF A SUDDEN?
SEUREUK (SSS)
CHALKAK (CLICK)
CHWAAK (SKIIIIID)

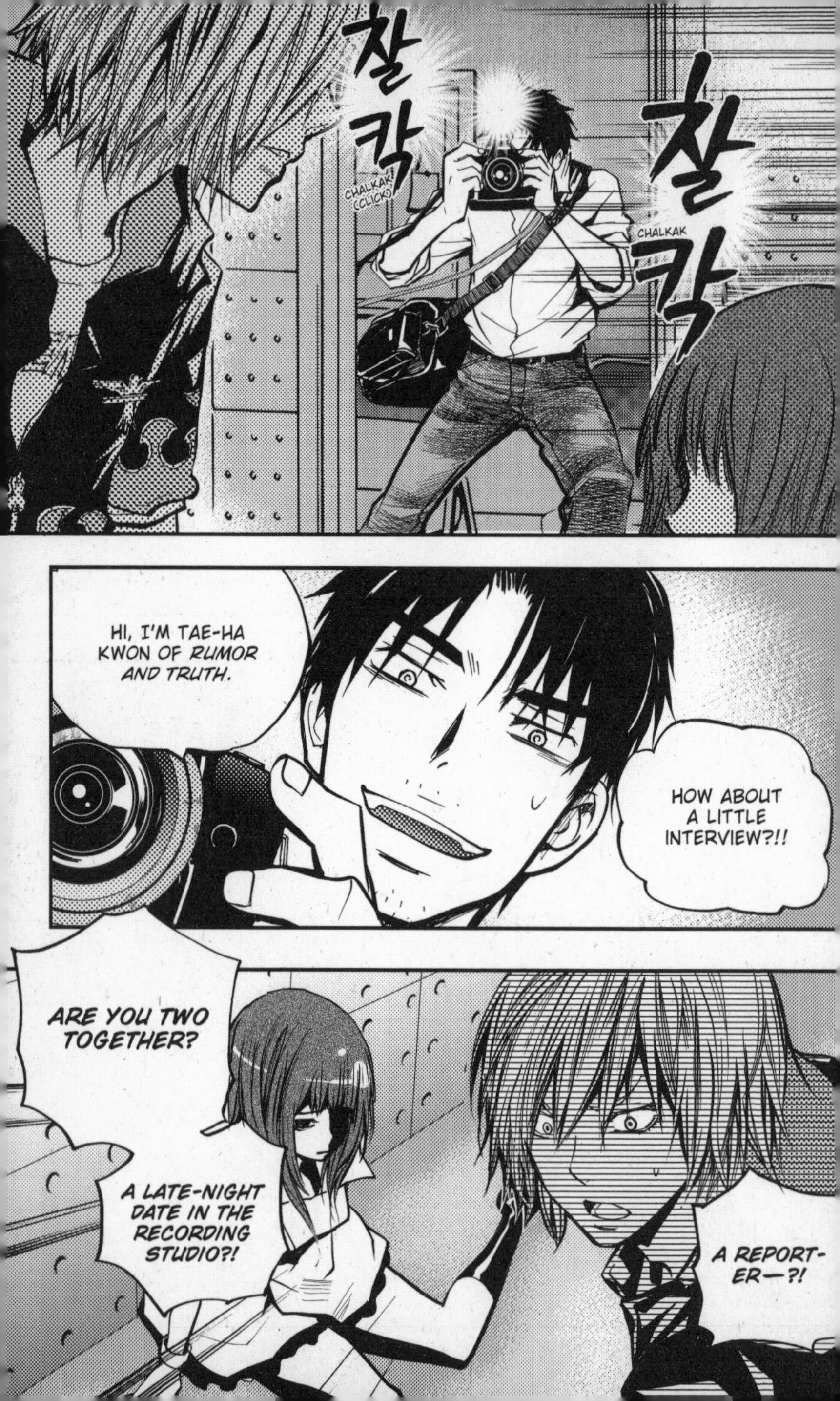

찰칵
CHALKAK (CLICK)
찰칵
CHALKAK
HI, I'M TAE-HA KWON OF *RUMOR AND TRUTH.*
HOW ABOUT A LITTLE INTERVIEW?!!
ARE YOU TWO TOGETHER?
A LATE-NIGHT DATE IN THE RECORDING STUDIO?!
A REPORTER—?!

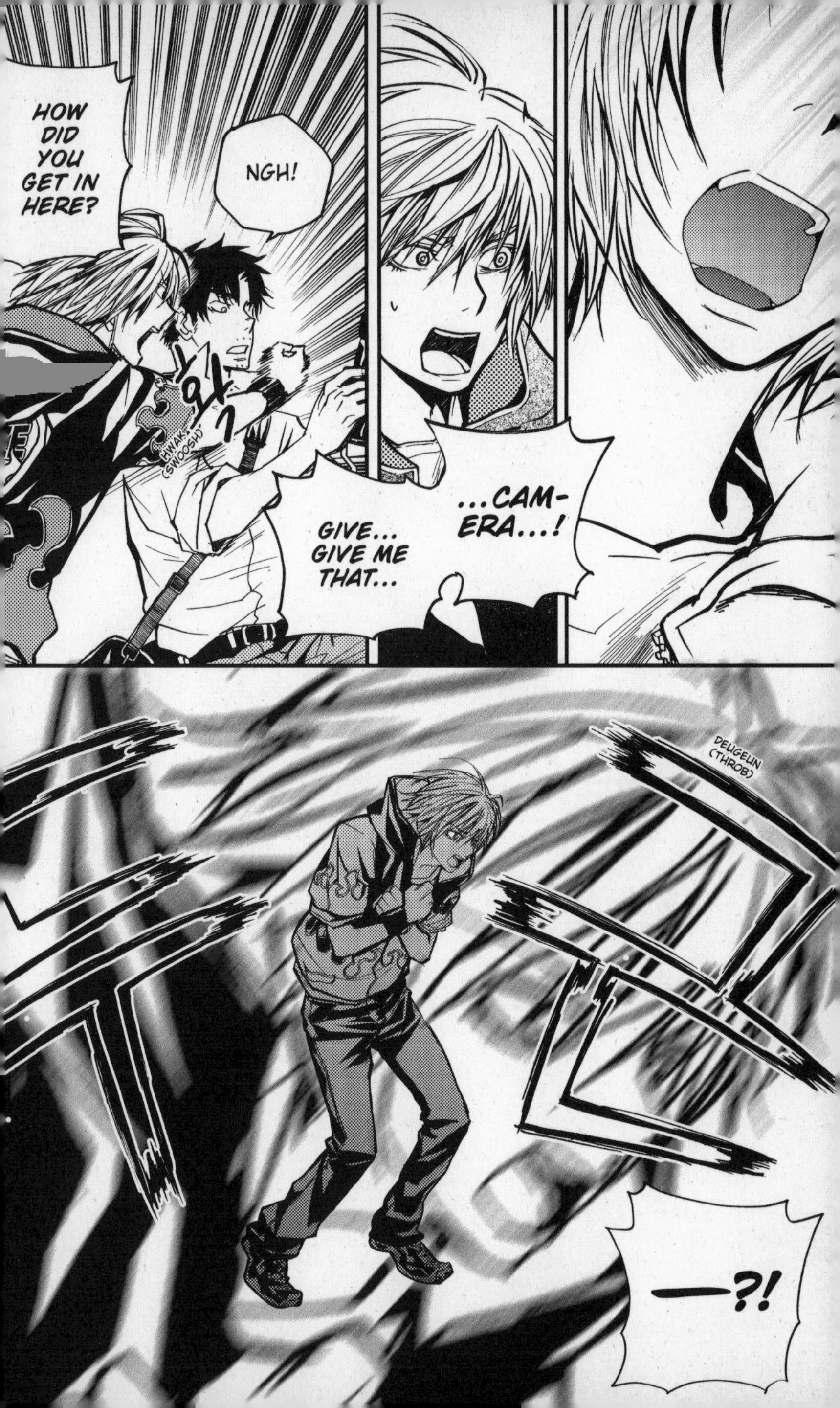
HOW DID YOU GET IN HERE?
NGH!
HWAK (SWOOSH)
GIVE... GIVE ME THAT...
...CAM-ERA...!
DEUGEUN (THROB)
—?!

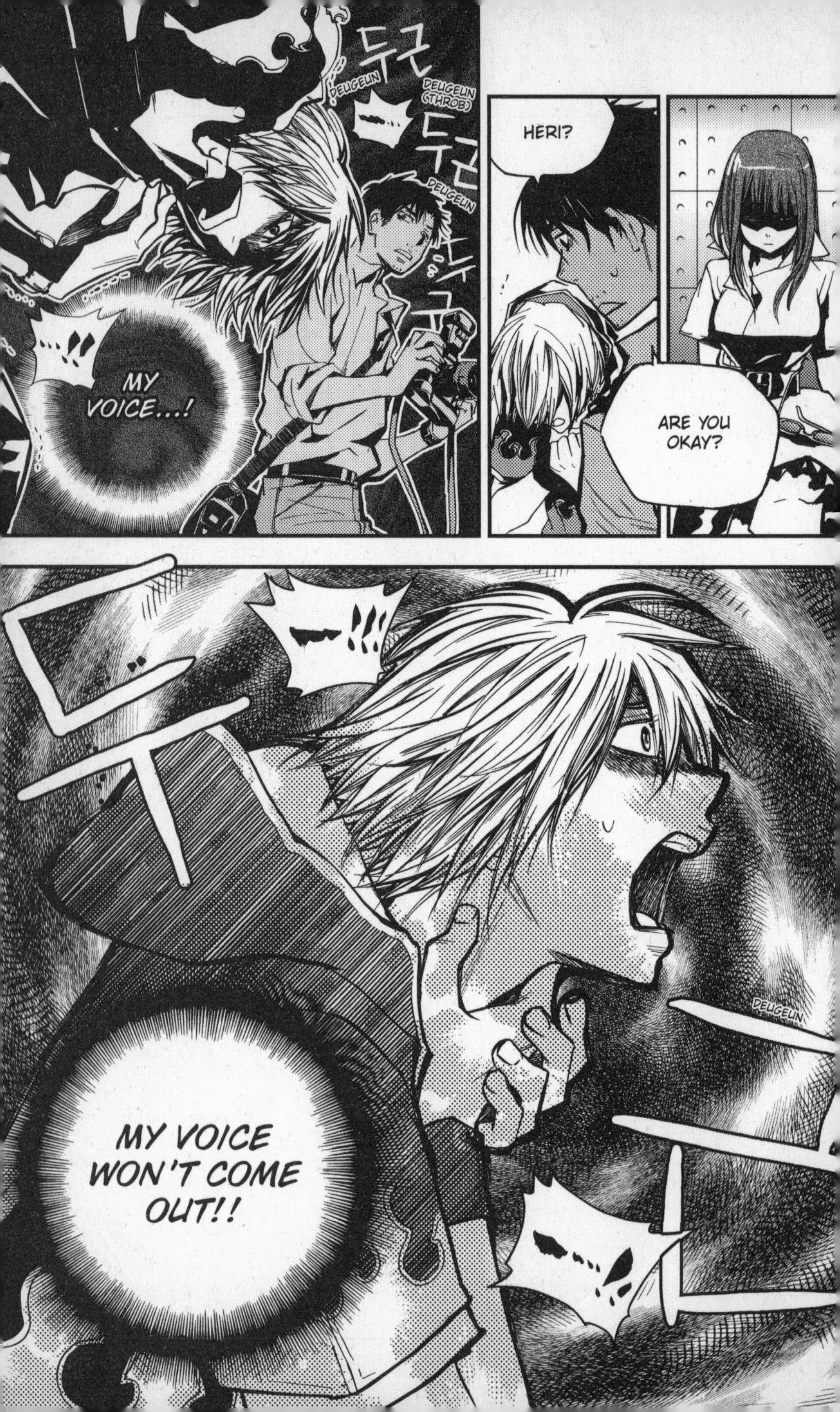
두근
DEUGEUN
DEUGEUN (THROB)
...
두근
DEUGEUN
...!!
MY VOICE...!
HERI?
ARE YOU OKAY?
—!!
MY VOICE WON'T COME OUT!!
DEUGEUN
...!

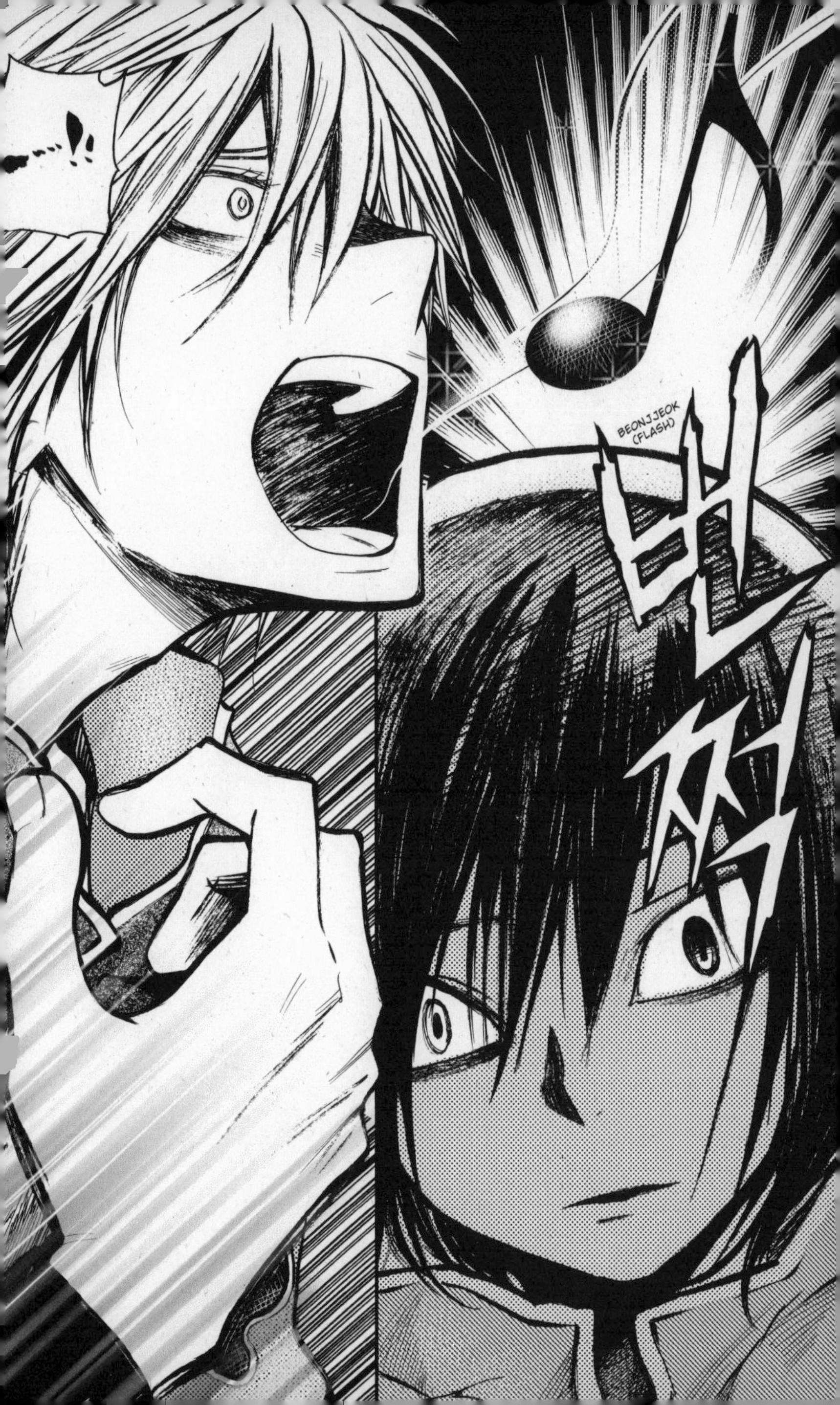
...!!
BEONJJEOK
(FLASH)
번쩍

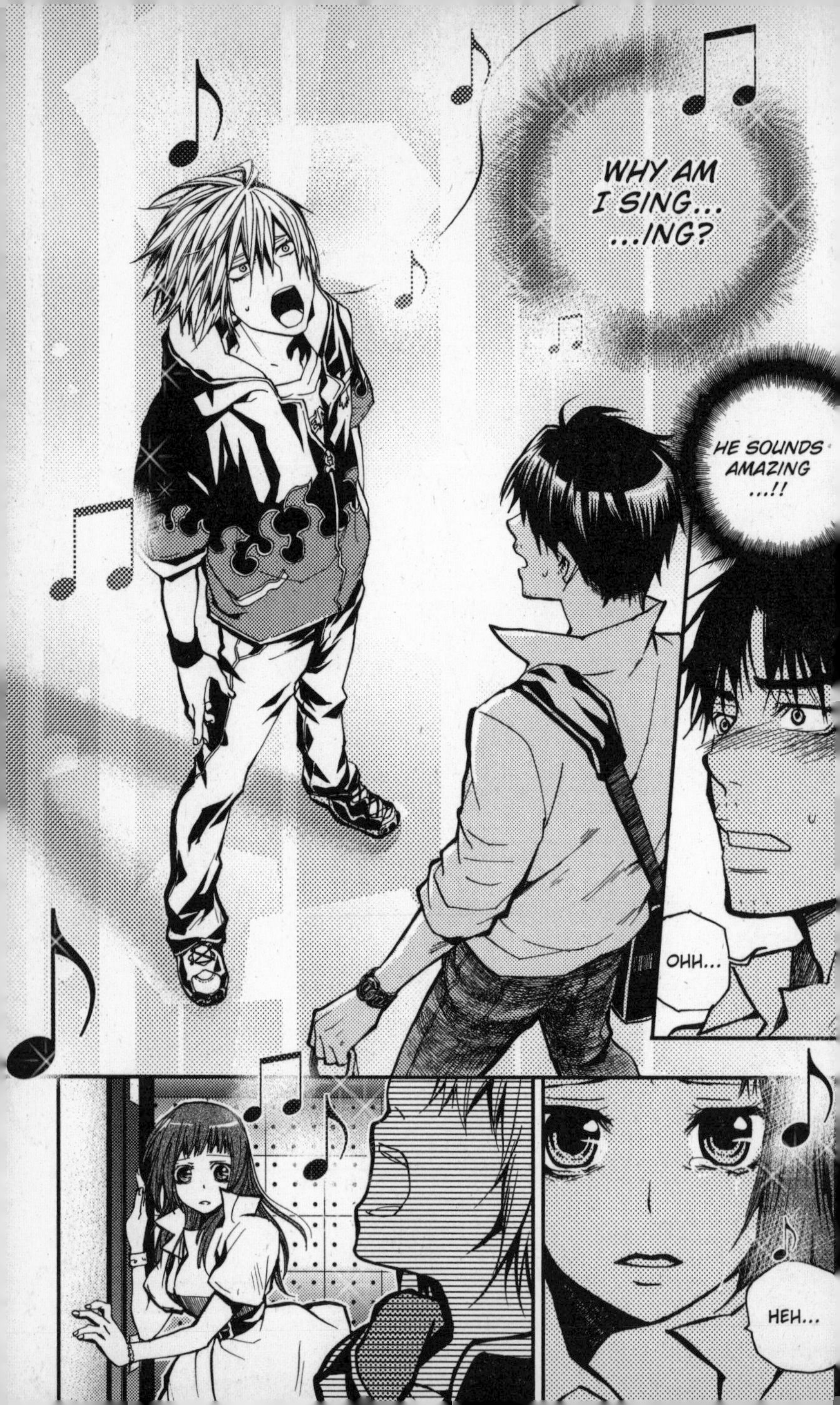
WHY AM I SING... ...ING?
HE SOUNDS AMAZING ...!!
OHH...
HEH...

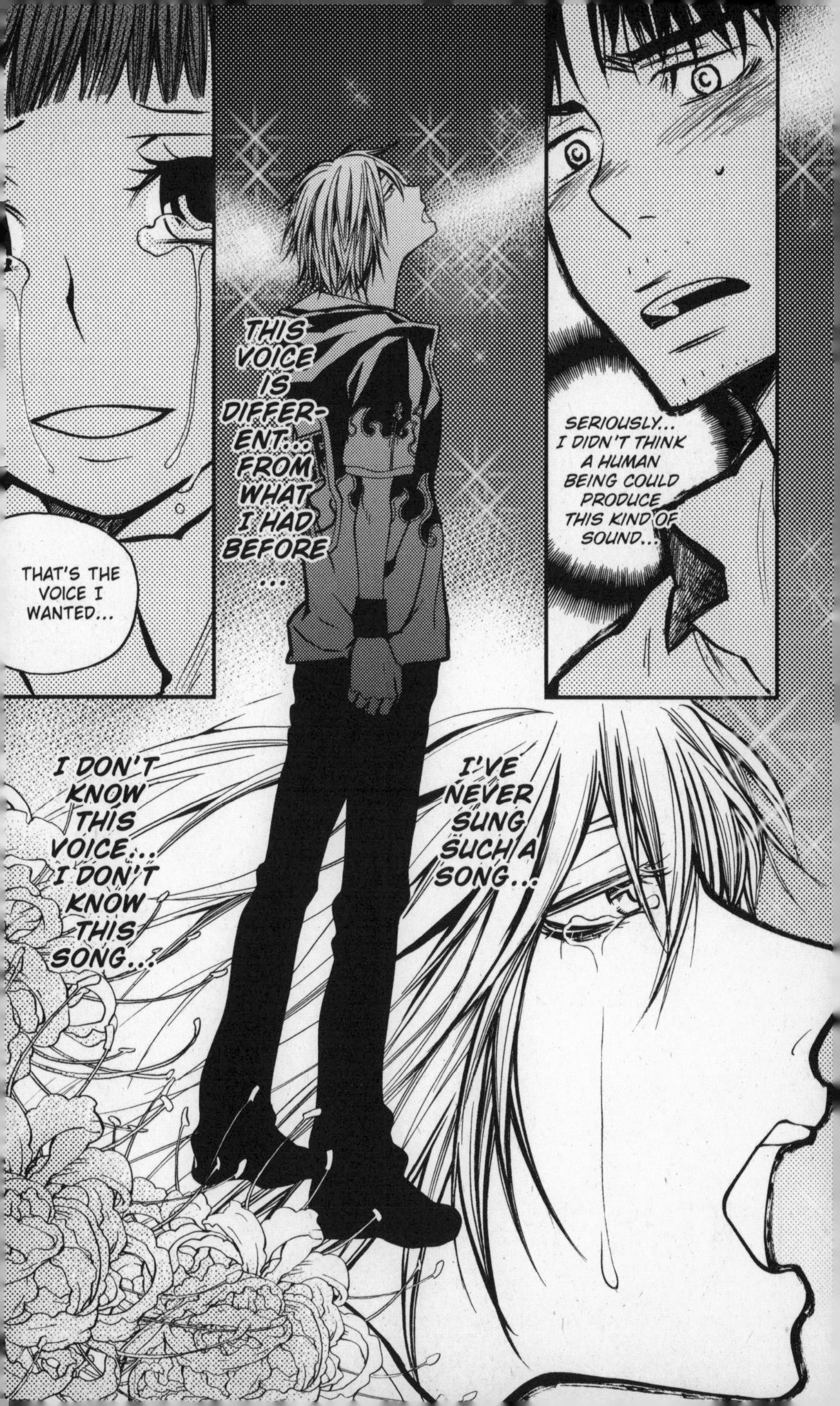
THAT'S THE VOICE I WANTED...
THIS VOICE IS DIFFER-ENT... FROM WHAT I HAD BEFORE ...
SERIOUSLY... I DIDN'T THINK A HUMAN BEING COULD PRODUCE THIS KIND OF SOUND...
I DON'T KNOW THIS VOICE... I DON'T KNOW THIS SONG...
I'VE NEVER SUNG SUCH A SONG...

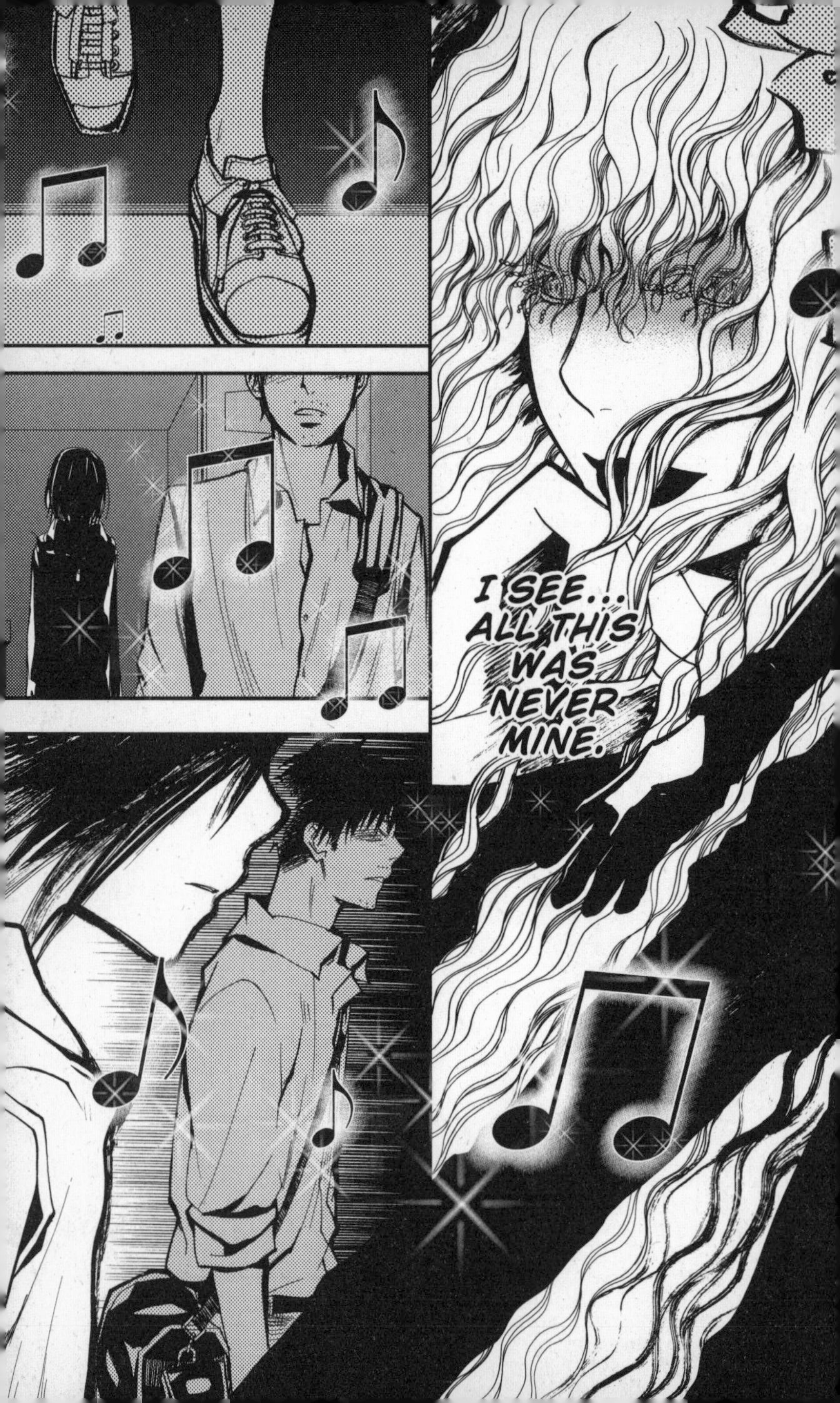
I SEE... ALL THIS WAS NEVER MINE.

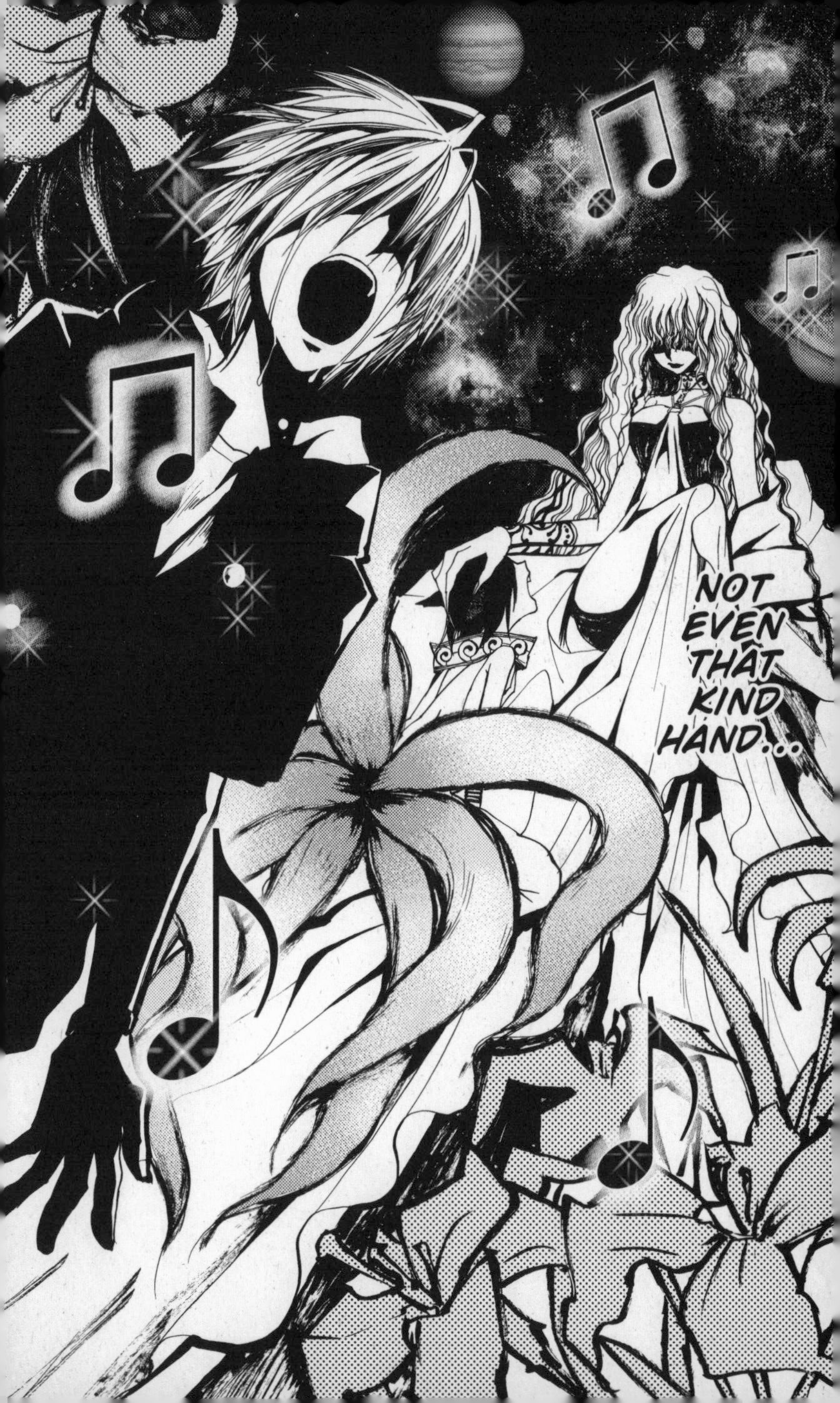
NOT EVEN THAT KIND HAND...

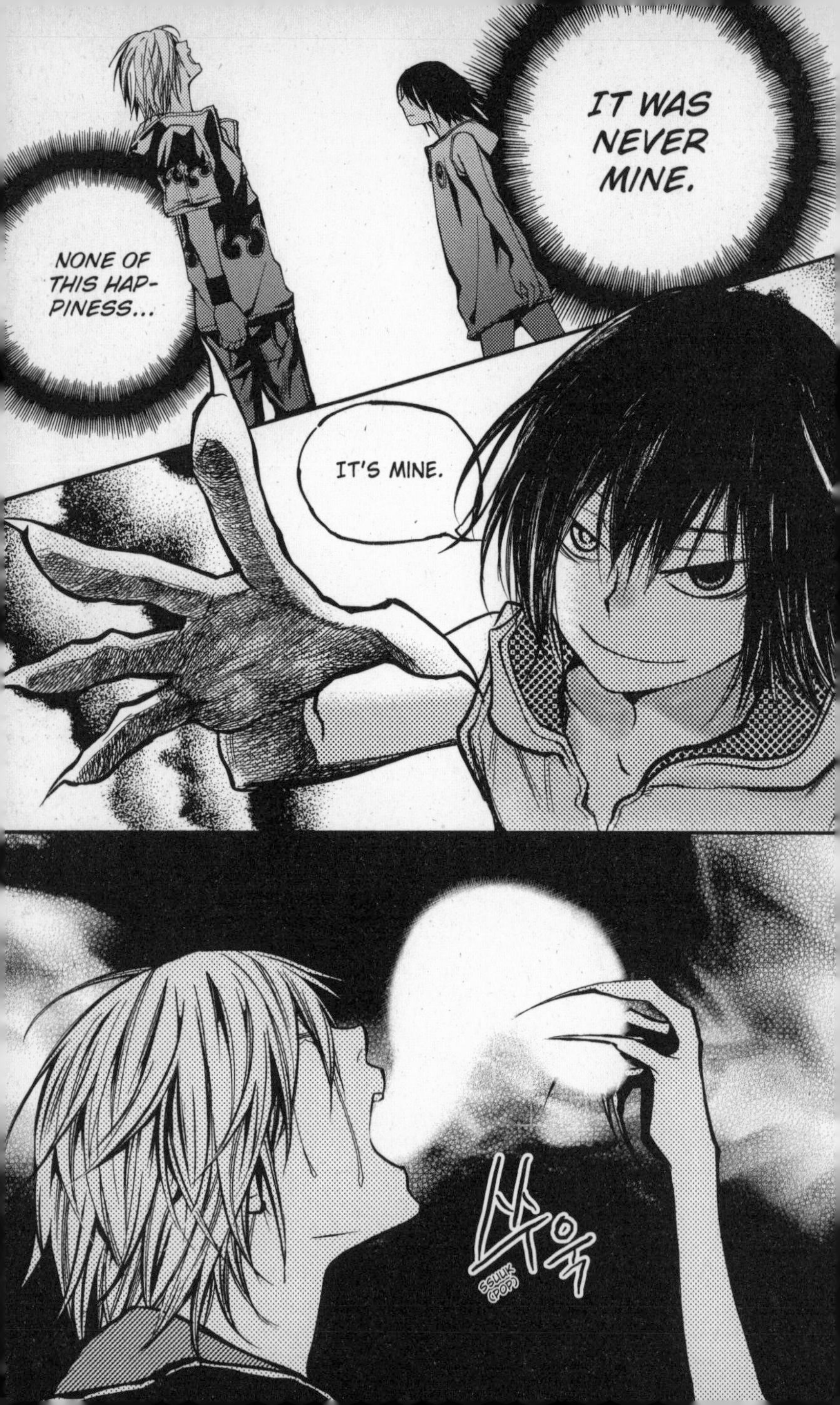
NONE OF THIS HAP-PINESS...
IT WAS NEVER MINE.
IT'S MINE.
SSUUK (POP)

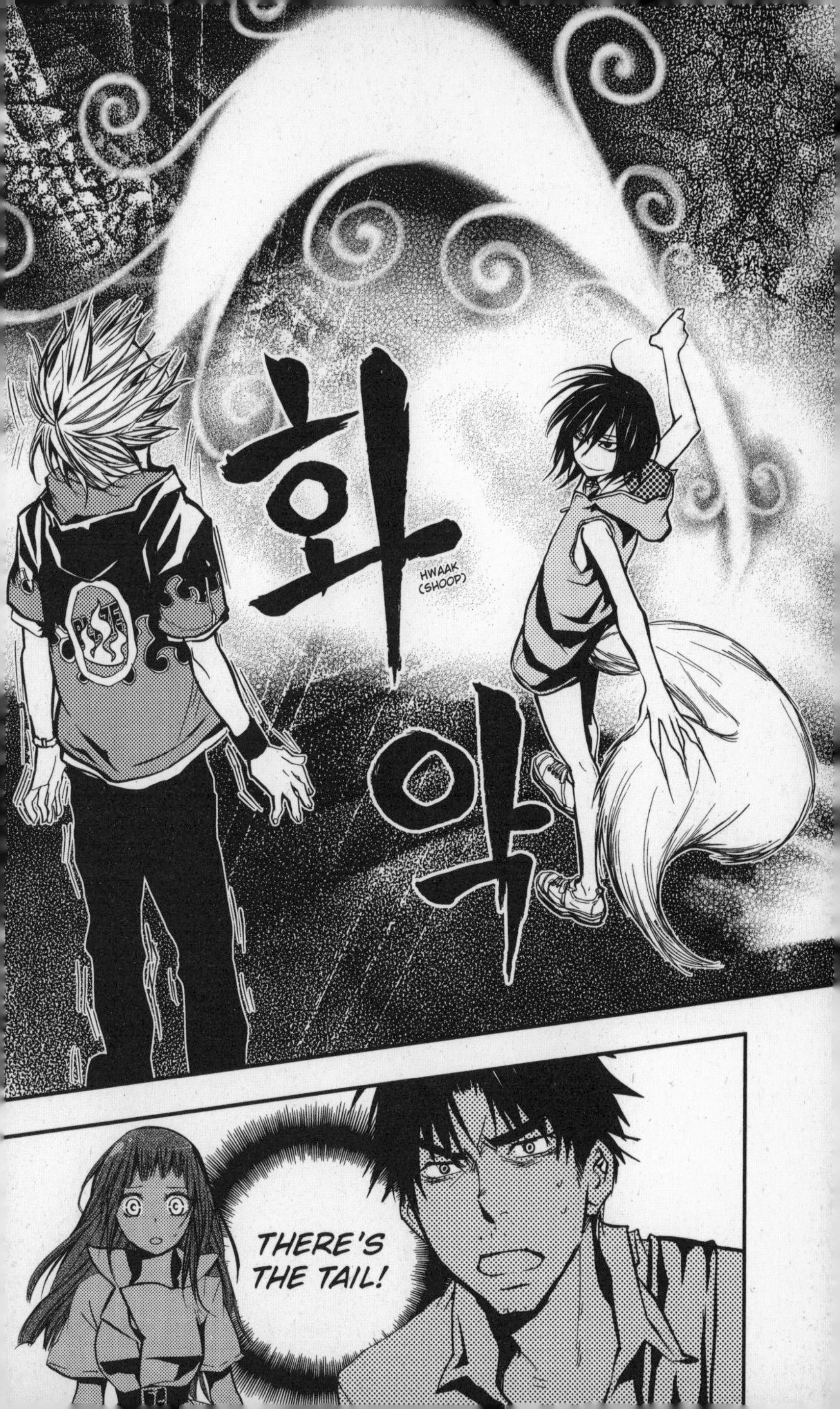
HWAAK (SHOOP)
THERE'S THE TAIL!

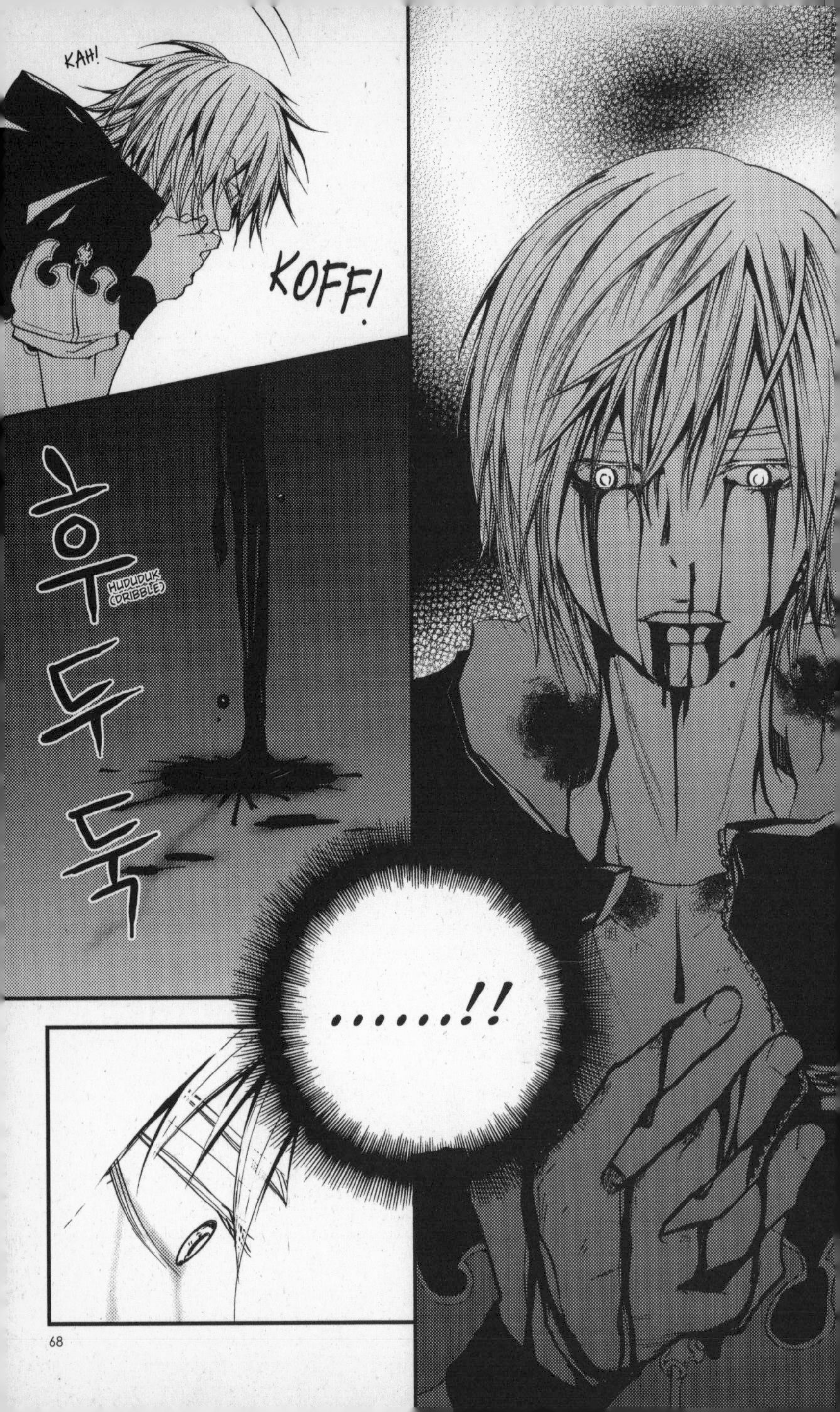
KAH!
KOFF!
후두둑
HUDUDUK (DRIBBLE)
......!!

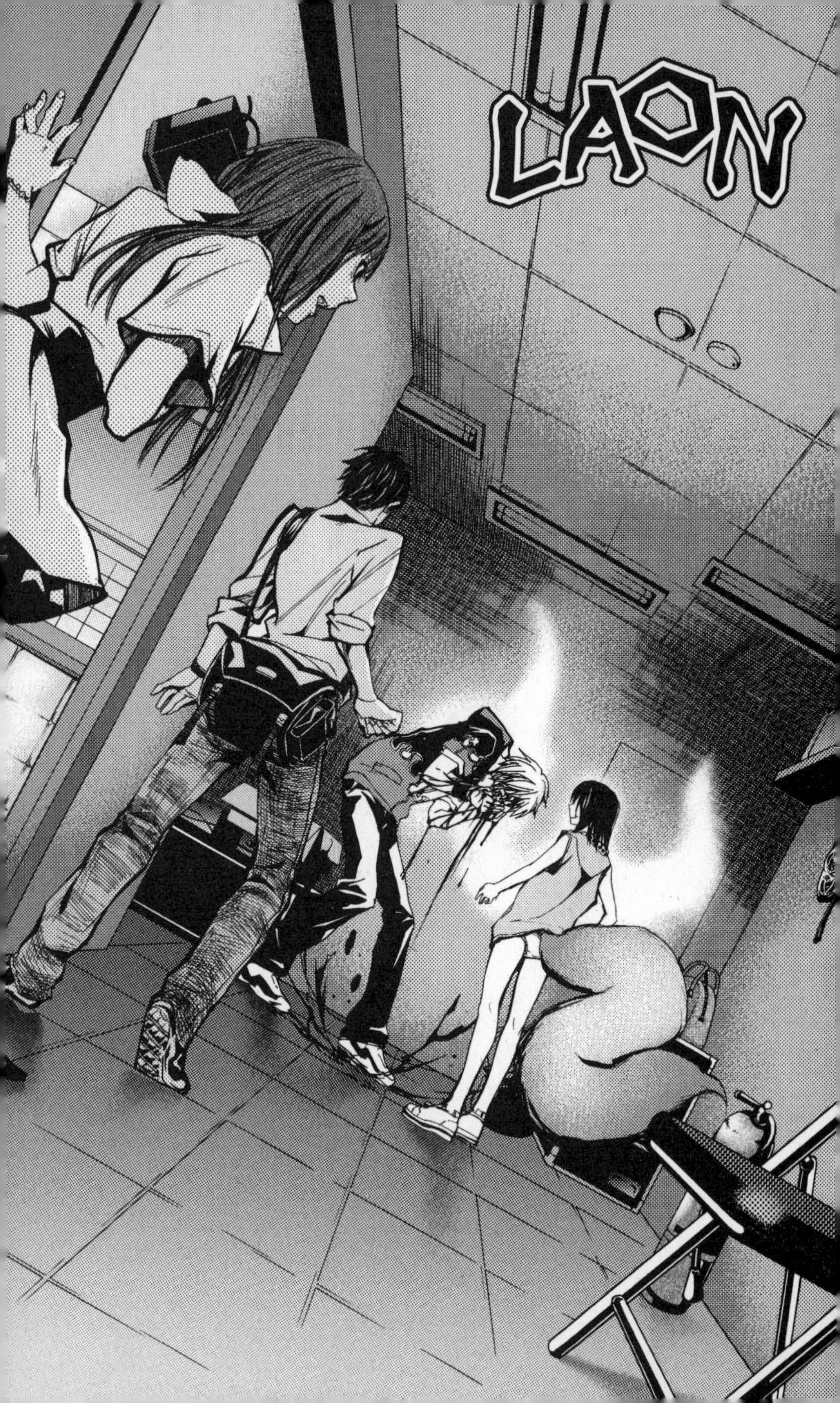
LAON

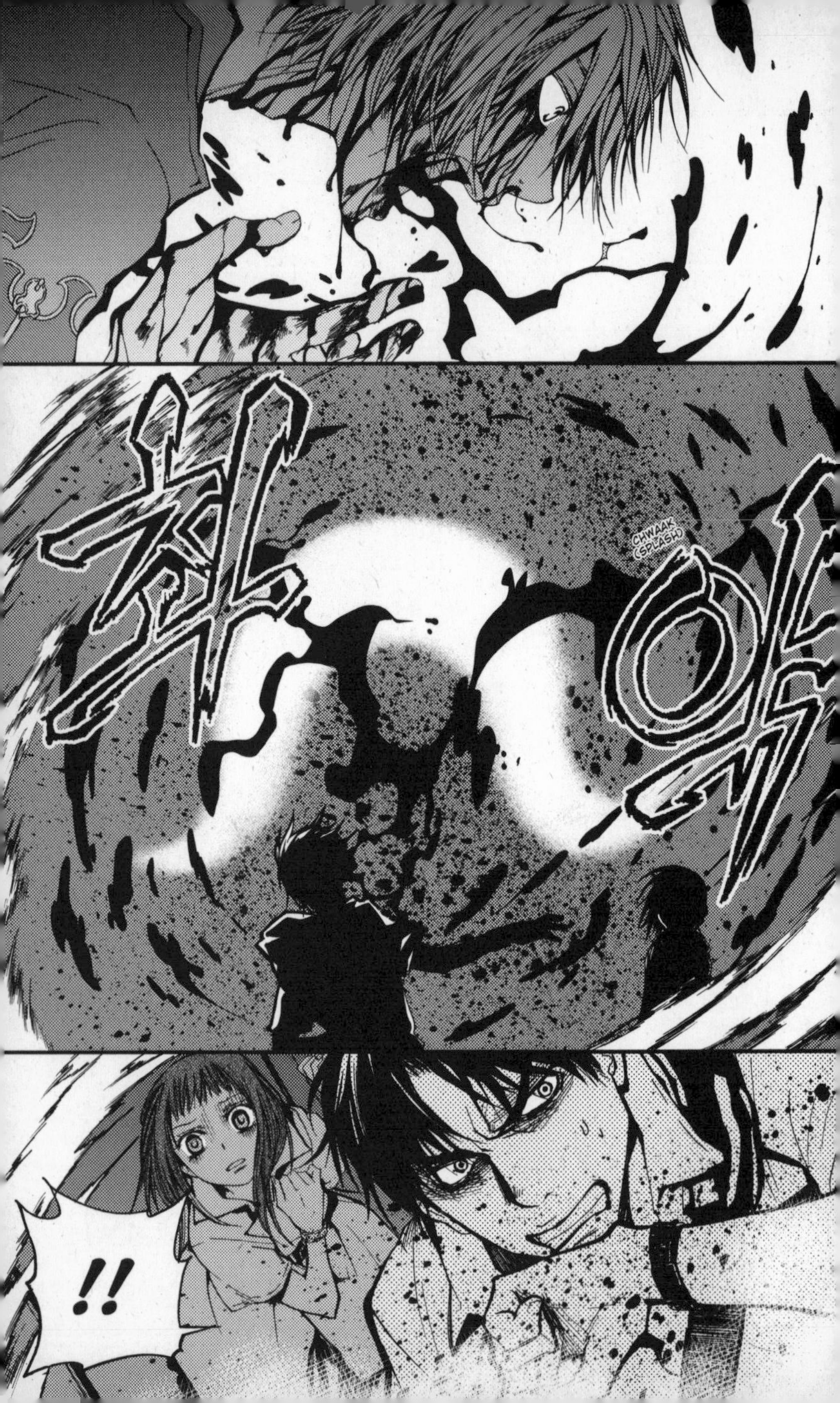
촤악
CHWAAK (SPLASH)
!!

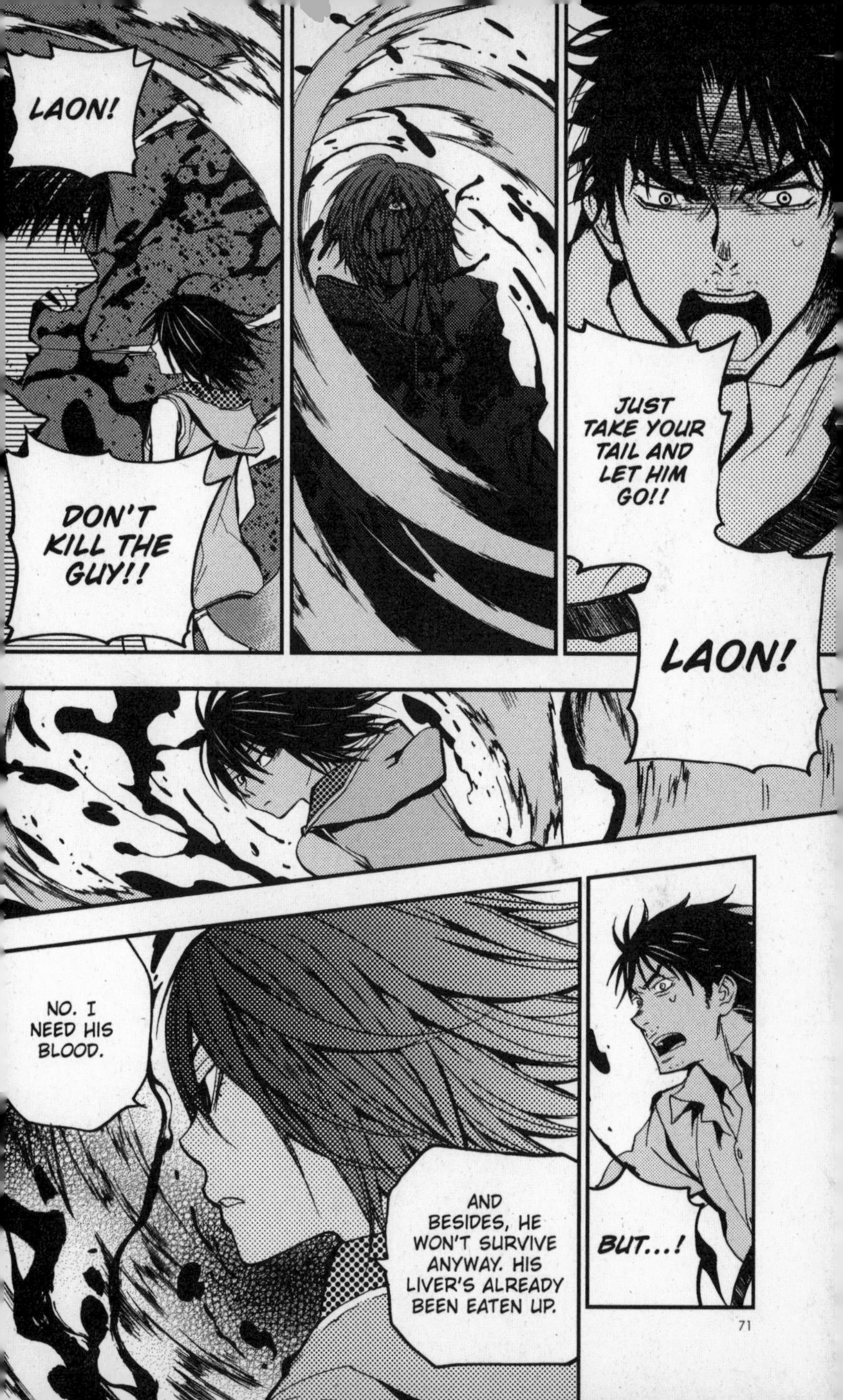
LAON!
DON'T KILL THE GUY!!
JUST TAKE YOUR TAIL AND LET HIM GO!!
LAON!
NO. I NEED HIS BLOOD.
AND BESIDES, HE WON'T SURVIVE ANYWAY. HIS LIVER'S ALREADY BEEN EATEN UP.
BUT...!

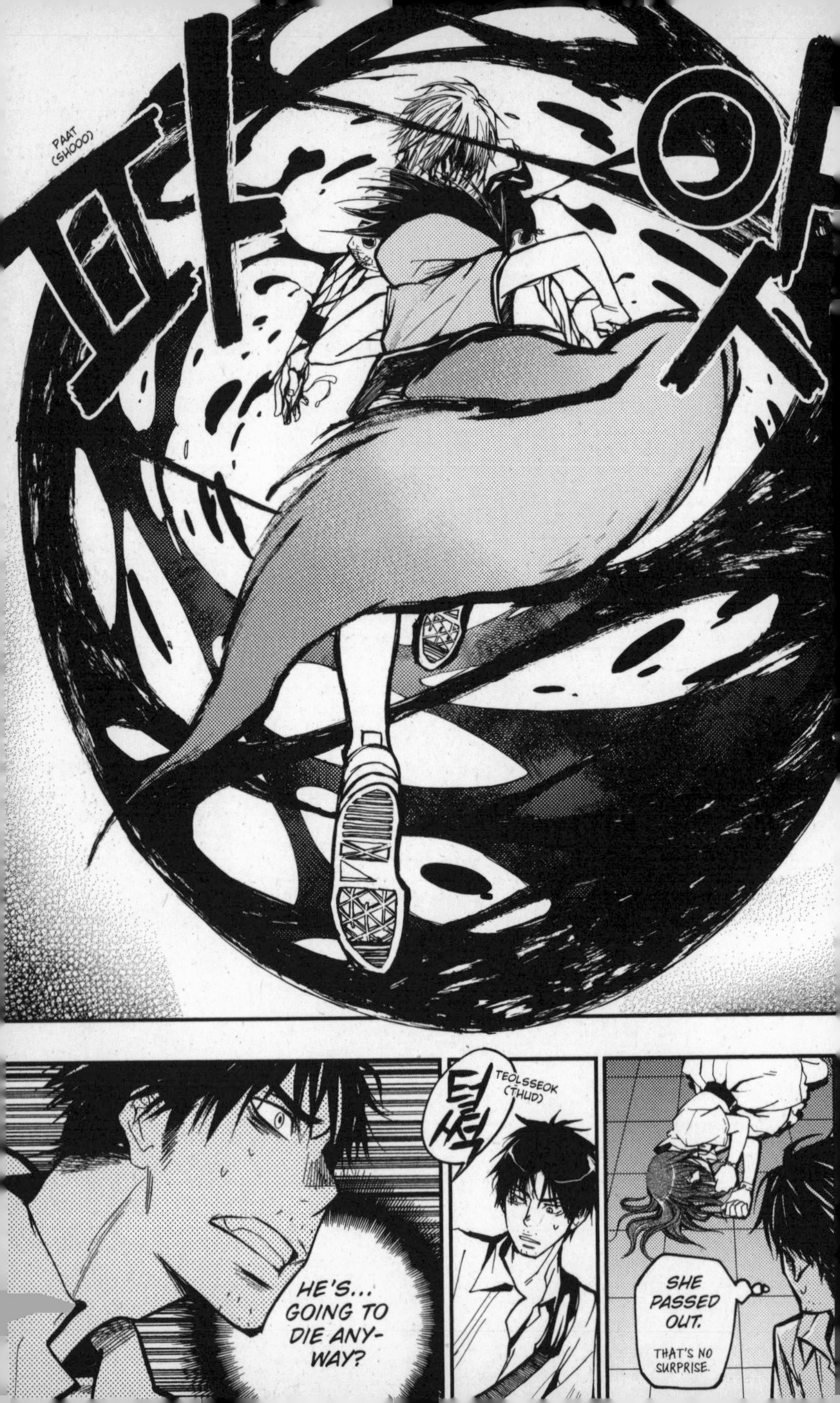
PAAT (SHOOO)
HE'S... GOING TO DIE ANY-WAY?
TEOLSSEOK (THUD)
털썩
SHE PASSED OUT.
THAT'S NO SURPRISE.

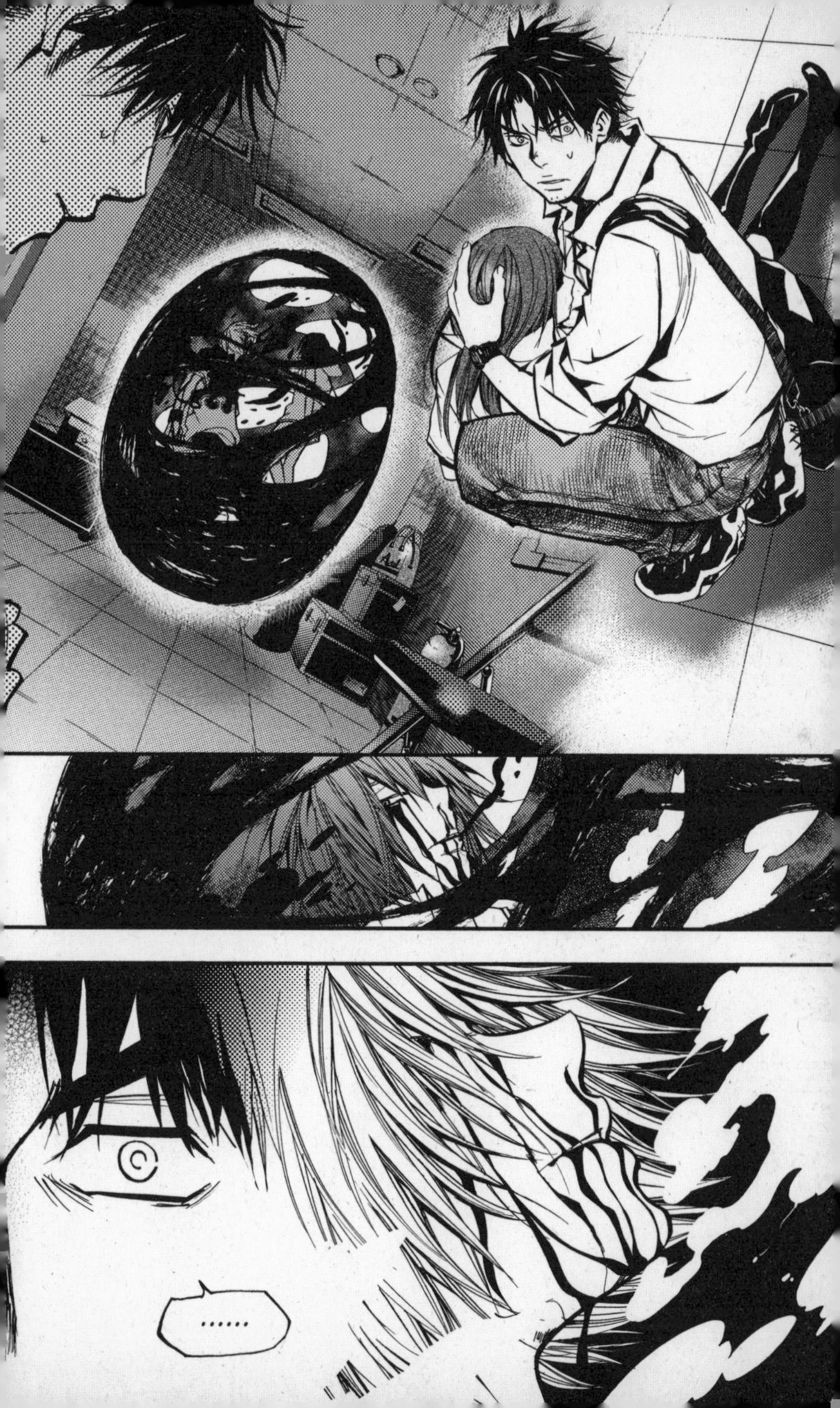
......

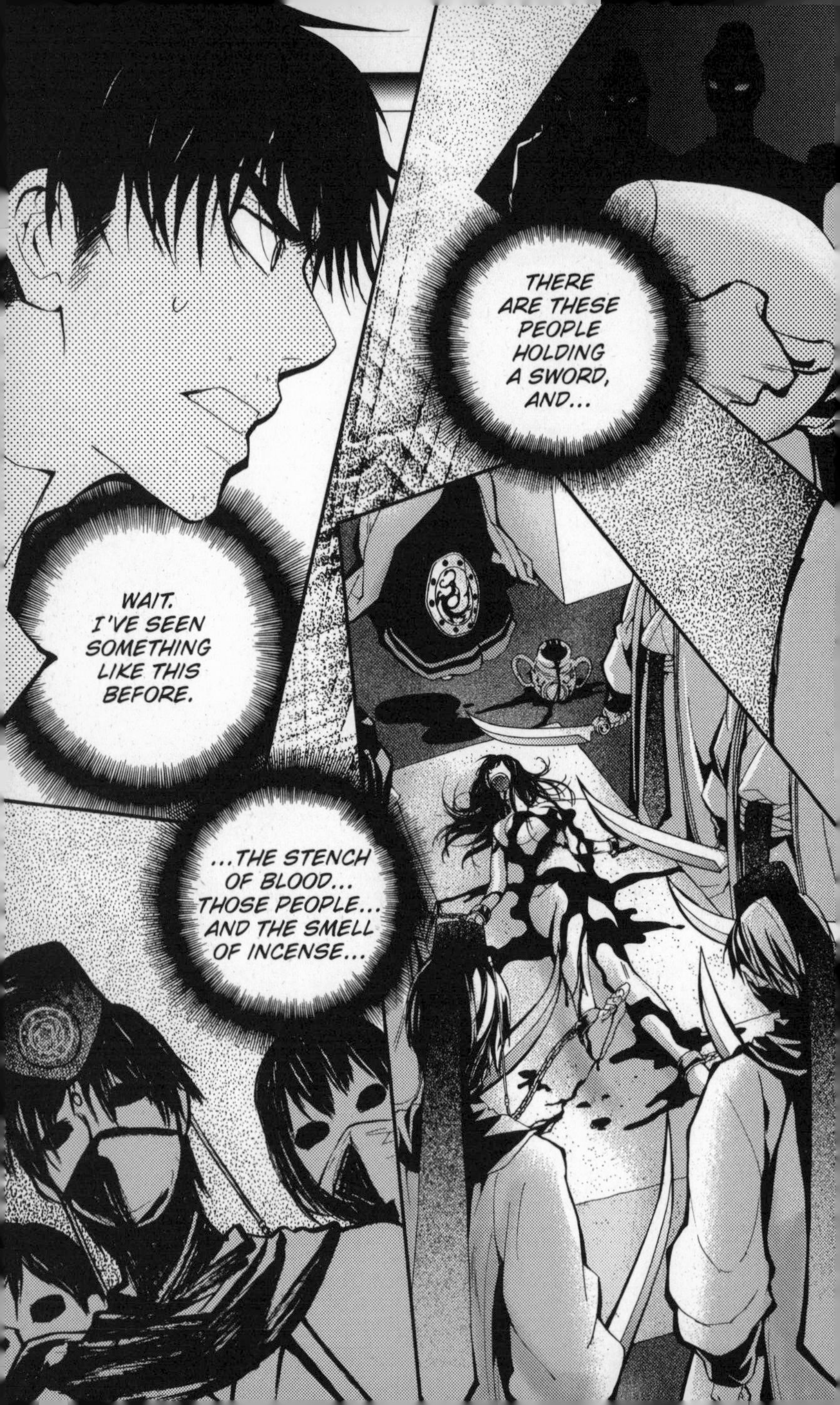
WAIT. I'VE SEEN SOMETHING LIKE THIS BEFORE.
THERE ARE THESE PEOPLE HOLDING A SWORD, AND...
...THE STENCH OF BLOOD... THOSE PEOPLE... AND THE SMELL OF INCENSE...

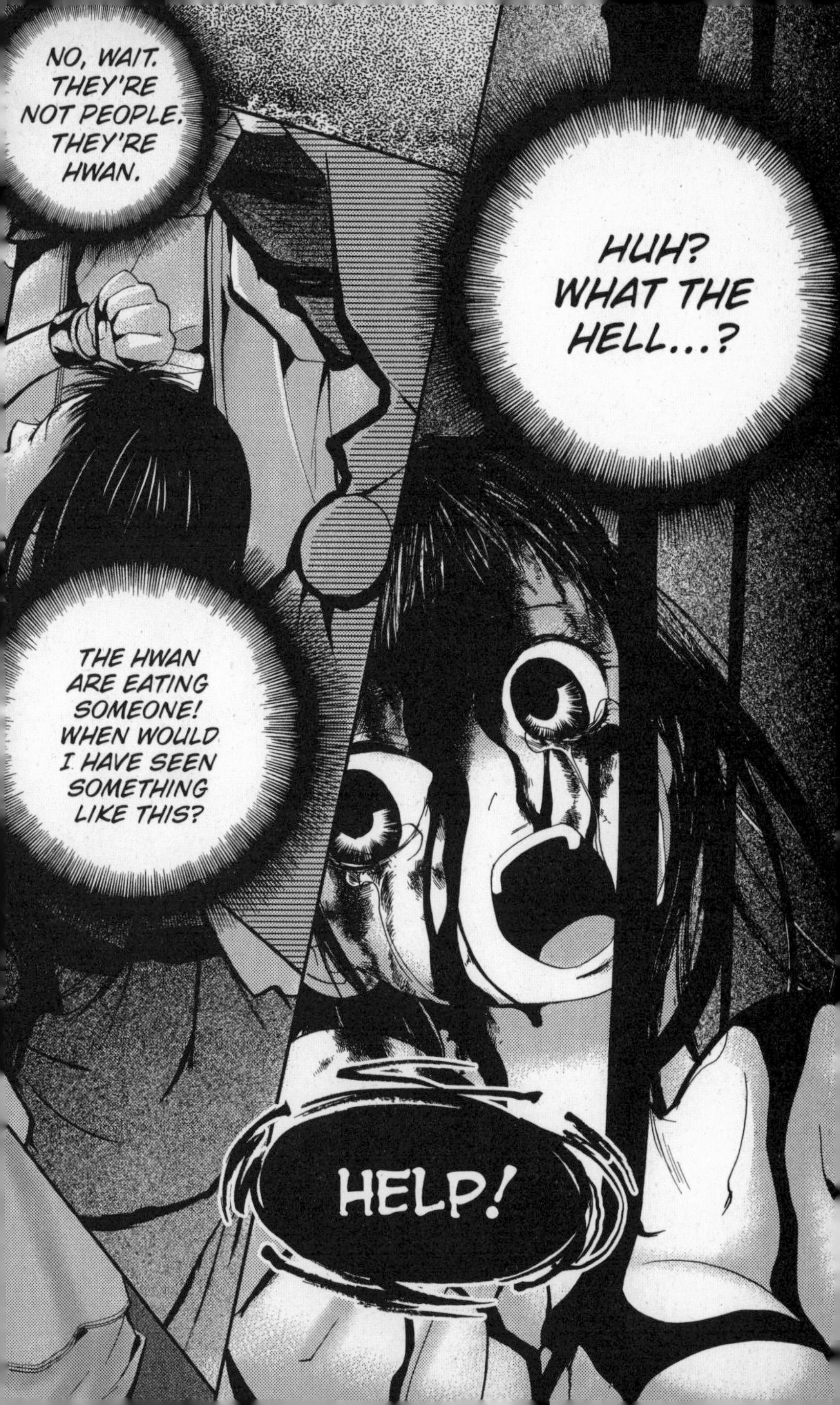
NO, WAIT. THEY'RE NOT PEOPLE. THEY'RE HWAN.
THE HWAN ARE EATING SOMEONE! WHEN WOULD I HAVE SEEN SOMETHING LIKE THIS?
HUH? WHAT THE HELL...?
HELP!

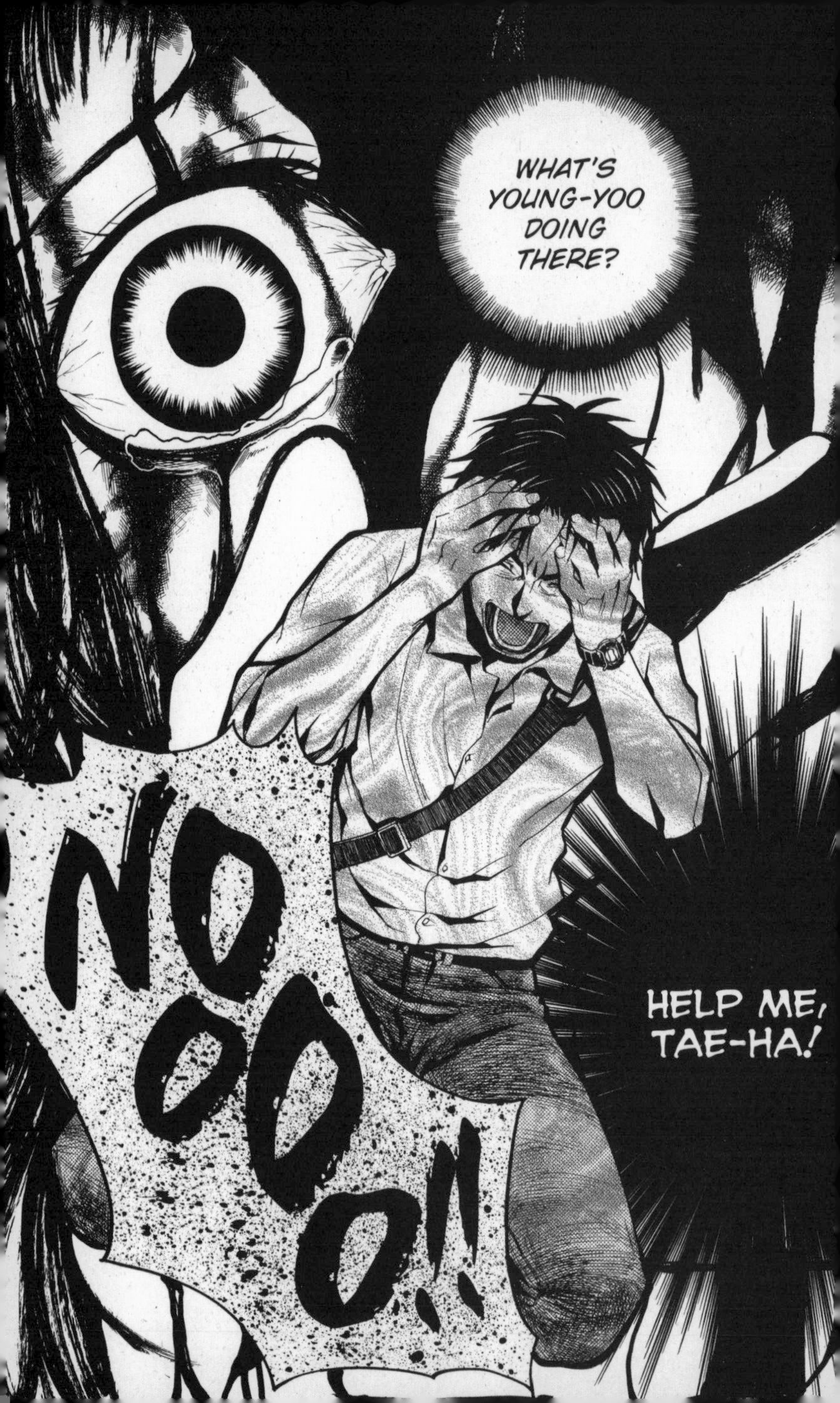
WHAT'S YOUNG-YOO DOING THERE?
NOOOOO!!
HELP ME, TAE-HA!

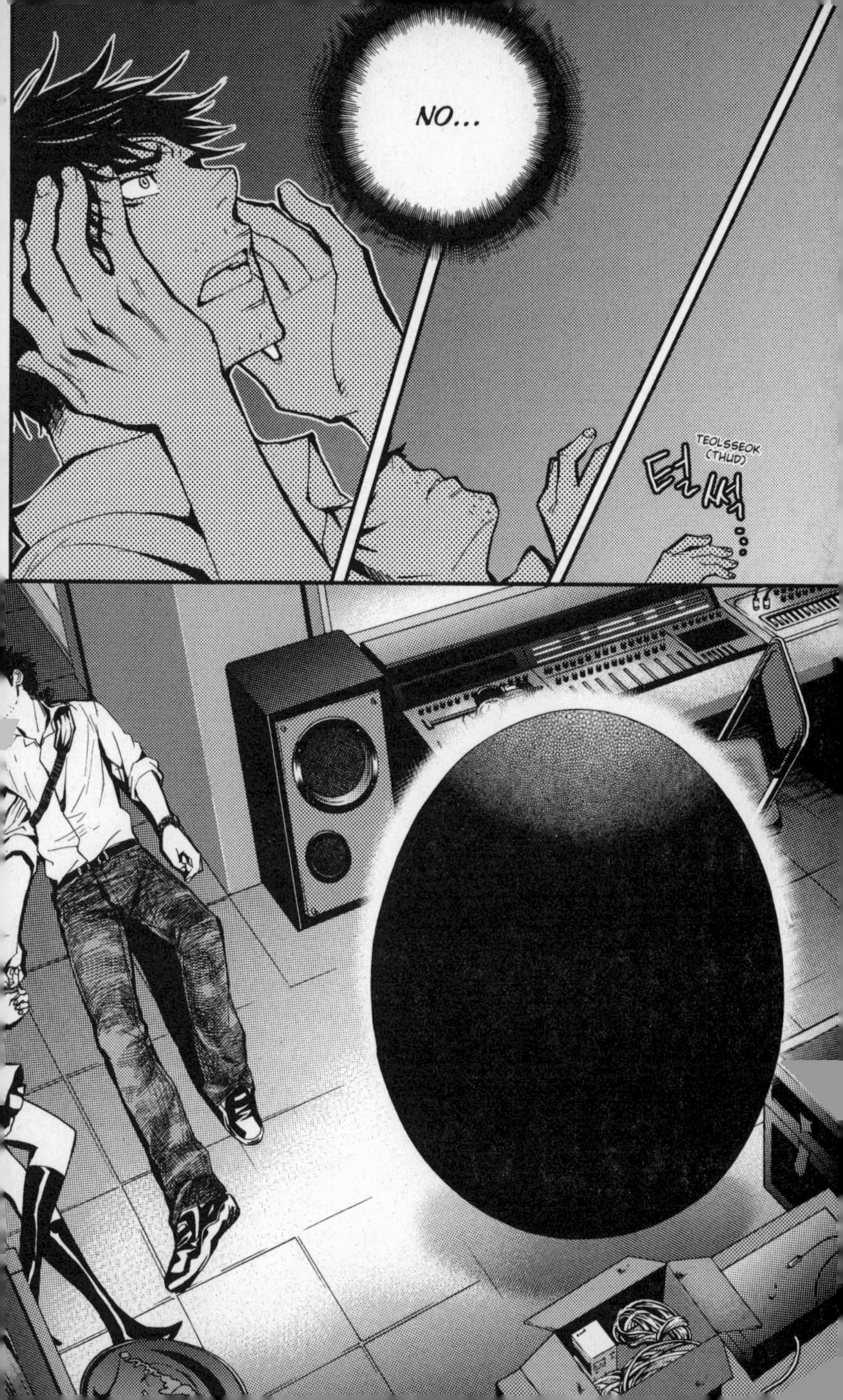
NO...
TEOLSSEOK (THUD)
털썩

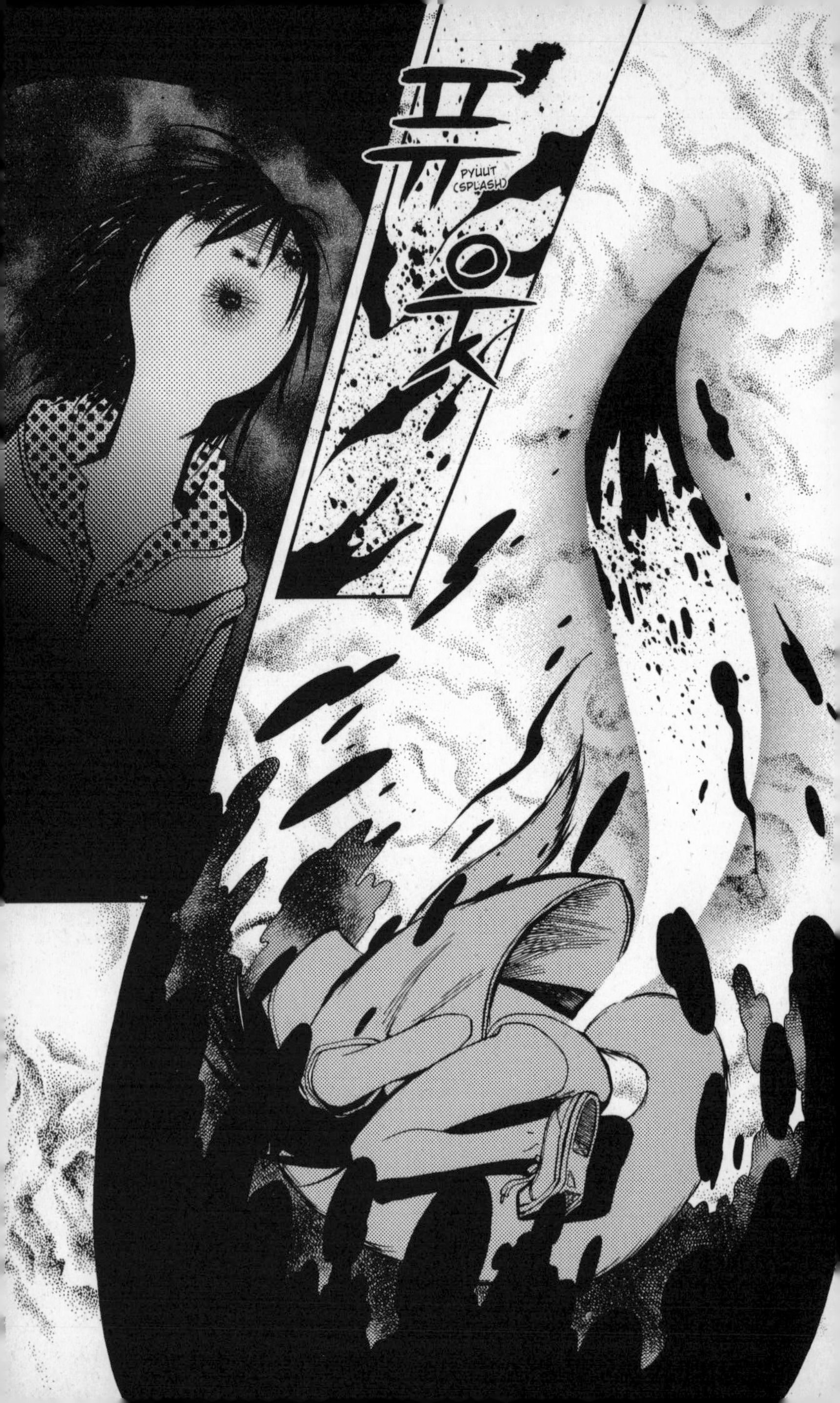
PYUUT
(SPLASH)

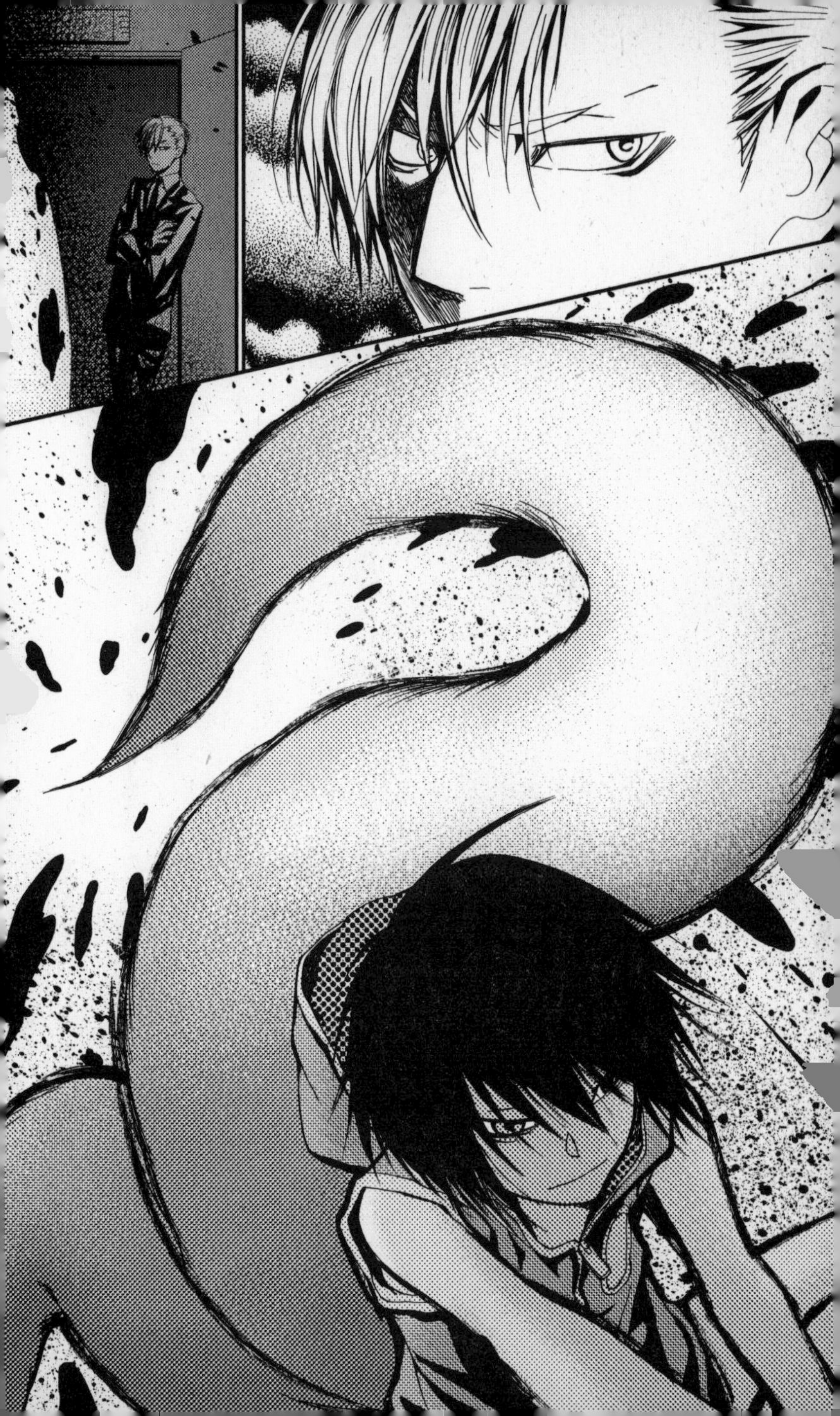

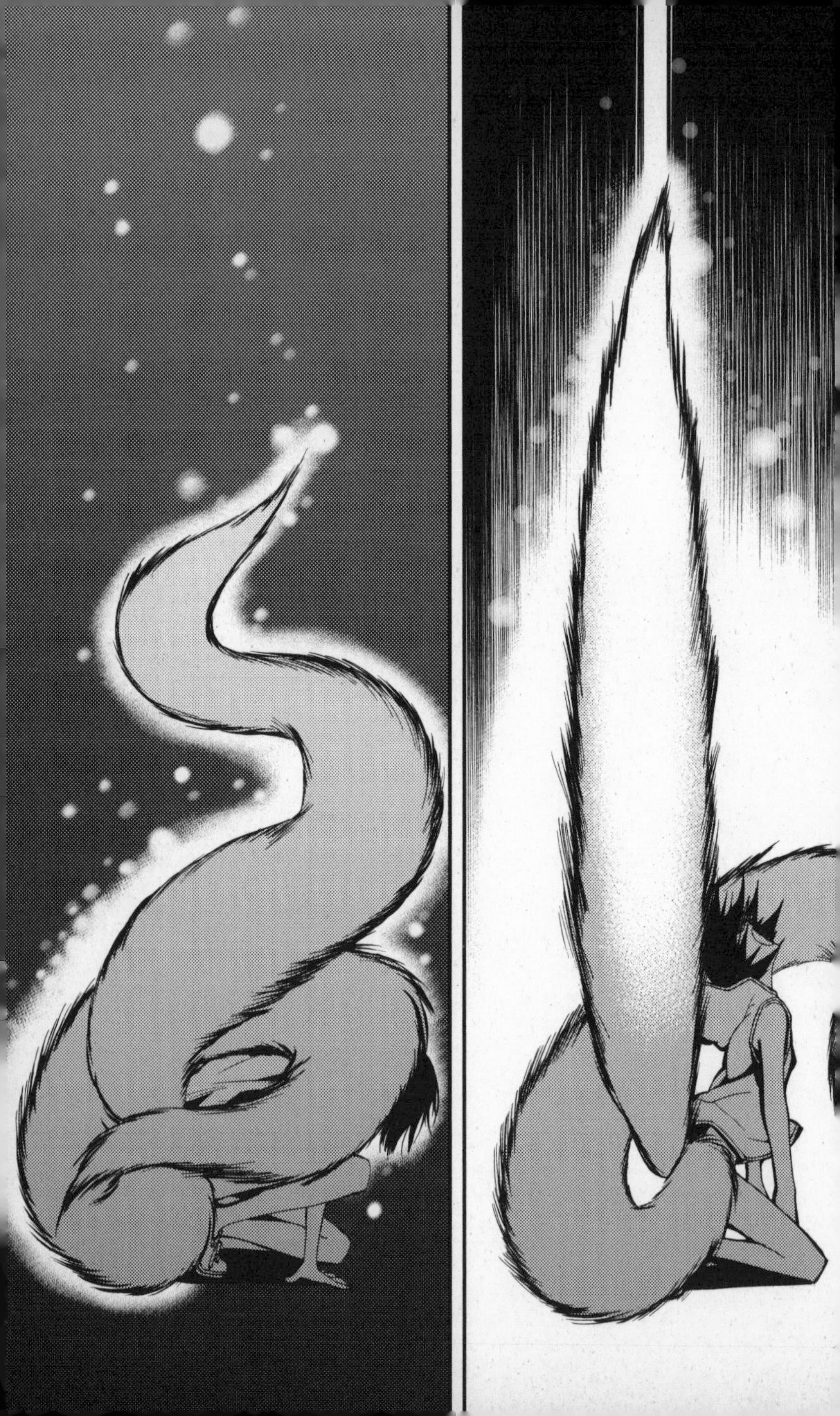

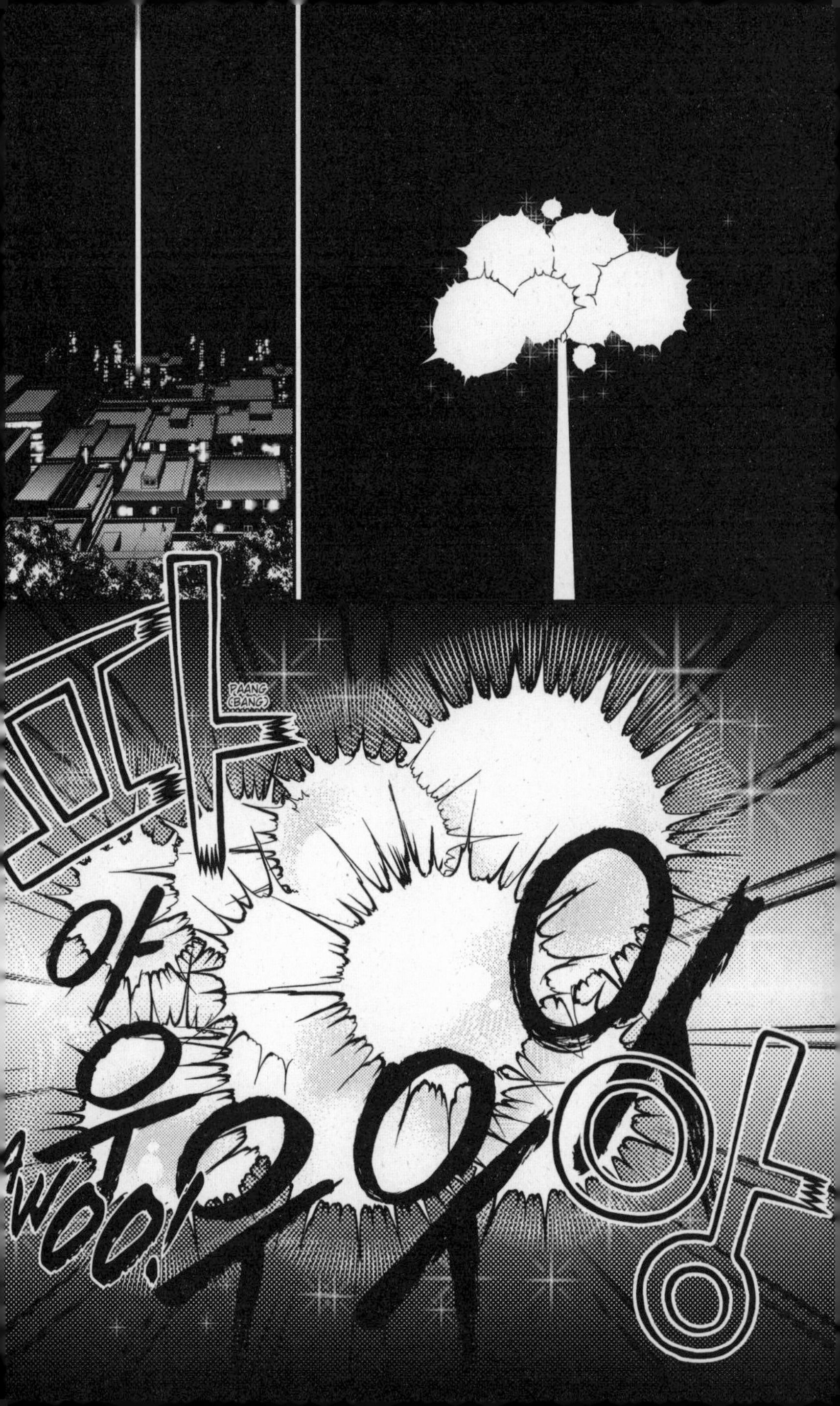
PAANG
(BANG)
WOO!

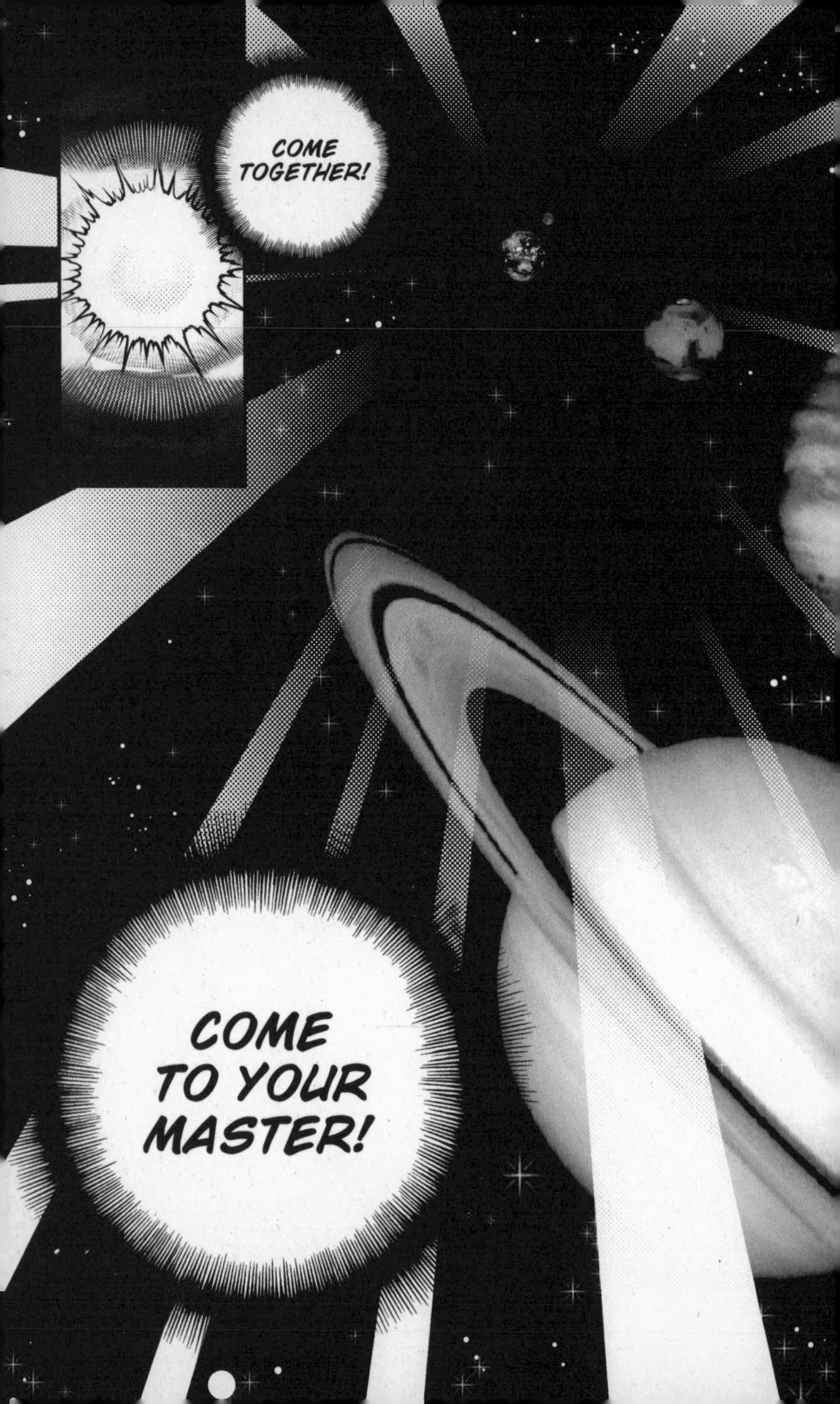
COME TOGETHER!
COME TO YOUR MASTER!

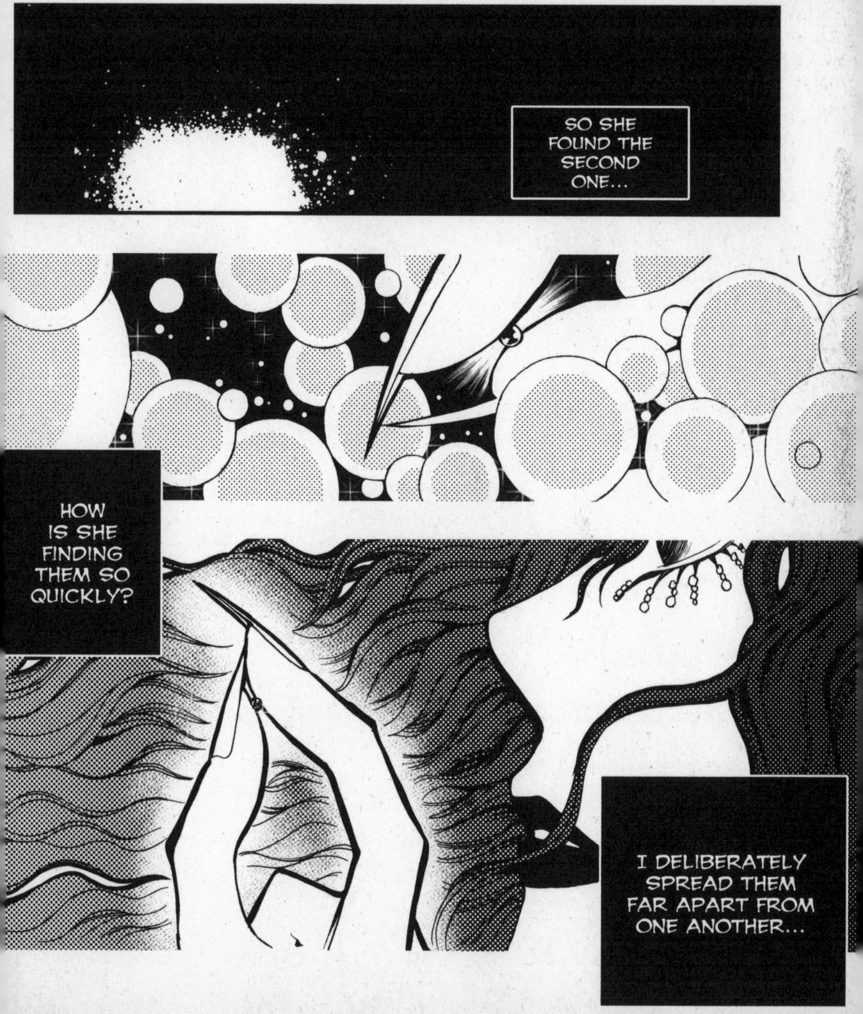
SO SHE FOUND THE SECOND ONE...
HOW IS SHE FINDING THEM SO QUICKLY?
I DELIBERATELY SPREAD THEM FAR APART FROM ONE ANOTHER...

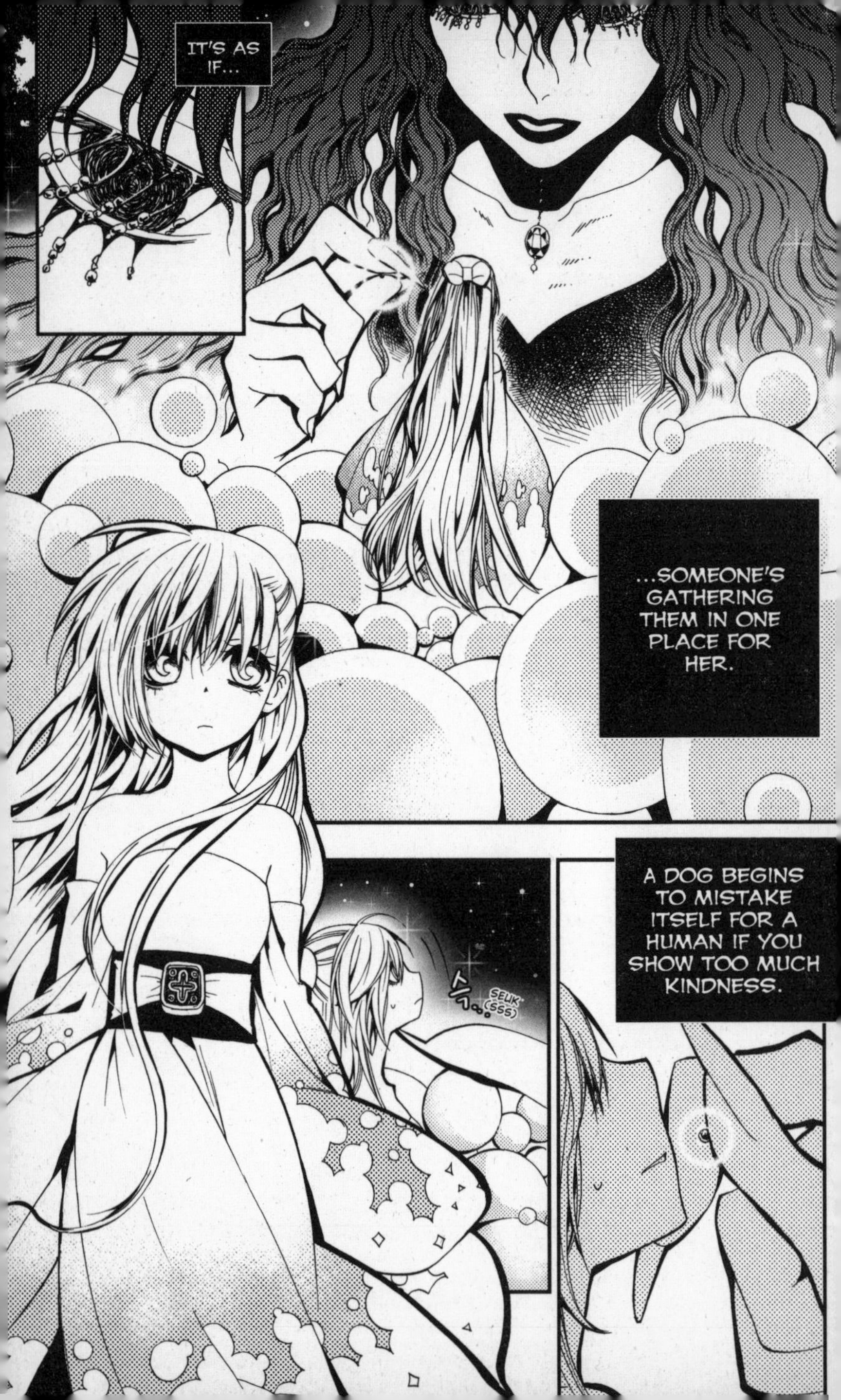
IT'S AS IF...
...SOMEONE'S GATHERING THEM IN ONE PLACE FOR HER.
SEUK (SSS)
A DOG BEGINS TO MISTAKE ITSELF FOR A HUMAN IF YOU SHOW TOO MUCH KINDNESS.

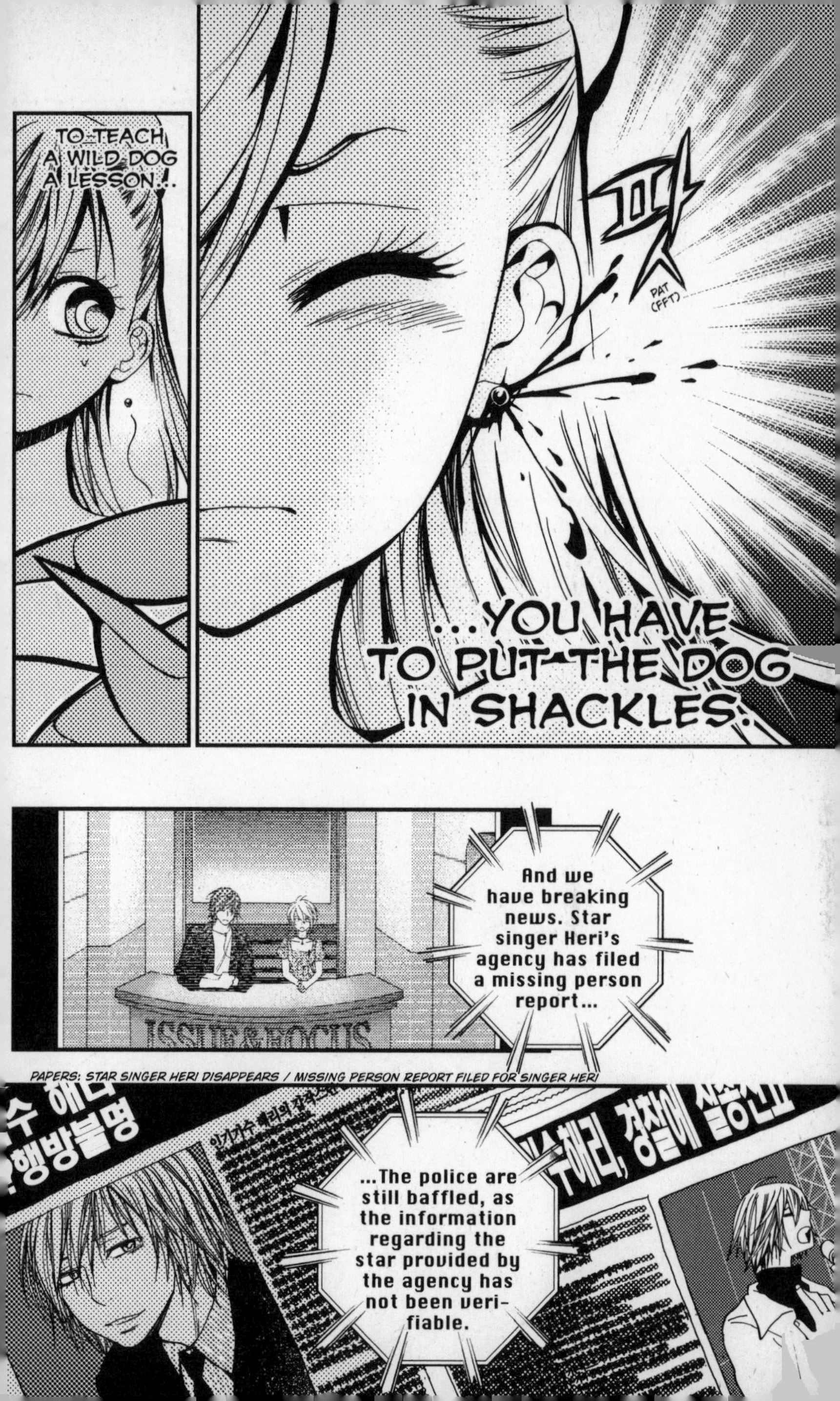
TO TEACH A WILD DOG A LESSON...
PAT (FFT)
...YOU HAVE TO PUT THE DOG IN SHACKLES.
And we have breaking news. Star singer Heri's agency has filed a missing person report...
PAPERS: STAR SINGER HERI DISAPPEARS / MISSING PERSON REPORT FILED FOR SINGER HERI
...The police are still baffled, as the information regarding the star provided by the agency has not been veri-fiable.

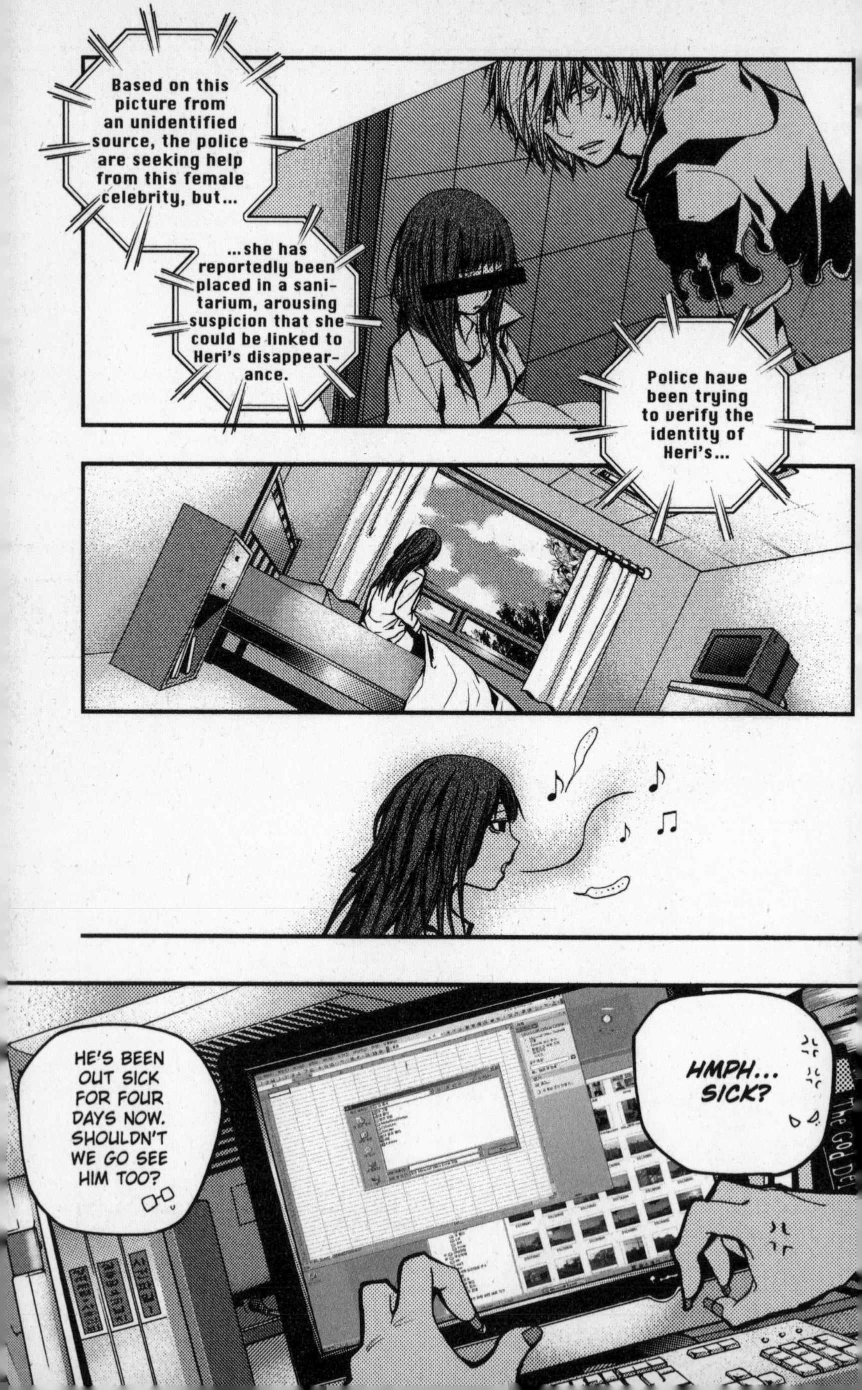
Based on this picture from an unidentified source, the police are seeking help from this female celebrity, but...
...she has reportedly been placed in a sani-tarium, arousing suspicion that she could be linked to Heri's disappear-ance.
Police have been trying to verify the identity of Heri's...
HE'S BEEN OUT SICK FOR FOUR DAYS NOW. SHOULDN'T WE GO SEE HIM TOO?
HMPH... SICK?

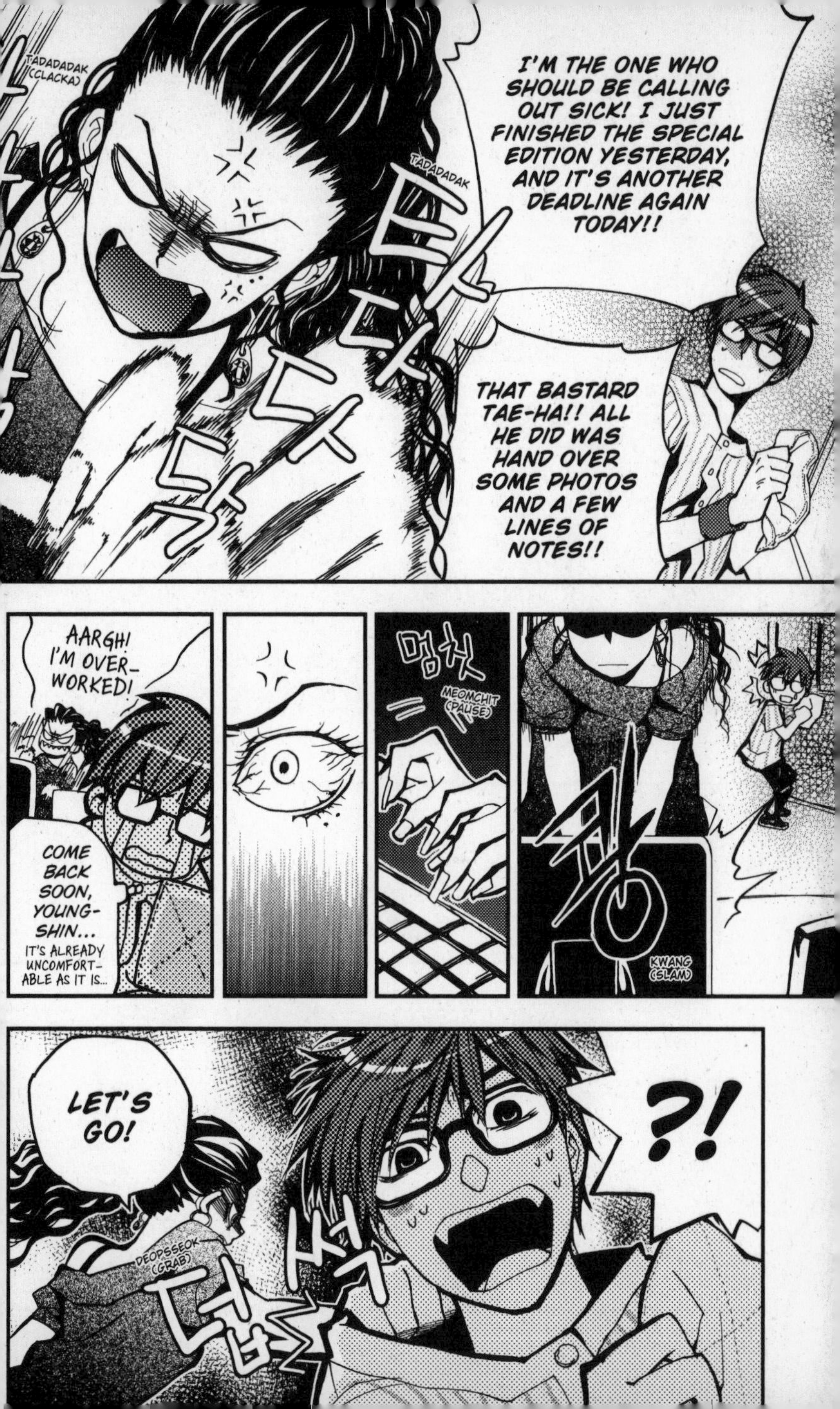
TADADADAK (CLACKA)
TADADADAK
I'M THE ONE WHO SHOULD BE CALLING OUT SICK! I JUST FINISHED THE SPECIAL EDITION YESTERDAY, AND IT'S ANOTHER DEADLINE AGAIN TODAY!!
THAT BASTARD TAE-HA!! ALL HE DID WAS HAND OVER SOME PHOTOS AND A FEW LINES OF NOTES!!
AARGH! I'M OVER-WORKED!
COME BACK SOON, YOUNG-SHIN...
IT'S ALREADY UNCOMFORT-ABLE AS IT IS...
멈칫
MEOMCHIT (PAUSE)
KWANG (SLAM)
LET'S GO!
?!
DEOPSSEOK (GRAB)

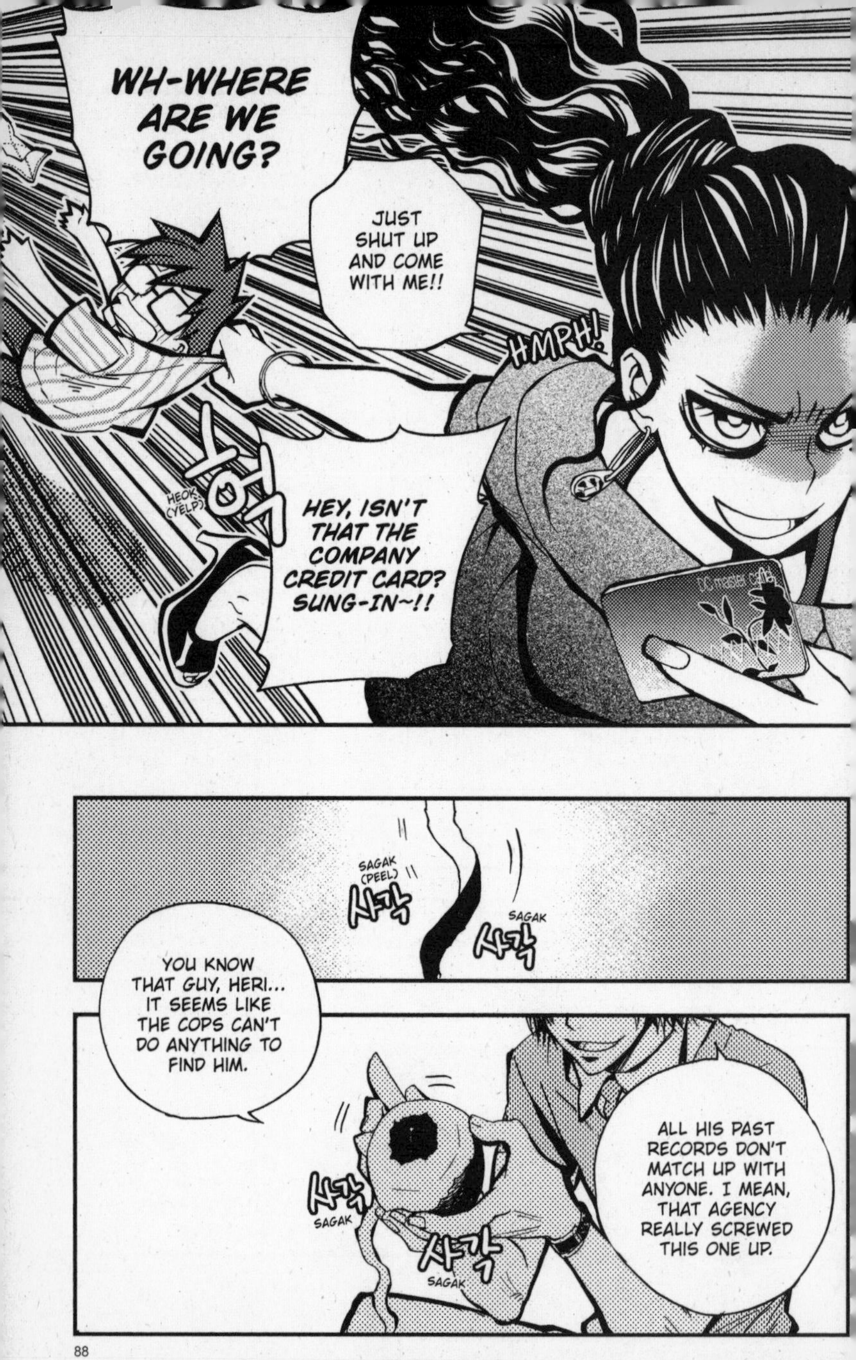
WH-WHERE ARE WE GOING?
JUST SHUT UP AND COME WITH ME!!
HMPH!
헉
HEOK (YELP)
HEY, ISN'T THAT THE COMPANY CREDIT CARD? SUNG-IN~!!
SAGAK (PEEL)
사각
SAGAK
사각
YOU KNOW THAT GUY, HERI... IT SEEMS LIKE THE COPS CAN'T DO ANYTHING TO FIND HIM.
사각
SAGAK
사각
SAGAK
ALL HIS PAST RECORDS DON'T MATCH UP WITH ANYONE. I MEAN, THAT AGENCY REALLY SCREWED THIS ONE UP.

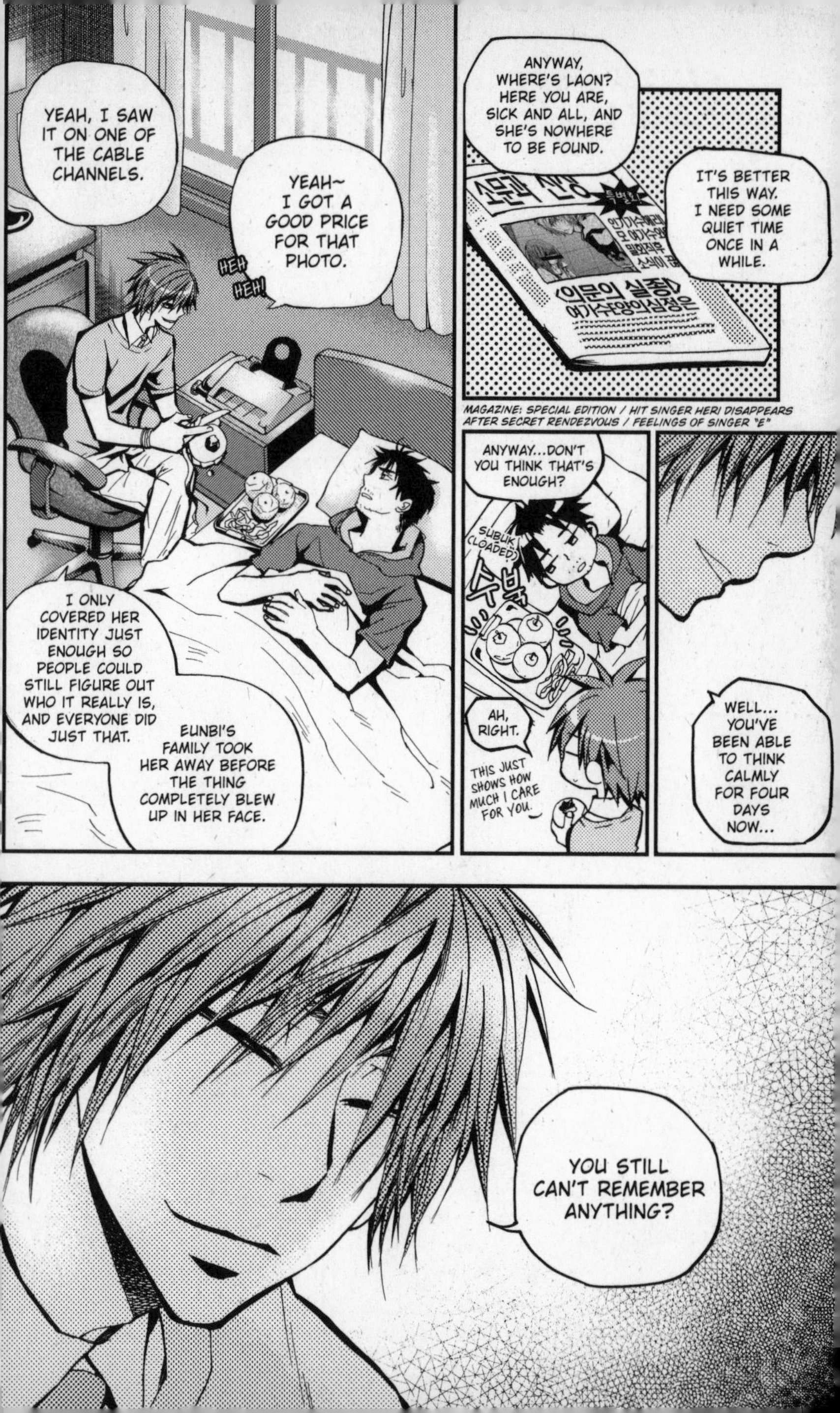
YEAH, I SAW IT ON ONE OF THE CABLE CHANNELS.
YEAH~ I GOT A GOOD PRICE FOR THAT PHOTO.
HEH HEH!
I ONLY COVERED HER IDENTITY JUST ENOUGH SO PEOPLE COULD STILL FIGURE OUT WHO IT REALLY IS, AND EVERYONE DID JUST THAT.
EUNBI'S FAMILY TOOK HER AWAY BEFORE THE THING COMPLETELY BLEW UP IN HER FACE.
ANYWAY, WHERE'S LAON? HERE YOU ARE, SICK AND ALL, AND SHE'S NOWHERE TO BE FOUND.
IT'S BETTER THIS WAY. I NEED SOME QUIET TIME ONCE IN A WHILE.
MAGAZINE: SPECIAL EDITION / HIT SINGER HERI DISAPPEARS AFTER SECRET RENDEZVOUS / FEELINGS OF SINGER "E"
ANYWAY...DON'T YOU THINK THAT'S ENOUGH?
SUBUK (LOADED)
수북
AH, RIGHT.
THIS JUST SHOWS HOW MUCH I CARE FOR YOU.
WELL... YOU'VE BEEN ABLE TO THINK CALMLY FOR FOUR DAYS NOW...
YOU STILL CAN'T REMEMBER ANYTHING?

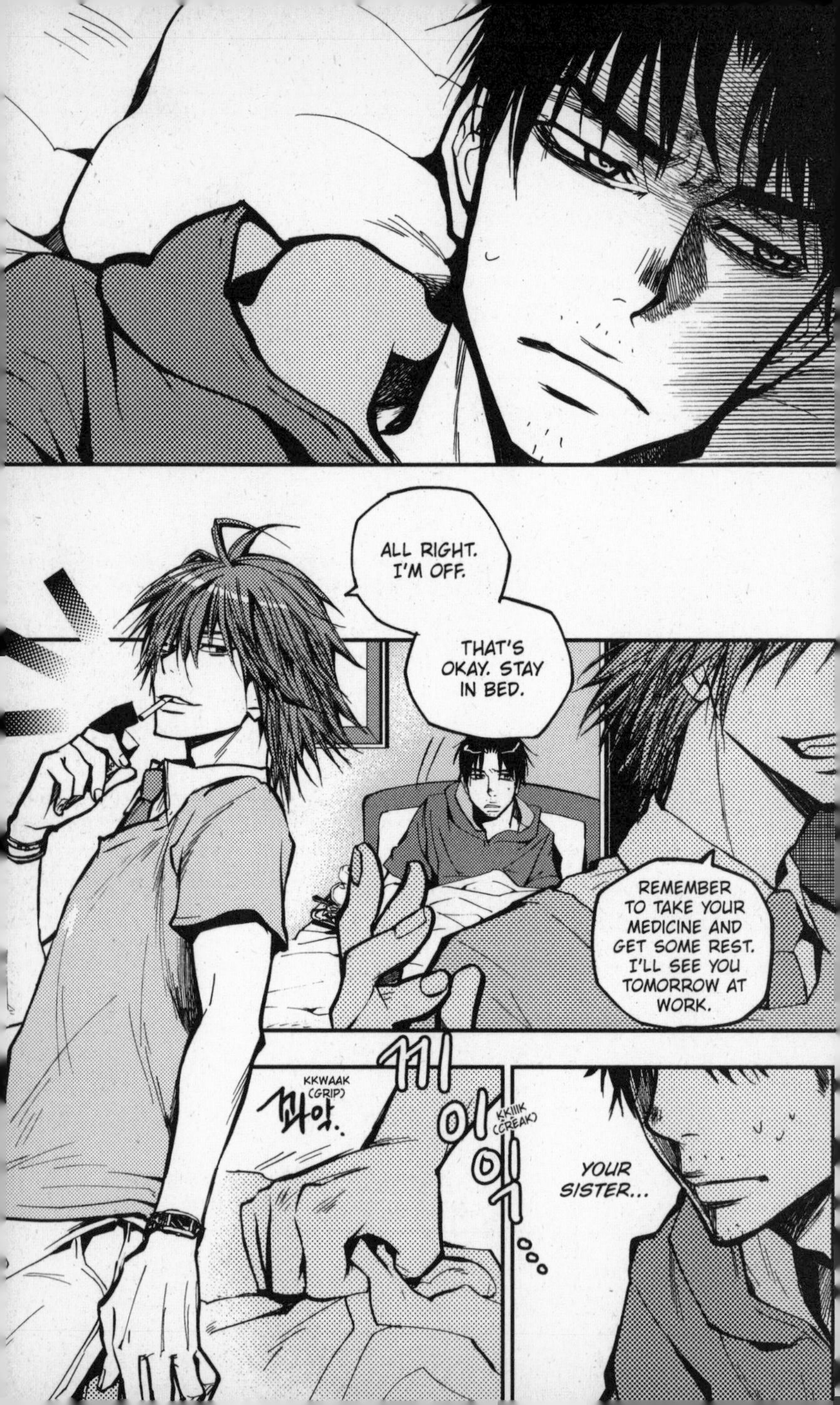

ALL RIGHT. I'M OFF.
THAT'S OKAY. STAY IN BED.
REMEMBER TO TAKE YOUR MEDICINE AND GET SOME REST. I'LL SEE YOU TOMORROW AT WORK.
콰악..
KKWAAK (GRIP)
끼이이이
KKIIIK (CREAK)
YOUR SISTER...

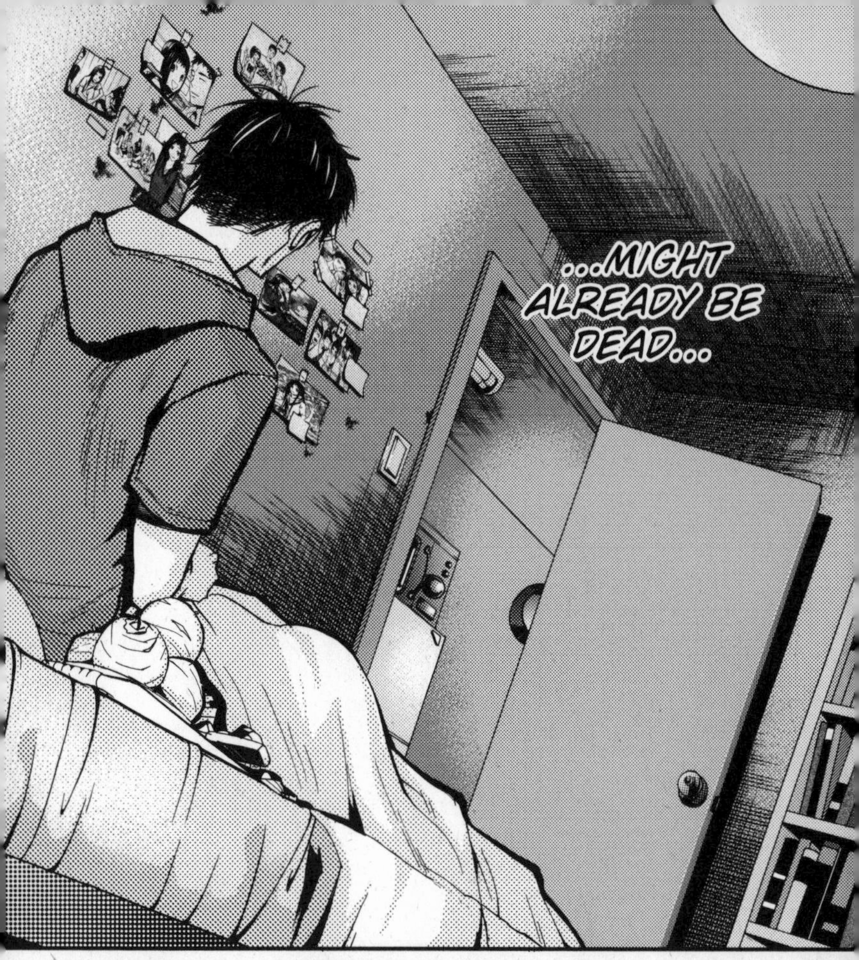
...MIGHT ALREADY BE DEAD...

NOTE: 1999, SCHOOL NEWSPAPER EXCHANGE EVENT

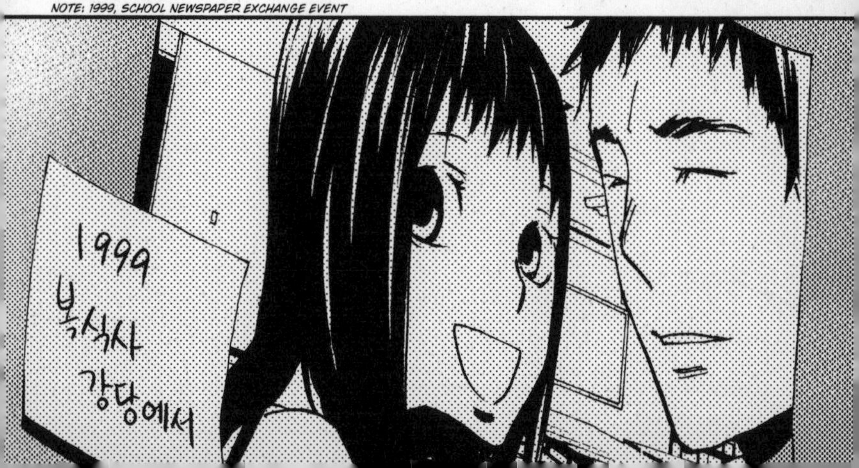
1999
복식사
강당에서

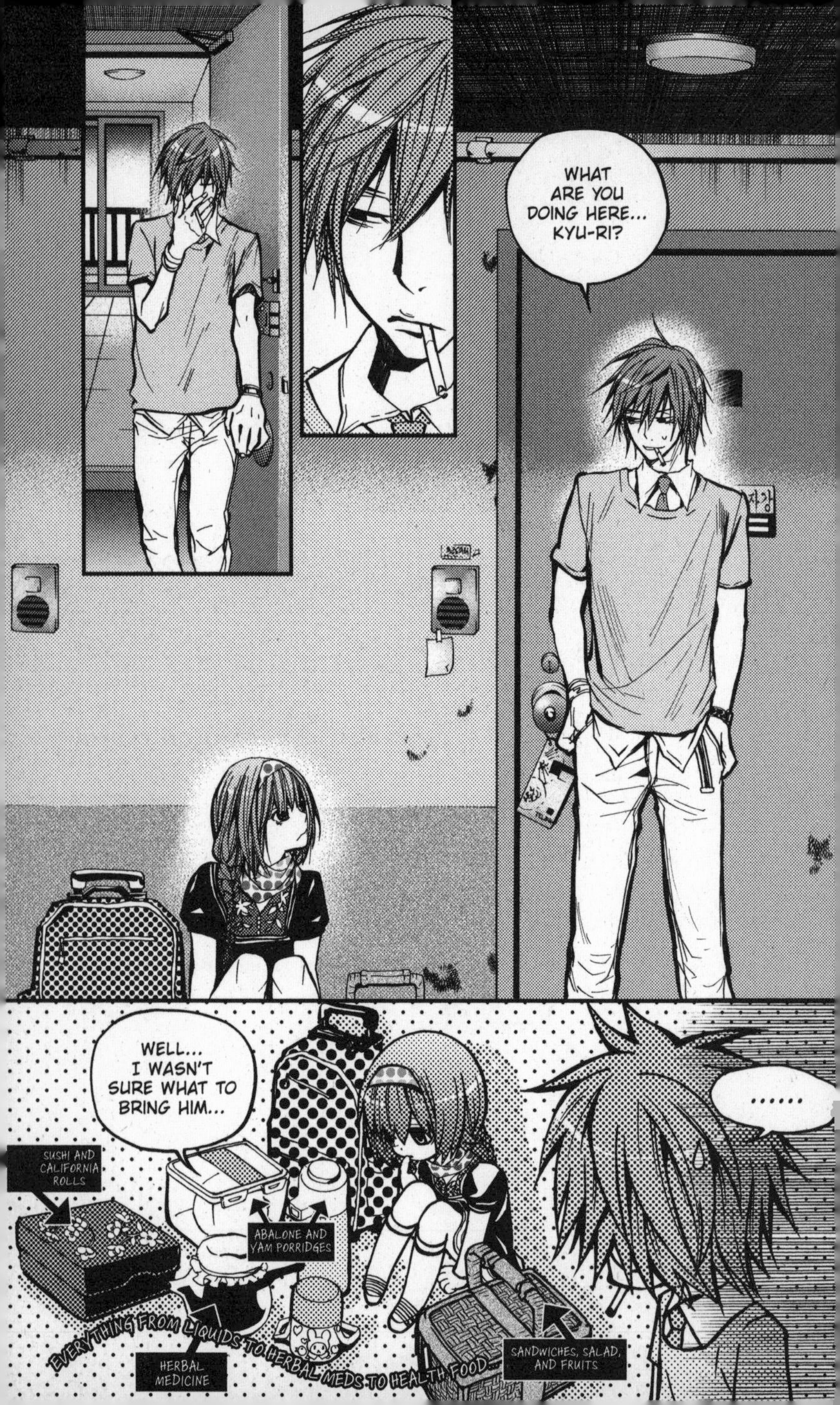
WHAT ARE YOU DOING HERE... KYU-RI?
WELL... I WASN'T SURE WHAT TO BRING HIM...
......
SUSHI AND CALIFORNIA ROLLS
ABALONE AND YAM PORRIDGES
EVERYTHING FROM LIQUIDS TO HERBAL MEDS TO HEALTH FOOD...
SANDWICHES, SALAD, AND FRUITS
HERBAL MEDICINE

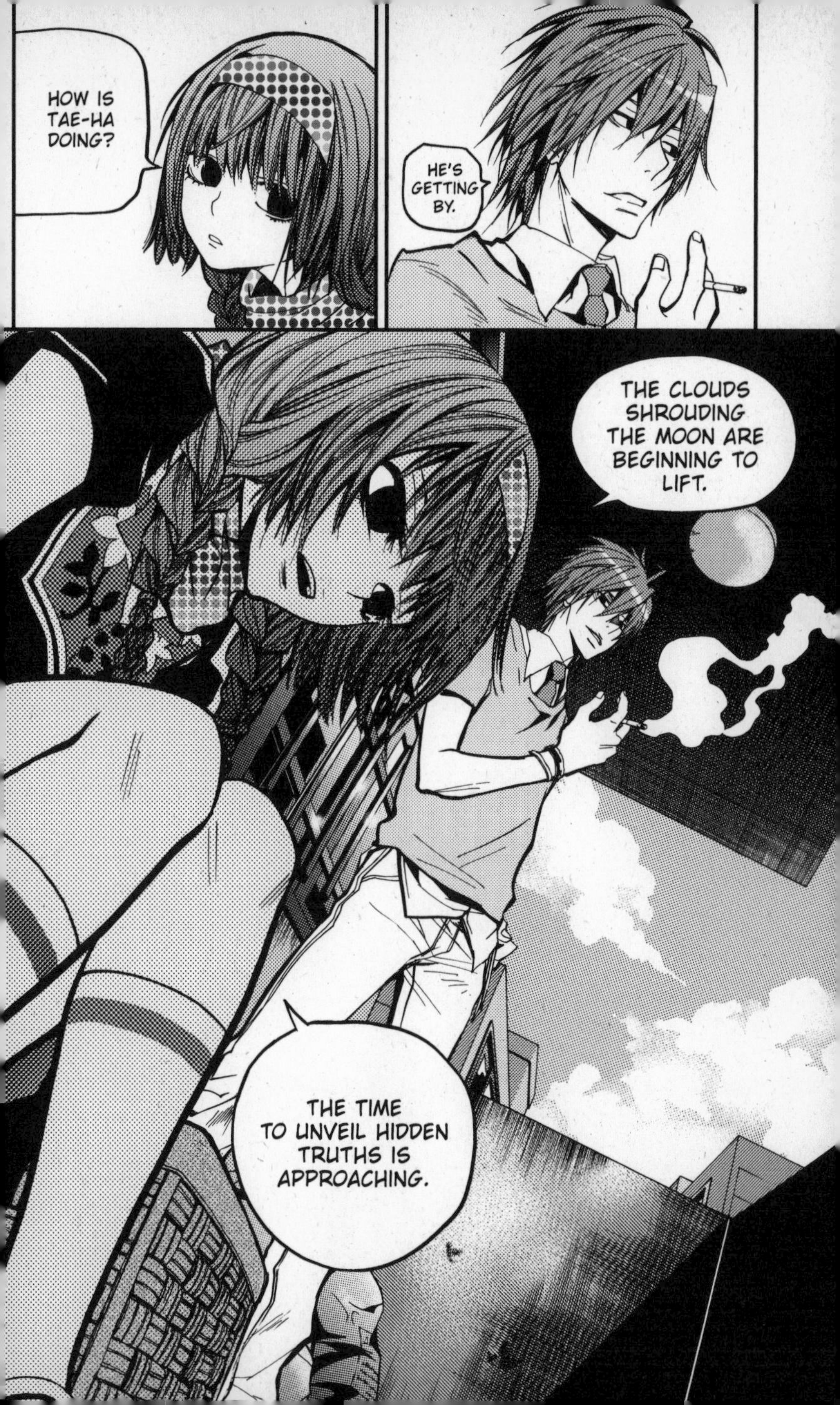
HOW IS TAE-HA DOING?
HE'S GETTING BY.
THE CLOUDS SHROUDING THE MOON ARE BEGINNING TO LIFT.
THE TIME TO UNVEIL HIDDEN TRUTHS IS APPROACHING.

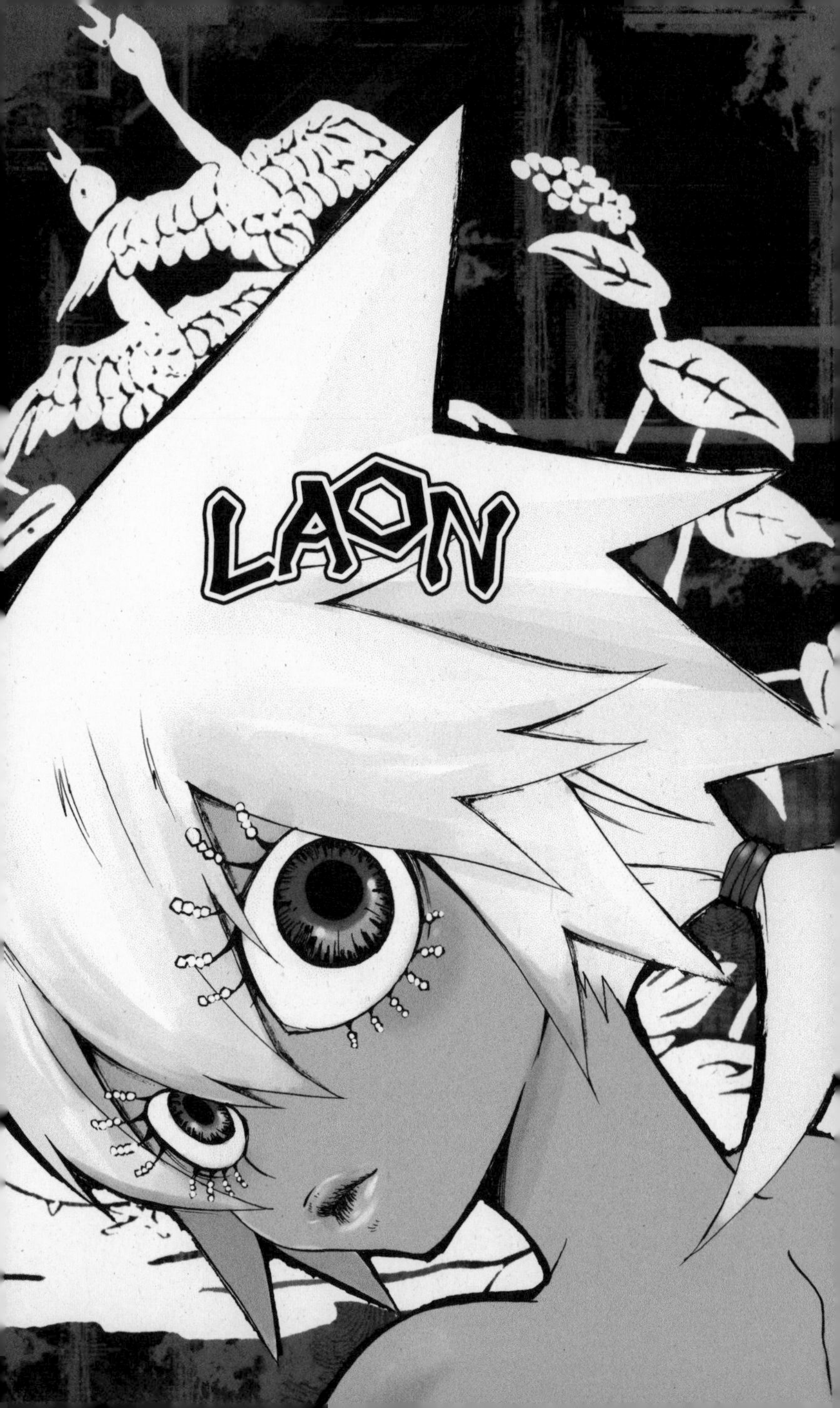
LAON

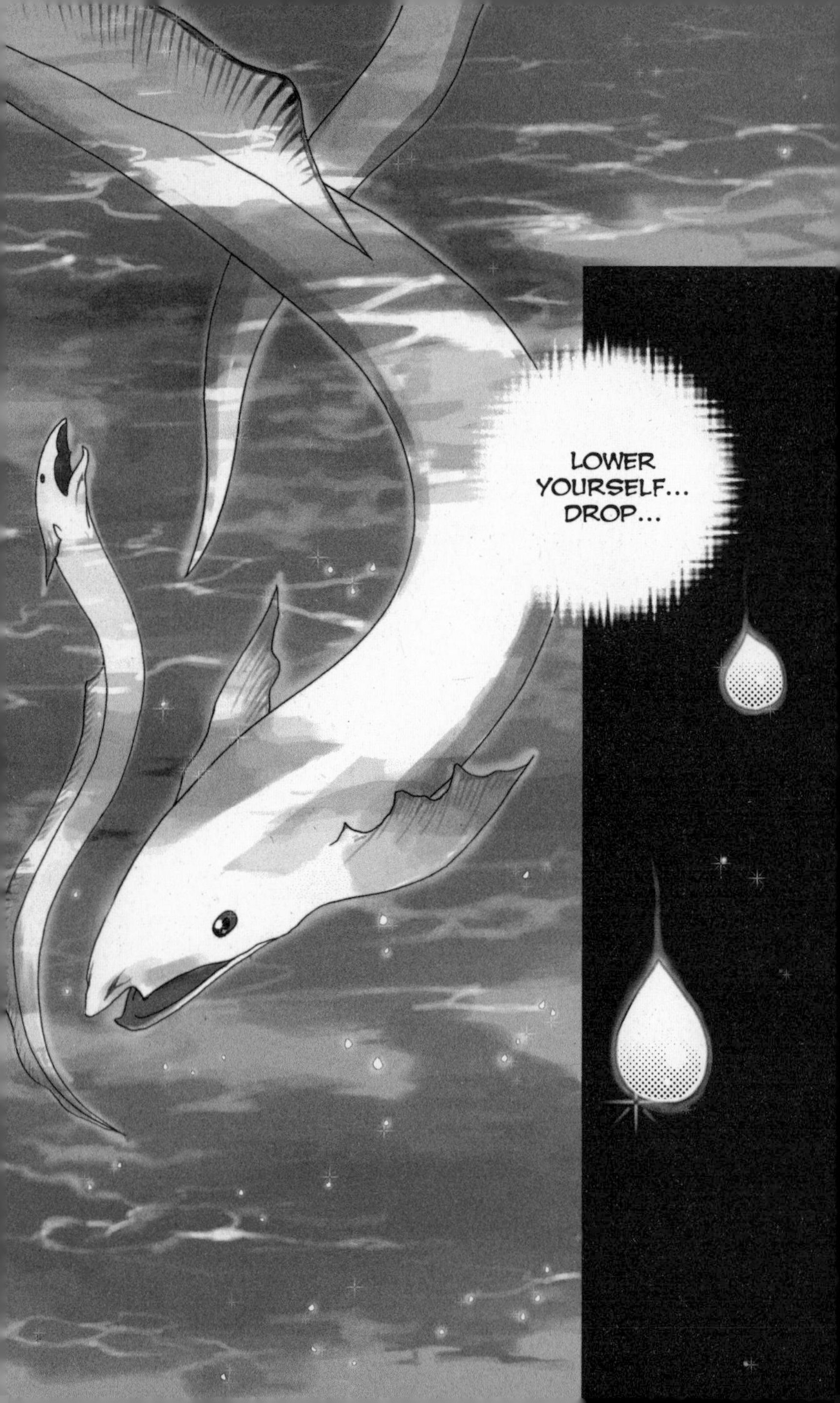
LOWER YOURSELF... DROP...

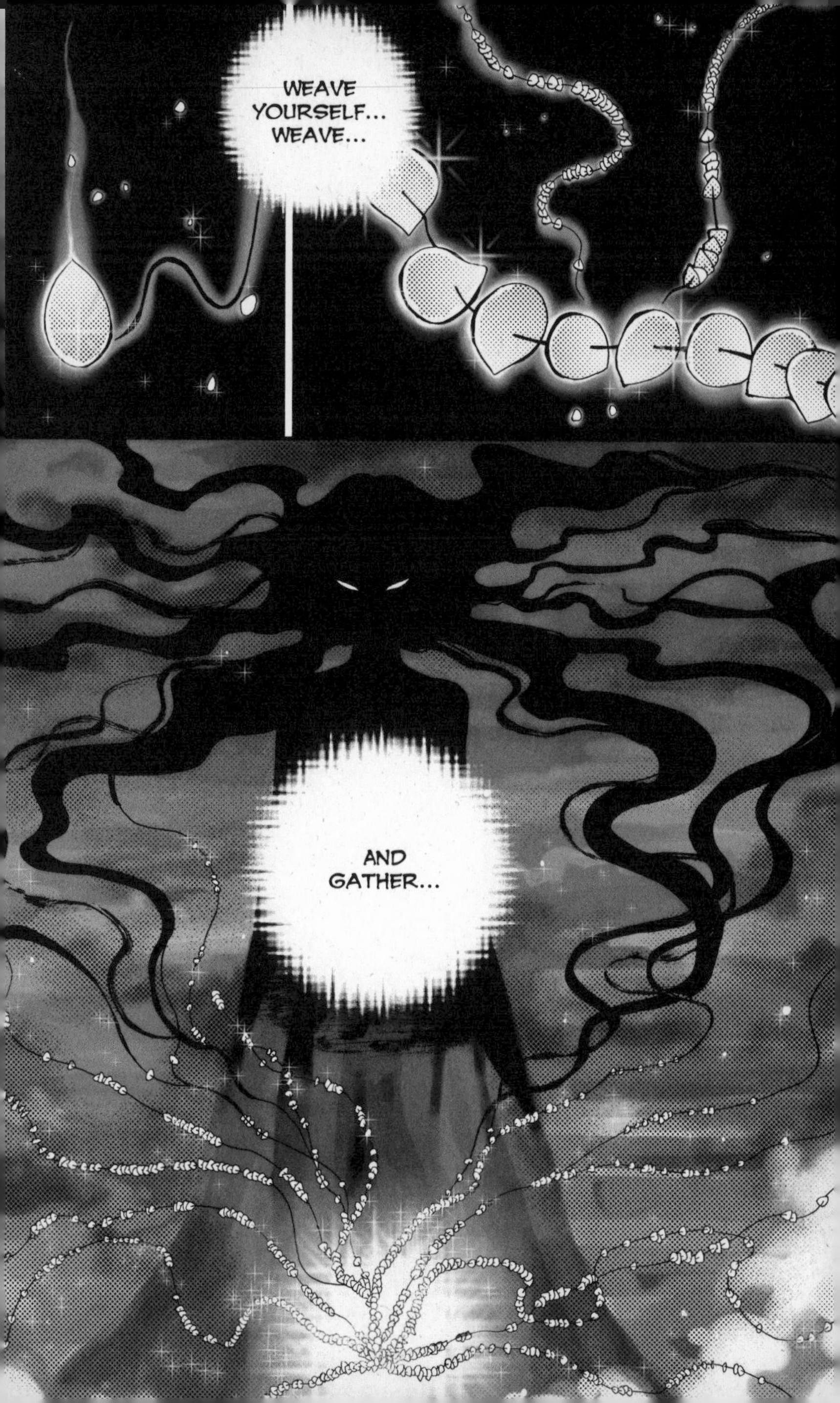
WEAVE YOURSELF... WEAVE...
AND GATHER...

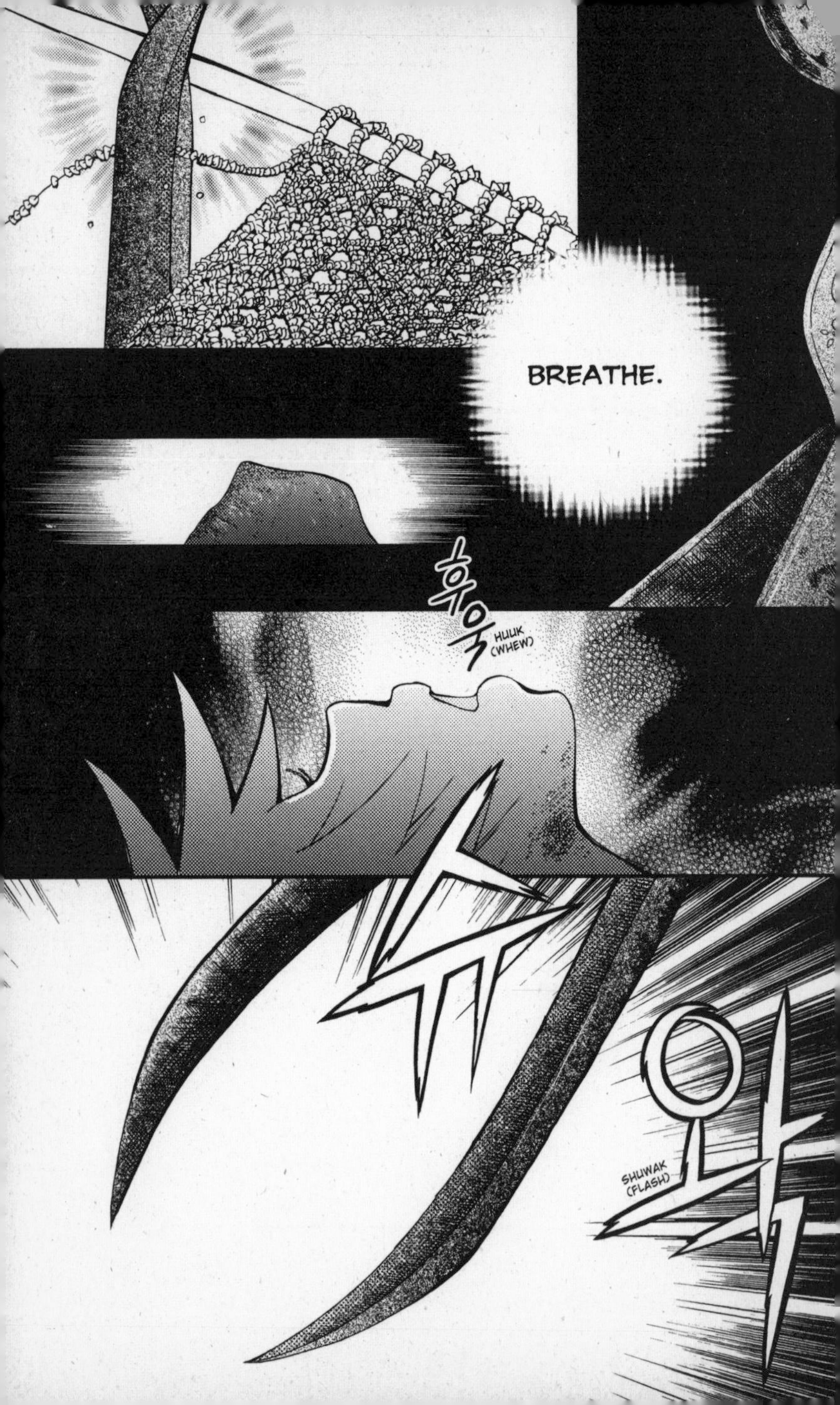
BREATHE.
후우욱
HUUK
(WHEW)
샤악
SHUWAK
(FLASH)

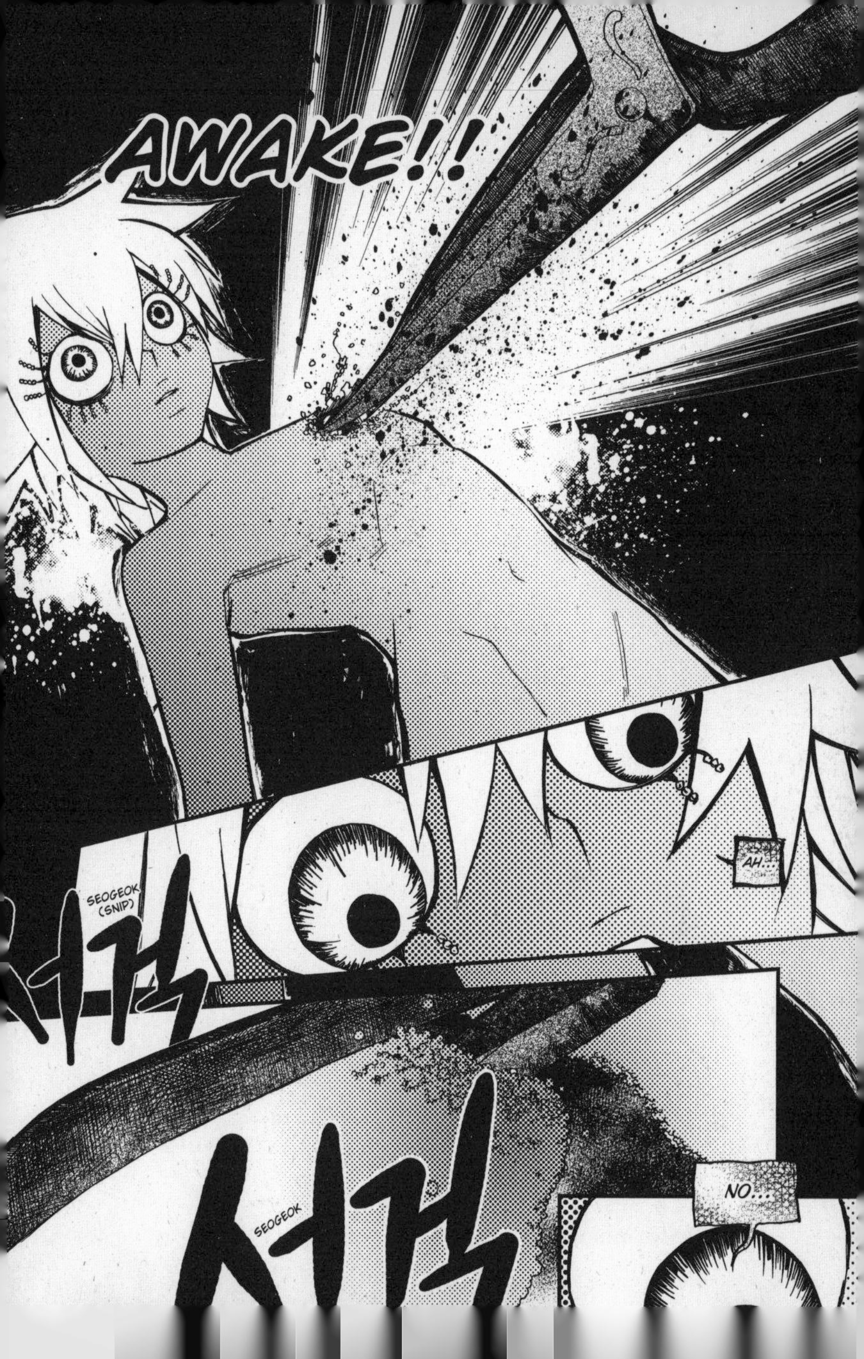
AWAKE!!
SEOGEOK
(SNIP)
서걱
AH...
SEOGEOK
서걱
NO...

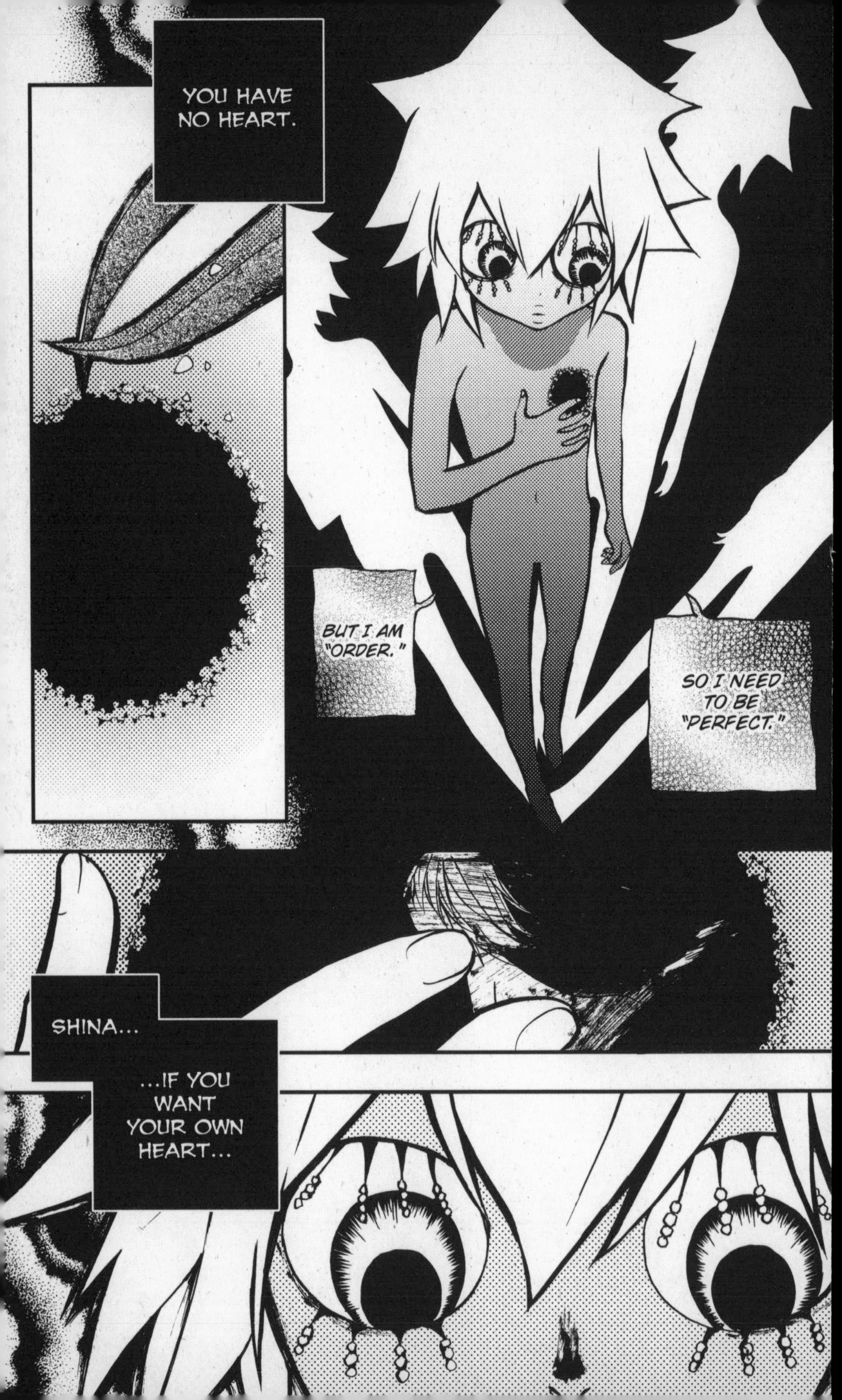
YOU HAVE NO HEART.
BUT I AM "ORDER."
SO I NEED TO BE "PERFECT."
SHINA...
...IF YOU WANT YOUR OWN HEART...

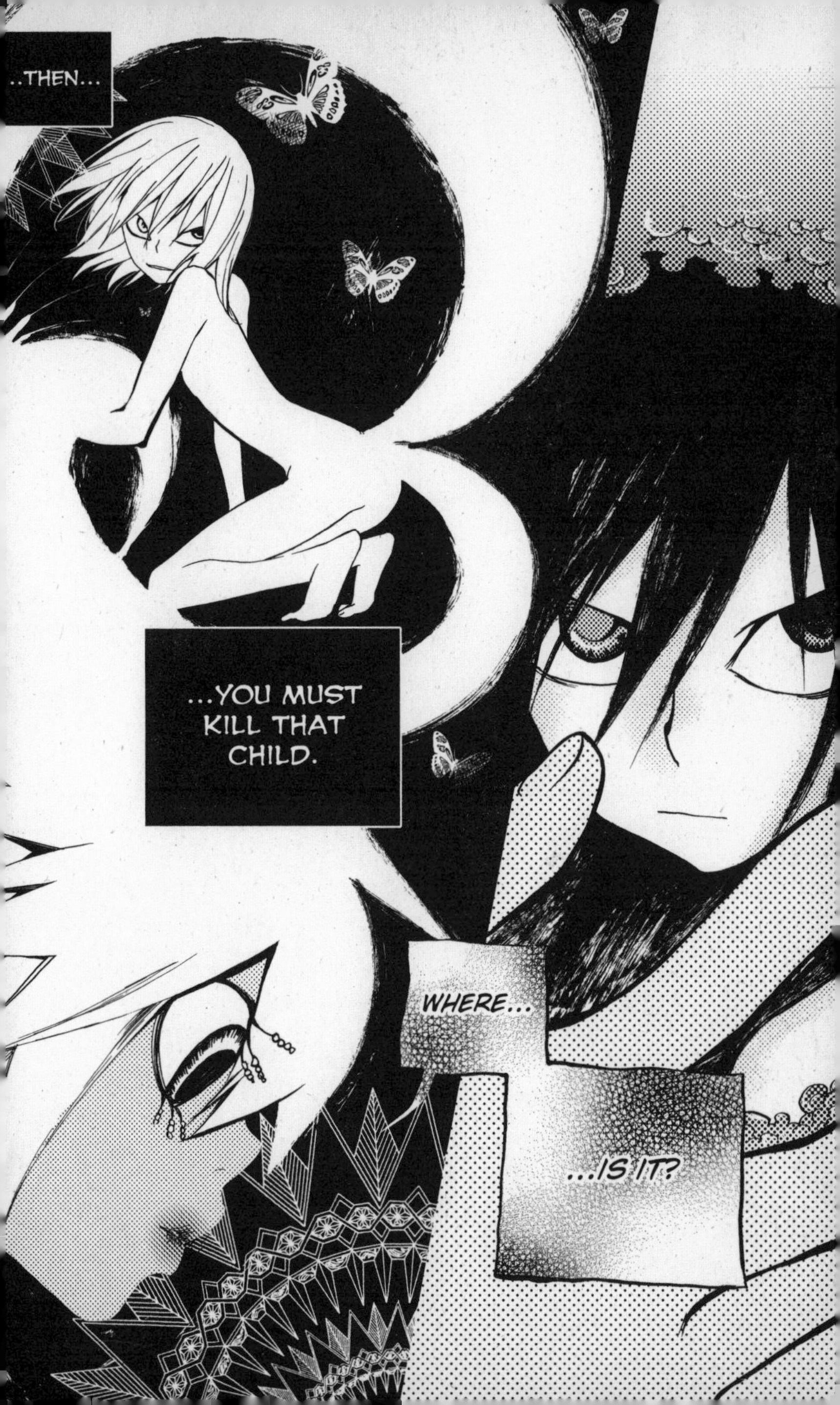
..THEN...
...YOU MUST KILL THAT CHILD.
WHERE...
...IS IT?

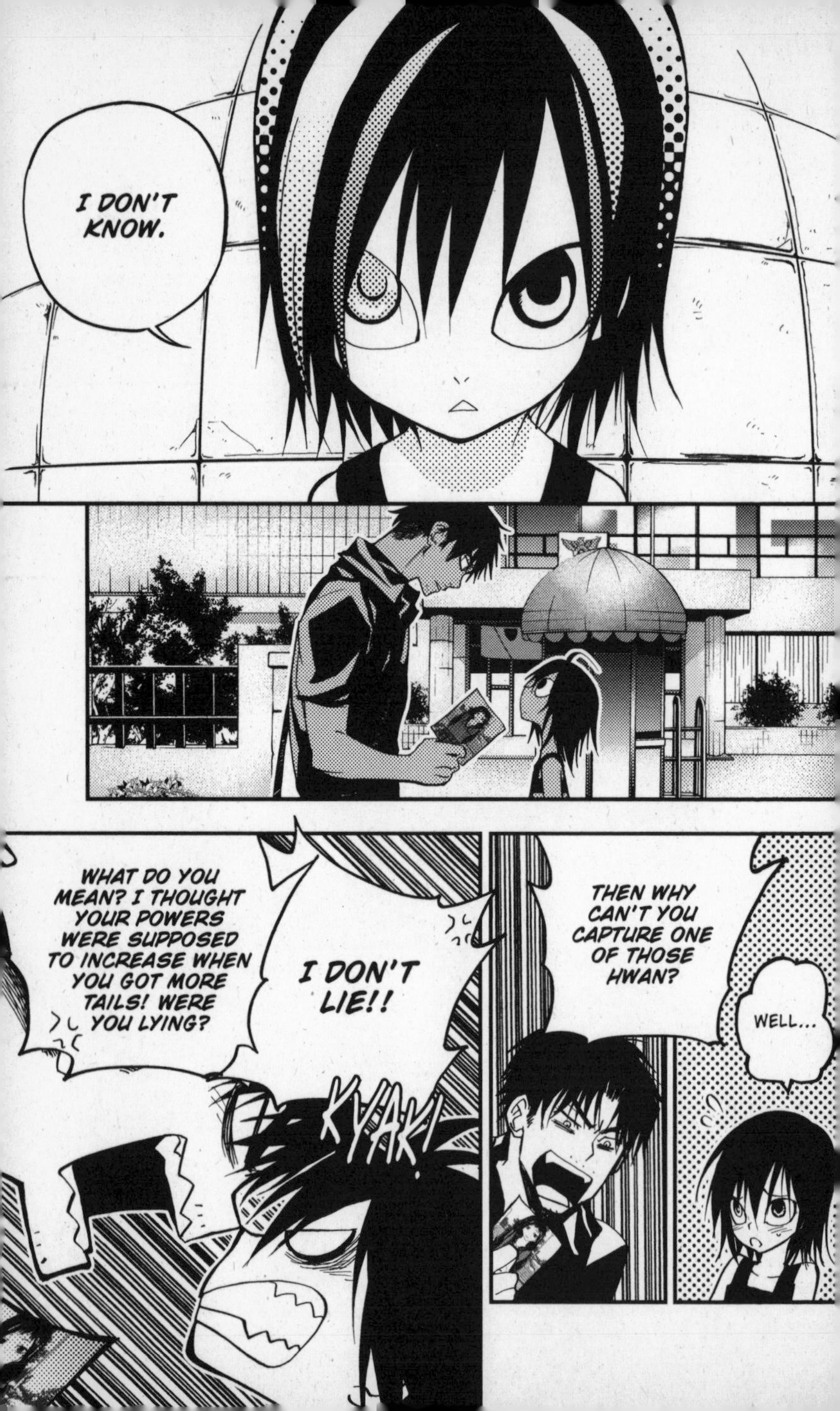
I DON'T KNOW.
WHAT DO YOU MEAN? I THOUGHT YOUR POWERS WERE SUPPOSED TO INCREASE WHEN YOU GOT MORE TAILS! WERE YOU LYING?
I DON'T LIE!!
KYAK!
THEN WHY CAN'T YOU CAPTURE ONE OF THOSE HWAN?
WELL...

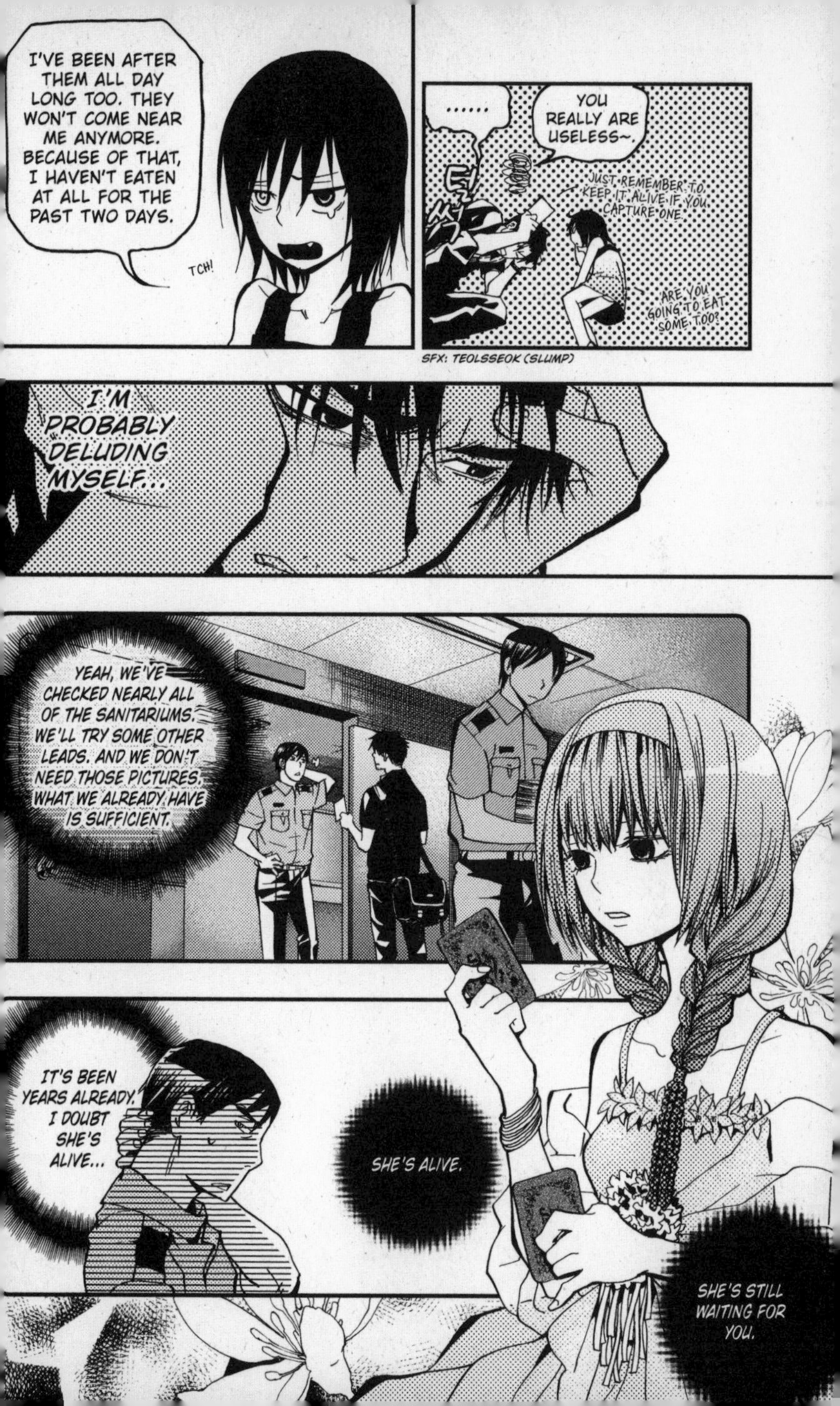
I'VE BEEN AFTER THEM ALL DAY LONG TOO. THEY WON'T COME NEAR ME ANYMORE. BECAUSE OF THAT, I HAVEN'T EATEN AT ALL FOR THE PAST TWO DAYS.
TCH!
......
YOU REALLY ARE USELESS~.
JUST REMEMBER TO KEEP IT ALIVE IF YOU CAPTURE ONE.
ARE YOU GOING TO EAT SOME TOO?
SFX: TEOLSSEOK (SLUMP)
I'M PROBABLY DELUDING MYSELF...
YEAH, WE'VE CHECKED NEARLY ALL OF THE SANITARIUMS. WE'LL TRY SOME OTHER LEADS. AND WE DON'T NEED THOSE PICTURES. WHAT WE ALREADY HAVE IS SUFFICIENT.
IT'S BEEN YEARS ALREADY. I DOUBT SHE'S ALIVE...
SHE'S ALIVE.
SHE'S STILL WAITING FOR YOU.

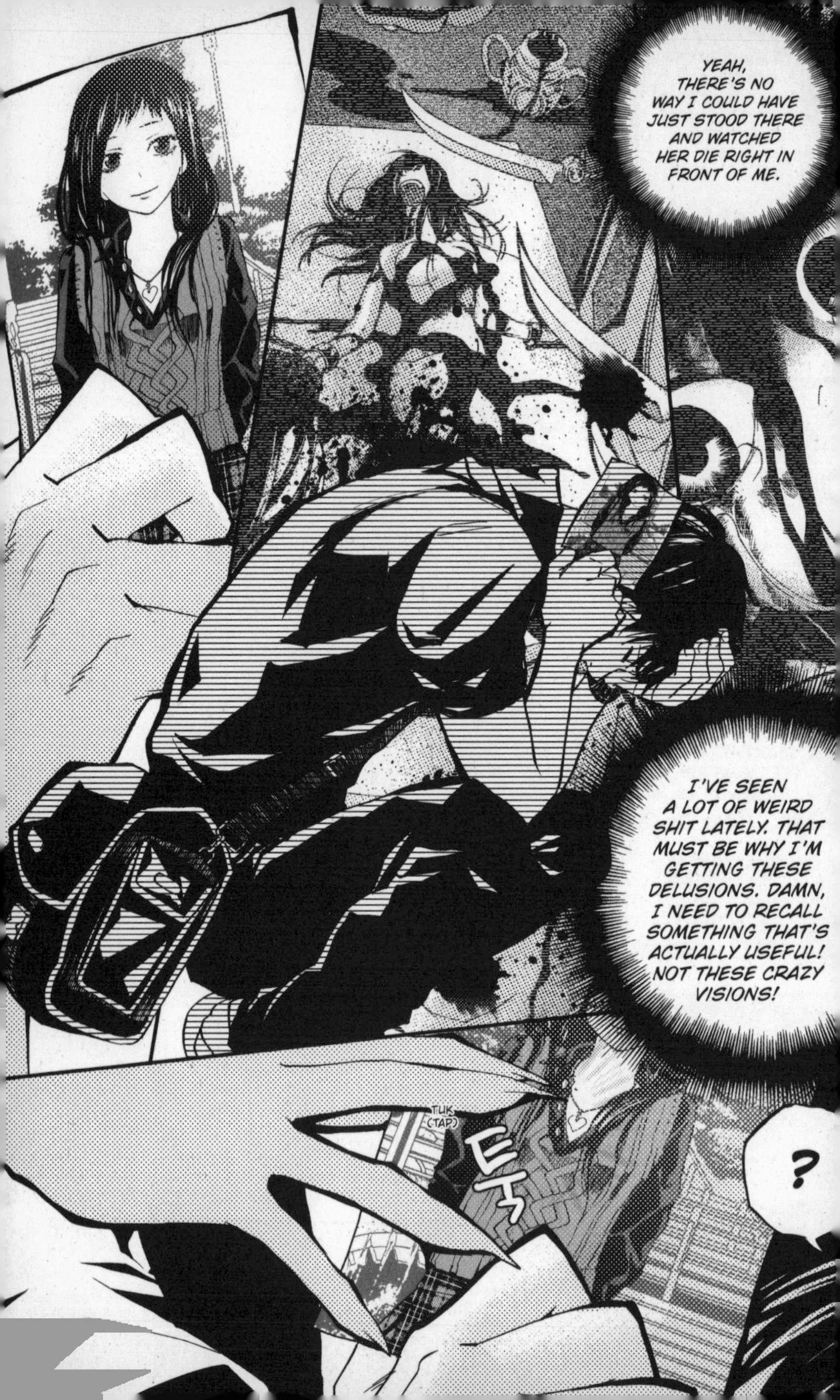
YEAH, THERE'S NO WAY I COULD HAVE JUST STOOD THERE AND WATCHED HER DIE RIGHT IN FRONT OF ME.
I'VE SEEN A LOT OF WEIRD SHIT LATELY. THAT MUST BE WHY I'M GETTING THESE DELUSIONS. DAMN, I NEED TO RECALL SOMETHING THAT'S ACTUALLY USEFUL! NOT THESE CRAZY VISIONS!
TUK (TAP)
?

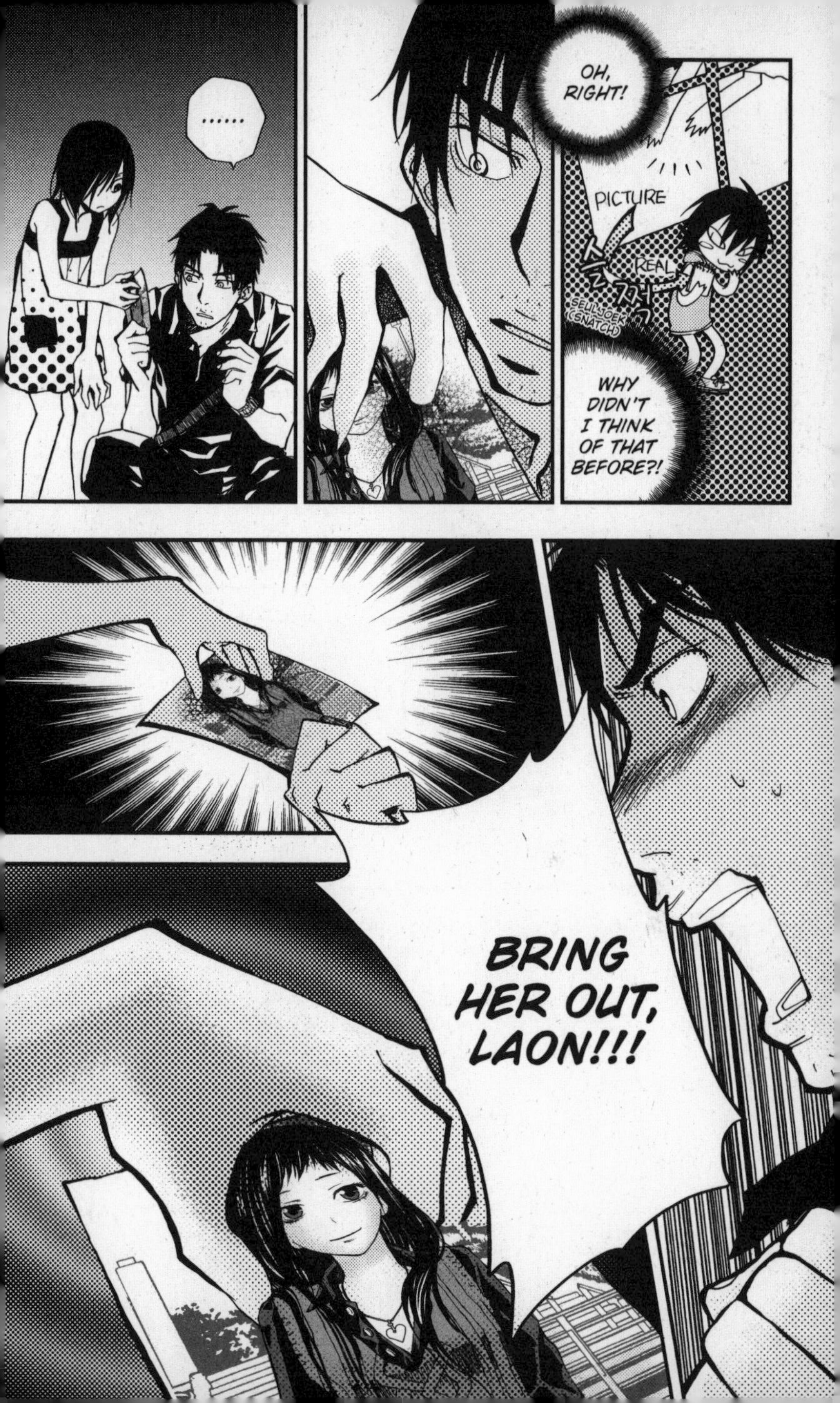
......
OH, RIGHT!
PICTURE
REAL
SEULJOEK (SNATCH)
WHY DIDN'T I THINK OF THAT BEFORE?!
BRING HER OUT, LAON!!!

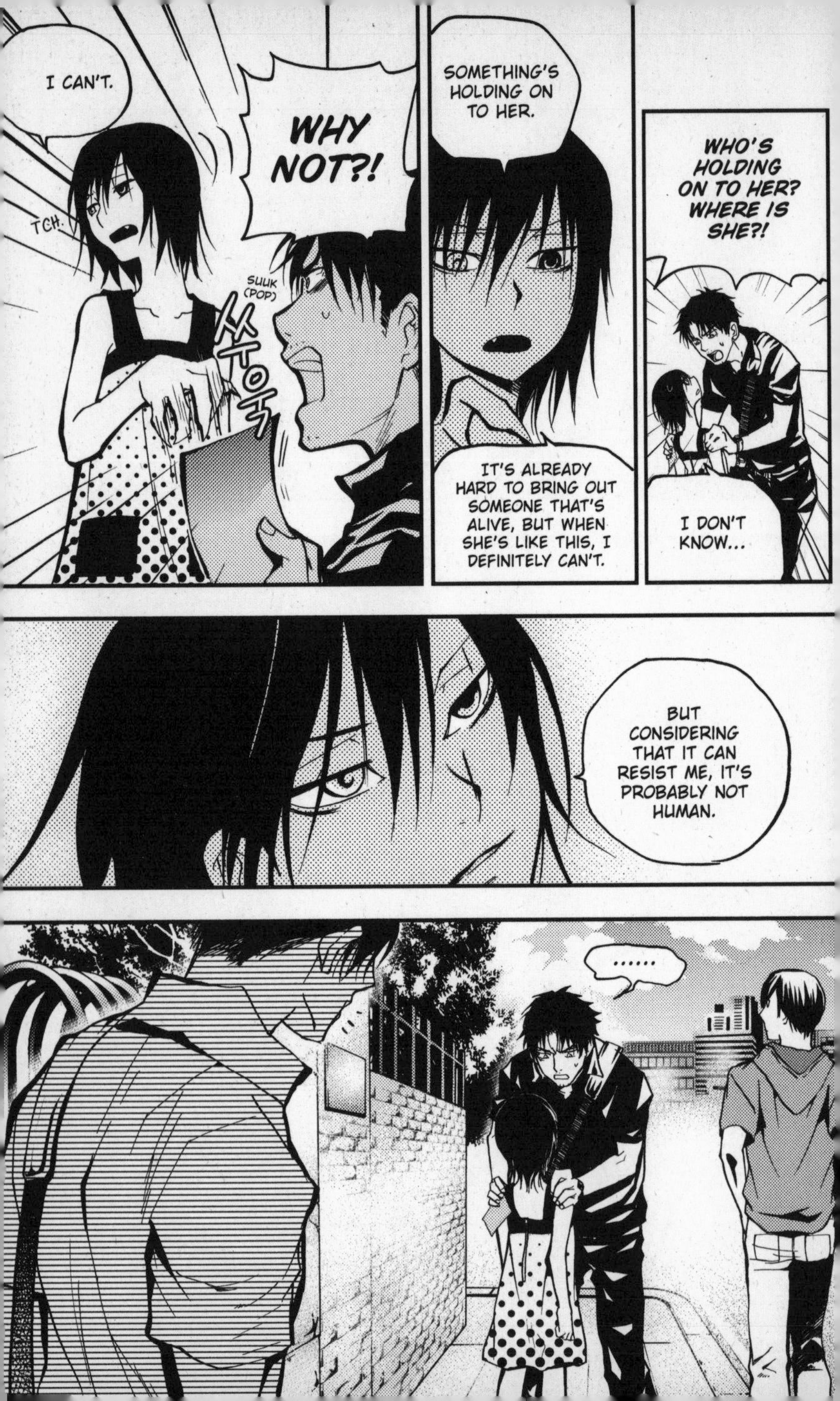
I CAN'T.
TCH.
WHY NOT?!
SUUK (POP)
SOMETHING'S HOLDING ON TO HER.
IT'S ALREADY HARD TO BRING OUT SOMEONE THAT'S ALIVE, BUT WHEN SHE'S LIKE THIS, I DEFINITELY CAN'T.
WHO'S HOLDING ON TO HER? WHERE IS SHE?!
I DON'T KNOW...
BUT CONSIDERING THAT IT CAN RESIST ME, IT'S PROBABLY NOT HUMAN.
......

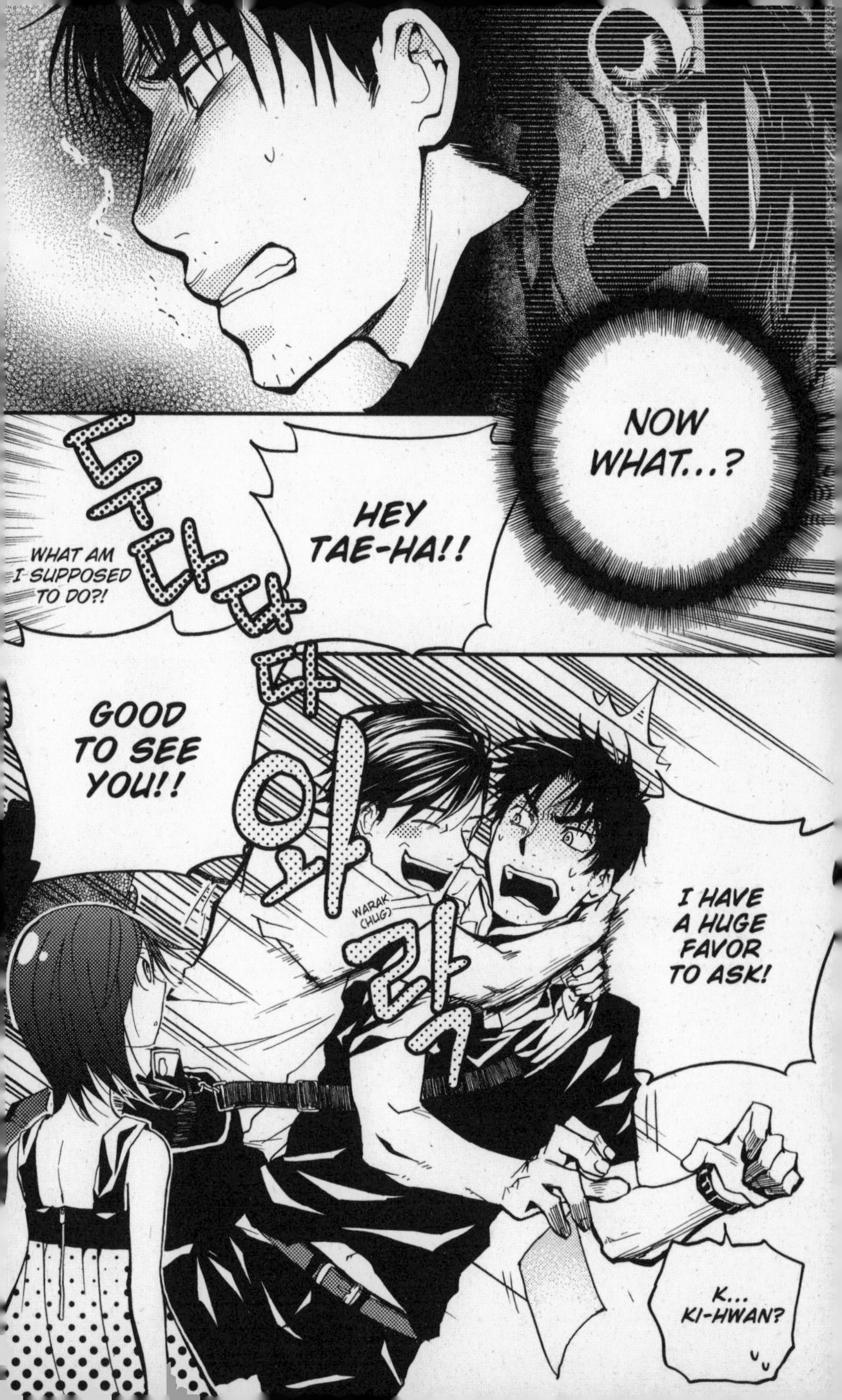
NOW WHAT...?
WHAT AM I SUPPOSED TO DO?!
HEY TAE-HA!!
GOOD TO SEE YOU!!
WARAK (HUG)
I HAVE A HUGE FAVOR TO ASK!
K... KI-HWAN?

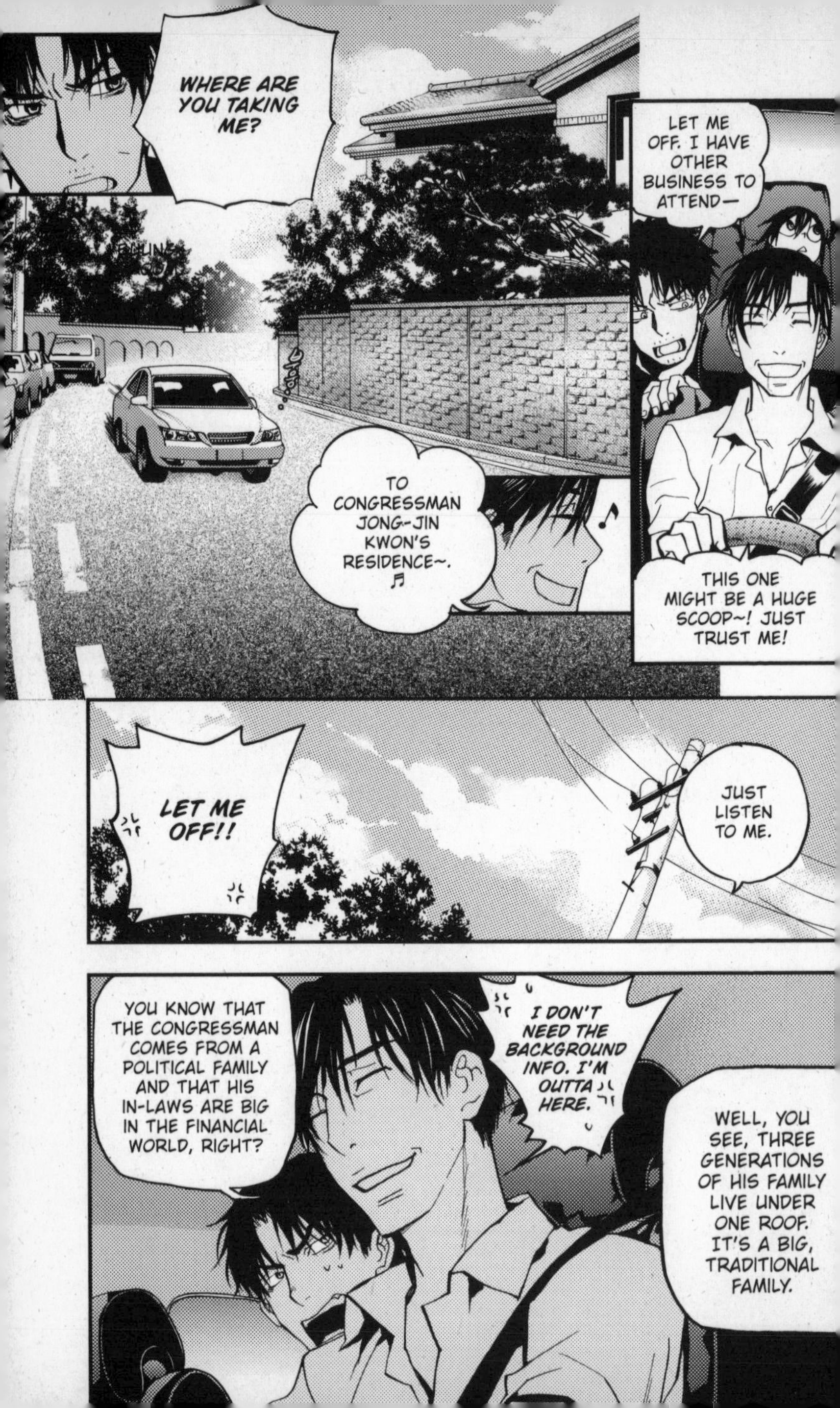
WHERE ARE YOU TAKING ME?
TO CONGRESSMAN JONG-JIN KWON'S RESIDENCE~. ♬
LET ME OFF. I HAVE OTHER BUSINESS TO ATTEND—
THIS ONE MIGHT BE A HUGE SCOOP~! JUST TRUST ME!
LET ME OFF!!
JUST LISTEN TO ME.
YOU KNOW THAT THE CONGRESSMAN COMES FROM A POLITICAL FAMILY AND THAT HIS IN-LAWS ARE BIG IN THE FINANCIAL WORLD, RIGHT?
I DON'T NEED THE BACKGROUND INFO. I'M OUTTA HERE.
WELL, YOU SEE, THREE GENERATIONS OF HIS FAMILY LIVE UNDER ONE ROOF. IT'S A BIG, TRADITIONAL FAMILY.

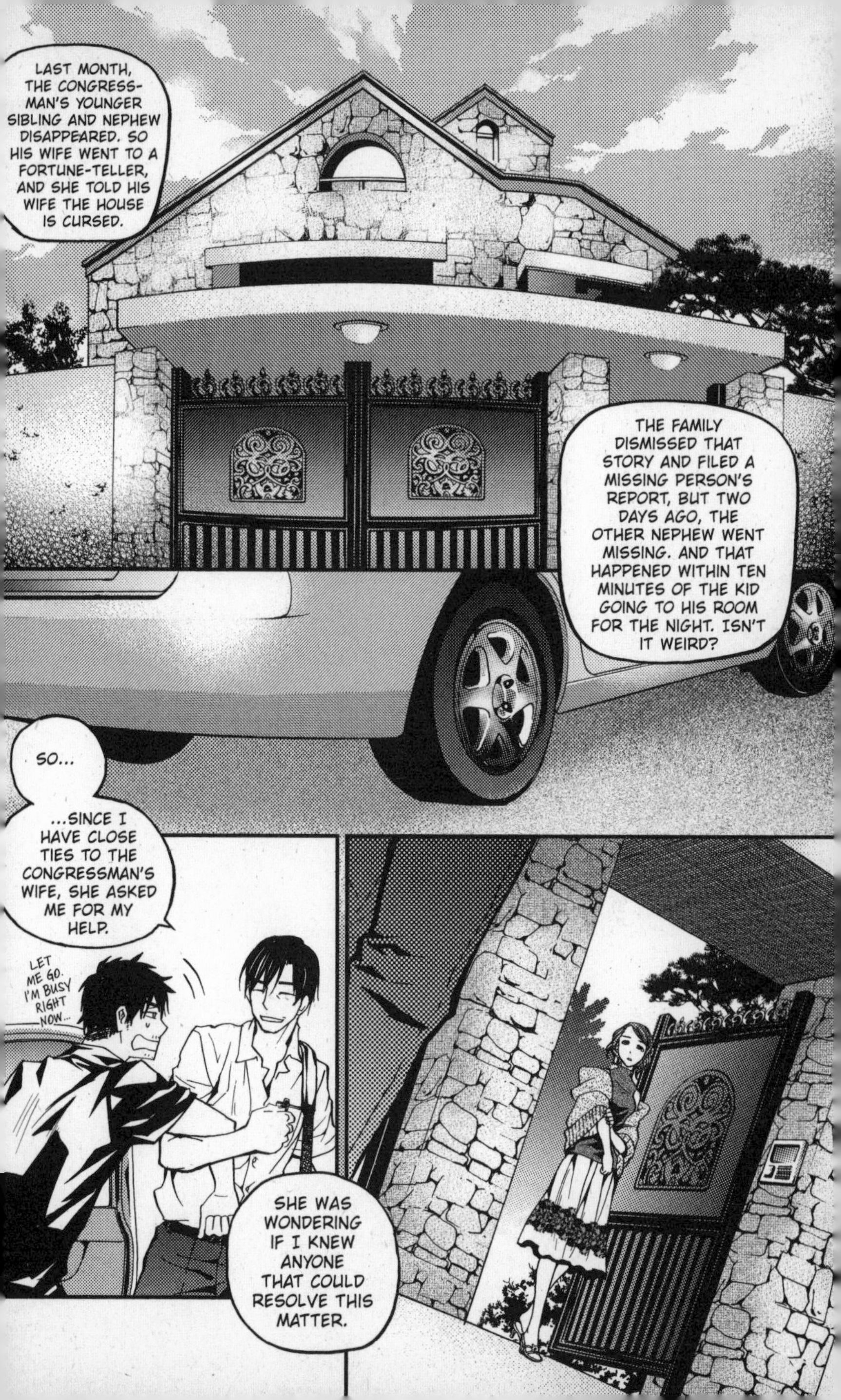
LAST MONTH, THE CONGRESS-MAN'S YOUNGER SIBLING AND NEPHEW DISAPPEARED. SO HIS WIFE WENT TO A FORTUNE-TELLER, AND SHE TOLD HIS WIFE THE HOUSE IS CURSED.
THE FAMILY DISMISSED THAT STORY AND FILED A MISSING PERSON'S REPORT, BUT TWO DAYS AGO, THE OTHER NEPHEW WENT MISSING. AND THAT HAPPENED WITHIN TEN MINUTES OF THE KID GOING TO HIS ROOM FOR THE NIGHT. ISN'T IT WEIRD?
SO...
...SINCE I HAVE CLOSE TIES TO THE CONGRESSMAN'S WIFE, SHE ASKED ME FOR MY HELP.
LET ME GO. I'M BUSY RIGHT NOW...
SHE WAS WONDERING IF I KNEW ANYONE THAT COULD RESOLVE THIS MATTER.

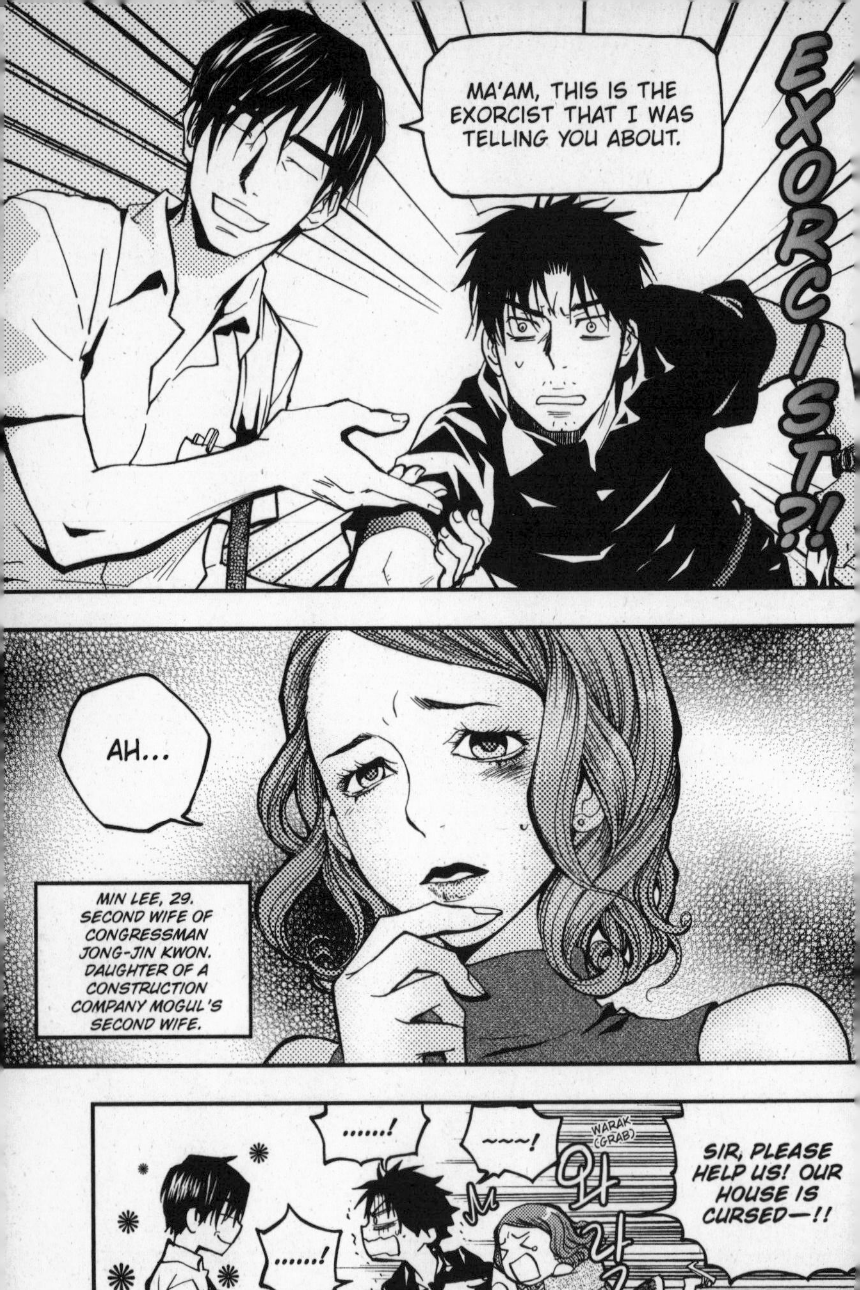
MA'AM, THIS IS THE EXORCIST THAT I WAS TELLING YOU ABOUT.
EXORCIST?!
AH...
MIN LEE, 29. SECOND WIFE OF CONGRESSMAN JONG-JIN KWON. DAUGHTER OF A CONSTRUCTION COMPANY MOGUL'S SECOND WIFE.
......!
~~~!
WARAK (GRAB)
......!
SIR, PLEASE HELP US! OUR HOUSE IS CURSED—!!
~~~

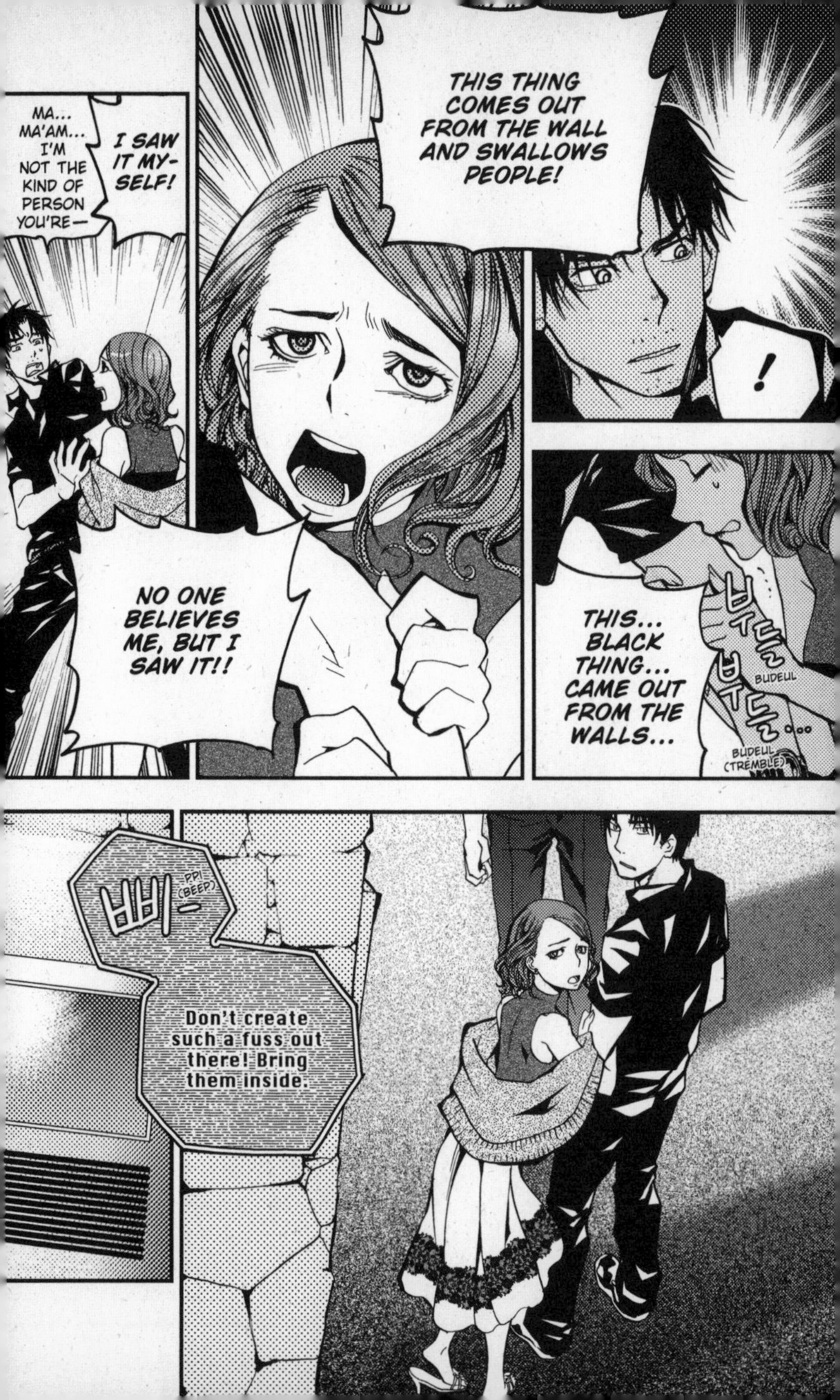
MA... MA'AM... I'M NOT THE KIND OF PERSON YOU'RE—
I SAW IT MY-SELF!
THIS THING COMES OUT FROM THE WALL AND SWALLOWS PEOPLE!
NO ONE BELIEVES ME, BUT I SAW IT!!
!
THIS... BLACK THING... CAME OUT FROM THE WALLS...
부들
BUDEUL
부들...
BUDEUL (TREMBLE)
삐-
PPI (BEEP)
Don't create such a fuss out there! Bring them inside.

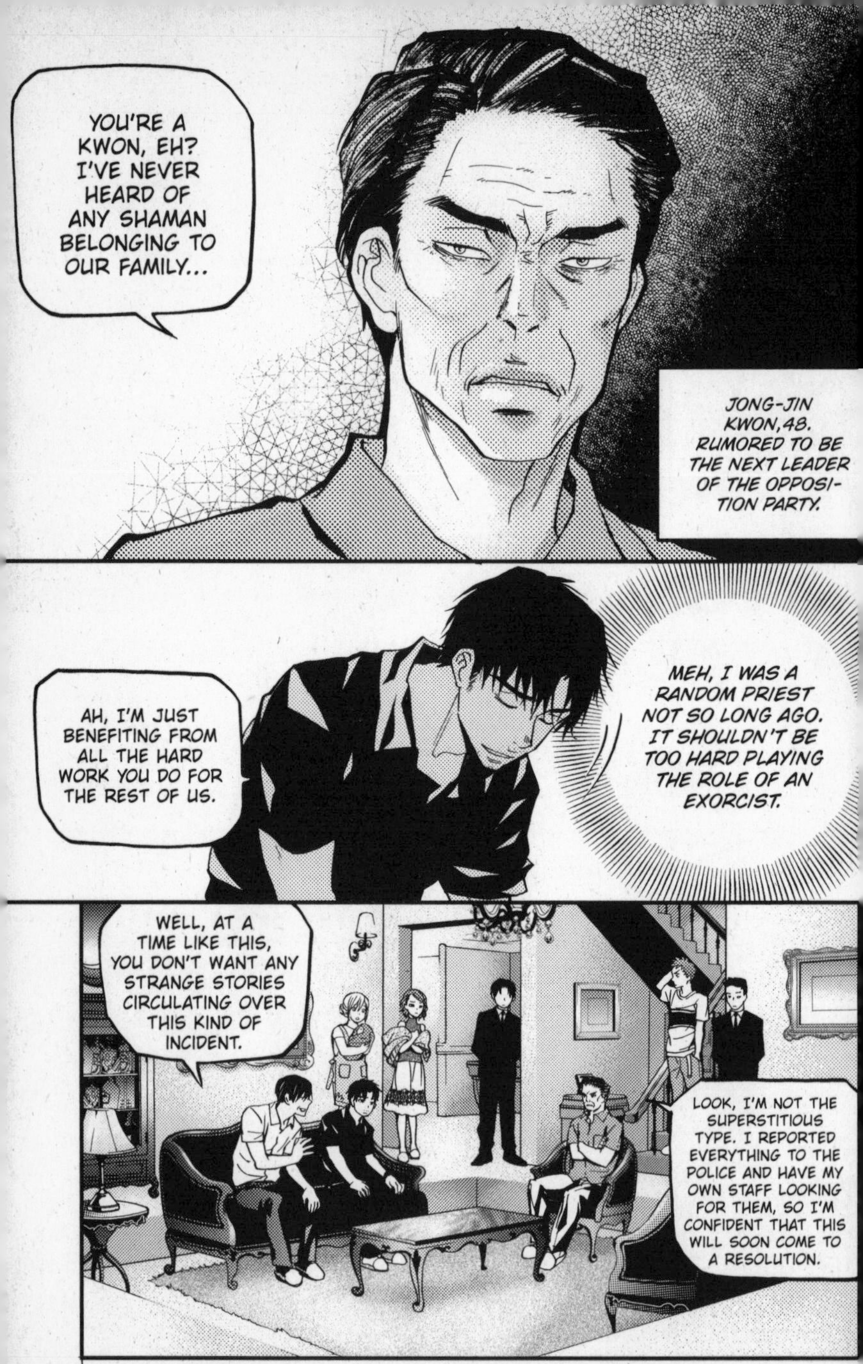

YOU'RE A KWON, EH? I'VE NEVER HEARD OF ANY SHAMAN BELONGING TO OUR FAMILY...
JONG-JIN KWON, 48. RUMORED TO BE THE NEXT LEADER OF THE OPPOSI-TION PARTY.
AH, I'M JUST BENEFITING FROM ALL THE HARD WORK YOU DO FOR THE REST OF US.
MEH, I WAS A RANDOM PRIEST NOT SO LONG AGO. IT SHOULDN'T BE TOO HARD PLAYING THE ROLE OF AN EXORCIST.
WELL, AT A TIME LIKE THIS, YOU DON'T WANT ANY STRANGE STORIES CIRCULATING OVER THIS KIND OF INCIDENT.
LOOK, I'M NOT THE SUPERSTITIOUS TYPE. I REPORTED EVERYTHING TO THE POLICE AND HAVE MY OWN STAFF LOOKING FOR THEM, SO I'M CONFIDENT THAT THIS WILL SOON COME TO A RESOLUTION.

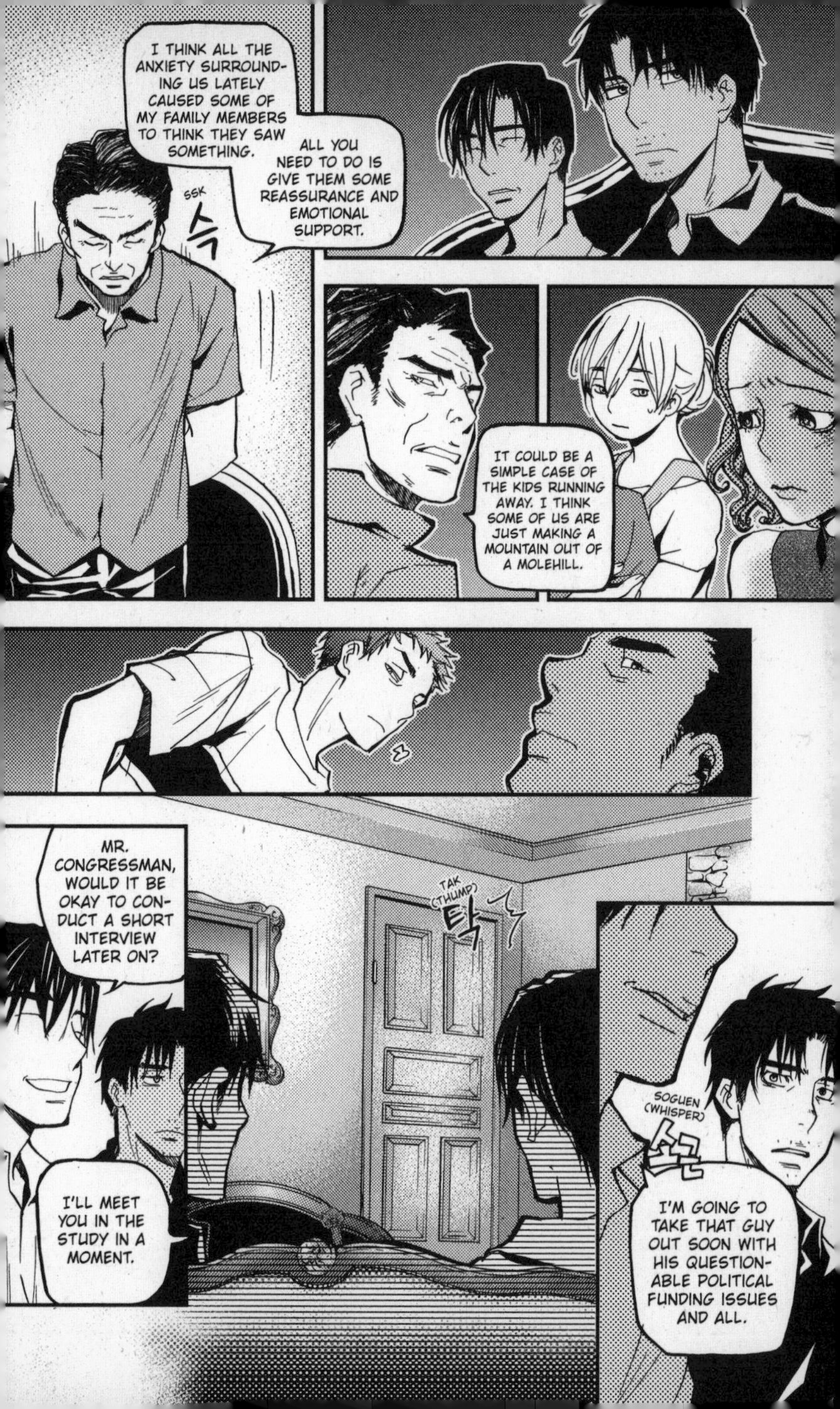
I THINK ALL THE ANXIETY SURROUNDING US LATELY CAUSED SOME OF MY FAMILY MEMBERS TO THINK THEY SAW SOMETHING.
ALL YOU NEED TO DO IS GIVE THEM SOME REASSURANCE AND EMOTIONAL SUPPORT.
SSK
스극
IT COULD BE A SIMPLE CASE OF THE KIDS RUNNING AWAY. I THINK SOME OF US ARE JUST MAKING A MOUNTAIN OUT OF A MOLEHILL.
MR. CONGRESSMAN, WOULD IT BE OKAY TO CONDUCT A SHORT INTERVIEW LATER ON?
I'LL MEET YOU IN THE STUDY IN A MOMENT.
TAK (THUMP)
탁
SOGUEN (WHISPER)
소근
I'M GOING TO TAKE THAT GUY OUT SOON WITH HIS QUESTIONABLE POLITICAL FUNDING ISSUES AND ALL.

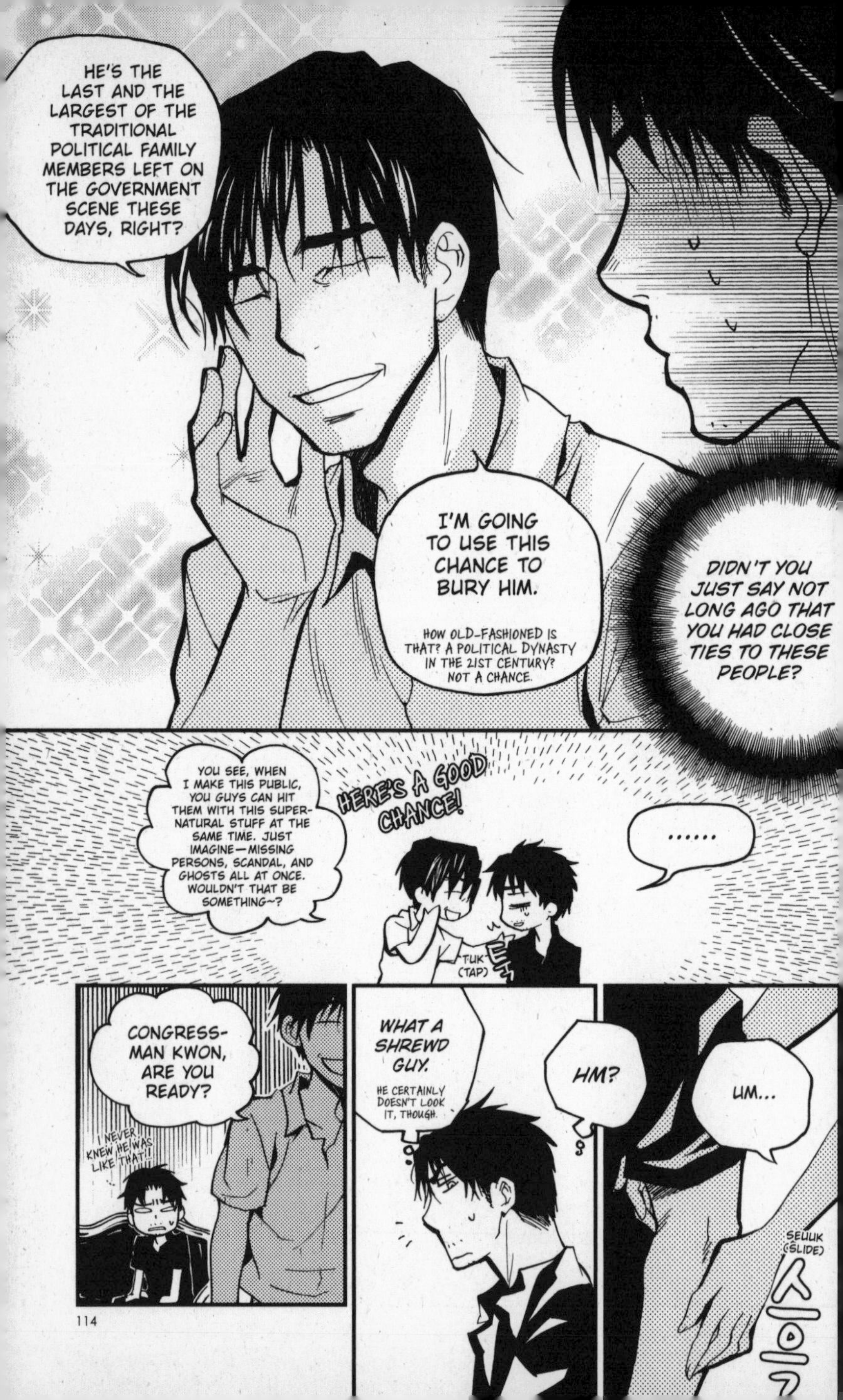
HE'S THE LAST AND THE LARGEST OF THE TRADITIONAL POLITICAL FAMILY MEMBERS LEFT ON THE GOVERNMENT SCENE THESE DAYS, RIGHT?
I'M GOING TO USE THIS CHANCE TO BURY HIM.
HOW OLD-FASHIONED IS THAT? A POLITICAL DYNASTY IN THE 21ST CENTURY? NOT A CHANCE.
DIDN'T YOU JUST SAY NOT LONG AGO THAT YOU HAD CLOSE TIES TO THESE PEOPLE?
YOU SEE, WHEN I MAKE THIS PUBLIC, YOU GUYS CAN HIT THEM WITH THIS SUPER-NATURAL STUFF AT THE SAME TIME. JUST IMAGINE—MISSING PERSONS, SCANDAL, AND GHOSTS ALL AT ONCE. WOULDN'T THAT BE SOMETHING~?
HERE'S A GOOD CHANCE!
TUK (TAP)
......
CONGRESS-MAN KWON, ARE YOU READY?
I NEVER KNEW HE WAS LIKE THAT...
WHAT A SHREWD GUY.
HE CERTAINLY DOESN'T LOOK IT, THOUGH.
HM?
UM...
SEUUK (SLIDE)

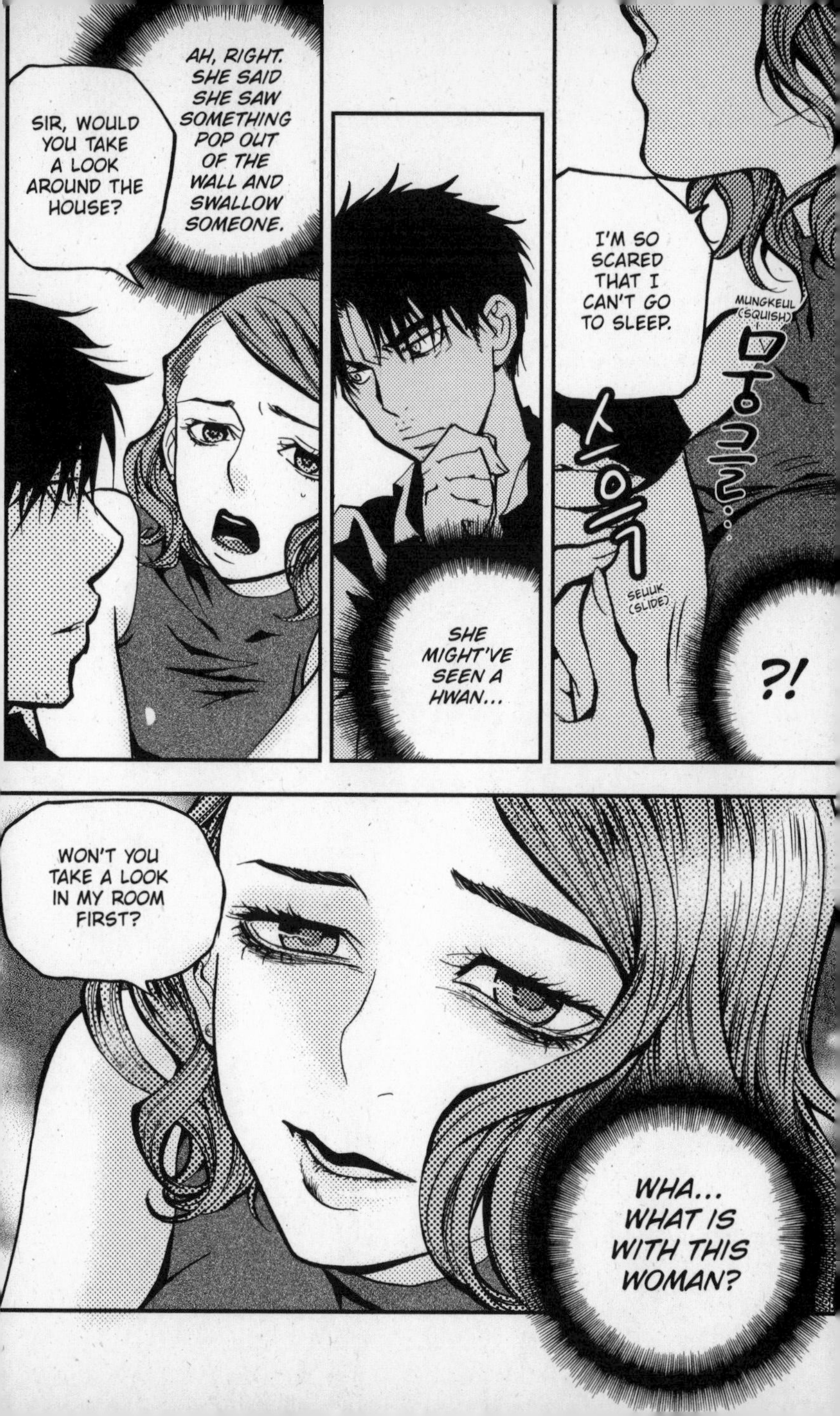
SIR, WOULD YOU TAKE A LOOK AROUND THE HOUSE?
AH, RIGHT. SHE SAID SHE SAW SOMETHING POP OUT OF THE WALL AND SWALLOW SOMEONE.
SHE MIGHT'VE SEEN A HWAN...
I'M SO SCARED THAT I CAN'T GO TO SLEEP.
MUNGKEUL (SQUISH)
뭉클...
스윽
SEUUK (SLIDE)
?!
WON'T YOU TAKE A LOOK IN MY ROOM FIRST?
WHA... WHAT IS WITH THIS WOMAN?

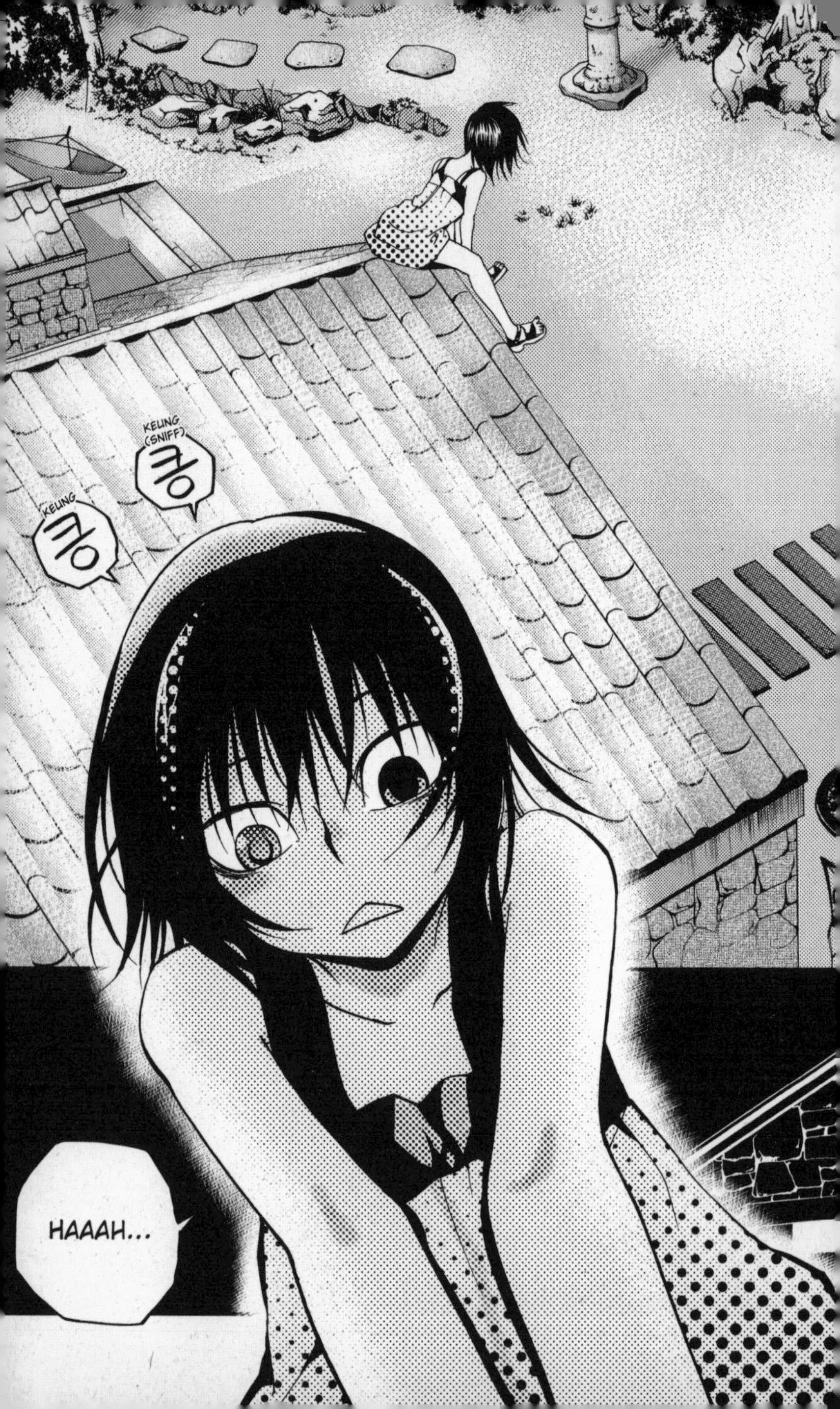
KEUNG
쿵
KEUNG (SNIFF)
쿵
HAAAH...

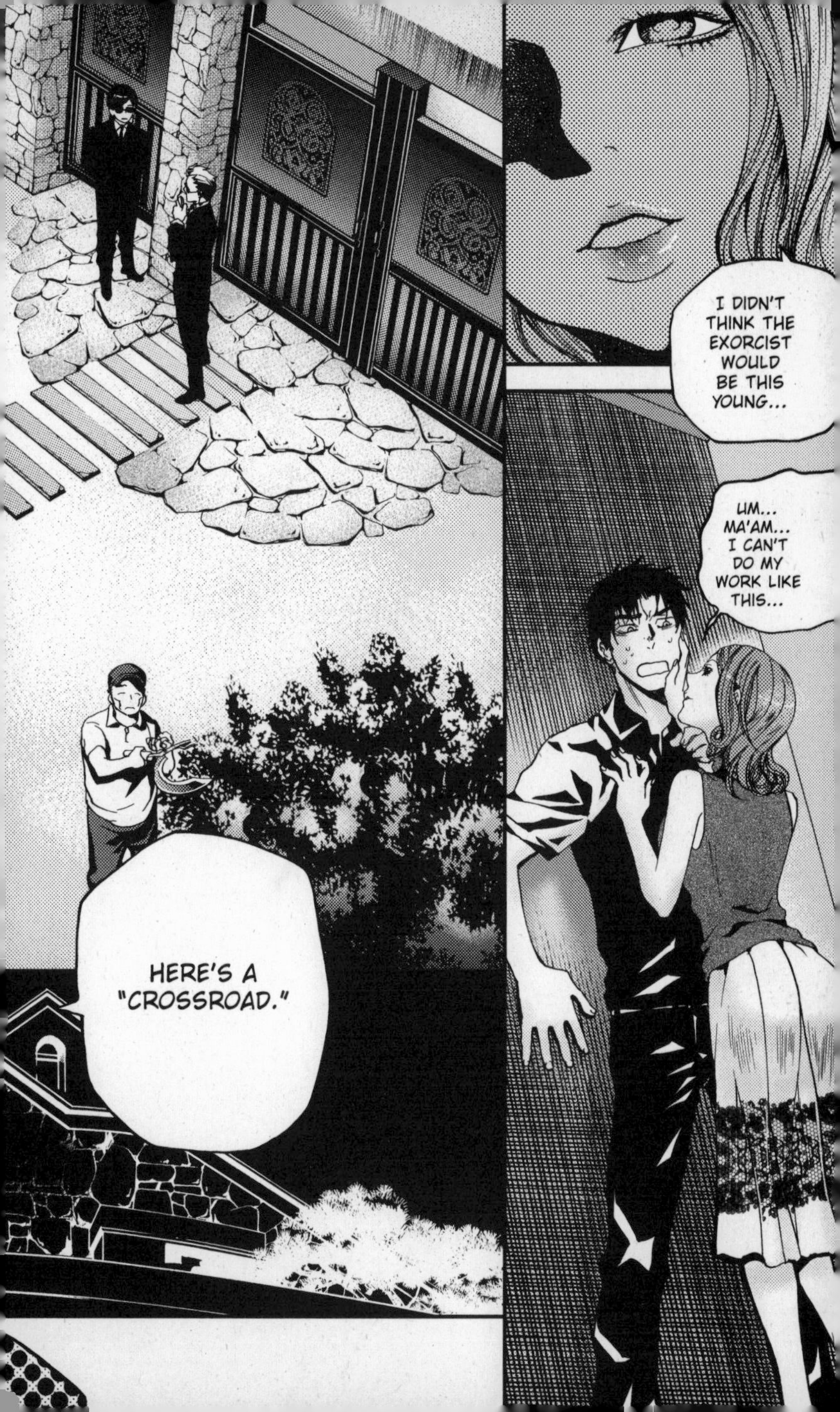
I DIDN'T THINK THE EXORCIST WOULD BE THIS YOUNG...
HERE'S A "CROSSROAD."
UM... MA'AM... I CAN'T DO MY WORK LIKE THIS...

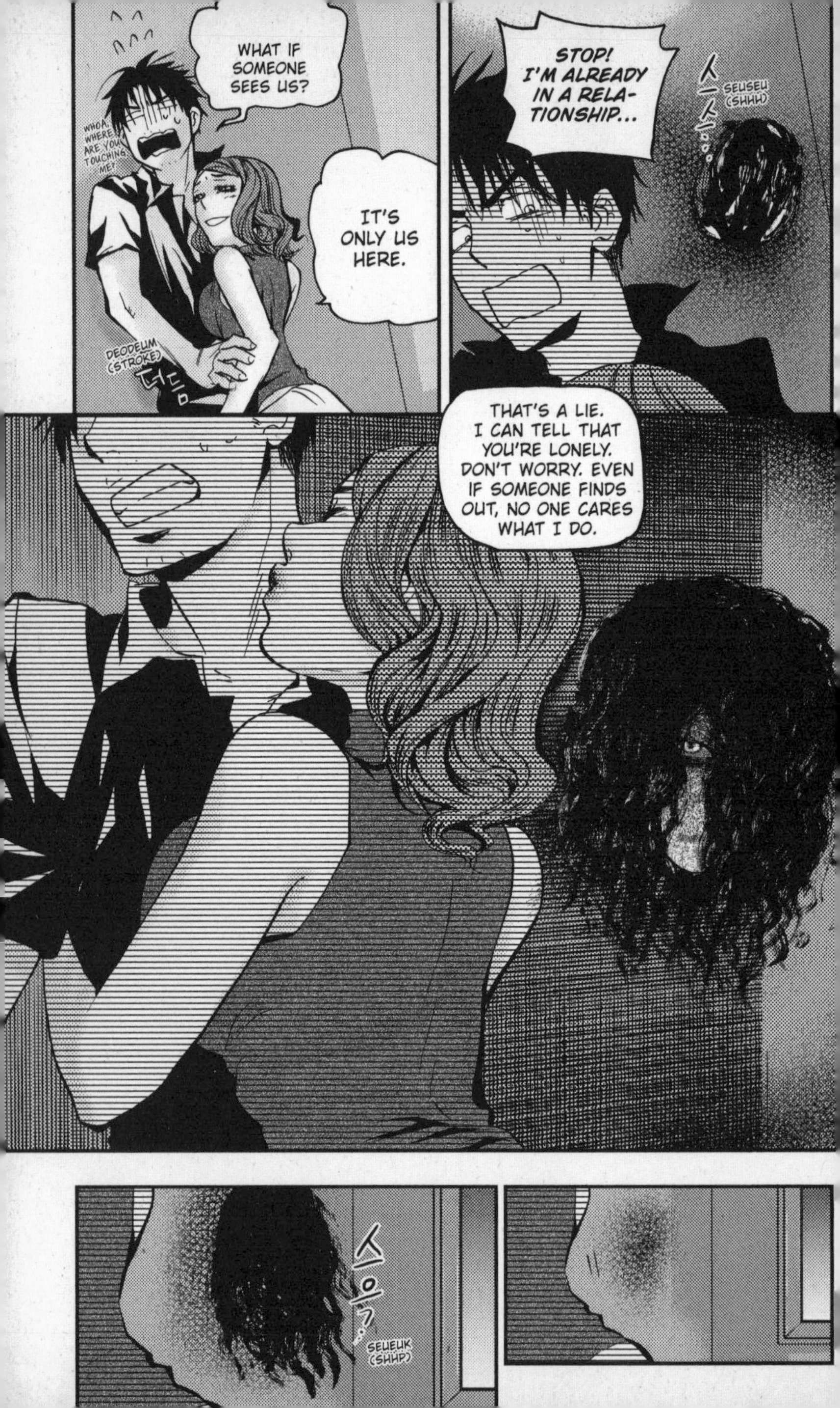
WHOA, WHERE ARE YOU TOUCHING ME?
WHAT IF SOMEONE SEES US?
IT'S ONLY US HERE.
DEODEUM (STROKE)
STOP! I'M ALREADY IN A RELATIONSHIP...
SEUSEU (SHHH)
THAT'S A LIE. I CAN TELL THAT YOU'RE LONELY. DON'T WORRY. EVEN IF SOMEONE FINDS OUT, NO ONE CARES WHAT I DO.
SEUEUK (SHHP)

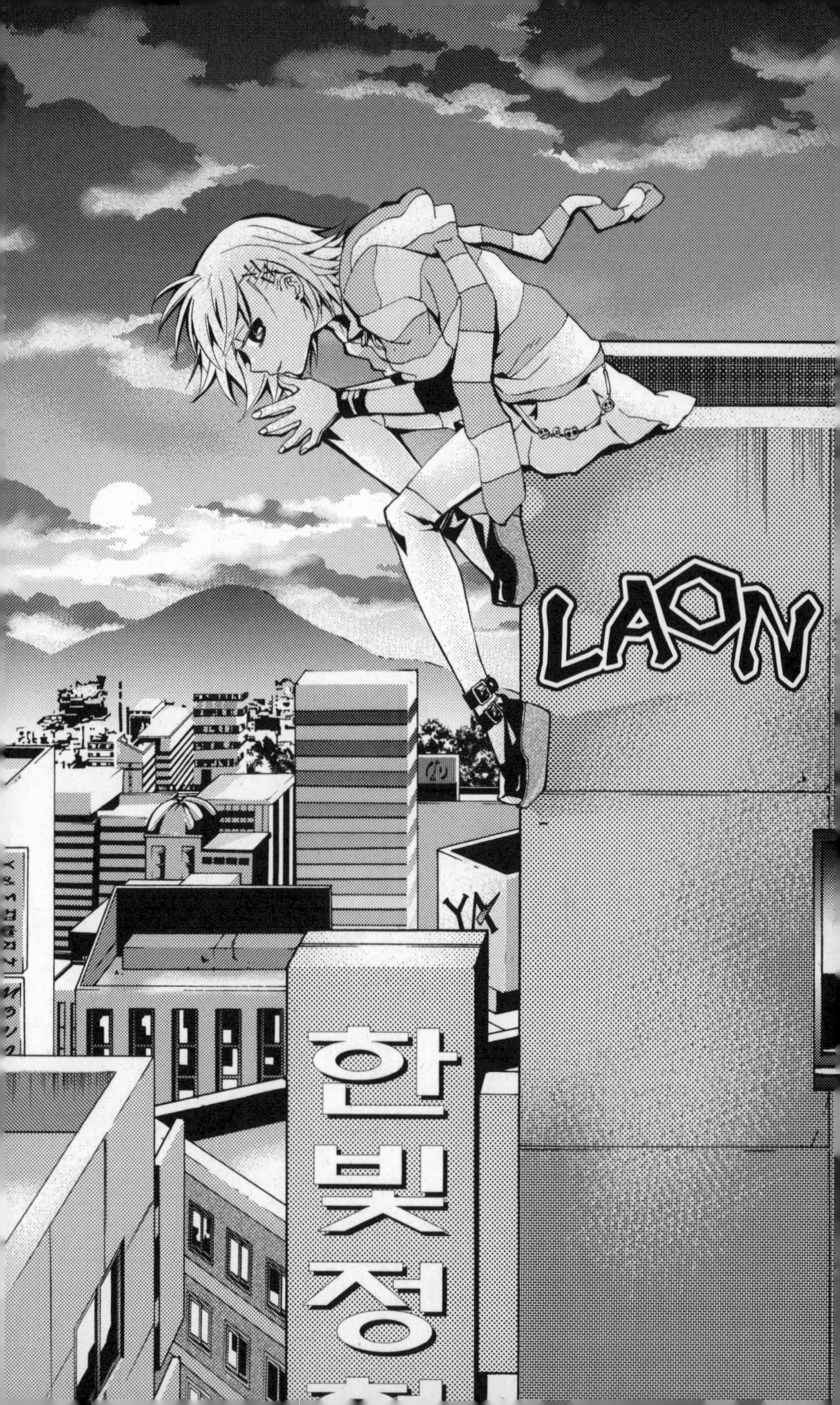
LAON
한빛정

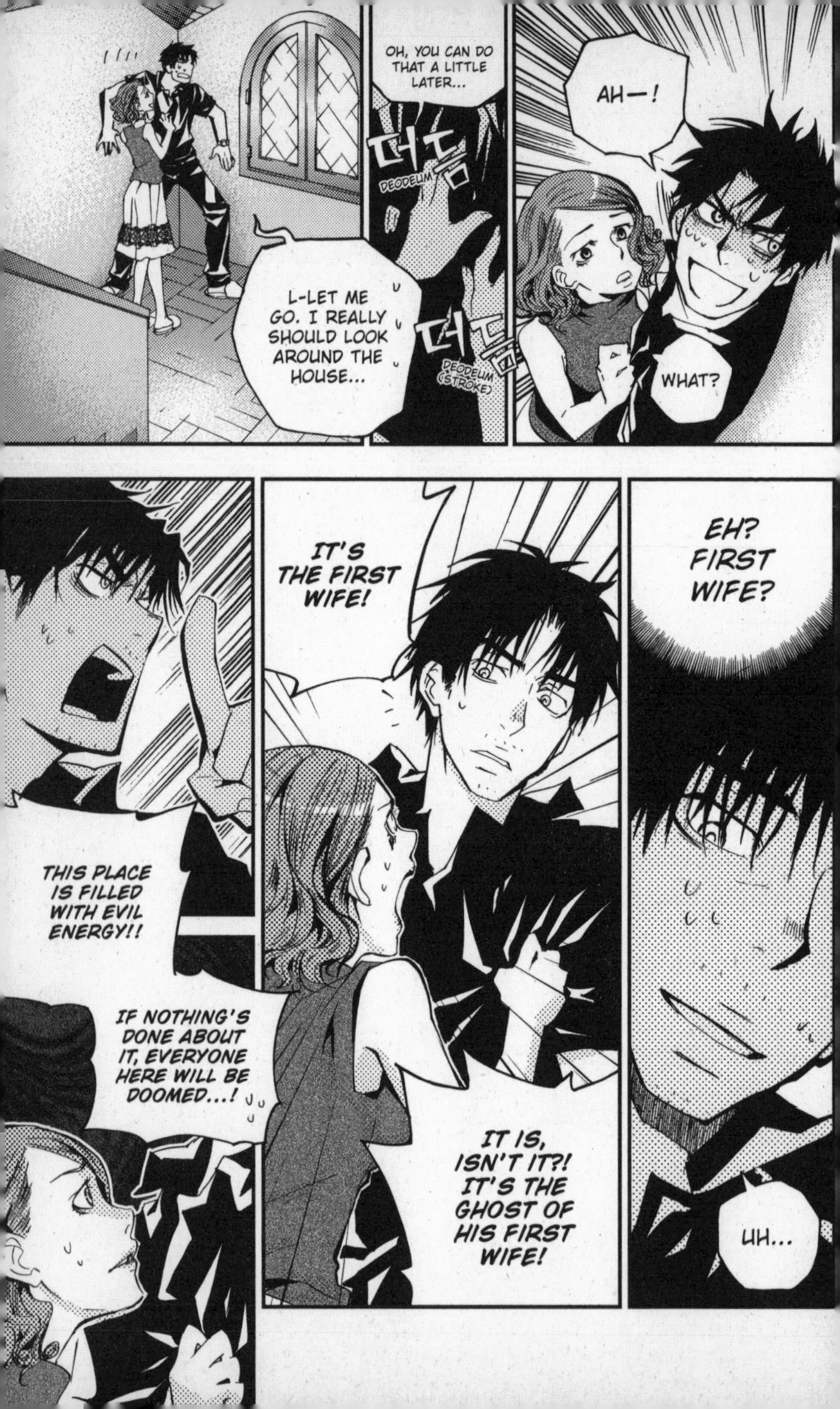
L-LET ME GO. I REALLY SHOULD LOOK AROUND THE HOUSE...
OH, YOU CAN DO THAT A LITTLE LATER...
더듬
DEODEUM
더듬
DEODEUM (STROKE)
AH—!
WHAT?
THIS PLACE IS FILLED WITH EVIL ENERGY!!
IF NOTHING'S DONE ABOUT IT, EVERYONE HERE WILL BE DOOMED...!
IT'S THE FIRST WIFE!
IT IS, ISN'T IT?! IT'S THE GHOST OF HIS FIRST WIFE!
EH? FIRST WIFE?
UH...

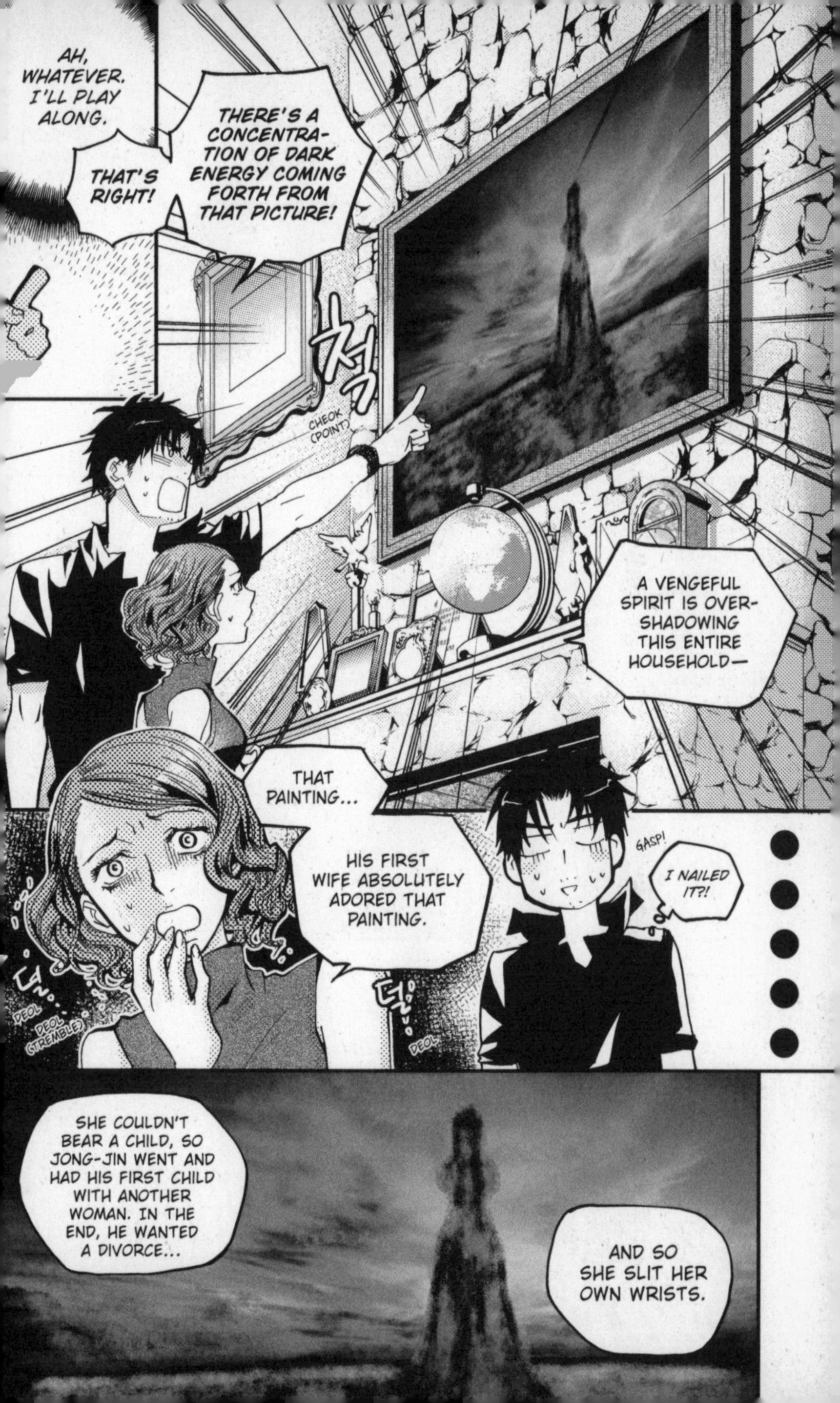
AH, WHATEVER. I'LL PLAY ALONG.
THAT'S RIGHT!
THERE'S A CONCENTRATION OF DARK ENERGY COMING FORTH FROM THAT PICTURE!
척
CHEOK (POINT)
A VENGEFUL SPIRIT IS OVERSHADOWING THIS ENTIRE HOUSEHOLD—
THAT PAINTING...
HIS FIRST WIFE ABSOLUTELY ADORED THAT PAINTING.
DEOL DEOL (TREMBLE)
GASP!
I NAILED IT?!
DEOL
SHE COULDN'T BEAR A CHILD, SO JONG-JIN WENT AND HAD HIS FIRST CHILD WITH ANOTHER WOMAN. IN THE END, HE WANTED A DIVORCE...
AND SO SHE SLIT HER OWN WRISTS.

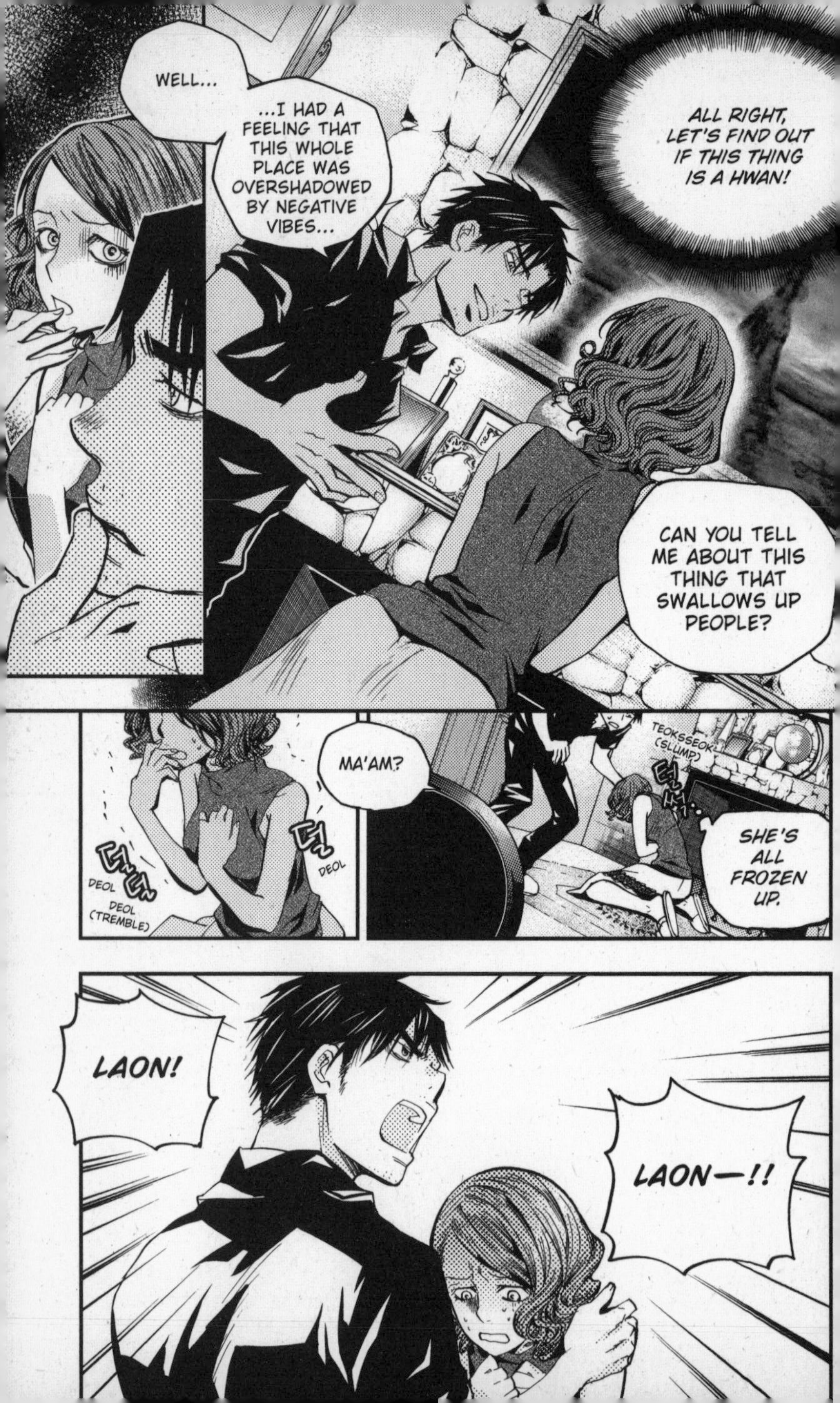
WELL...
...I HAD A FEELING THAT THIS WHOLE PLACE WAS OVERSHADOWED BY NEGATIVE VIBES...
ALL RIGHT, LET'S FIND OUT IF THIS THING IS A HWAN!
CAN YOU TELL ME ABOUT THIS THING THAT SWALLOWS UP PEOPLE?
DEOL DEOL (TREMBLE)
MA'AM?
DEOL
TEOKSSEOK (SLUMP)
SHE'S ALL FROZEN UP.
LAON!
LAON—!!

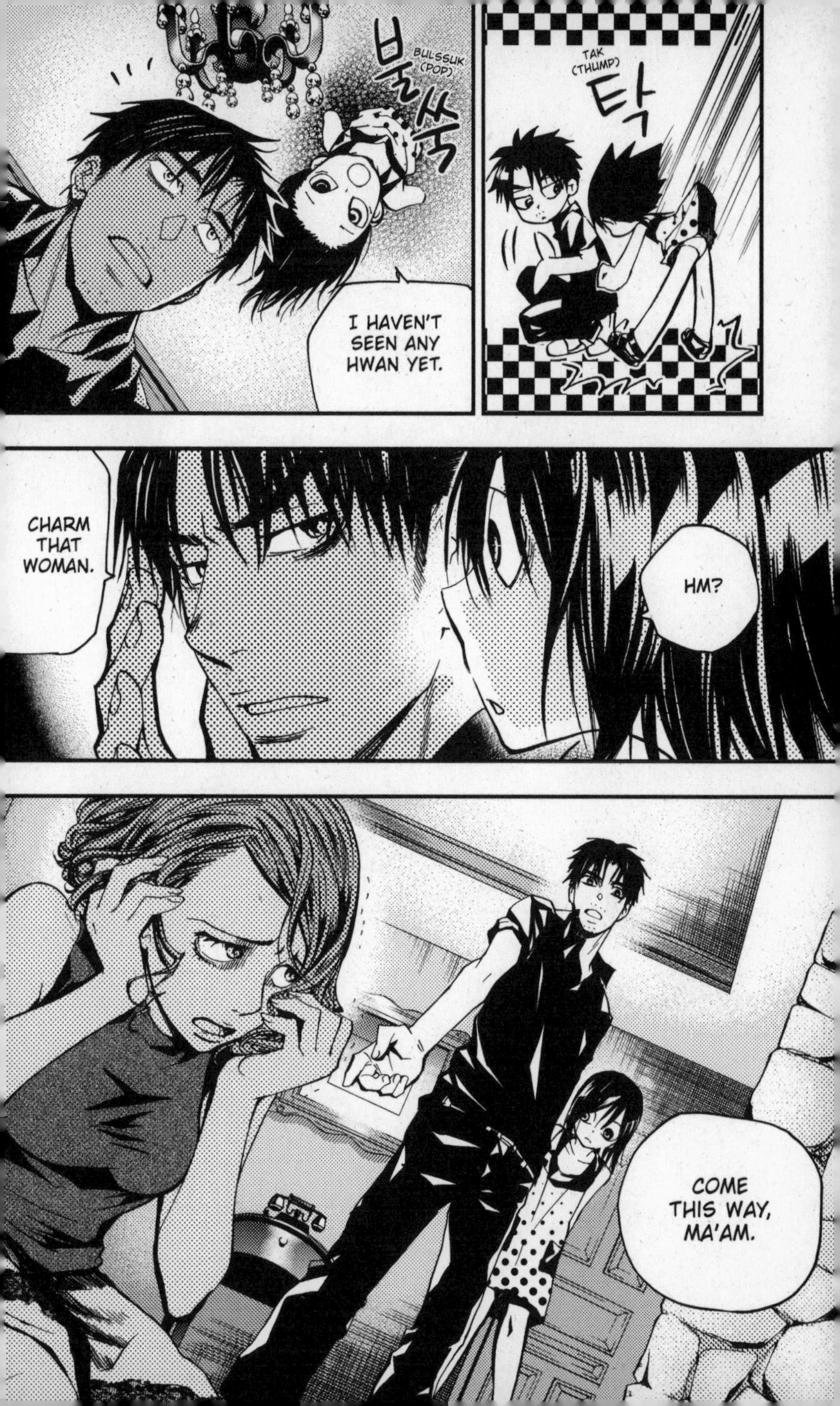
불쑥
BULSSUK (POP)
I HAVEN'T SEEN ANY HWAN YET.
TAK (THUMP)
탁
CHARM THAT WOMAN.
HM?
COME THIS WAY, MA'AM.

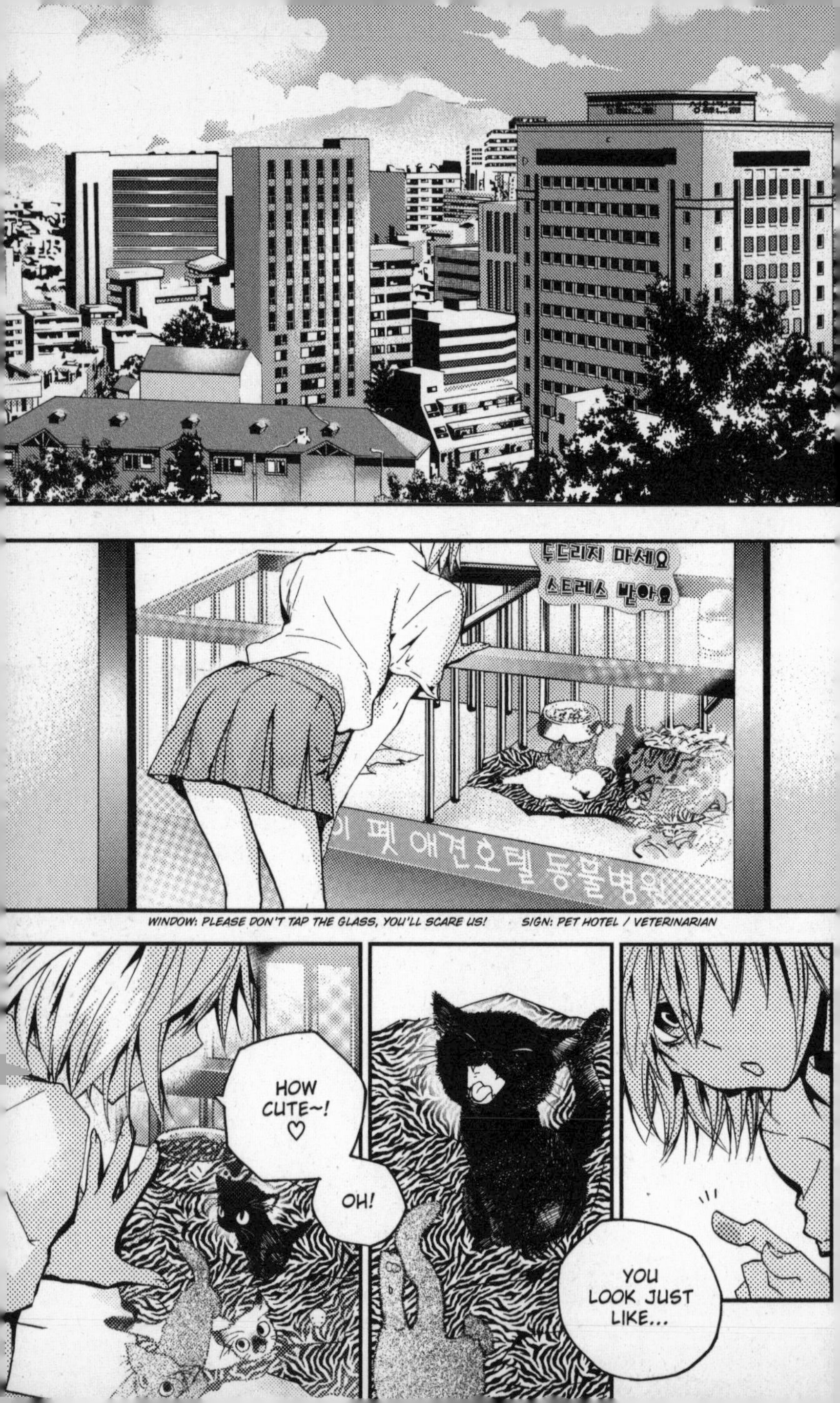

두드리지 마세요
스트레스 받아요
이 펫 애견호텔 동물병원
WINDOW: PLEASE DON'T TAP THE GLASS, YOU'LL SCARE US!
SIGN: PET HOTEL / VETERINARIAN
HOW CUTE~! ♡
OH!
YOU LOOK JUST LIKE...

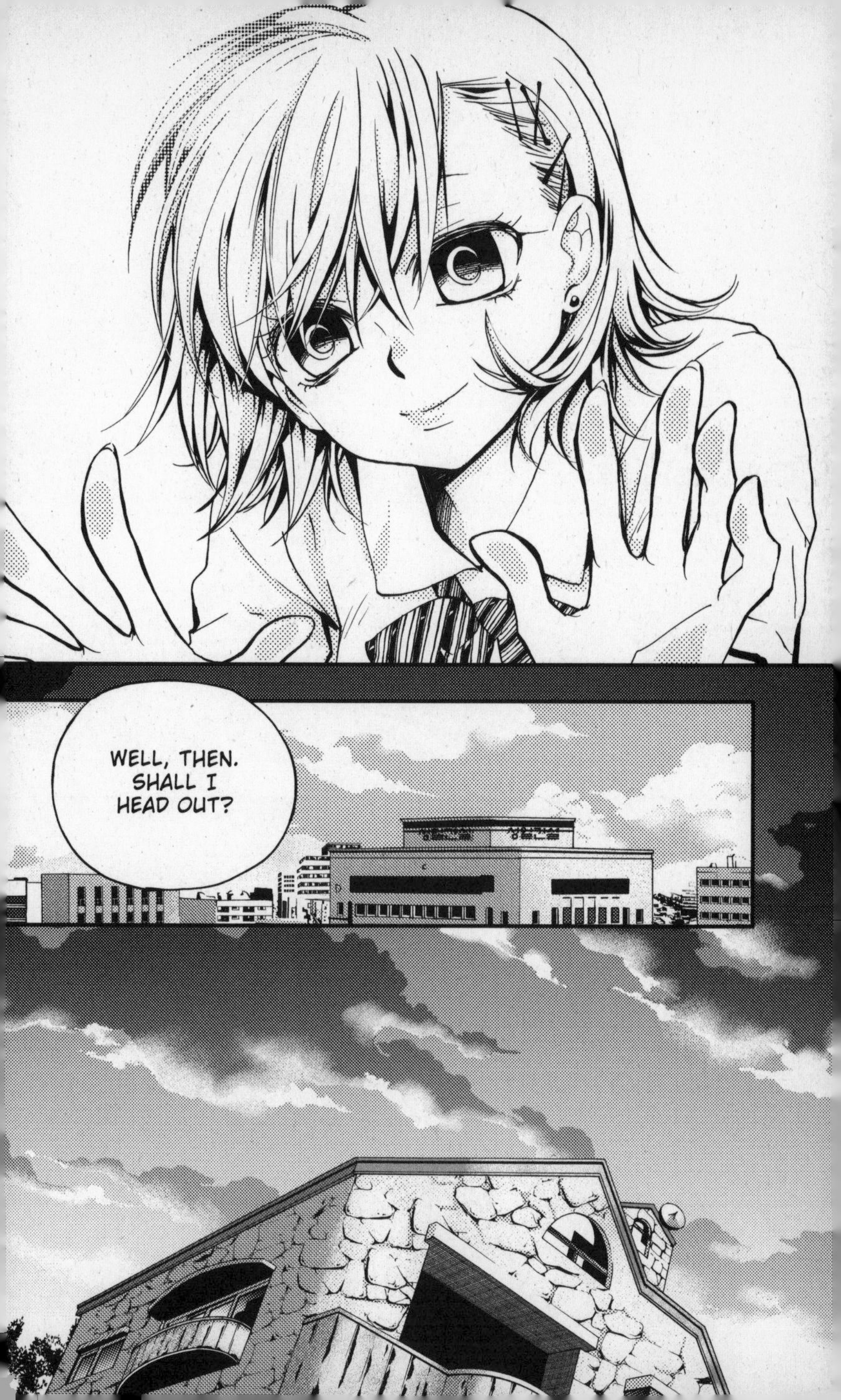
WELL, THEN. SHALL I HEAD OUT?

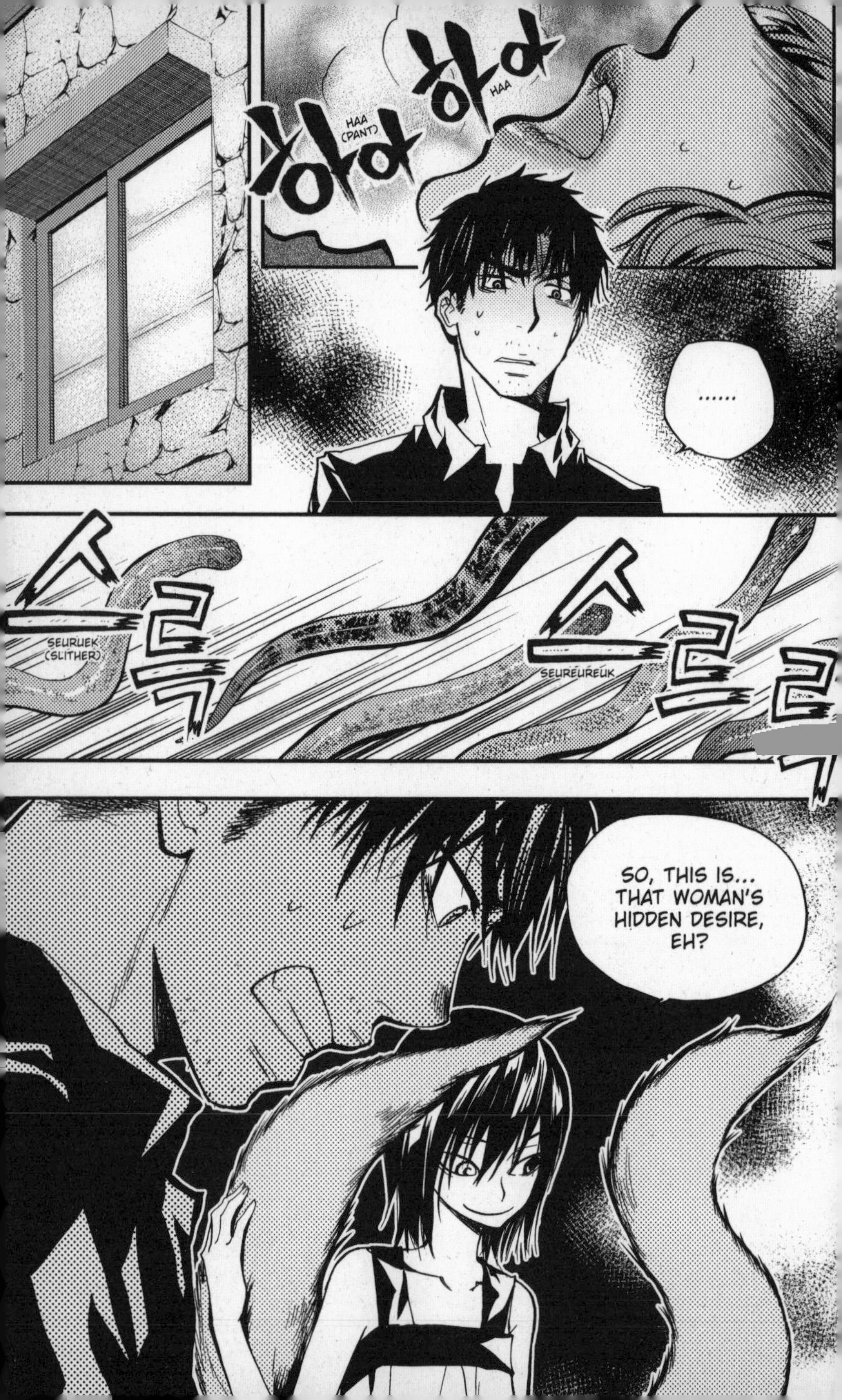
하아
HAA (PANT)
하아
HAA
......
스르륵
SEURUEK (SLITHER)
스르르륵
SEUREUREUK
SO, THIS IS... THAT WOMAN'S HIDDEN DESIRE, EH?

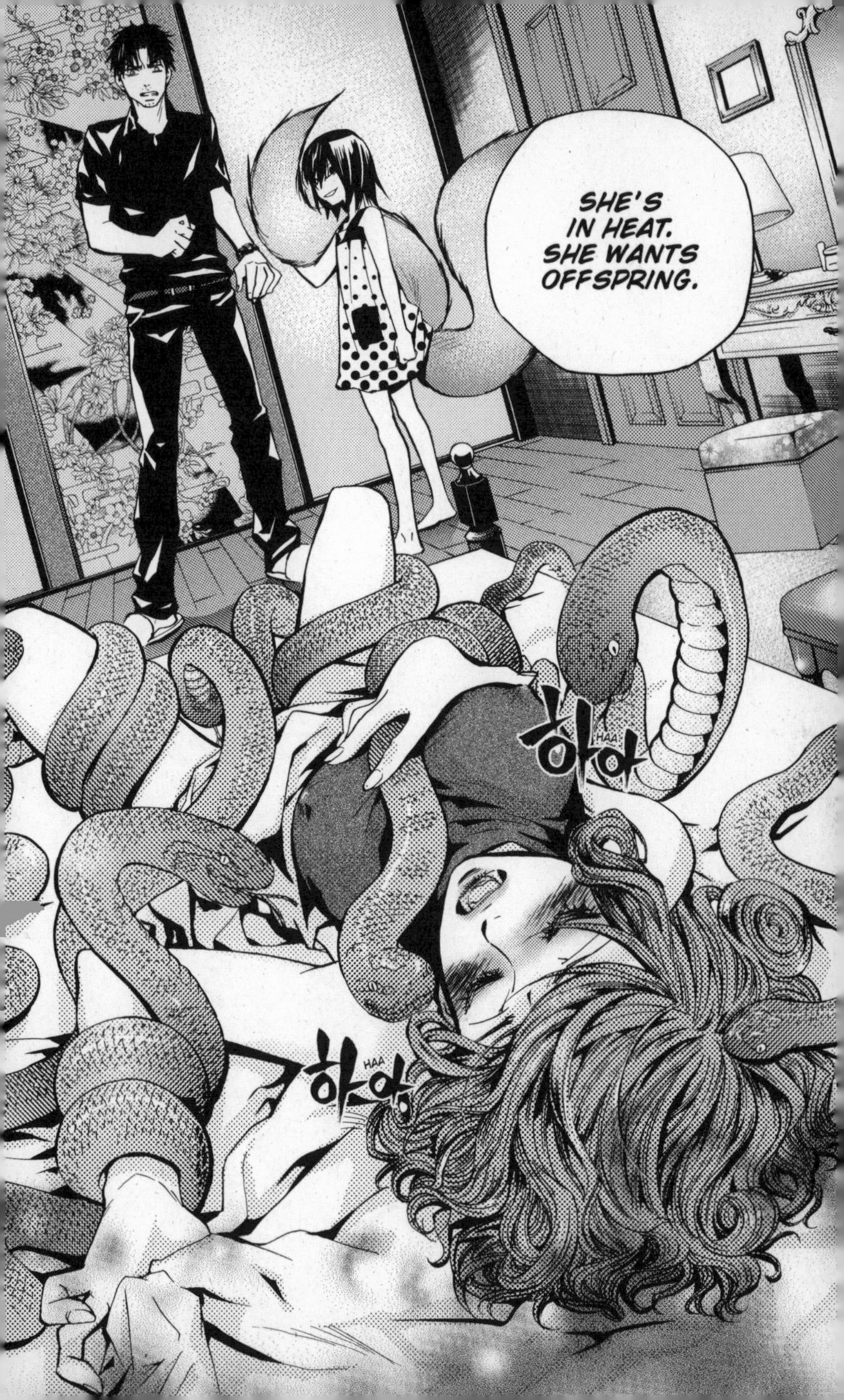
SHE'S IN HEAT. SHE WANTS OFFSPRING.
하아
HAA
하아
HAA

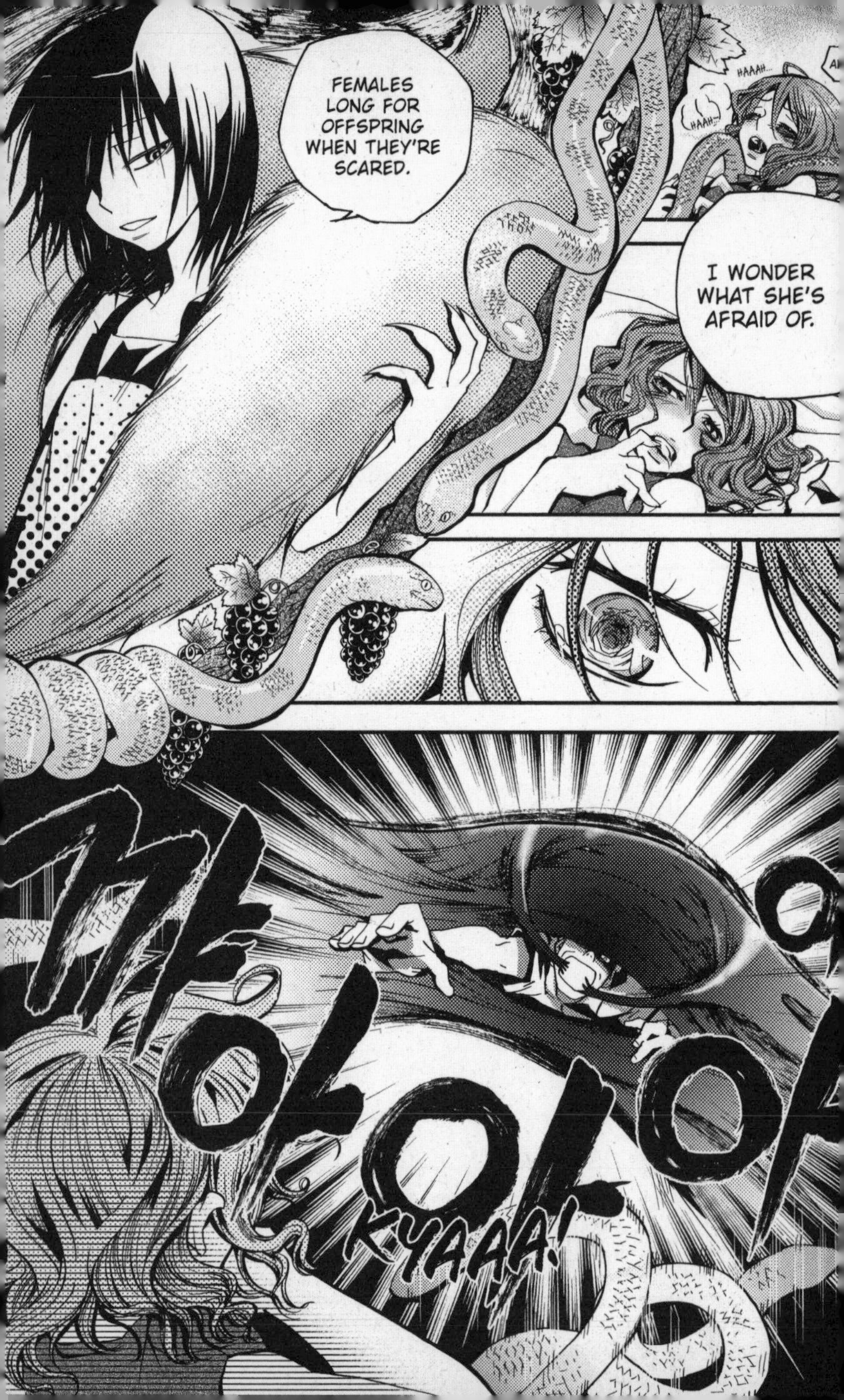
FEMALES LONG FOR OFFSPRING WHEN THEY'RE SCARED.
HAAAH...
HAAAH...
I WONDER WHAT SHE'S AFRAID OF.
KYAAA!

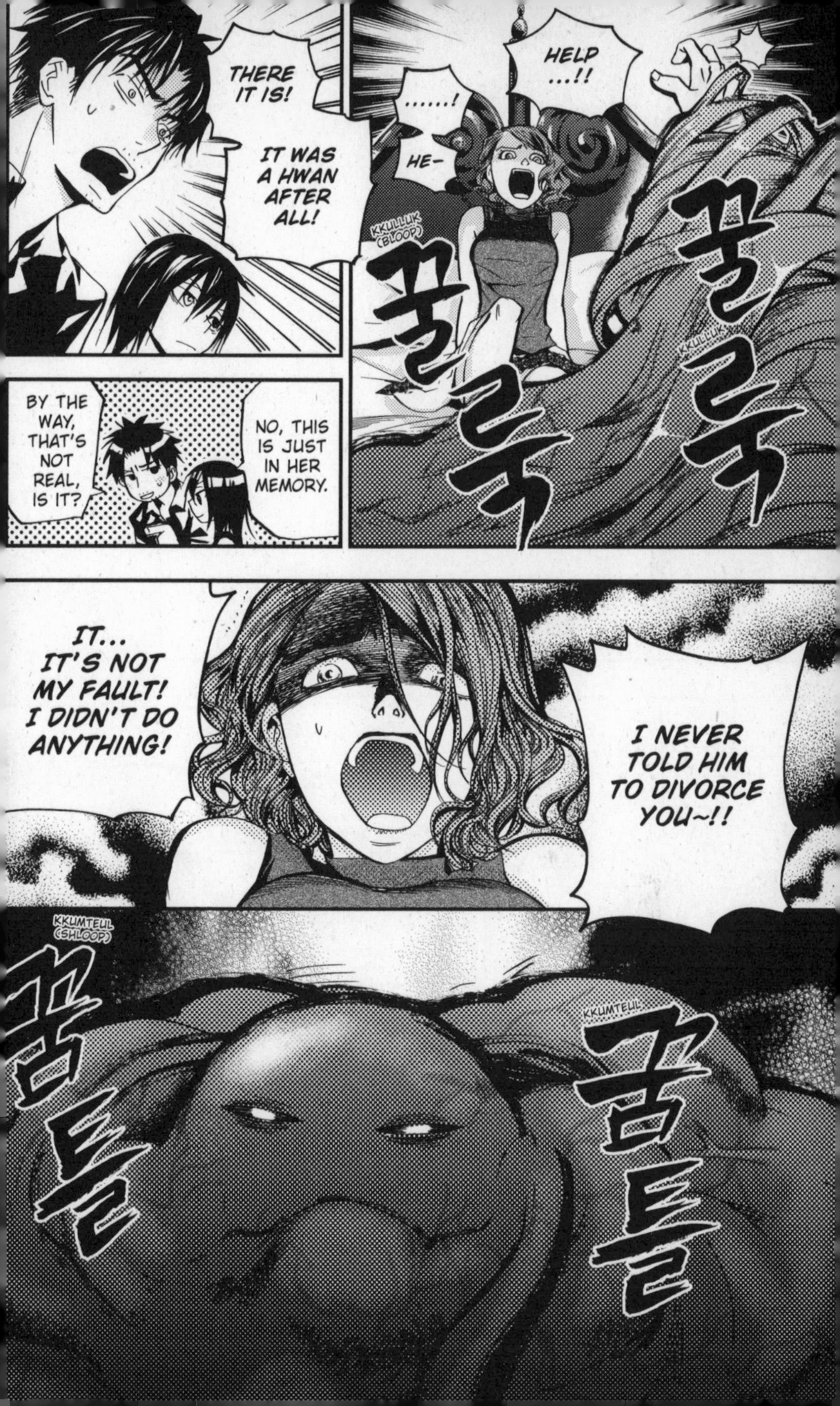
THERE IT IS!
IT WAS A HWAN AFTER ALL!
HELP ...!!
......!
HE-
KKULLUK (BLOOP)
KKULLUK
BY THE WAY, THAT'S NOT REAL, IS IT?
NO, THIS IS JUST IN HER MEMORY.
IT... IT'S NOT MY FAULT! I DIDN'T DO ANYTHING!
I NEVER TOLD HIM TO DIVORCE YOU~!!
KKUMTEUL (SHLOOP)
KKUMTEUL

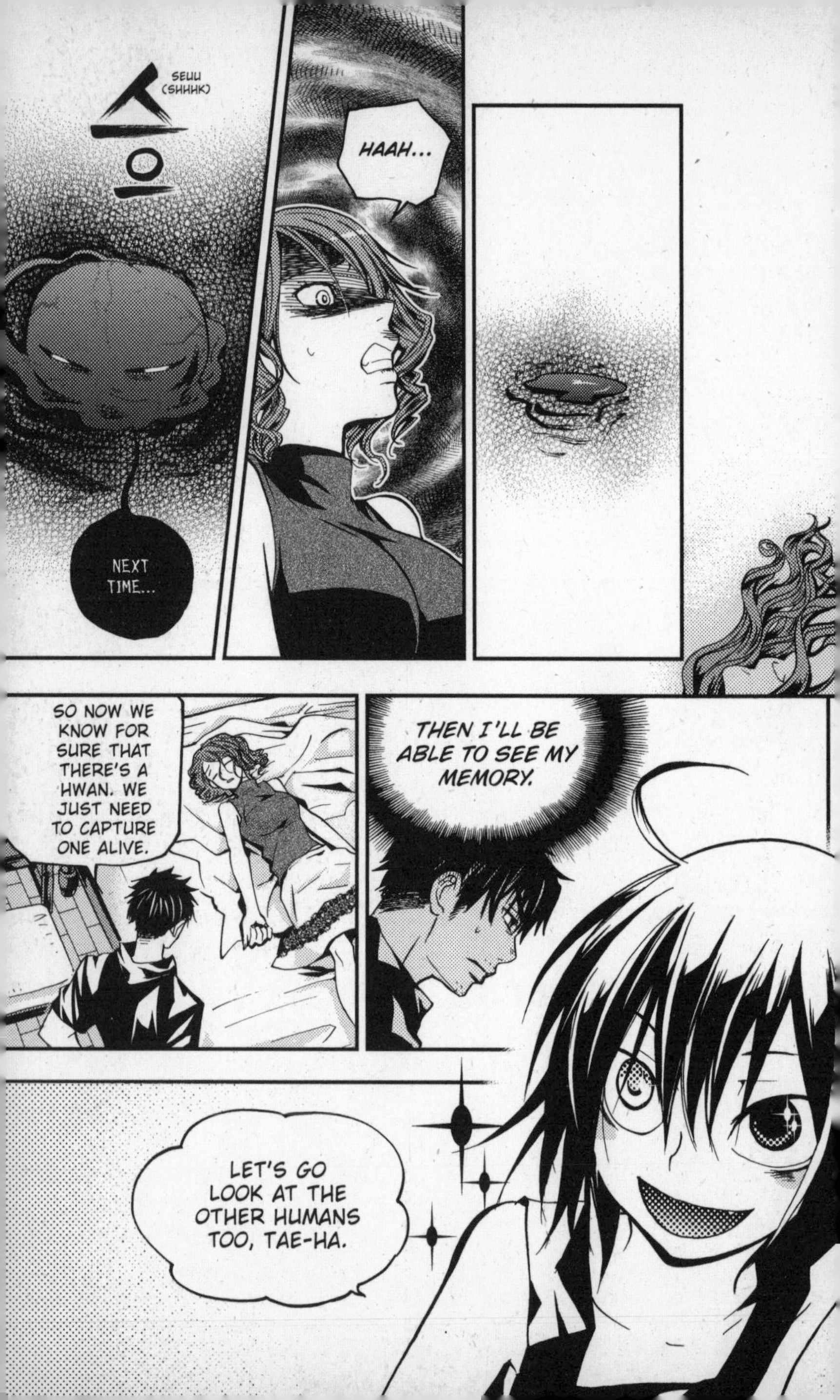
SEUU (SHHHK)
NEXT TIME...
HAAH...
SO NOW WE KNOW FOR SURE THAT THERE'S A HWAN. WE JUST NEED TO CAPTURE ONE ALIVE.
THEN I'LL BE ABLE TO SEE MY MEMORY.
LET'S GO LOOK AT THE OTHER HUMANS TOO, TAE-HA.

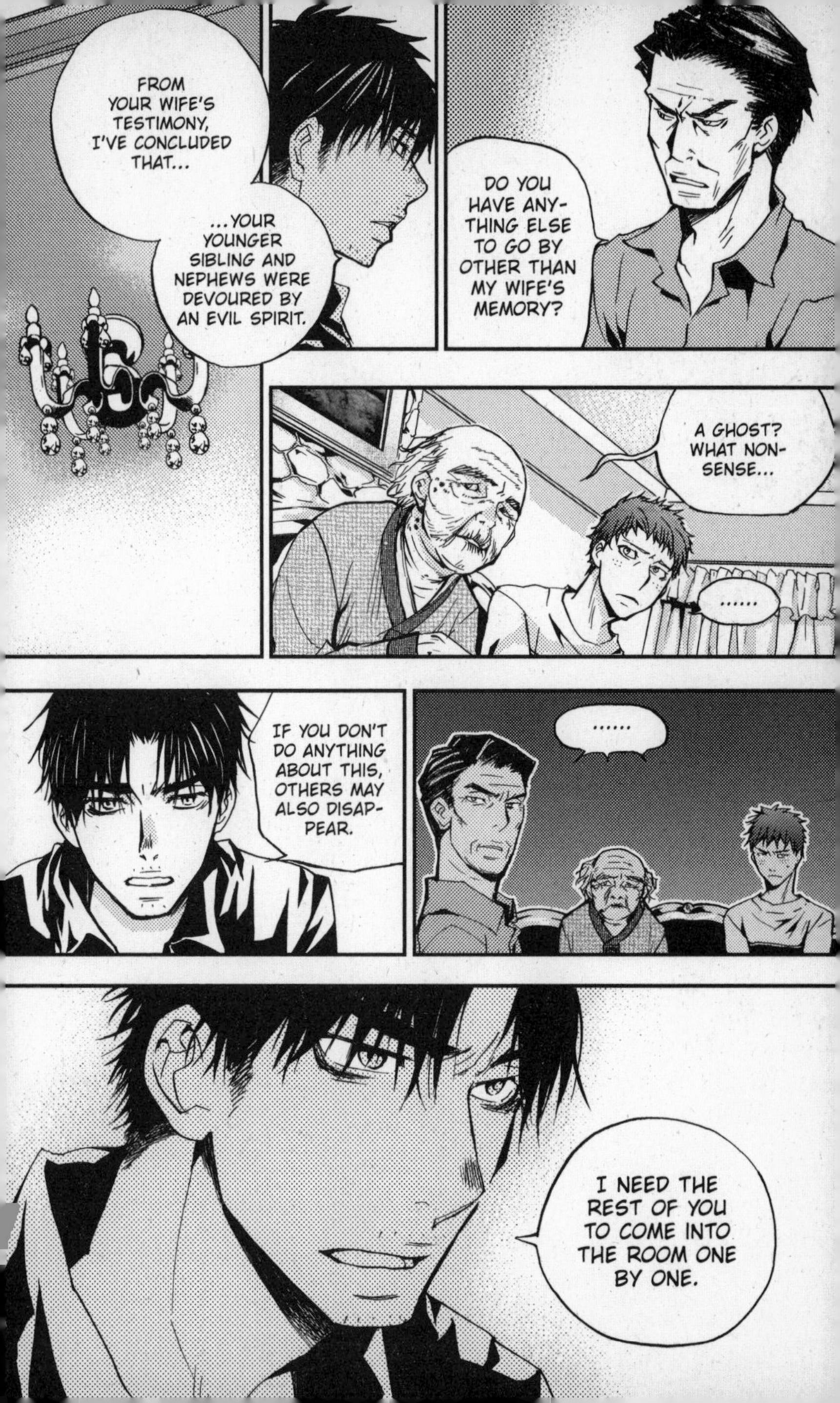
FROM YOUR WIFE'S TESTIMONY, I'VE CONCLUDED THAT...
...YOUR YOUNGER SIBLING AND NEPHEWS WERE DEVOURED BY AN EVIL SPIRIT.
DO YOU HAVE ANY-THING ELSE TO GO BY OTHER THAN MY WIFE'S MEMORY?
A GHOST? WHAT NON-SENSE...
......
IF YOU DON'T DO ANYTHING ABOUT THIS, OTHERS MAY ALSO DISAP-PEAR.
......
I NEED THE REST OF YOU TO COME INTO THE ROOM ONE BY ONE.

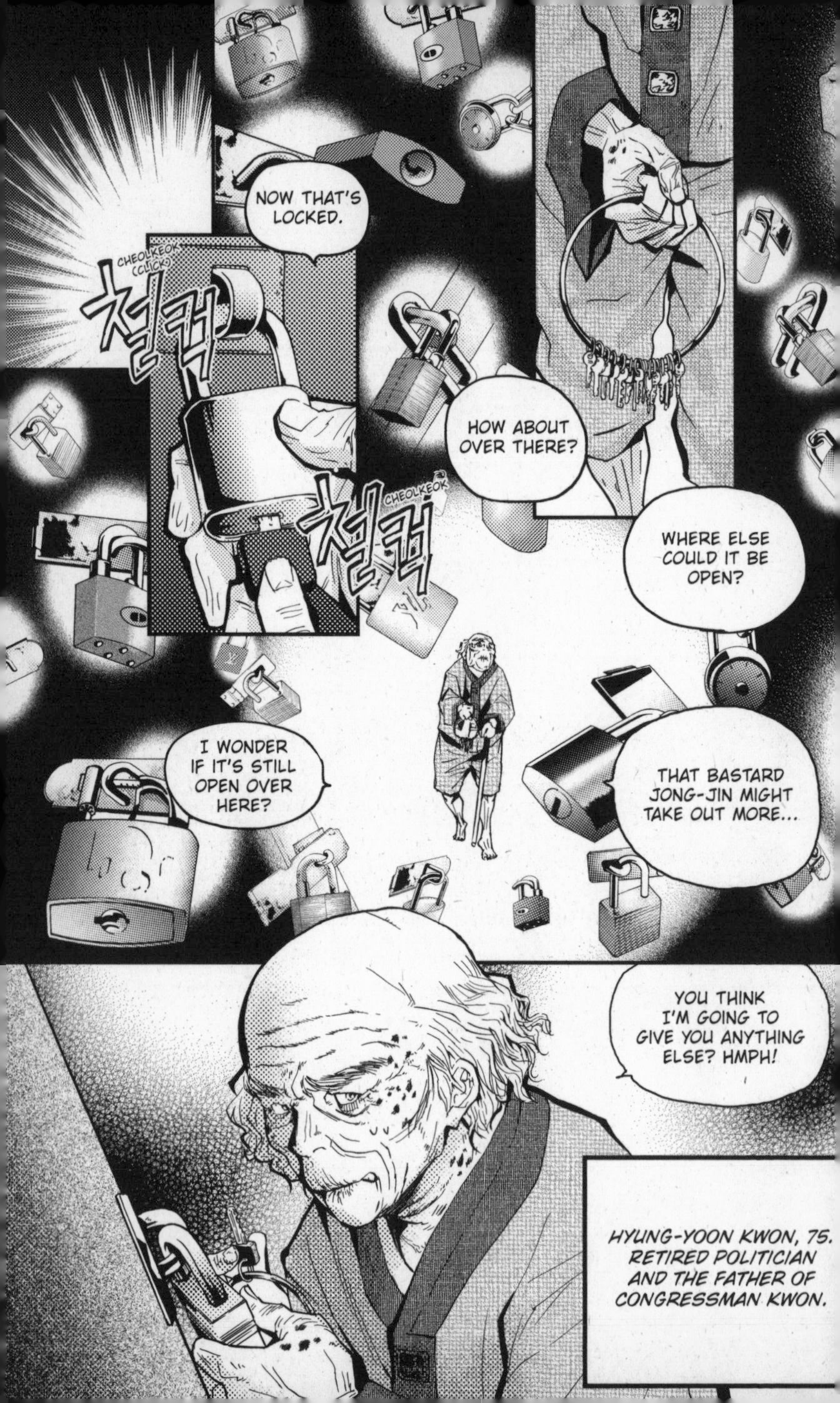
NOW THAT'S LOCKED.
CHEOLKEOK (CLICK)
철컥
CHEOLKEOK
철컥
HOW ABOUT OVER THERE?
WHERE ELSE COULD IT BE OPEN?
I WONDER IF IT'S STILL OPEN OVER HERE?
THAT BASTARD JONG-JIN MIGHT TAKE OUT MORE...
YOU THINK I'M GOING TO GIVE YOU ANYTHING ELSE? HMPH!
HYUNG-YOON KWON, 75. RETIRED POLITICIAN AND THE FATHER OF CONGRESSMAN KWON.

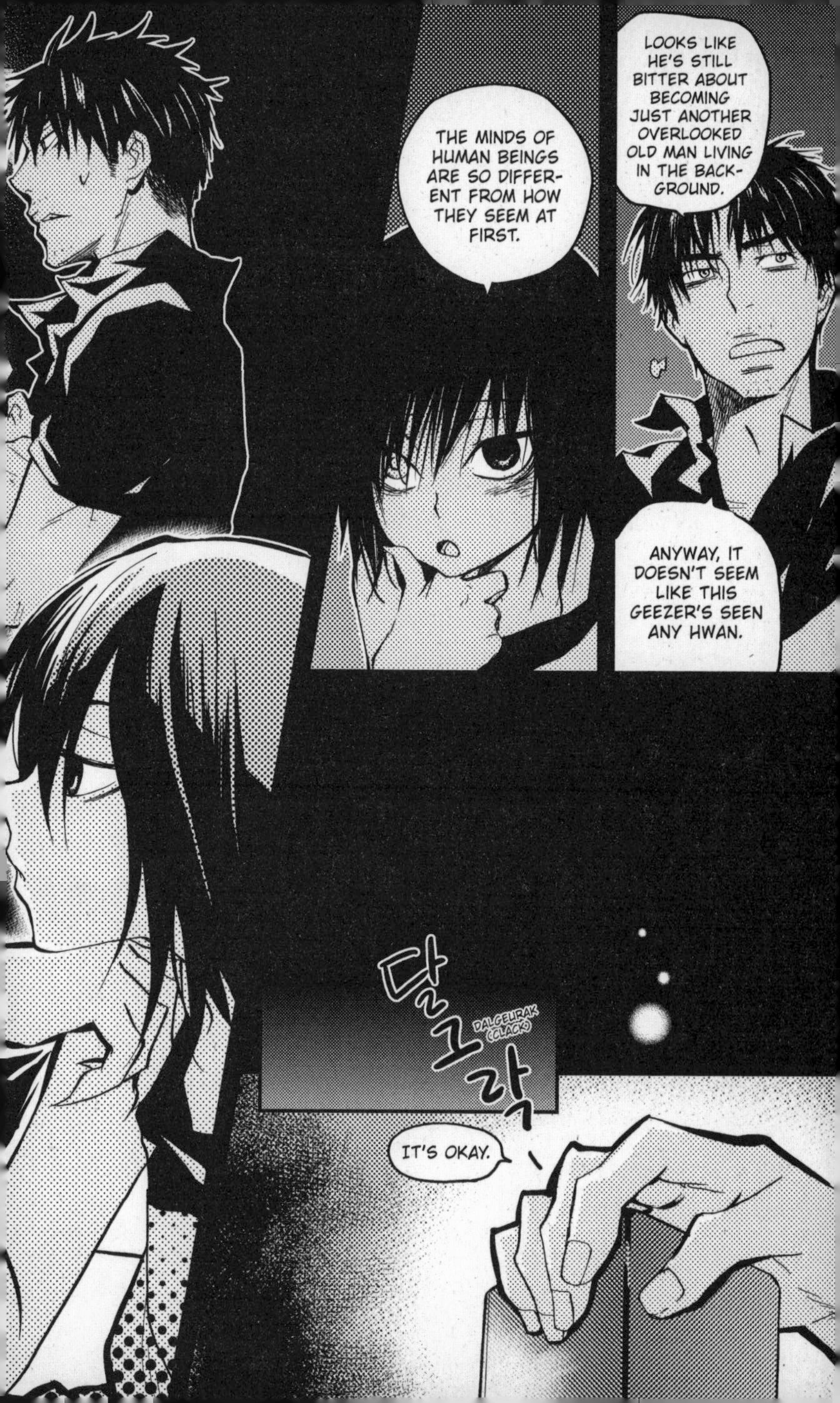
THE MINDS OF HUMAN BEINGS ARE SO DIFFER-ENT FROM HOW THEY SEEM AT FIRST.
LOOKS LIKE HE'S STILL BITTER ABOUT BECOMING JUST ANOTHER OVERLOOKED OLD MAN LIVING IN THE BACK-GROUND.
ANYWAY, IT DOESN'T SEEM LIKE THIS GEEZER'S SEEN ANY HWAN.
달그락
DALGEURAK (CLACK)
IT'S OKAY.

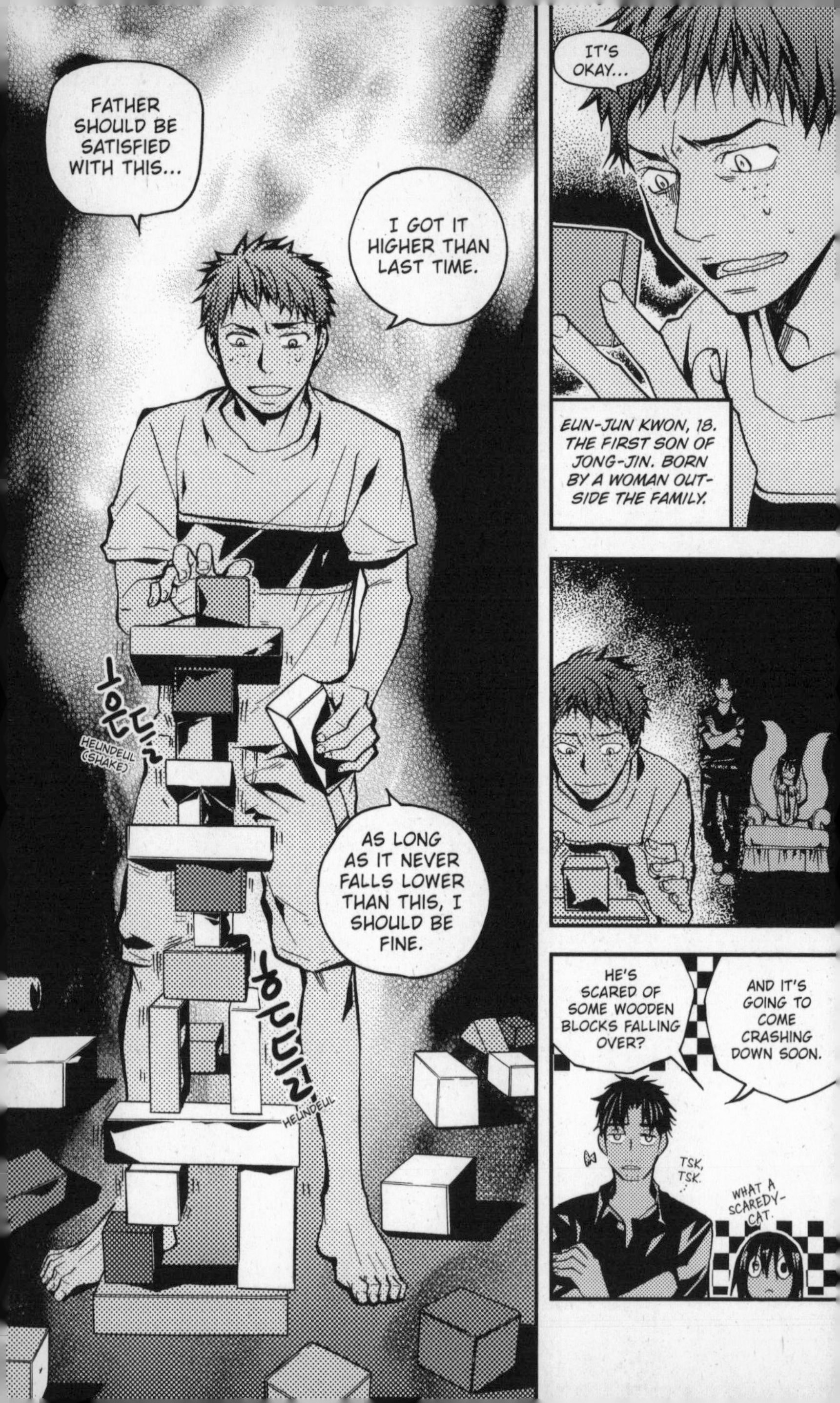
FATHER SHOULD BE SATISFIED WITH THIS...
I GOT IT HIGHER THAN LAST TIME.
흔들
HEUNDEUL (SHAKE)
AS LONG AS IT NEVER FALLS LOWER THAN THIS, I SHOULD BE FINE.
흔들
HEUNDEUL
IT'S OKAY...
EUN-JUN KWON, 18. THE FIRST SON OF JONG-JIN. BORN BY A WOMAN OUT-SIDE THE FAMILY.
HE'S SCARED OF SOME WOODEN BLOCKS FALLING OVER?
AND IT'S GOING TO COME CRASHING DOWN SOON.
TSK, TSK.
WHAT A SCAREDY-CAT.

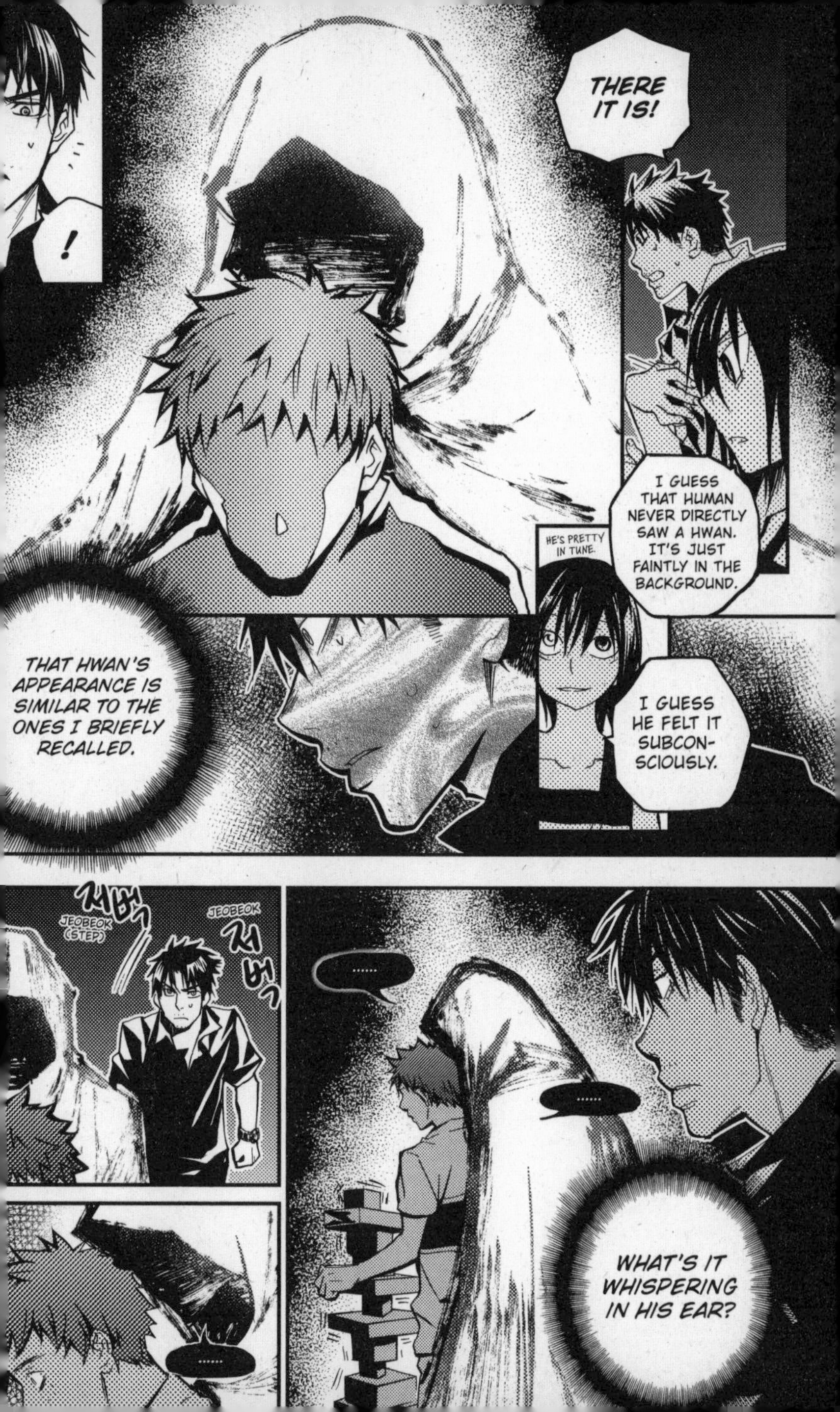
!
THERE IT IS!
I GUESS THAT HUMAN NEVER DIRECTLY SAW A HWAN. IT'S JUST FAINTLY IN THE BACKGROUND.
THAT HWAN'S APPEARANCE IS SIMILAR TO THE ONES I BRIEFLY RECALLED.
HE'S PRETTY IN TUNE.
I GUESS HE FELT IT SUBCONSCIOUSLY.
저벅
JEOBEOK (STEP)
저벅
JEOBEOK
......
......
......
WHAT'S IT WHISPERING IN HIS EAR?

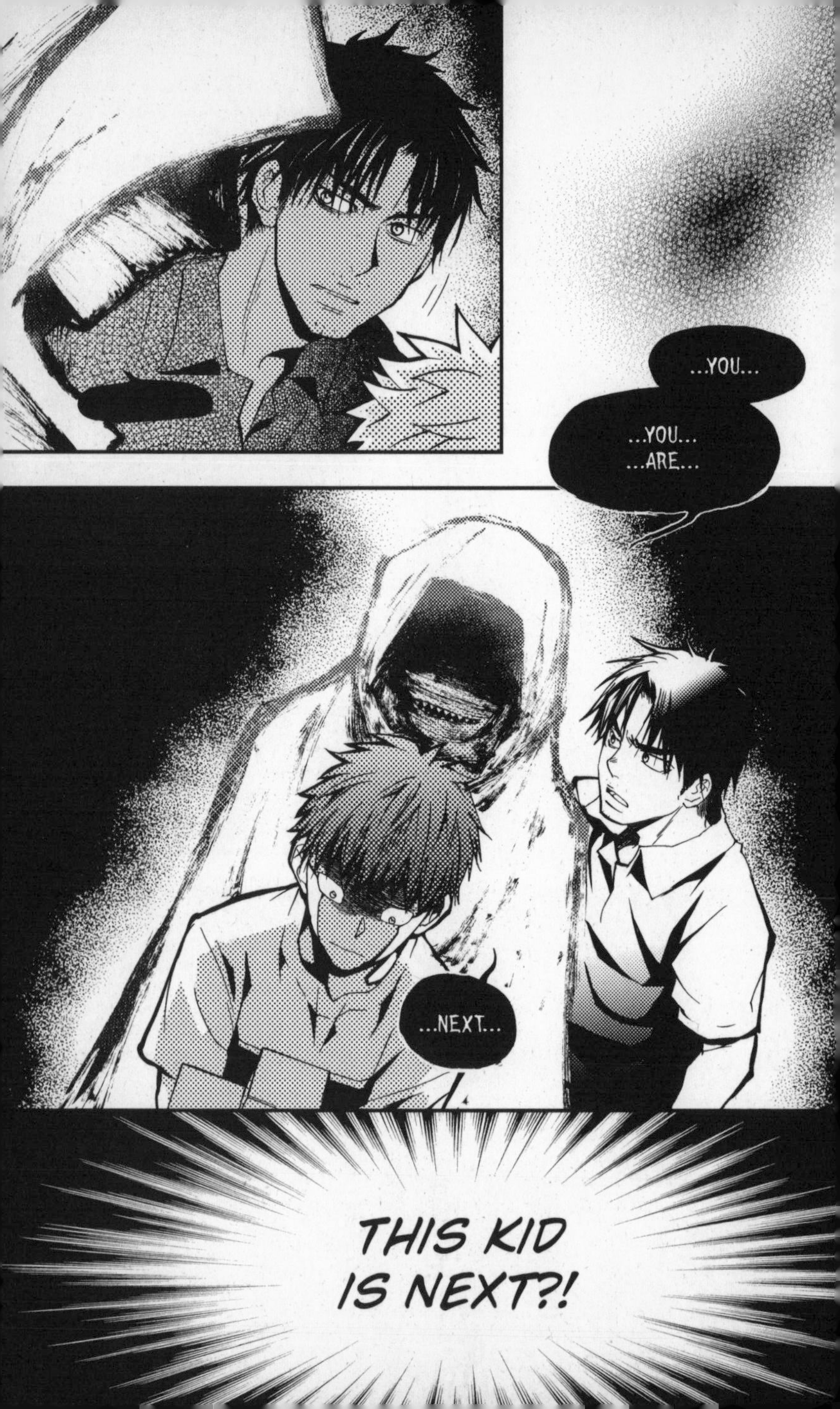
...YOU...
...YOU... ...ARE...
...NEXT...
THIS KID IS NEXT?!

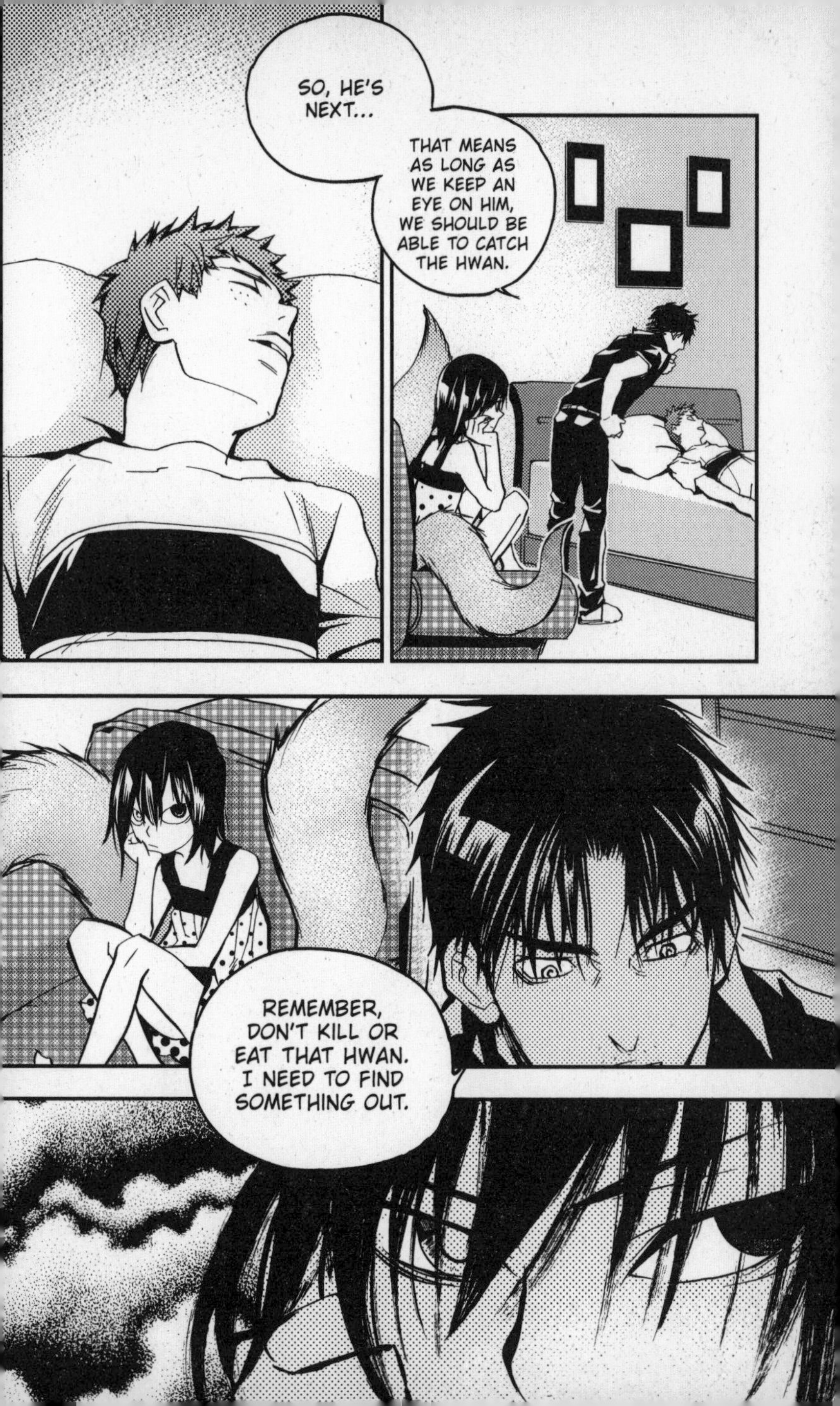
SO, HE'S NEXT...
THAT MEANS AS LONG AS WE KEEP AN EYE ON HIM, WE SHOULD BE ABLE TO CATCH THE HWAN.
REMEMBER, DON'T KILL OR EAT THAT HWAN. I NEED TO FIND SOMETHING OUT.

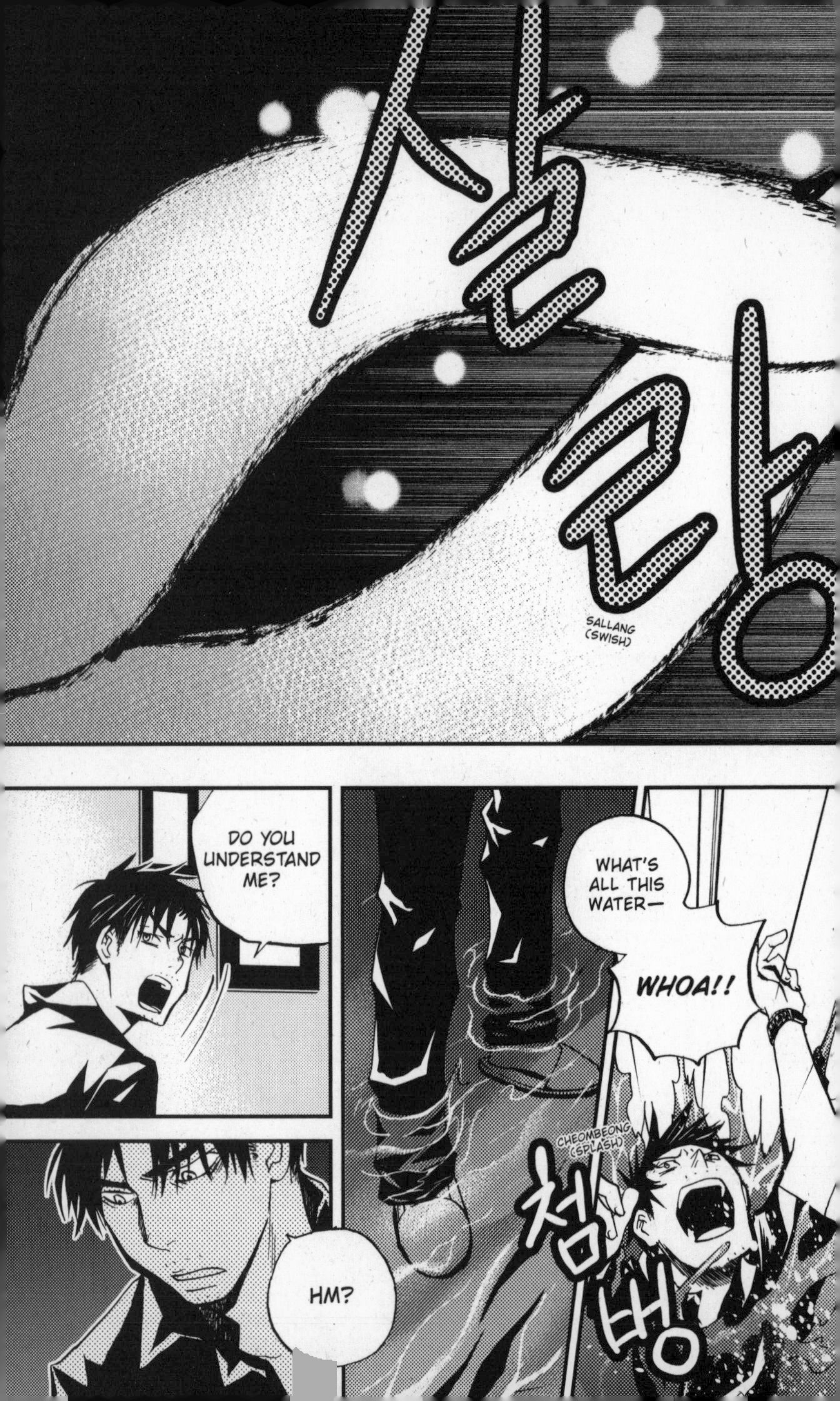
살랑
SALLANG
(SWISH)
DO YOU UNDERSTAND ME?
HM?
WHAT'S ALL THIS WATER—
WHOA!!
CHEOMBEONG
(SPLASH)
첨벙

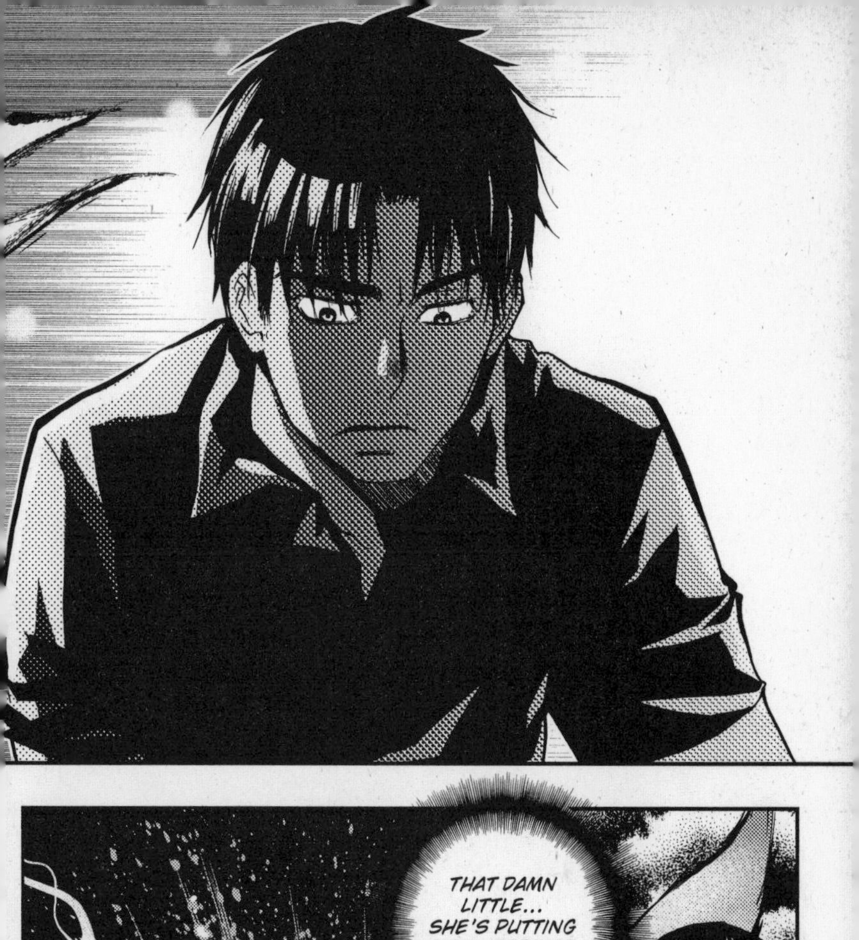

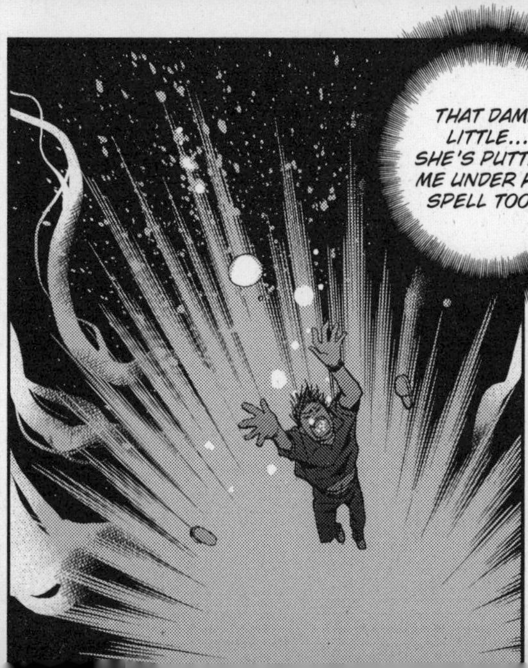
THAT DAMN LITTLE... SHE'S PUTTING ME UNDER HER SPELL TOO?!

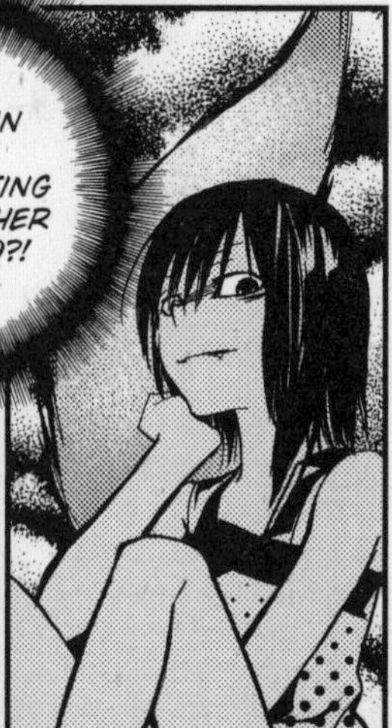

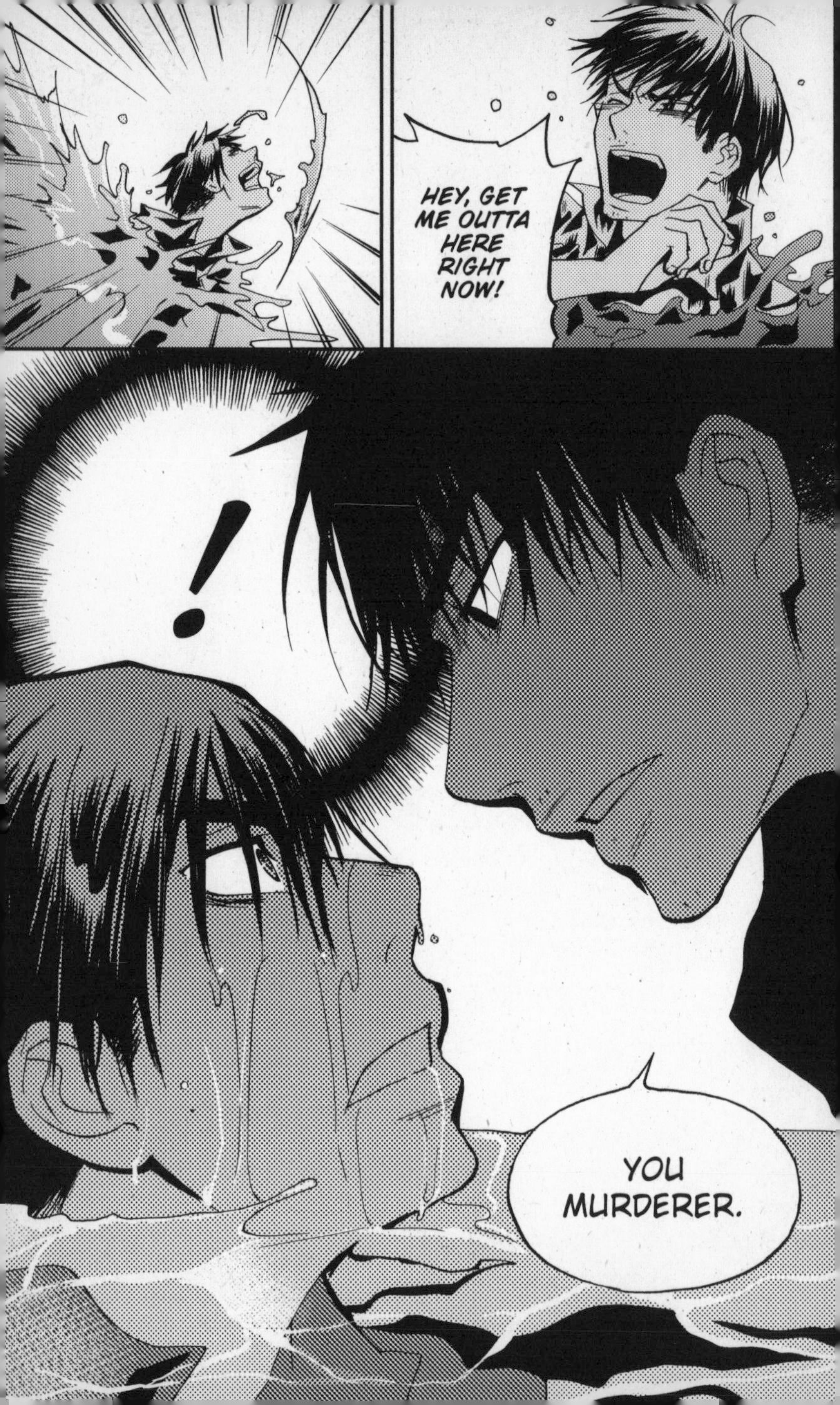
HEY, GET ME OUTTA HERE RIGHT NOW!
!
YOU MURDERER.

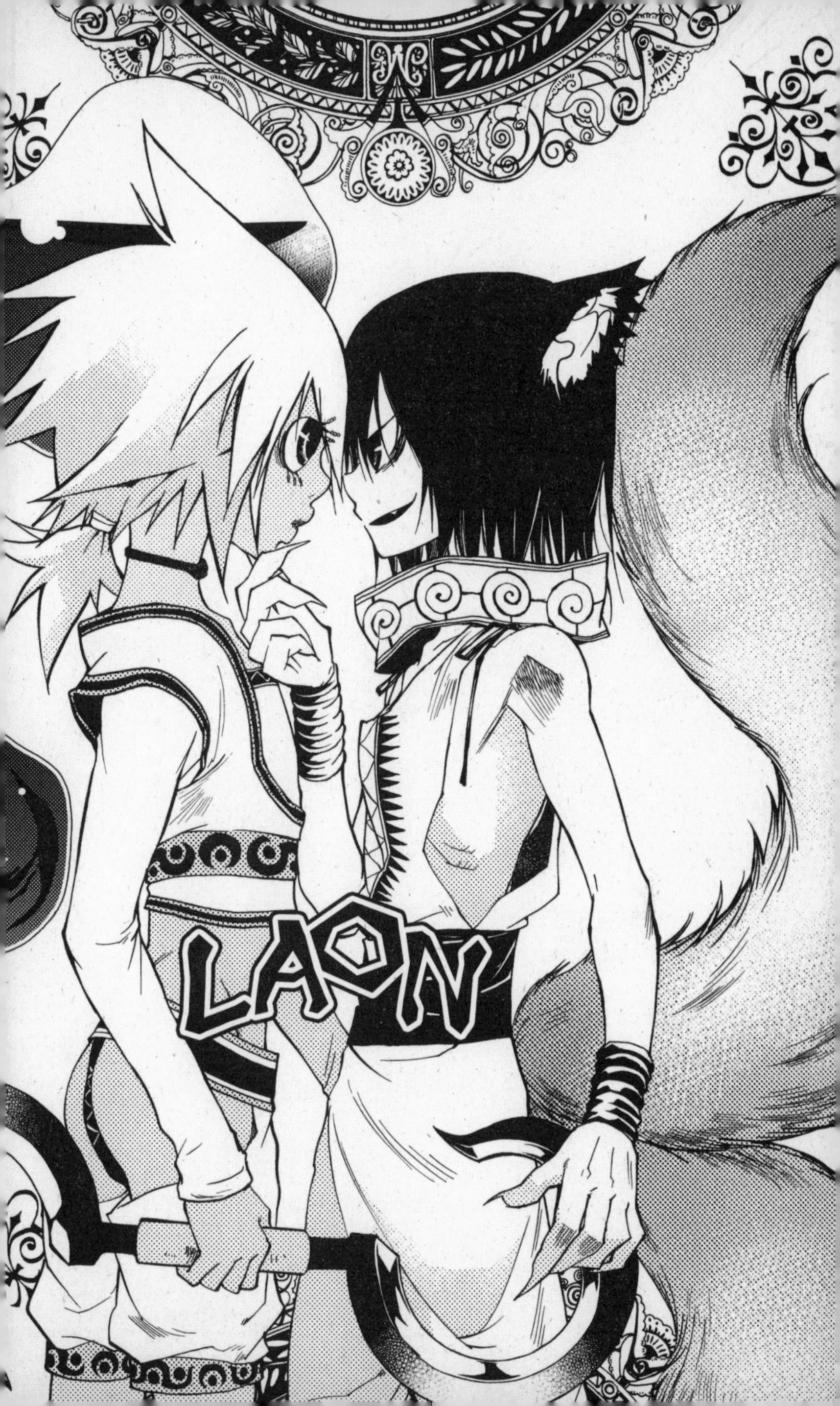
LAON

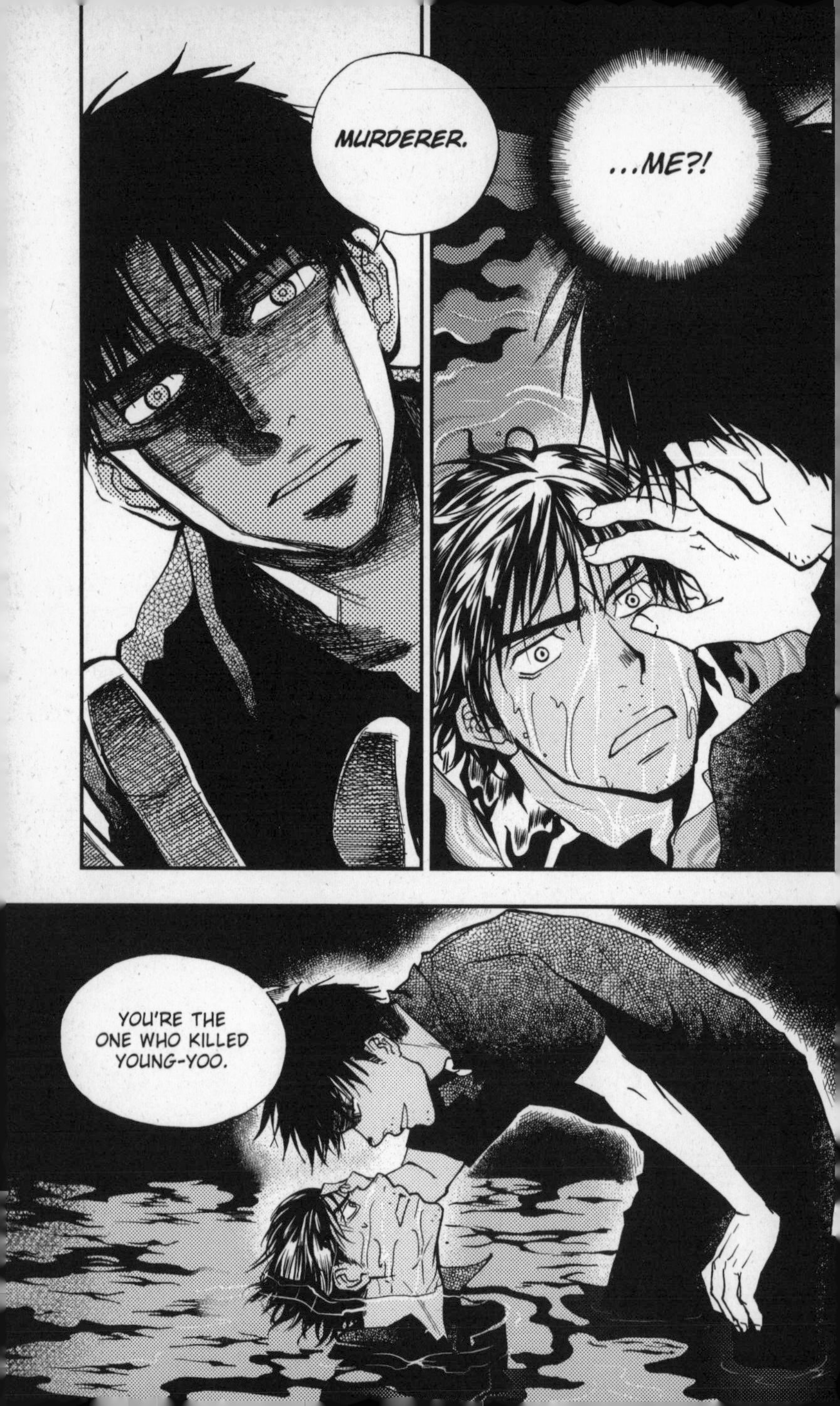
MURDERER.
...ME?!
YOU'RE THE ONE WHO KILLED YOUNG-YOO.

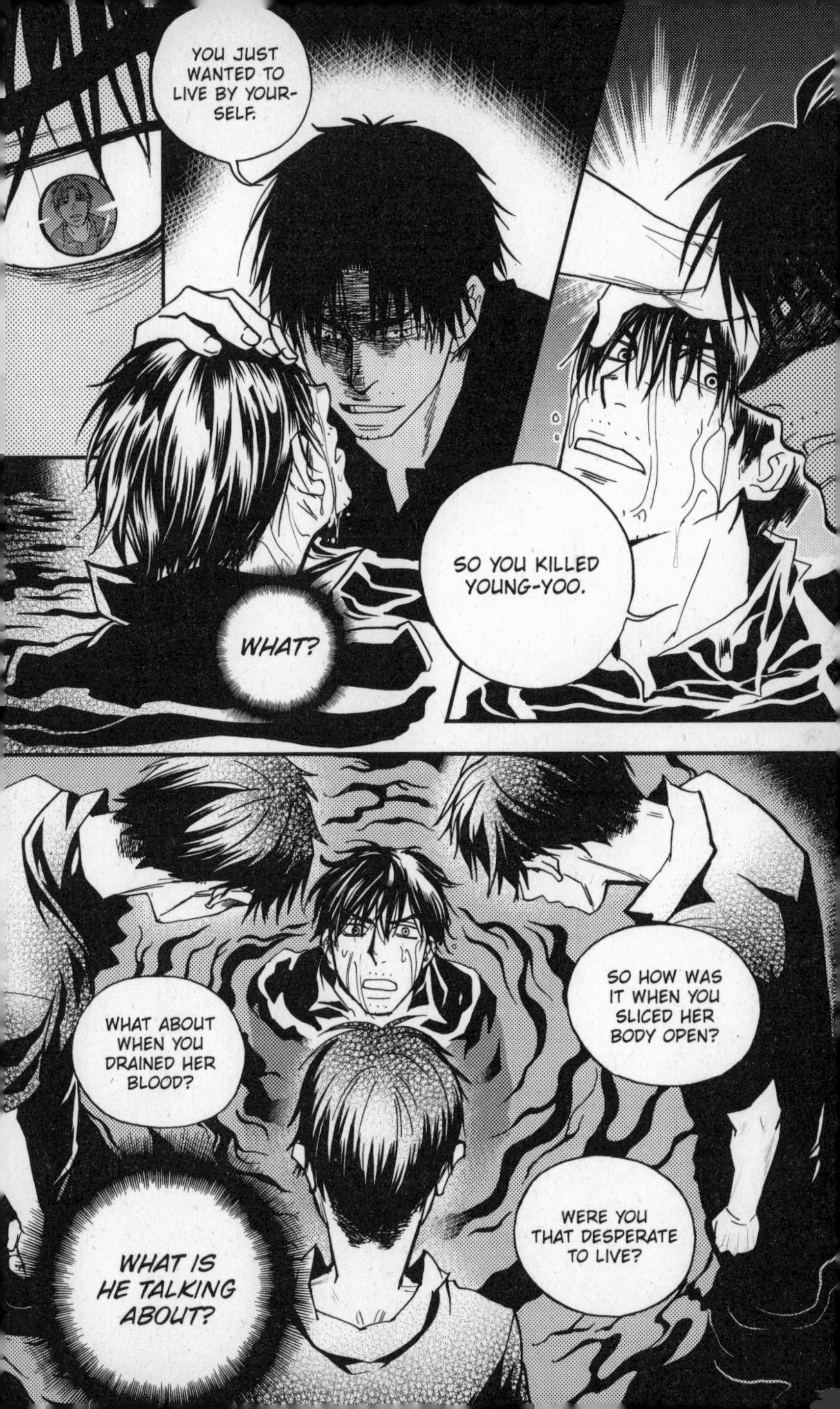
YOU JUST WANTED TO LIVE BY YOUR-SELF.
SO YOU KILLED YOUNG-YOO.
WHAT?
SO HOW WAS IT WHEN YOU SLICED HER BODY OPEN?
WHAT ABOUT WHEN YOU DRAINED HER BLOOD?
WERE YOU THAT DESPERATE TO LIVE?
WHAT IS HE TALKING ABOUT?

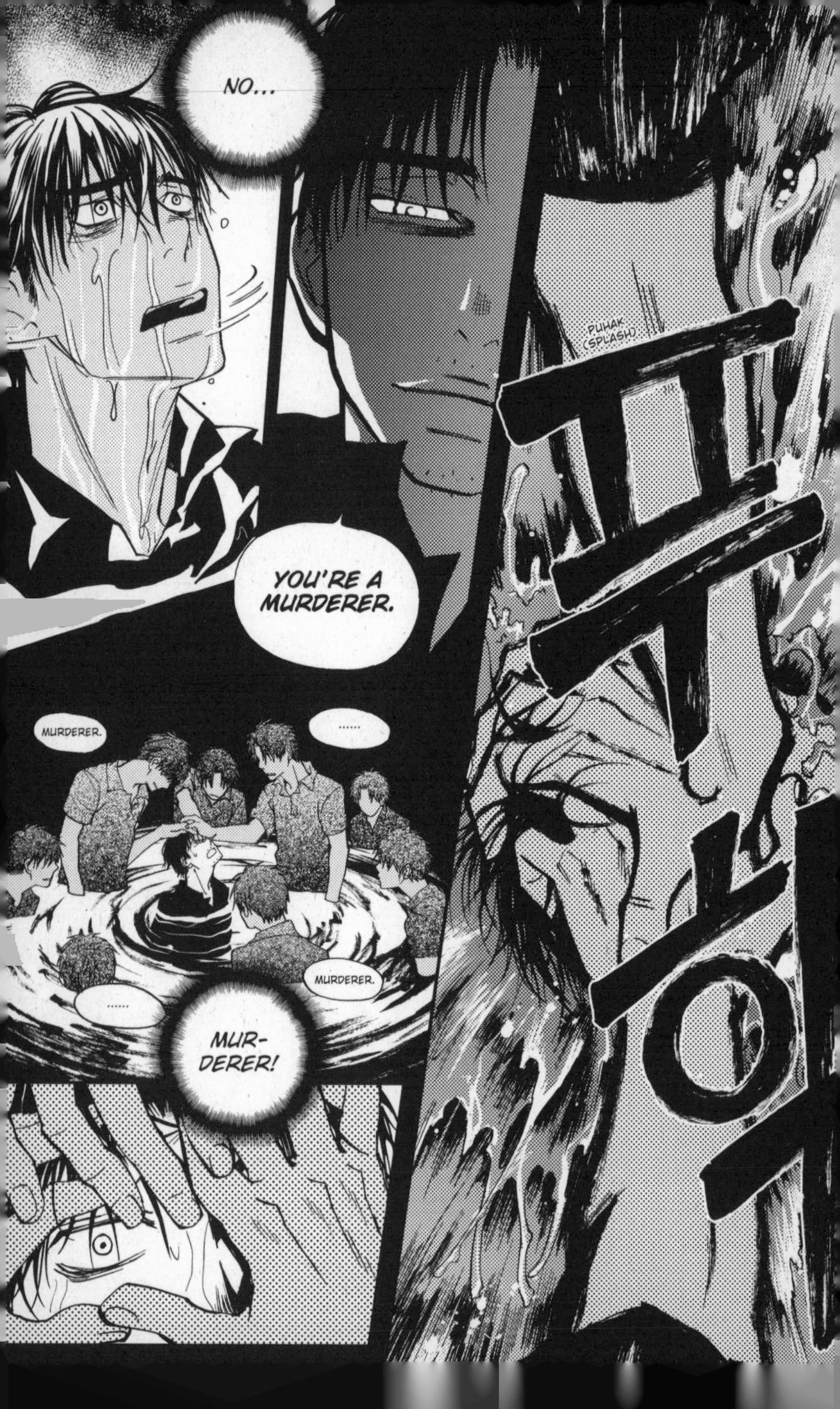
NO...
YOU'RE A MURDERER.
MURDERER.
......
......
MURDERER.
MUR-DERER!
PUHAK (SPLASH)

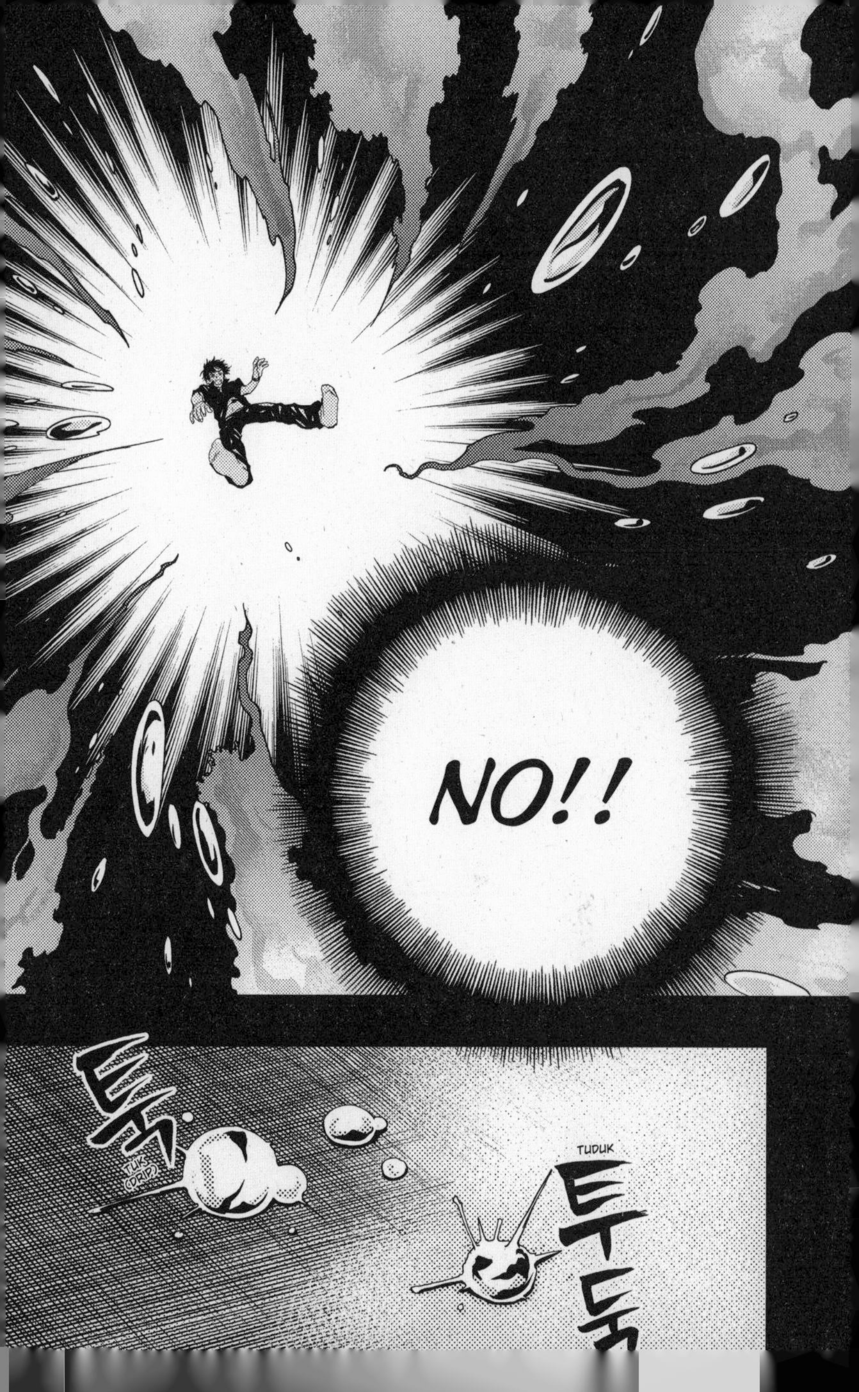
NO!!
뚝
TUKS (DRIP)
TUDUK
투둑

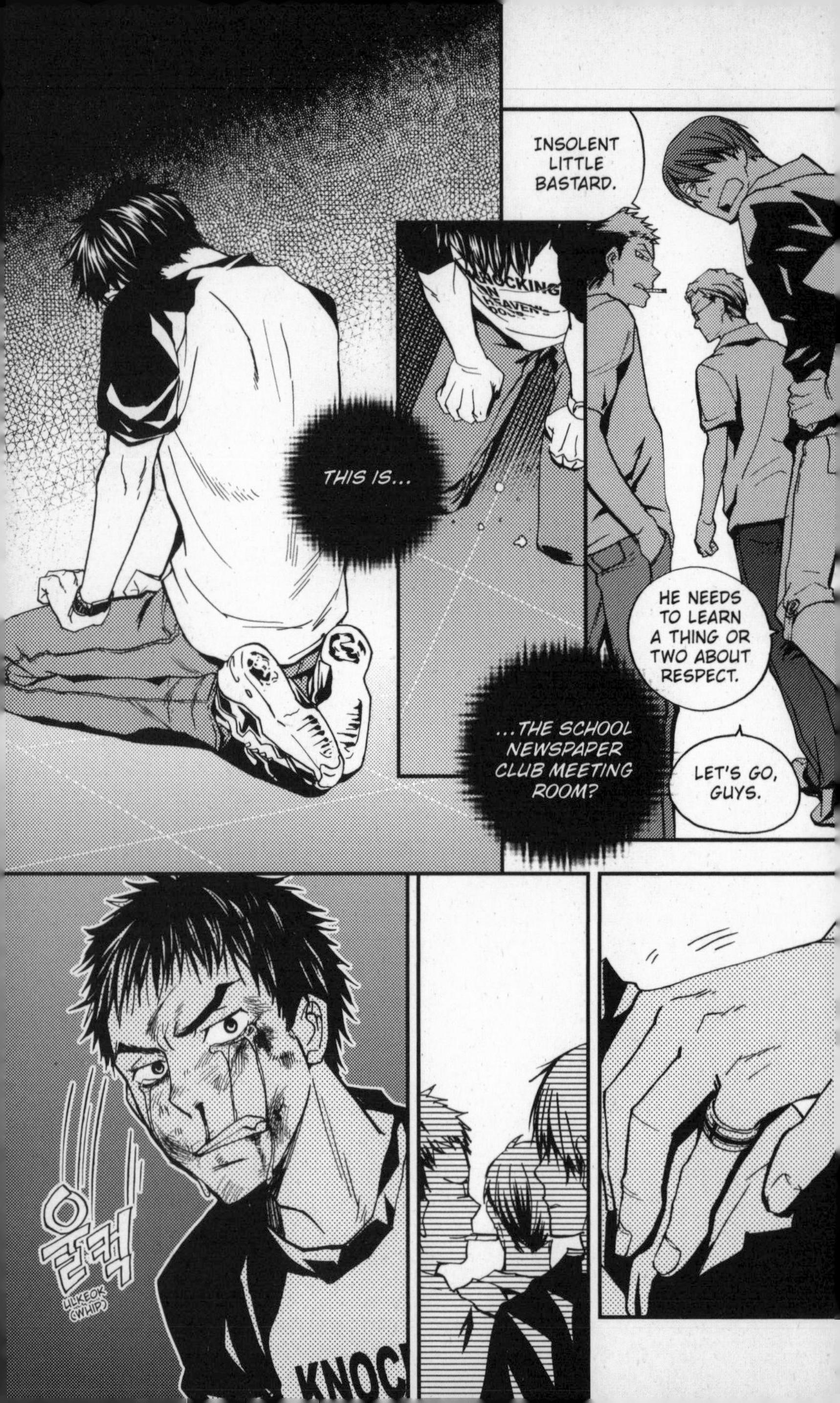
THIS IS...
INSOLENT LITTLE BASTARD.
HE NEEDS TO LEARN A THING OR TWO ABOUT RESPECT.
...THE SCHOOL NEWSPAPER CLUB MEETING ROOM?
LET'S GO, GUYS.
울컥
ULKEOK (WHIP)

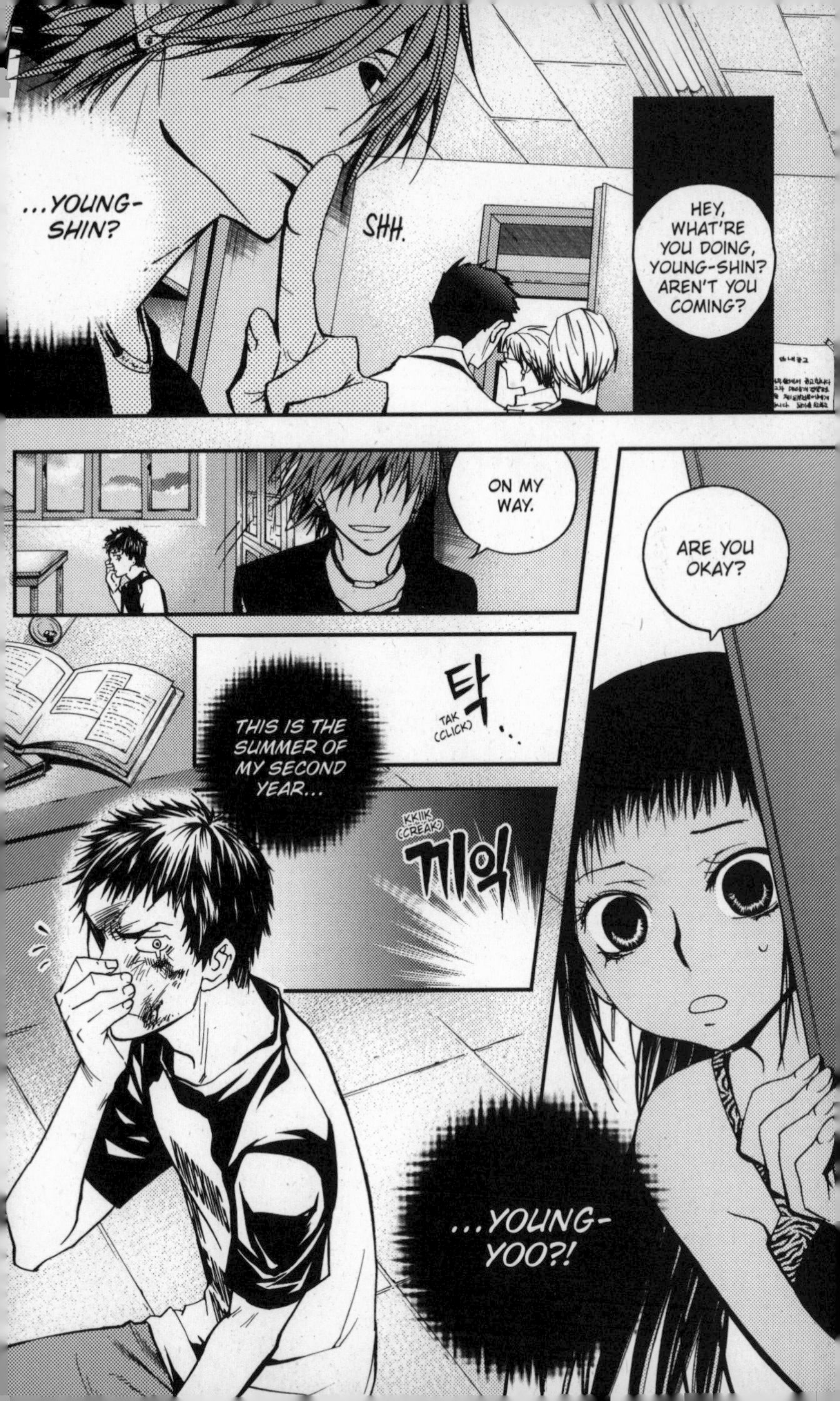
...YOUNG-SHIN?
SHH.
HEY, WHAT'RE YOU DOING, YOUNG-SHIN? AREN'T YOU COMING?
ON MY WAY.
THIS IS THE SUMMER OF MY SECOND YEAR...
탁
TAK (CLICK)
KKIIK (CREAK)
끼익
ARE YOU OKAY?
...YOUNG-YOO?!

WHY STICK YOUR NOSE IN EVERYTHING? JUST LET THEM DO THEIR THING.

JJIIK
(RIP)
찌익

THE SENIORS WERE GONNA BLOW THE CLUB FUNDS ON A DRINKING NIGHT. SO? YOU SHOULDA JUST PLAYED ALONG AND HAD A DRINK OR TWO YOURSELF. BUT NO, YOU'D RATHER GET BEATEN UP?

DID YOUNG-SHIN SEND YOU IN? HERE, GIVE IT TO ME. I HAVE HANDS TOO. I DON'T NEED YOUR HELP.

OUCH.

WOW, YOU SURE KNOW HOW TO CHARM A LADY~.

IS THAT HOW YOU NORMALLY TREAT GIRLS?

AH, NEVER MIND. NOT LIKE YOU'VE EVER HUNG AROUND GIRLS, HM?

I MEAN, WHAT KIND OF GIRL WOULD WANT TO BE WITH YOU?

WHAT?

RIGHT...I REMEMBER THIS...

YOU'VE NEVER EVEN KISSED A GIRL, HAVE YOU?

KNOCKIN ON HEAVEN DOOR

KNOCKI

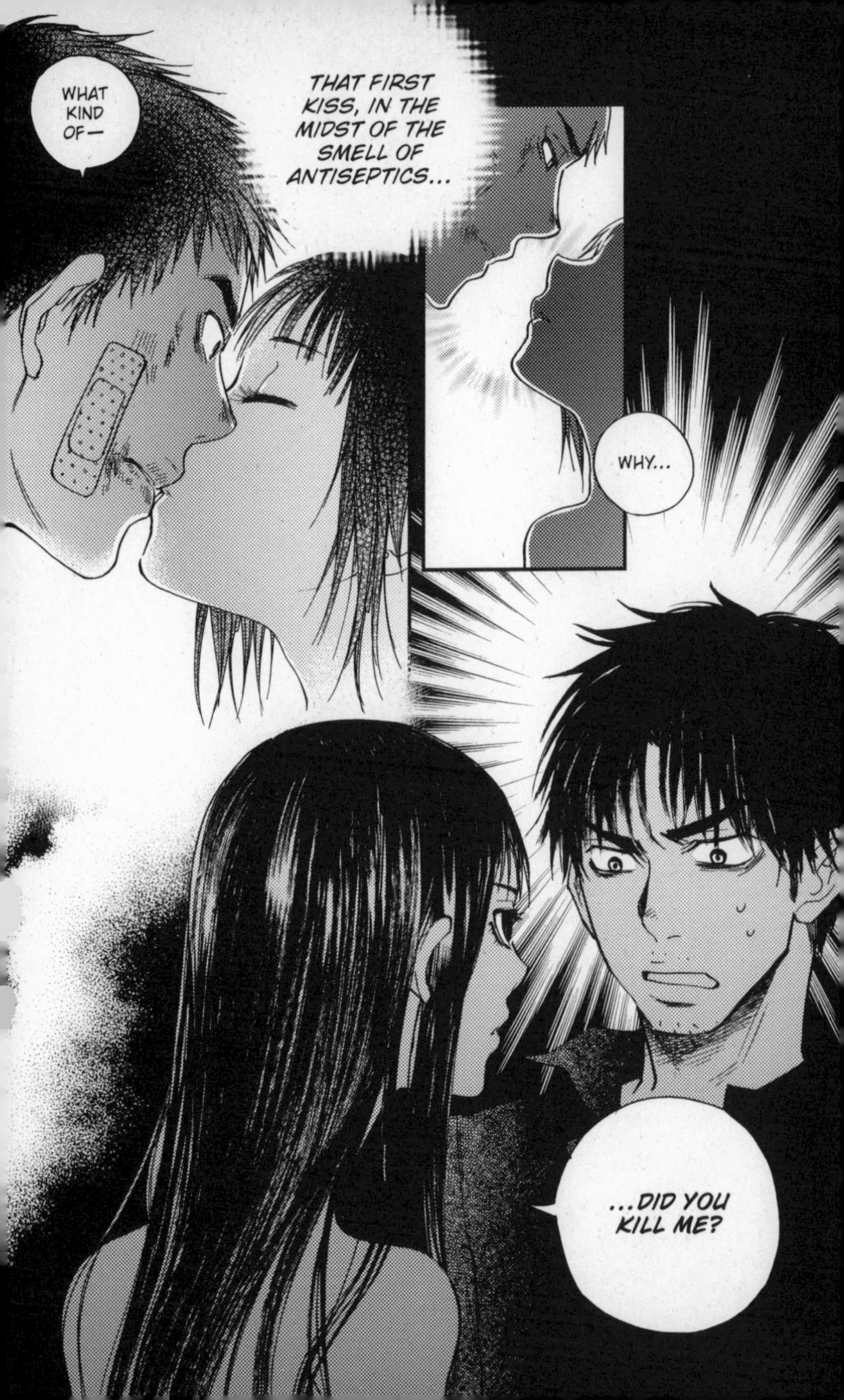
WHAT KIND OF—
THAT FIRST KISS, IN THE MIDST OF THE SMELL OF ANTISEPTICS...
WHY...
...DID YOU KILL ME?

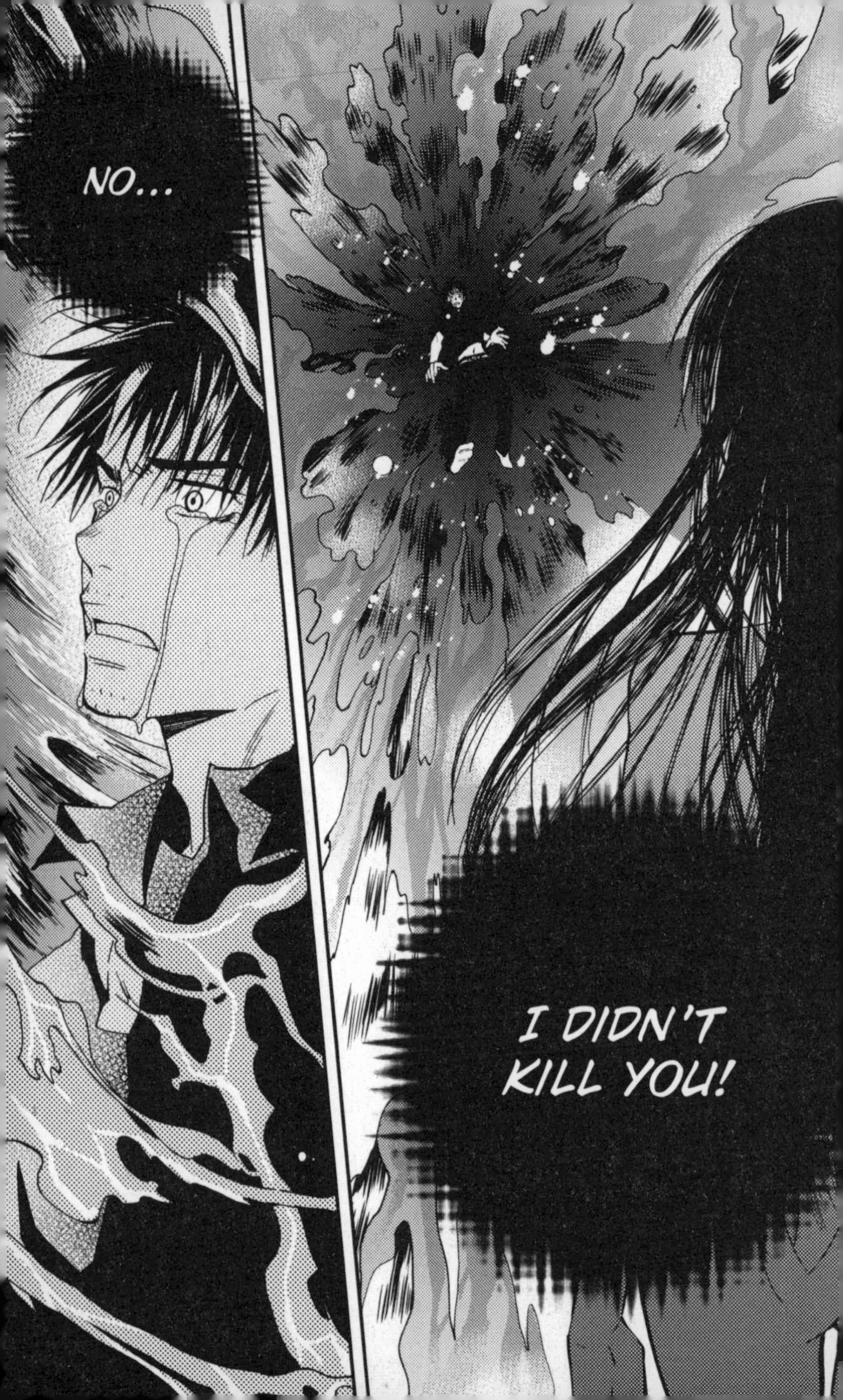
NO...
I DIDN'T KILL YOU!

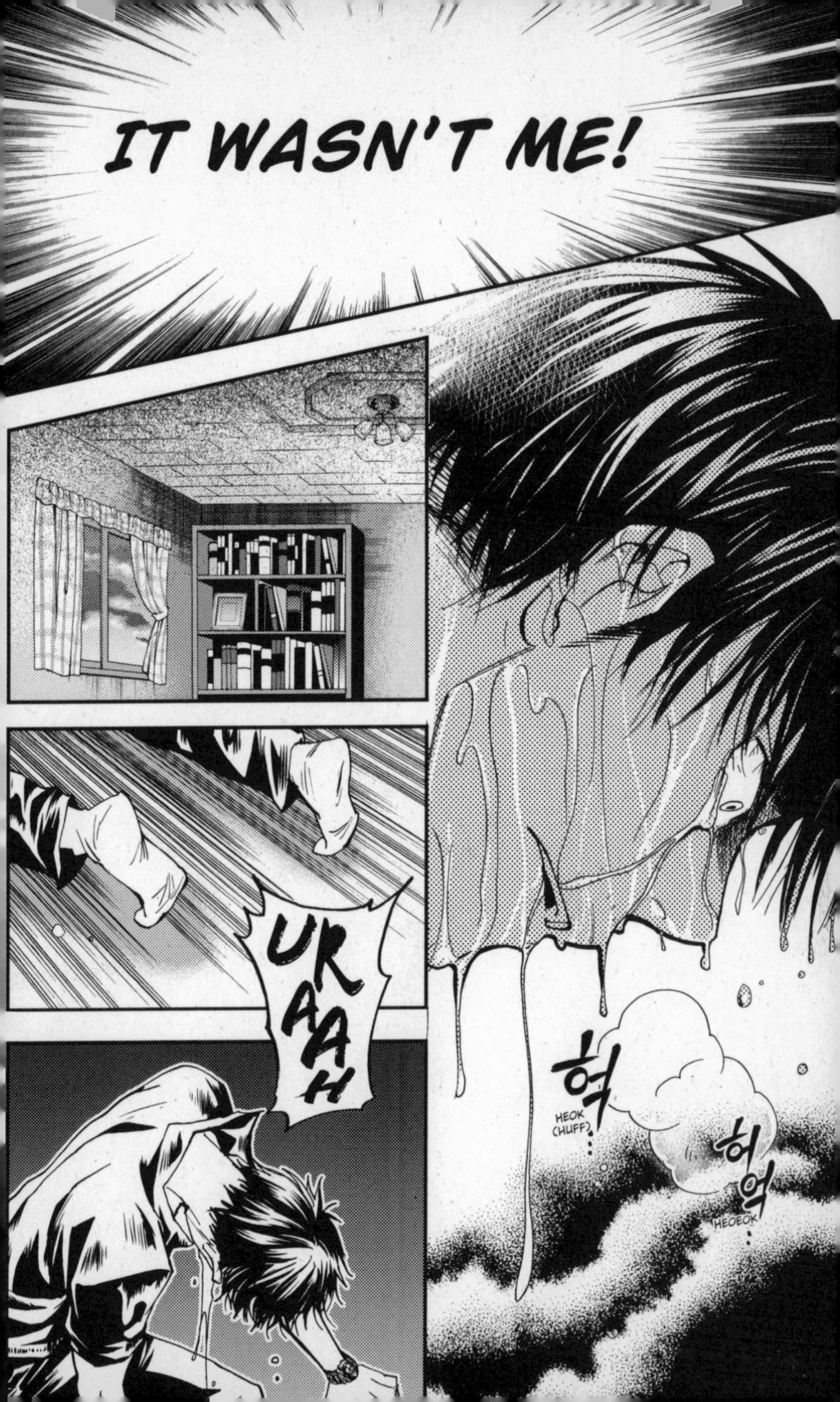
IT WASN'T ME!
URAAAH
헉
HEOK (HUFF)...
허억
HEOEOK...

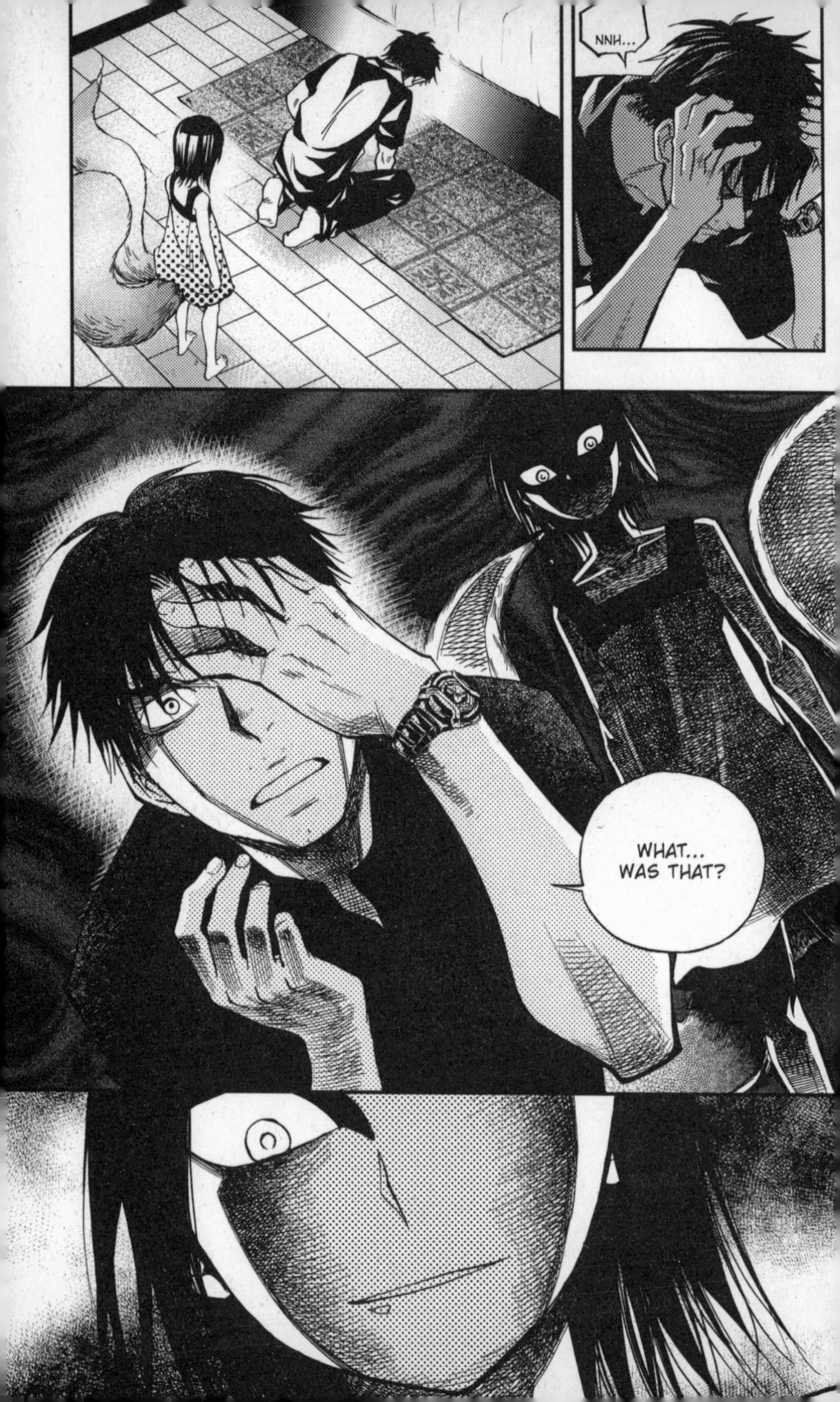
NNH...
WHAT... WAS THAT?

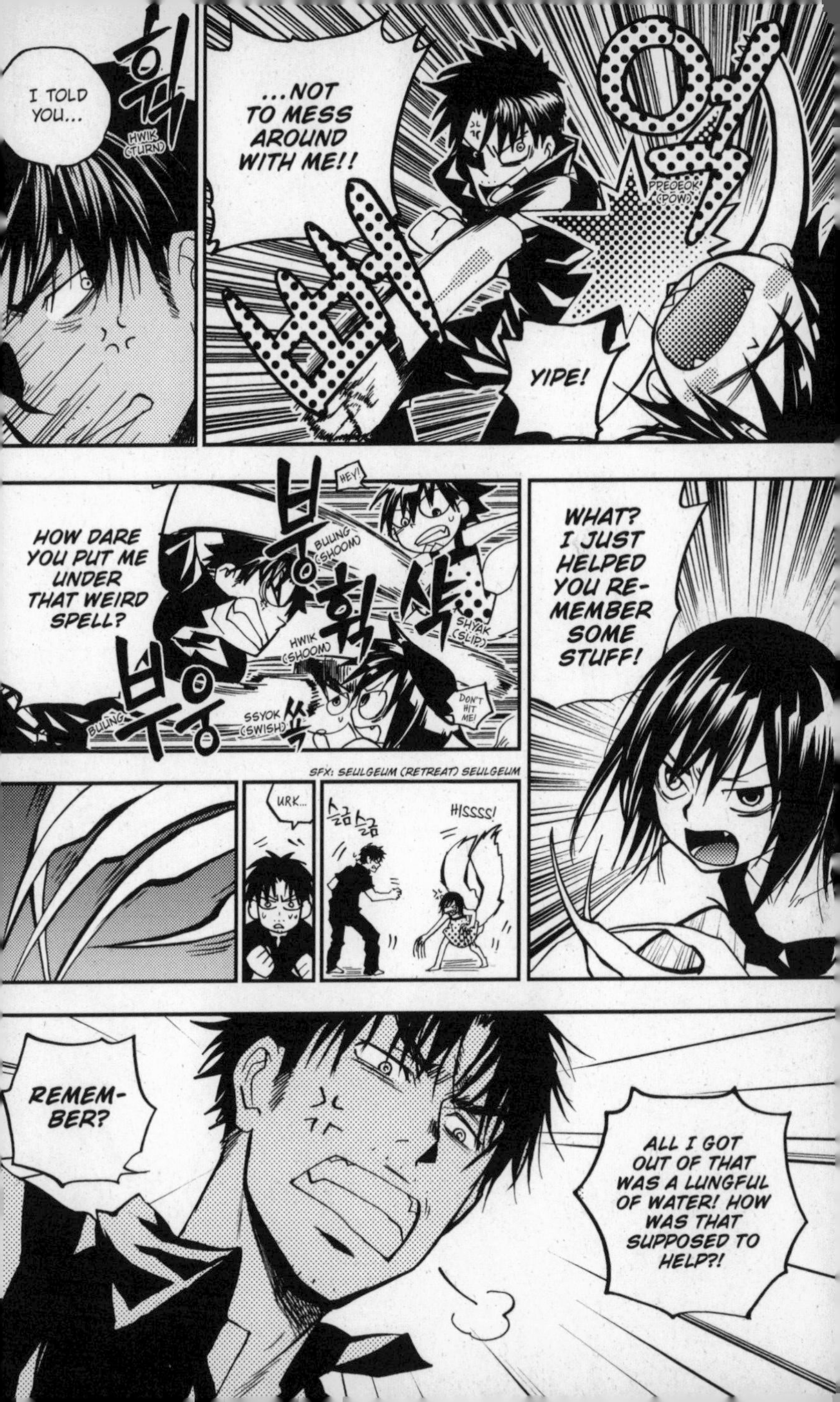

I TOLD YOU...
휙
HWIK (TURN)
...NOT TO MESS AROUND WITH ME!!
PREOEOK (POW)
YIPE!
HEY!
HOW DARE YOU PUT ME UNDER THAT WEIRD SPELL?
부웅
BUUNG (SHOOM)
휙
HWIK (SHOOM)
샥
SHYAK (SLIP)
부웅
BUUNG
쓱
SSYOK (SWISH)
DON'T HIT ME!
SFX: SEULGEUM (RETREAT) SEULGEUM
URK...
슬금슬금
HISSSS!
WHAT? I JUST HELPED YOU RE-MEMBER SOME STUFF!
REMEM-BER?
ALL I GOT OUT OF THAT WAS A LUNGFUL OF WATER! HOW WAS THAT SUPPOSED TO HELP?!

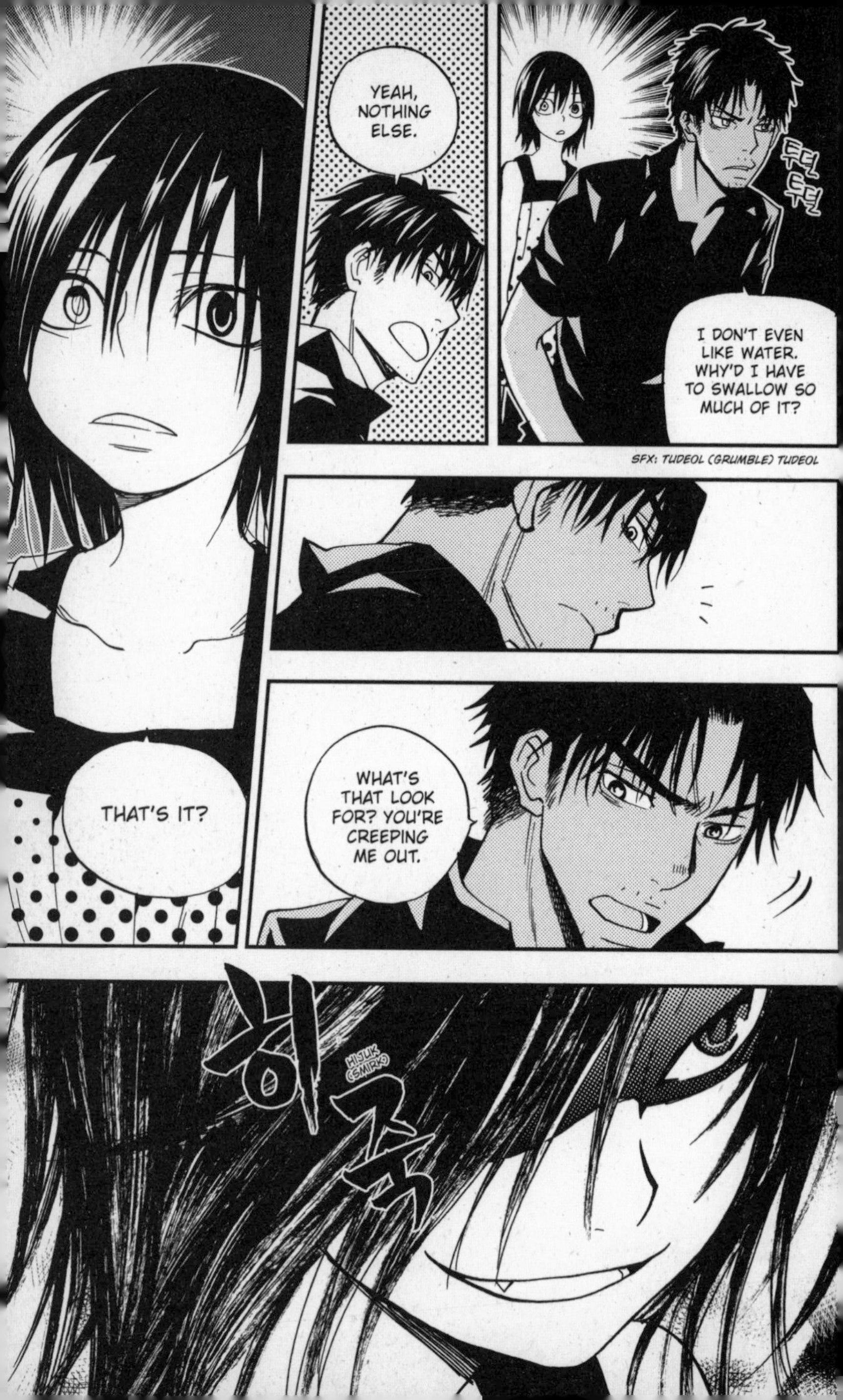
THAT'S IT?
YEAH, NOTHING ELSE.
투덜 투덜
I DON'T EVEN LIKE WATER. WHY'D I HAVE TO SWALLOW SO MUCH OF IT?
SFX: TUDEOL (GRUMBLE) TUDEOL
WHAT'S THAT LOOK FOR? YOU'RE CREEPING ME OUT.
히죽
HIJUK (SMIRK)

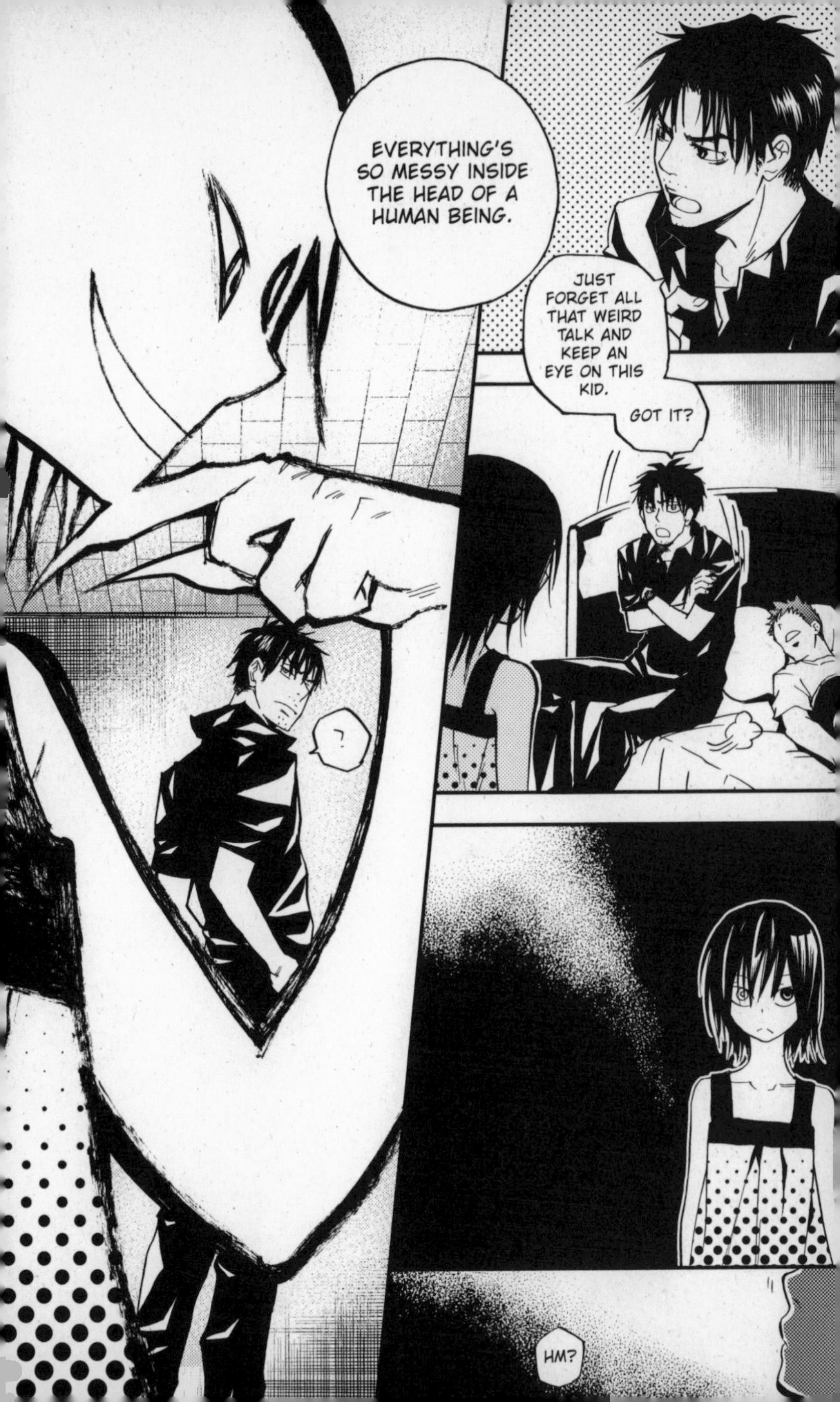
EVERYTHING'S SO MESSY INSIDE THE HEAD OF A HUMAN BEING.
?
JUST FORGET ALL THAT WEIRD TALK AND KEEP AN EYE ON THIS KID.
GOT IT?
HM?

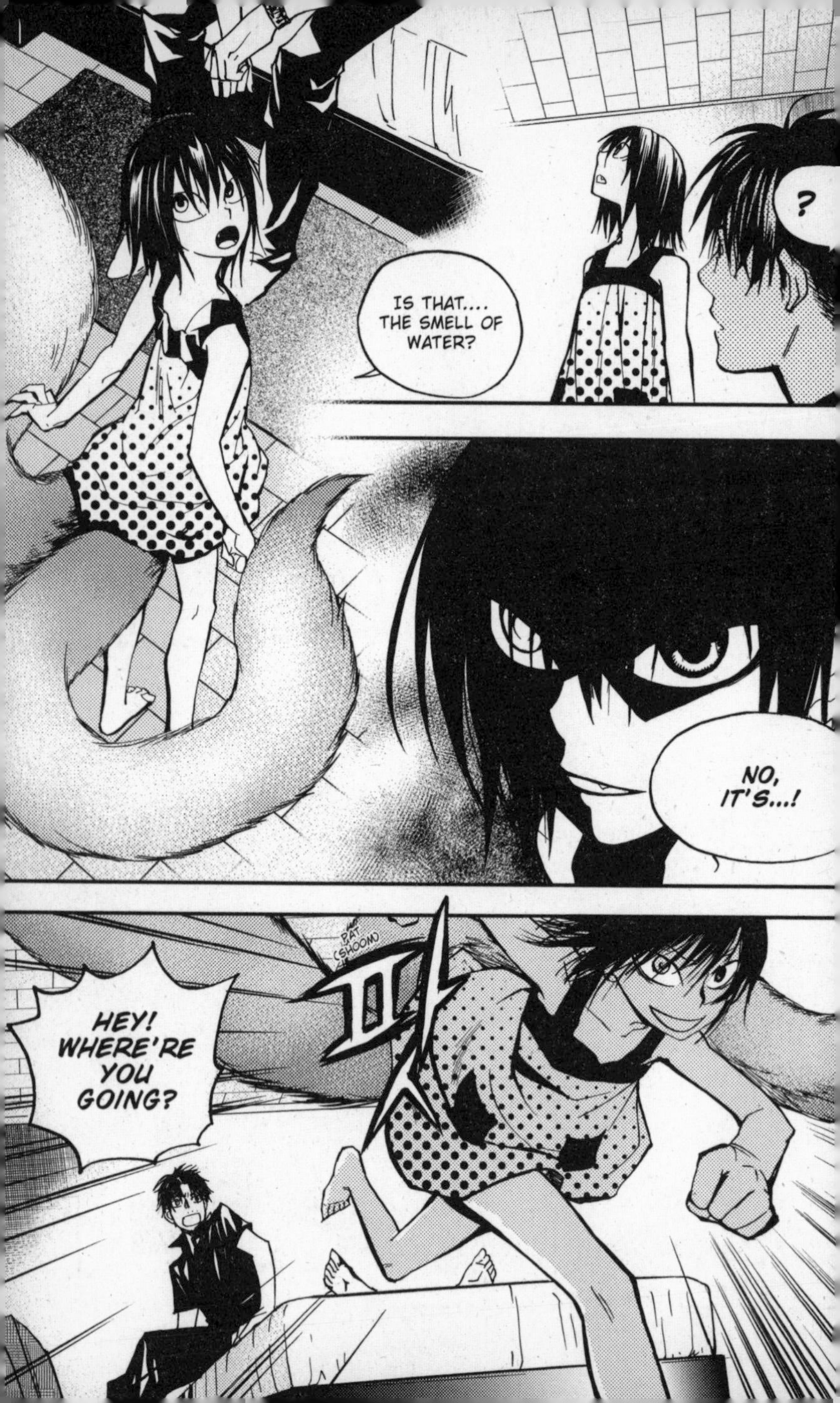
IS THAT.... THE SMELL OF WATER?
?
NO, IT'S...!
HEY! WHERE'RE YOU GOING?
PAT (SHOOM)

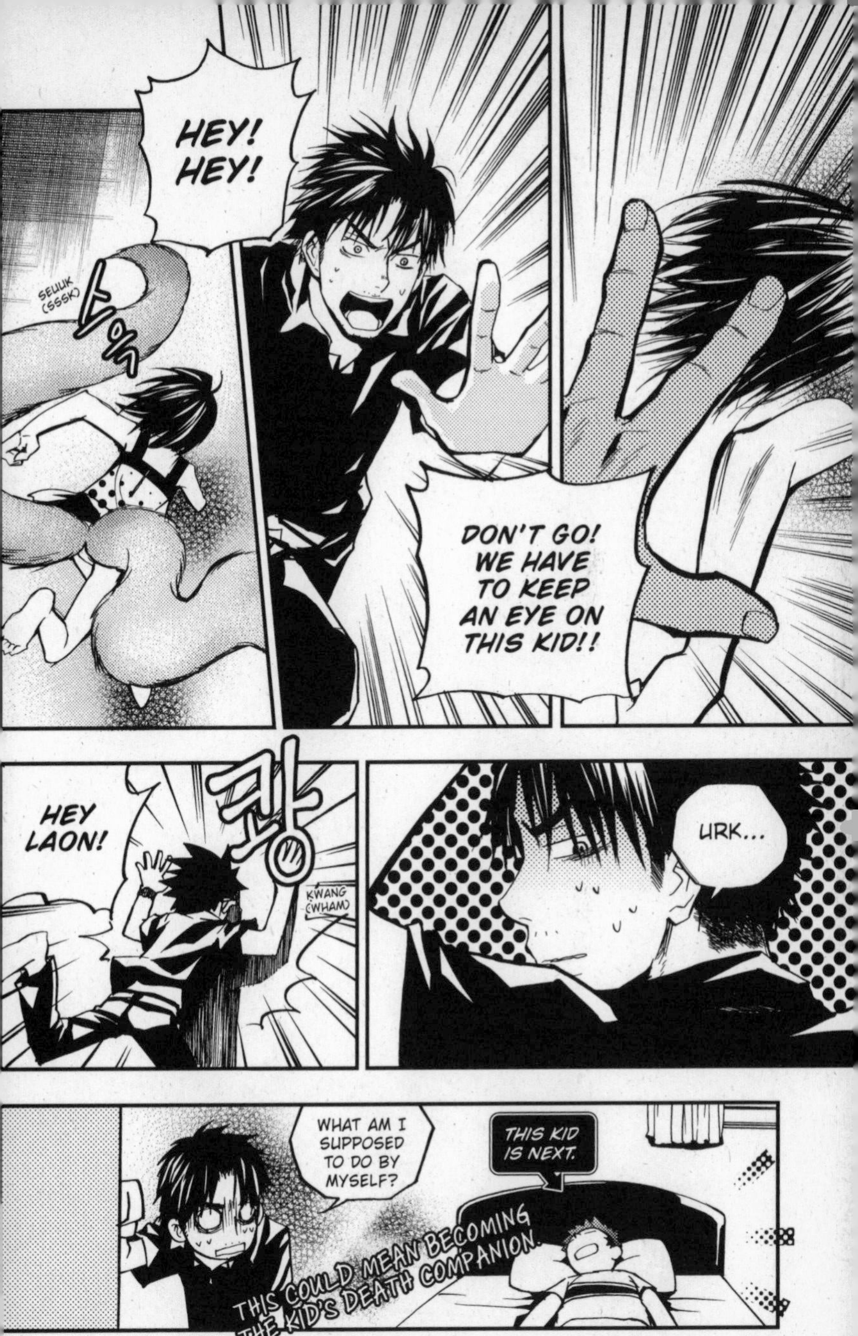

HEY! HEY!
스윽
SEULIK (SSSK)
DON'T GO! WE HAVE TO KEEP AN EYE ON THIS KID!!
HEY LAON!
쾅
KWANG (WHAM)
URK...
WHAT AM I SUPPOSED TO DO BY MYSELF?
THIS KID IS NEXT.
THIS COULD MEAN BECOMING THE KID'S DEATH COMPANION.

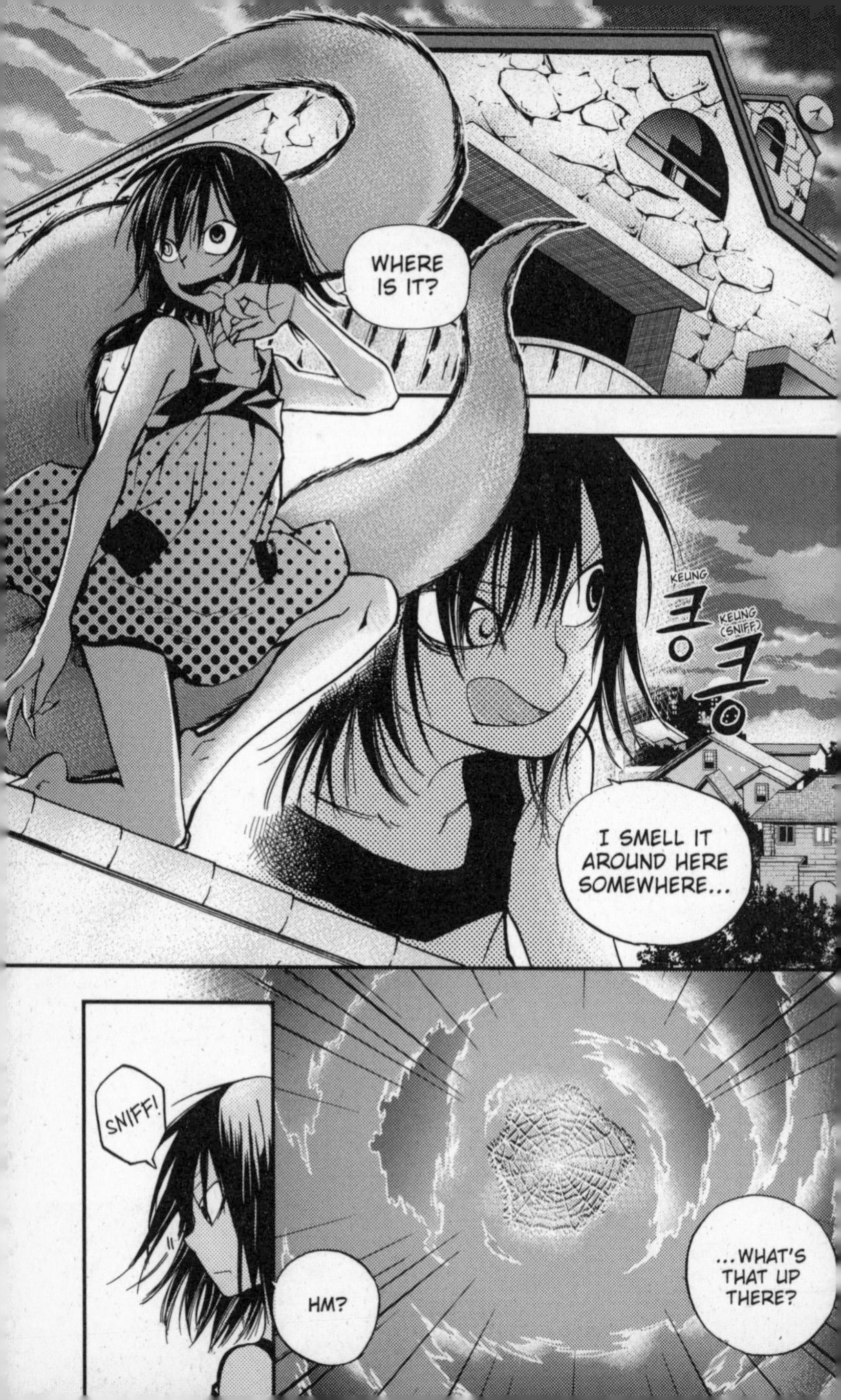
WHERE IS IT?
KEUNG
쿵
KEUNG (SNIFF)
킁
I SMELL IT AROUND HERE SOMEWHERE...
SNIFF!
HM?
...WHAT'S THAT UP THERE?

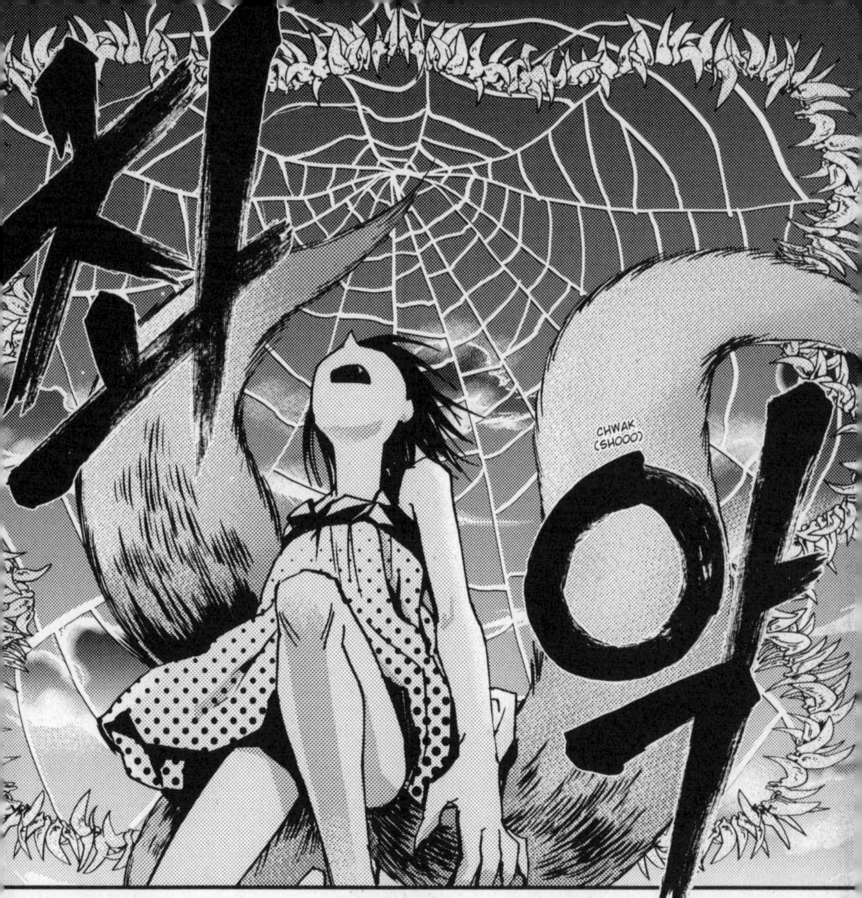
CHWAK
(SHOOO)
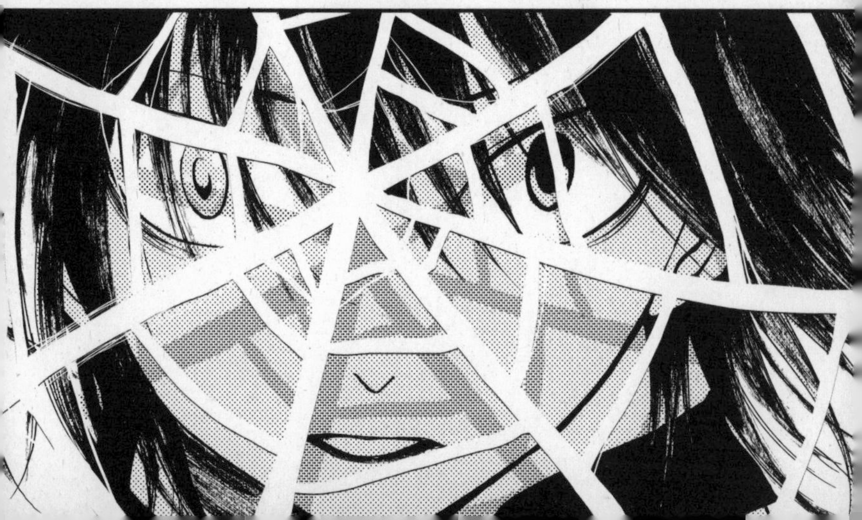

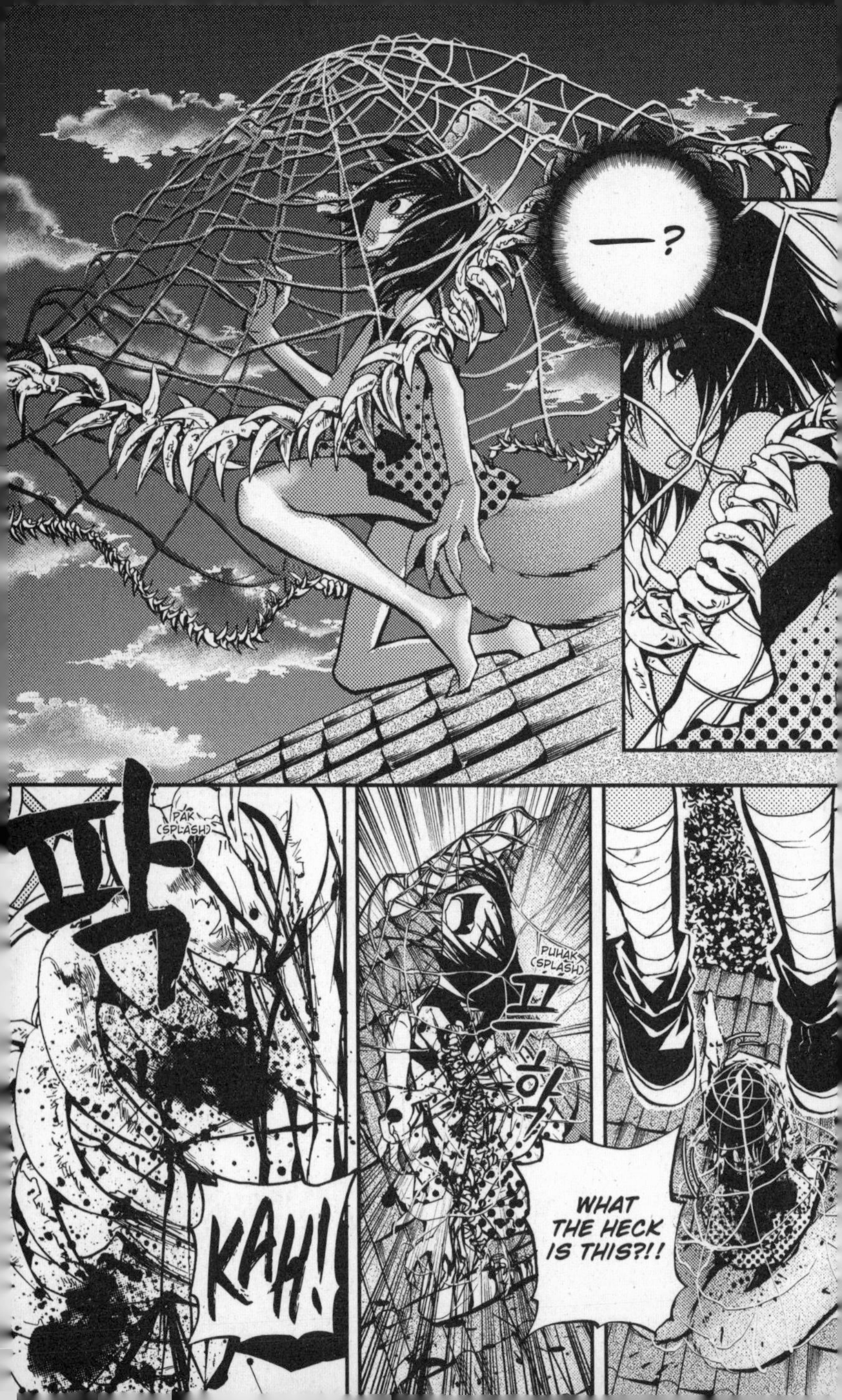

——?
PAK (SPLASH)
팍
KAH!
PUHAK (SPLASH)
푸학
WHAT THE HECK IS THIS?!!

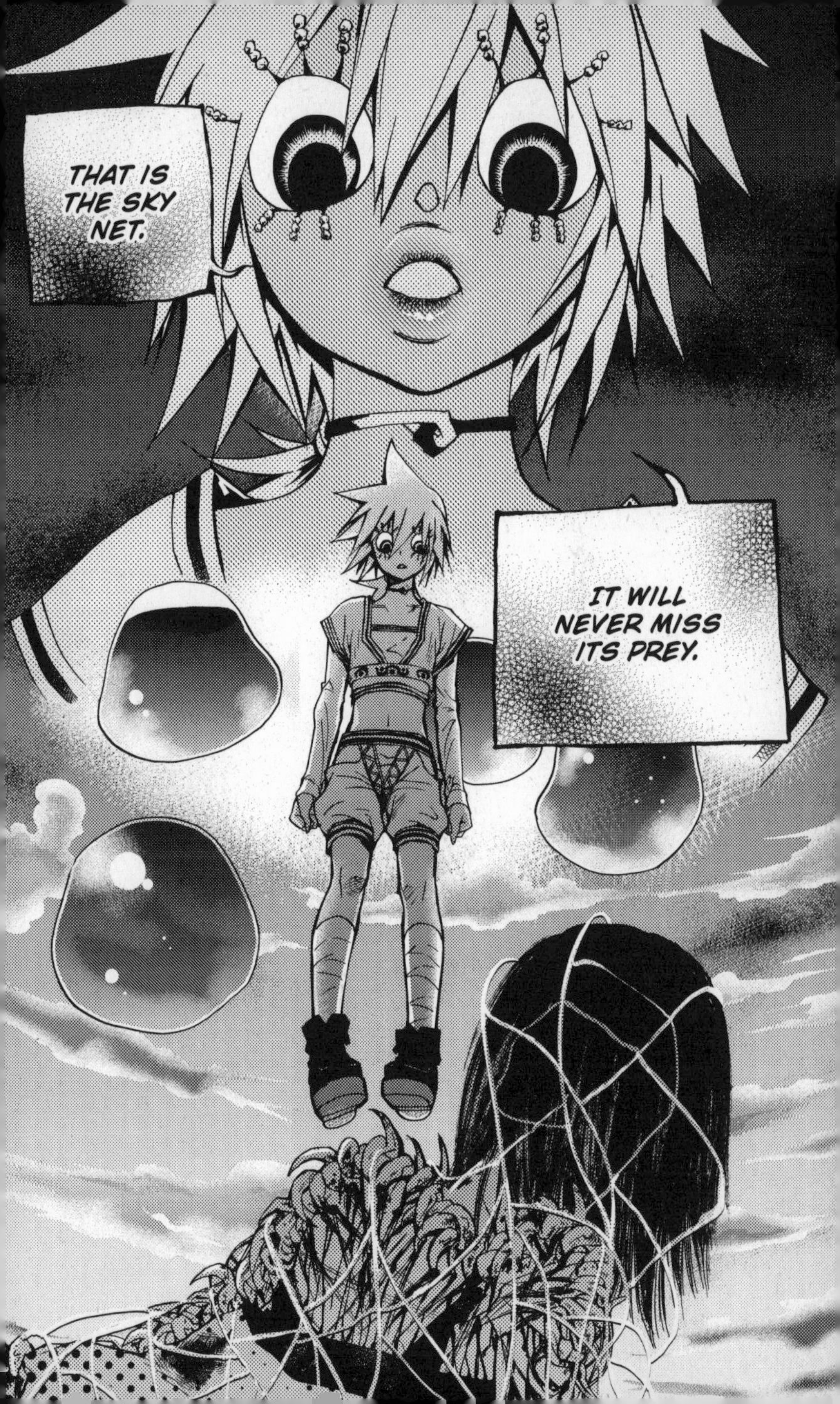
THAT IS THE SKY NET.
IT WILL NEVER MISS ITS PREY.

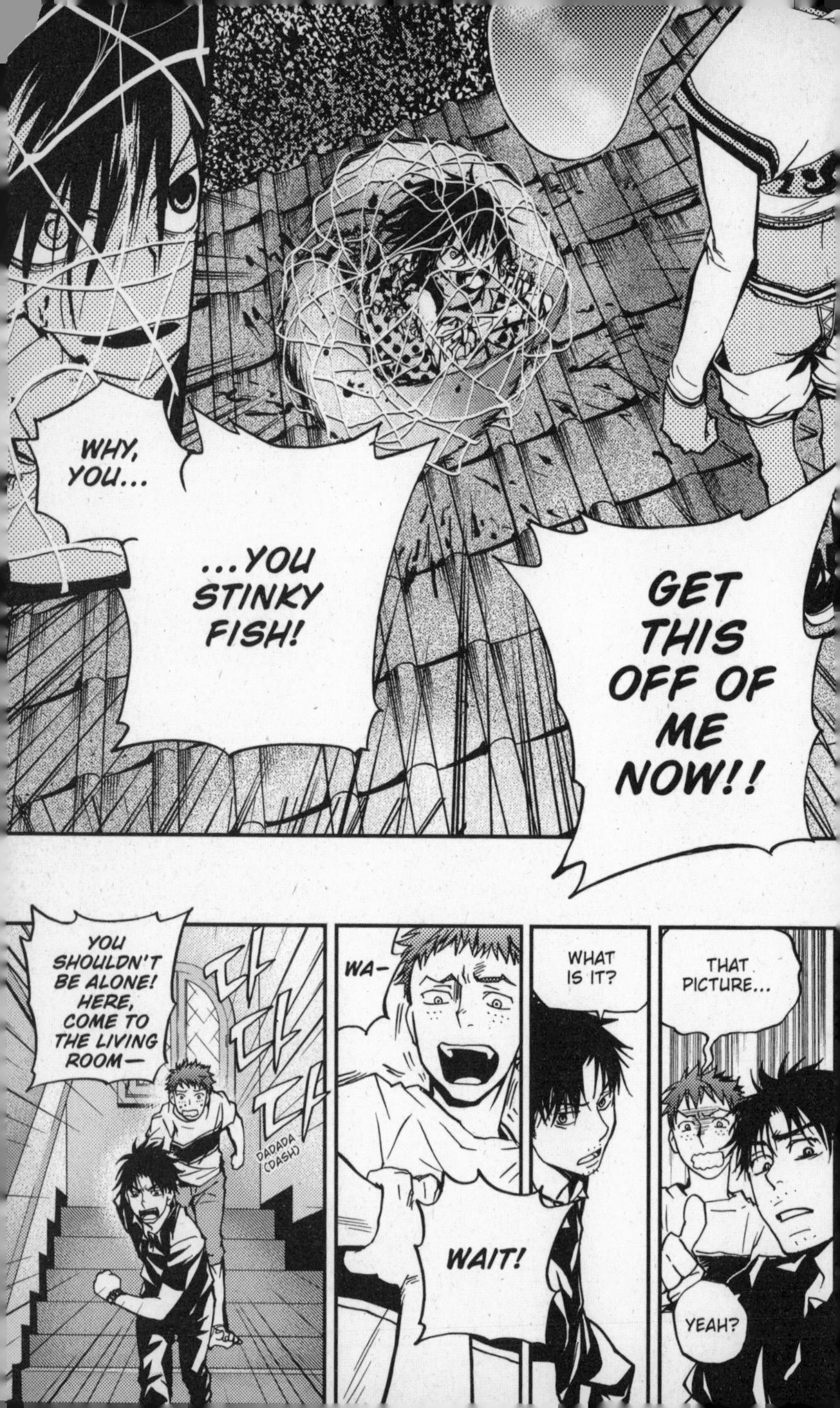
WHY, YOU...
...YOU STINKY FISH!
GET THIS OFF OF ME NOW!!
YOU SHOULDN'T BE ALONE! HERE, COME TO THE LIVING ROOM—
DADADA (DASH)
WA-
WAIT!
WHAT IS IT?
THAT PICTURE...
YEAH?

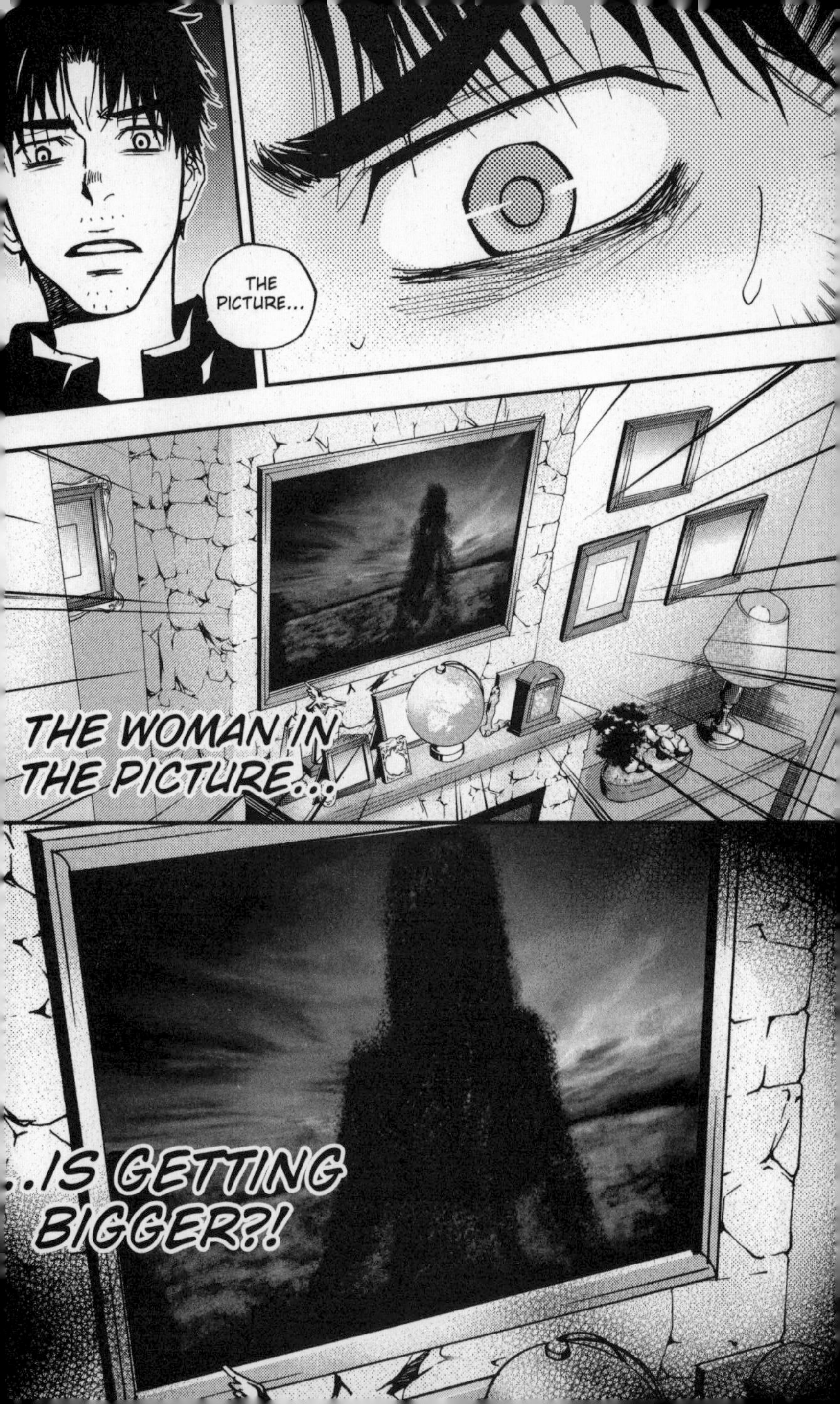
THE PICTURE...
THE WOMAN IN THE PICTURE...
...IS GETTING BIGGER?!

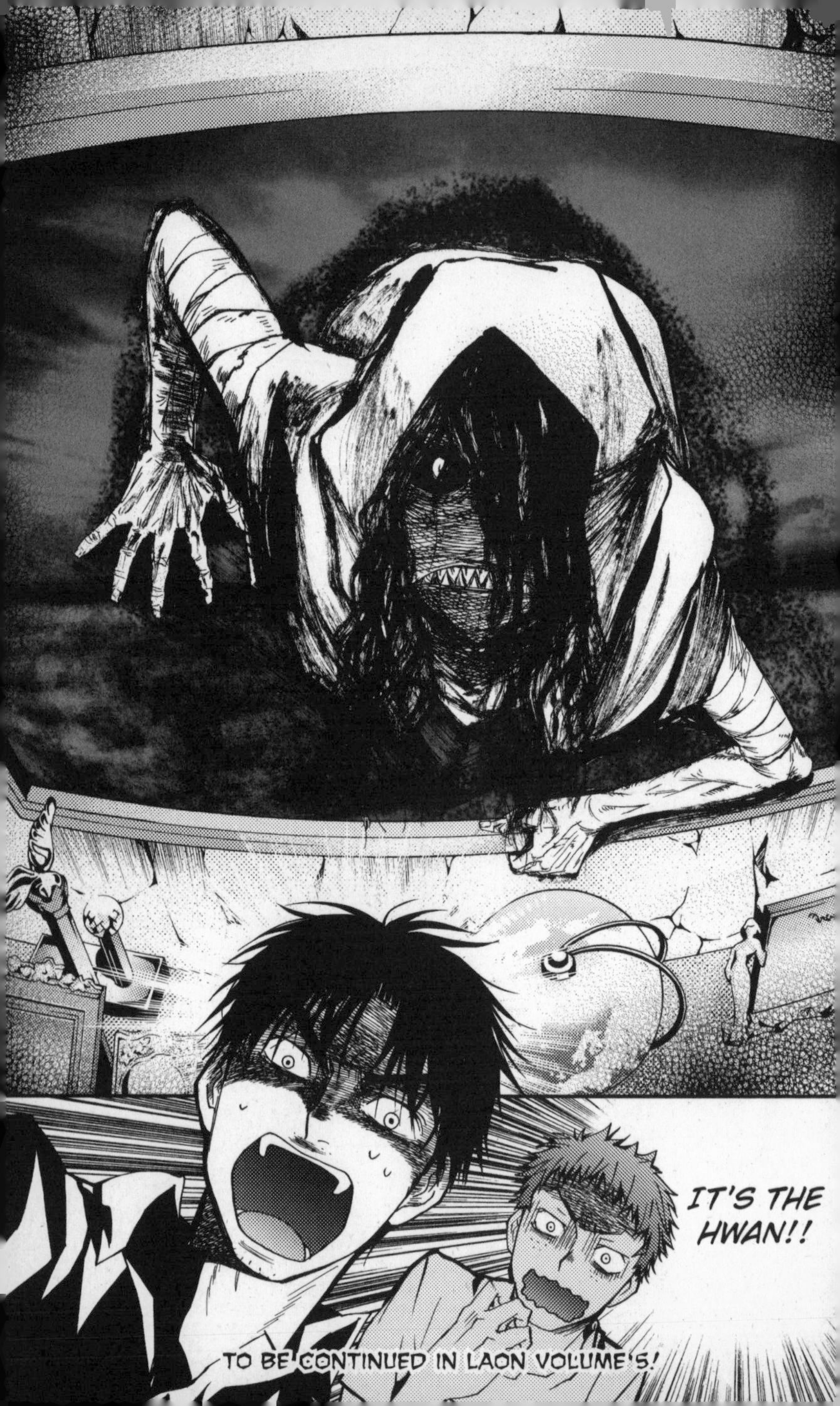
IT'S THE HWAN!!
TO BE CONTINUED IN LAON VOLUME 5!

Translation Notes

A *gumiho* (literally, a nine-tailed fox) is a mythical Korean fox creature with nine tails. Gumihos are able to transform into human form, generally beautiful women, in order to seduce men. Some versions have them eating human livers in order to regain their strength. This story follows the version that a fox creature becomes incrementally more powerful as it ages. From a common fox, it first becomes a white fox, then a red fox, then a gumiho, then finally rises to the level of a *cheonnyeonho* (literally, a 1,000-year-old fox). At this stage, it can ascend to the heavens, achieving the status of a god.

Hwan (幻) is a Chinese character used for words that indicate strangeness, change, illusion, and magic. In this series, it's used to describe parasitic supernatural creatures.

Page 26
The headline here, "A World Covered in Silver," is a reference to Eunbi's name, which literally means "silver rain" in Korean.

Page 100
The term "order" here is used in the sense of "public order," or those unspoken rules that the majority of a society considers the norm for behavior and morality.

Page 147
The Korean school year begins in March and ends in February of the following year, so the summer months actually do fall within the school year.

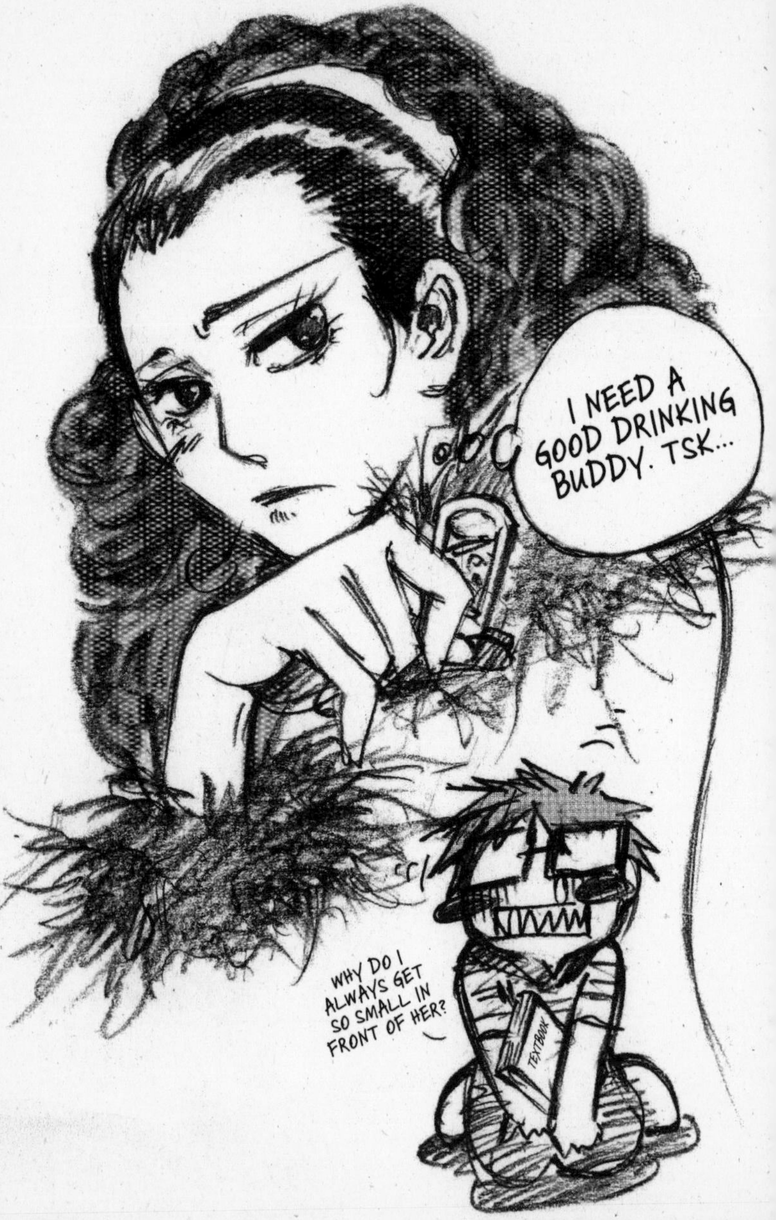
I NEED A GOOD DRINKING BUDDY. TSK...
WHY DO I ALWAYS GET SO SMALL IN FRONT OF HER?
TEXTBOOK

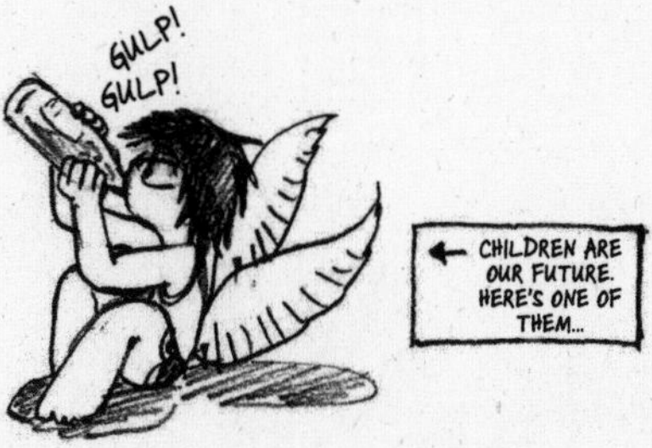
GULP! GULP!
CHILDREN ARE OUR FUTURE. HERE'S ONE OF THEM...

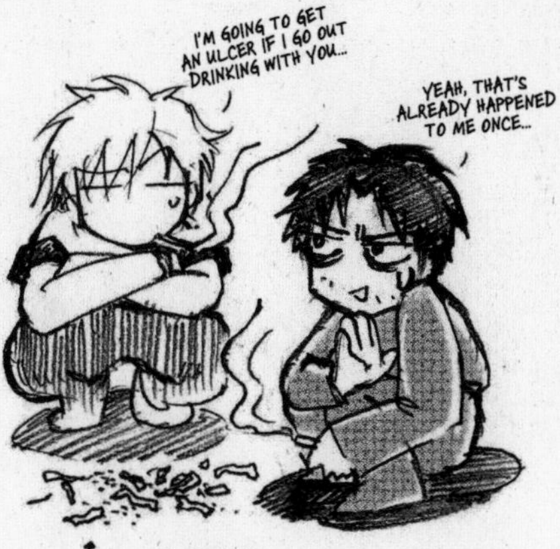
I'M GOING TO GET AN ULCER IF I GO OUT DRINKING WITH YOU...
YEAH, THAT'S ALREADY HAPPENED TO ME ONCE...
SO TRASHING YOUR LUNGS IS OKAY?

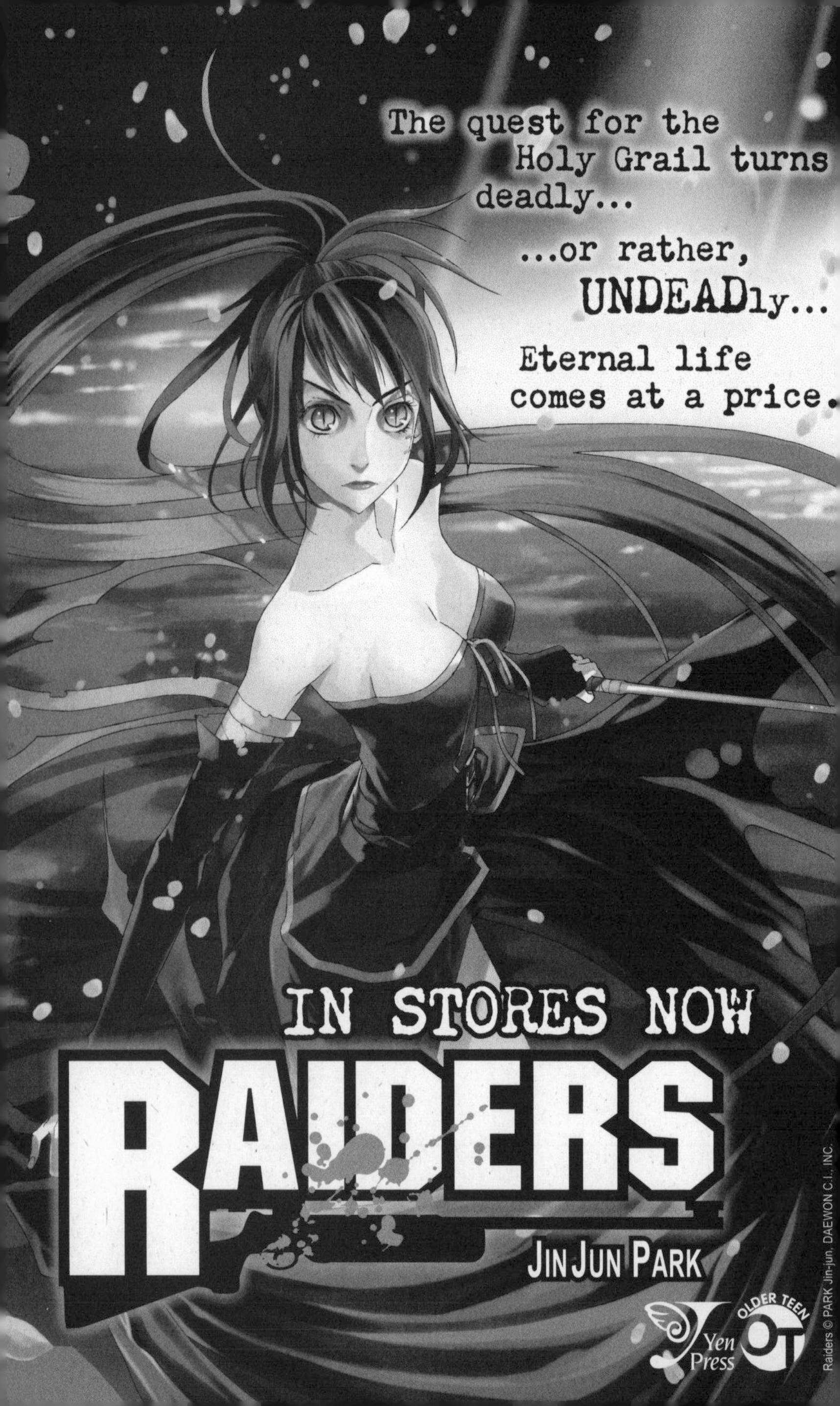

The quest for the Holy Grail turns deadly...
...or rather, UNDEADly...
Eternal life comes at a price.
IN STORES NOW
RAIDERS
JIN JUN PARK
Yen Press
OLDER TEEN OT
Raiders © PARK Jin-jun, DAEWON C.I. INC.

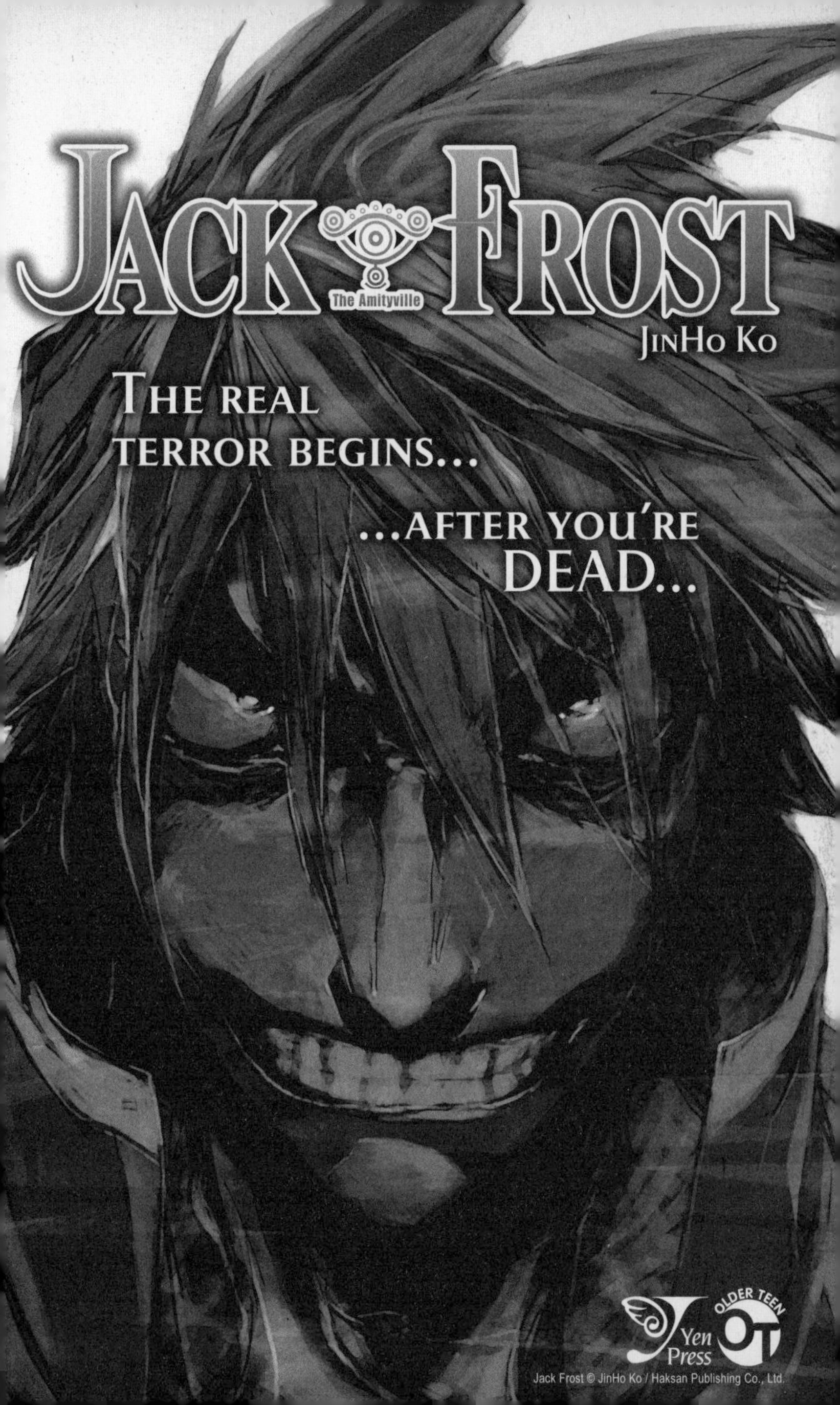
JACK FROST
The Amityville
JINHO KO
THE REAL
TERROR BEGINS...
...AFTER YOU'RE
DEAD...
OLDER TEEN
OT
Yen
Press
Jack Frost © JinHo Ko / Haksan Publishing Co., Ltd.

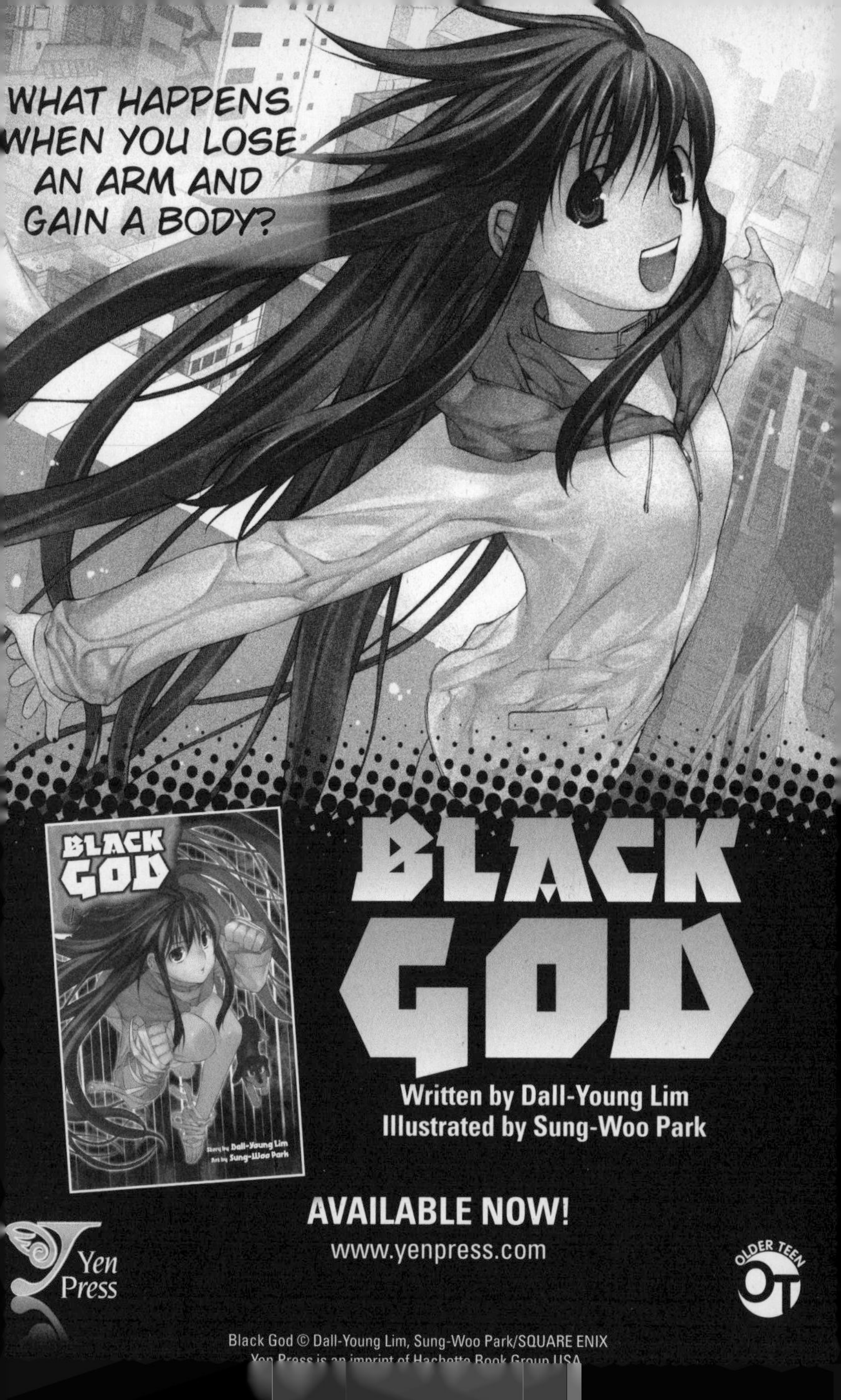
WHAT HAPPENS WHEN YOU LOSE AN ARM AND GAIN A BODY?
BLACK GOD
Story by Dall-Young Lim
Art by Sung-Woo Park
BLACK GOD
Written by Dall-Young Lim
Illustrated by Sung-Woo Park
AVAILABLE NOW!
www.yenpress.com
Yen Press
OLDER TEEN
OT
Black God © Dall-Young Lim, Sung-Woo Park/SQUARE ENIX
Yen Press is an imprint of Hachette Book Group USA

THE JOURNEY CONTINUES IN THE MANGA
ADAPTATION OF THE HIT NOVEL SERIES

IN STORES NOW

SPICE
&
WOLF

Kieli sees ghosts.
Harvey cannot die.
He will throw
her world into
chaos...
...and become her
one true friend.

STORY BY Yukako Kabei
ART BY Shiori Teshirogi

To become the ultimate weap
one boy must eat the souls
of 99 humans...

SOUL EATER

ATSUSHI OHKUBO

1

...and one wi

Maka is a scythemeister, working to perfect her demon scyth
enough to become Death's Weapon—the weapon used by S
spirit of Death himself. And if that isn't strange enough, her s
power to change form—into a human-looking boy!

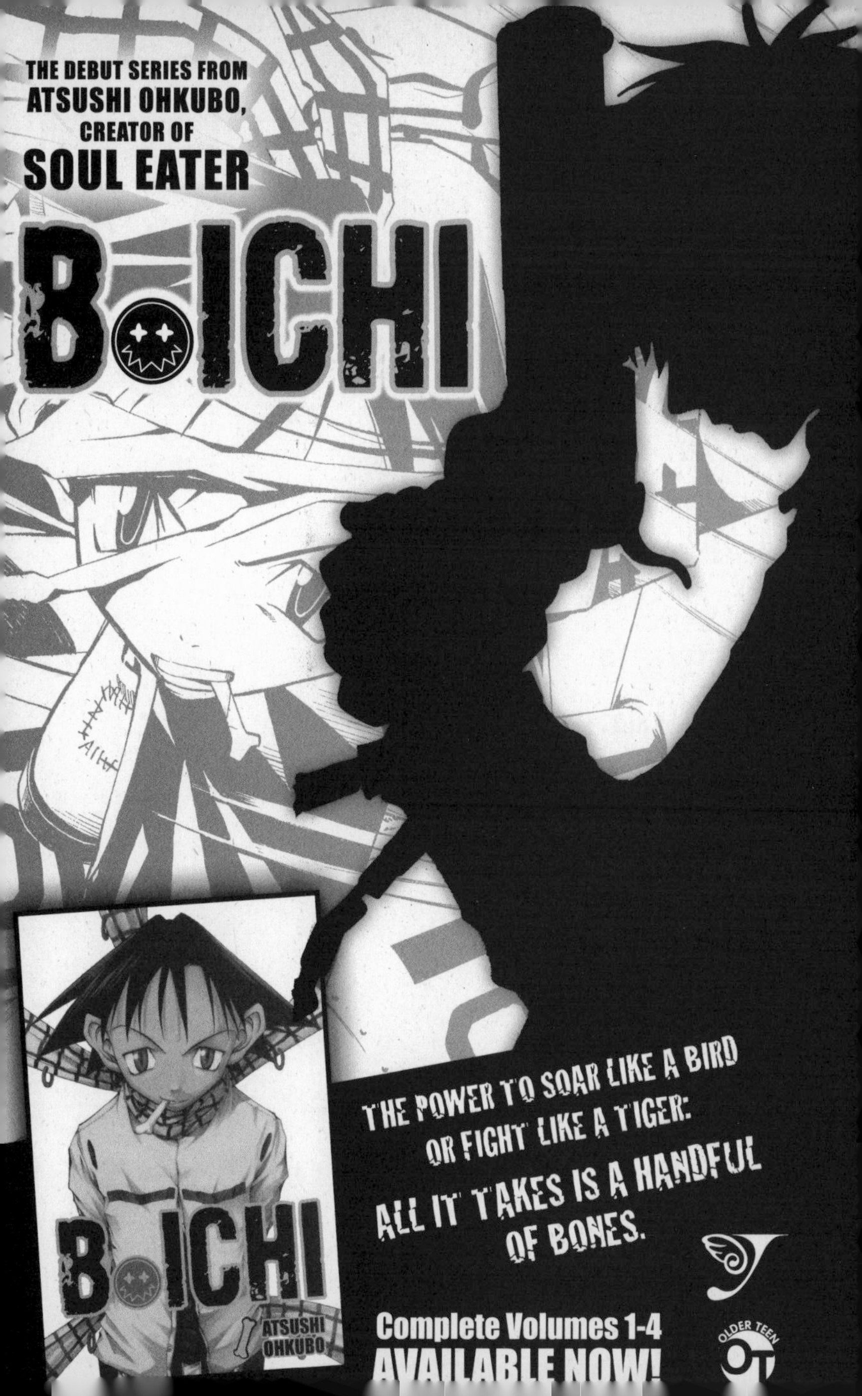
THE DEBUT SERIES FROM
ATSUSHI OHKUBO,
CREATOR OF
SOUL EATER
B ICHI
B ICHI
ATSUSHI OHKUBO
THE POWER TO SOAR LIKE A BIRD
OR FIGHT LIKE A TIGER:
ALL IT TAKES IS A HANDFUL
OF BONES.
Complete Volumes 1-4
AVAILABLE NOW!
OLDER TEEN
OT

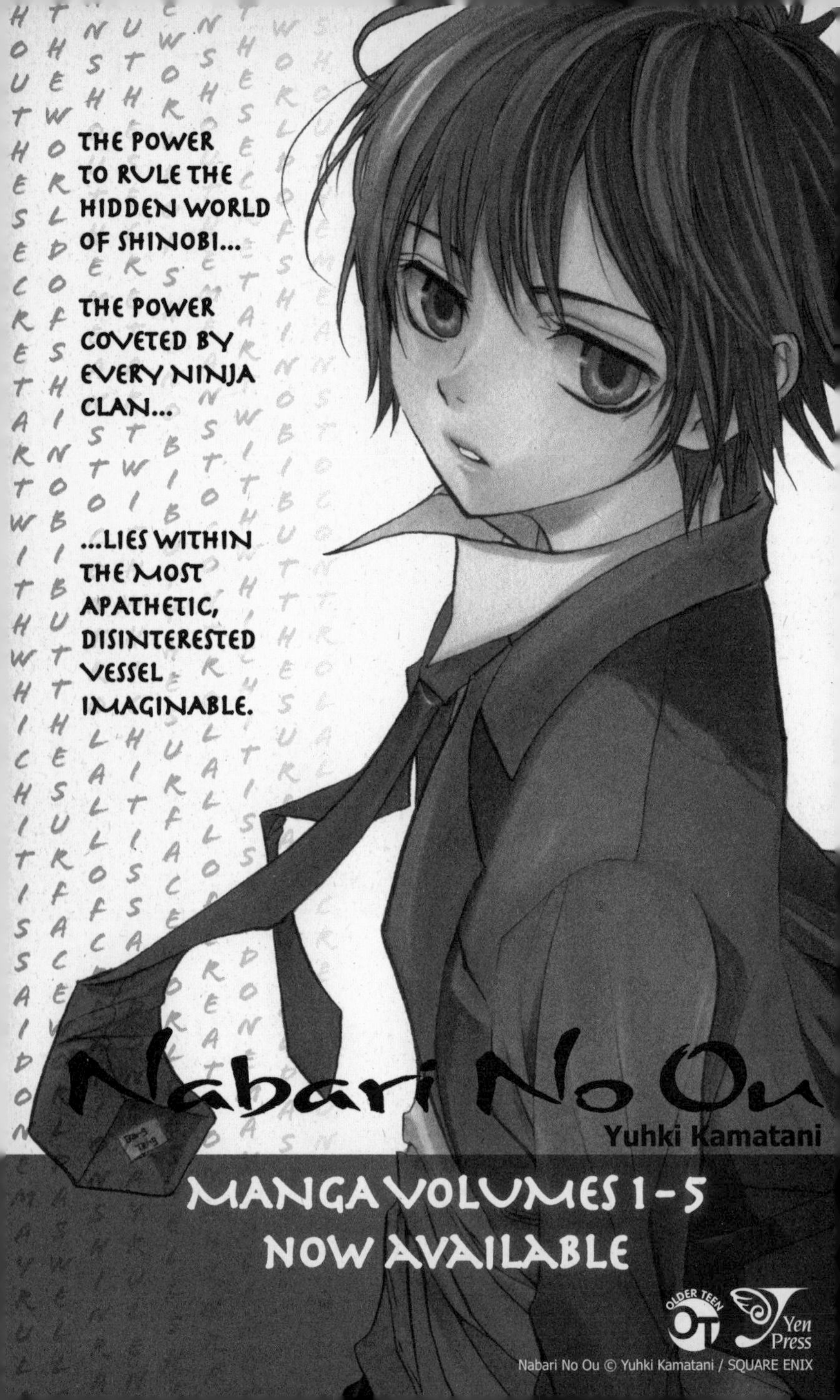
THE POWER TO RULE THE HIDDEN WORLD OF SHINOBI...
THE POWER COVETED BY EVERY NINJA CLAN...
...LIES WITHIN THE MOST APATHETIC, DISINTERESTED VESSEL IMAGINABLE.
Nabari No Ou
Yuhki Kamatani
MANGA VOLUMES 1-5
NOW AVAILABLE
OLDER TEEN
OT
Yen Press
Nabari No Ou © Yuhki Kamatani / SQUARE ENIX

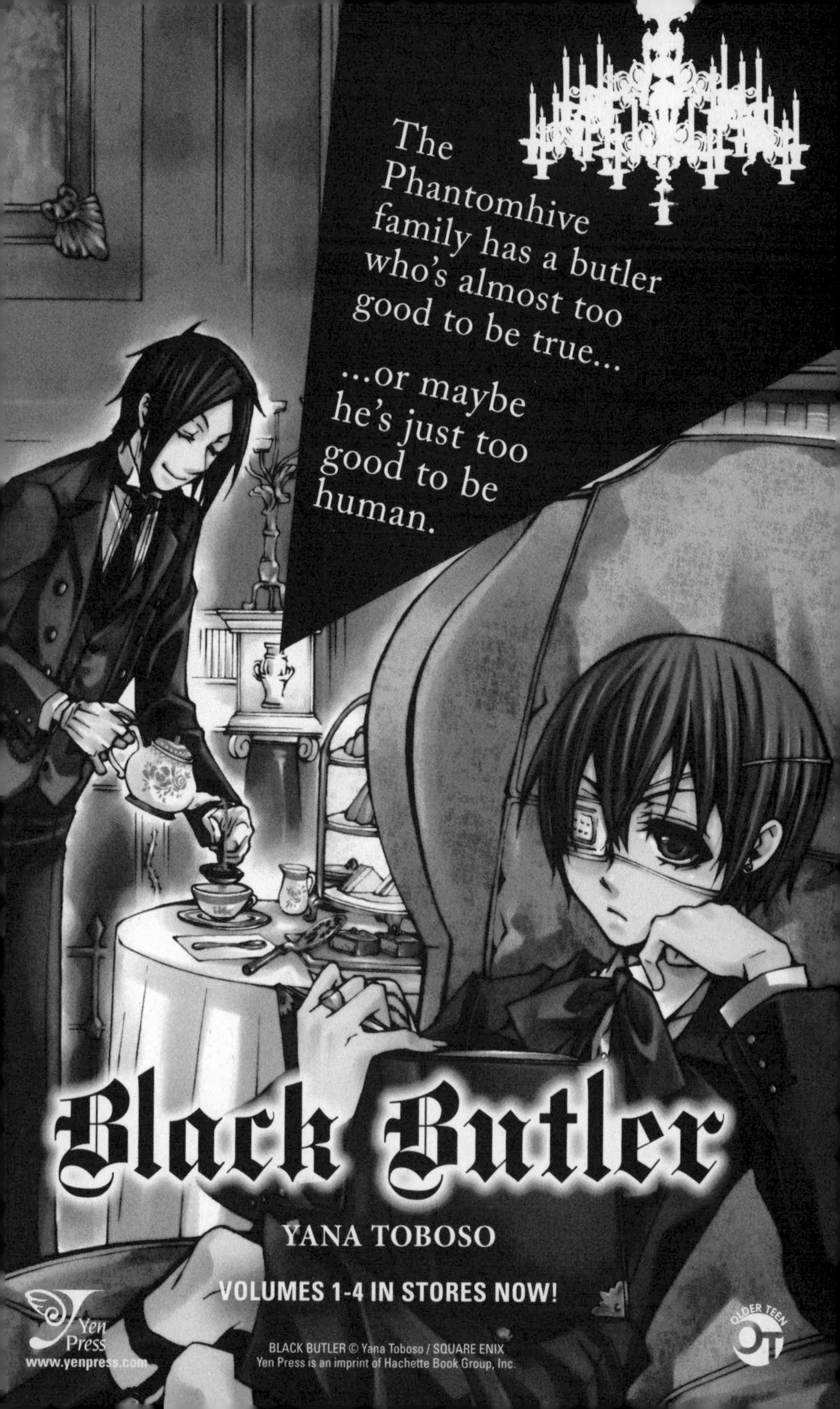

LAON ❹

YOUNGBIN KIM
HYUN YOU

Translation: Woo-Sok Park

Lettering: Abigail Blackman

LAON, vol. 4 © 2008 by KIM Young-bin and YOU Hyun, DAEWON C.I. Inc. All rights reserved. First published in Korea in 2008 by DAEWON C.I. Inc. English translation rights in USA, Canada, UK and Commonwealth arranged by Daewon C.I. Inc. through TOPAZ Agency Inc.

Translation © 2011 by Hachette Book Group, Inc.

Yen Press
Hachette Book Group
237 Park Avenue, New York, NY 10017

www.HachetteBookGroup.com
www.YenPress.com

Yen Press is an imprint of Hachette Book Group, Inc. The Yen Press name and logo are trademarks of Hachette Book Group, Inc.

First Yen Press Edition: January 2011

ISBN: 978-0-7595-3055-3

10 9 8 7 6 5 4 3 2 1

BVG

Printed in the United States of America